McDougal Littell
The
AMERICANS
Reconstruction through the 20th Century

P9-CSF-463

Reading Study Guide

McDougal Littell
A HOUGHTON MIFFLIN COMPANY
Evanston, Illinois • Boston • Dallas

Printed in the United States of America.

ISBN 0-395-92076-0

2 3 4 5 6 7 8 9 - CKI - 03 02 01 00 99 98

Contents

Chapter 18 Cold War Conflicts, 1945–1960

Chapter 19 The Postwar Boom, 1946–1960

UNIT 6 Living with Great Turmoil, 1954–1975

Chapter 20 The New Frontier and the Great Society, 1960–1968

Chapter 21 Civil Rights, 1954–1970

Chapter 22 The Vietnam War Years, 1954–1975

Chapter 23 An Era of Social Change, 1960–1975

UNIT 7 Passage to a New Century, 1968–1997

Being a Strategic Reader
Strategies for Reading Your History Book

UNDERSTANDING THE BIG PICTURE

History is filled with people, events, facts, and details. Sometimes you can get lost in all the details. This is why the most important strategy to remember as you read a history textbook is to form the "big picture" of history. As you read, keep asking yourself, "What is the main idea?" When you do this, the details will make more sense.

Use the strategies shown here to help you read *The Americans: Reconstruction through the 20th Century.*

Strategy: Look for key terms and names, which are in dark type in the section. The text gives clues to the important terms and names in the section.
Try This: Read the terms. Then look at pages 282 and 283. Which of the terms appear on these pages? How did you recognize them?

Strategy: Read "Learn About. . . to Understand" to begin forming the "big picture" of the section.
Try This: What do you think will be the subject of this section?

Strategy: Look closely at the photographs, art, and other illustrations in the text. Be sure to read the captions.
Try This: Look at the photograph. What does it show about life in American cities in the 1800s?

Strategy: Look at the heads and subheads in each section to get a general understanding of the subject.
Try This: Preview the head and subheads on pages 282 and 283. What do you expect to learn in this section?

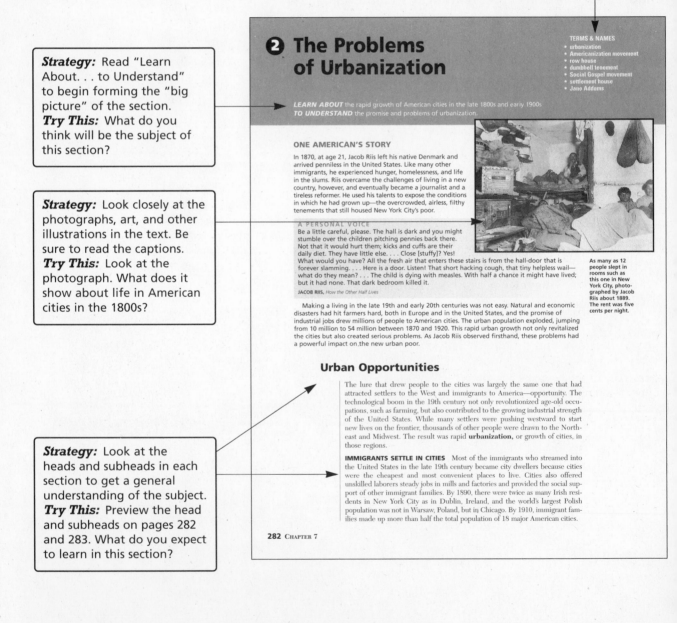

❷ The Problems of Urbanization

TERMS & NAMES
• urbanization
• Americanization movement
• row house
• dumbbell tenement
• Social Gospel movement
• settlement house
• Jane Addams

LEARN ABOUT the rapid growth of American cities in the late 1800s and early 1900s
TO UNDERSTAND the promise and problems of urbanization.

ONE AMERICAN'S STORY

In 1870, at age 21, Jacob Riis left his native Denmark and arrived penniless in the United States. Like many other immigrants, he experienced hunger, homelessness, and life in the slums. Riis overcame the challenges of living in a new country, however, and eventually became a journalist and a tireless reformer. He used his talents to expose the conditions in which he had grown up—the overcrowded, airless, filthy tenements that still housed New York City's poor.

A PERSONAL VOICE
Be a little careful, please. The hall is dark and you might stumble over the children pitching pennies back there. Not that it would hurt them; kicks and cuffs are their daily diet. They have little else. . . . Close [stuffy]? Yes! What would you have? All the fresh air that enters these stairs is from the hall-door that is forever slamming. . . . Here is a door. Listen! That short hacking cough, that tiny helpless wail—what do they mean? . . . The child is dying with measles. With half a chance it might have lived; but it had none. That dark bedroom killed it.

JACOB RIIS, *How the Other Half Lives*

As many as 12 people slept in rooms such as this one in New York City, photographed by Jacob Riis about 1889. The rent was five cents per night.

Making a living in the late 19th and early 20th centuries was not easy. Natural and economic disasters had hit farmers hard, both in Europe and in the United States, and the promise of industrial jobs drew millions of people to American cities. The urban population exploded, jumping from 10 million to 54 million between 1870 and 1920. This rapid urban growth not only revitalized the cities but also created serious problems. As Jacob Riis observed firsthand, these problems had a powerful impact on the new urban poor.

Urban Opportunities

The lure that drew people to the cities was largely the same one that had attracted settlers to the West and immigrants to America—opportunity. The technological boom in the 19th century not only revolutionized age-old occupations, such as farming, but also contributed to the growing industrial strength of the United States. While many settlers were pushing westward to start new lives on the frontier, thousands of other people were drawn to the Northeast and Midwest. The result was rapid **urbanization**, or growth of cities, in those regions.

IMMIGRANTS SETTLE IN CITIES Most of the immigrants who streamed into the United States in the late 19th century became city dwellers because cities were the cheapest and most convenient places to live. Cities also offered unskilled laborers steady jobs in mills and factories and provided the social support of other immigrant families. By 1890, there were twice as many Irish residents in New York City as in Dublin, Ireland, and the world's largest Polish population was not in Warsaw, Poland, but in Chicago. By 1910, immigrant families made up more than half the total population of 18 major American cities.

Immigrants often clustered in ethnic neighborhoods with others from the same country—or even from the same province or village. Living among people who shared their background enabled the newcomers to speak their own language and practice their customs and religion.

At the same time newcomers were able to learn about their new home through a program of education known as the **Americanization movement.** Schools and voluntary associations provided programs aimed at teaching immigrants the English language as well as American history and government—subjects that were necessary to help the newcomers become citizens. The movement also included the teaching of other subjects, such as cooking and social etiquette, designed to assist the immigrants in assimilating into American culture.

Unfortunately, many native-born Americans felt threatened by these mushrooming ethnic communities and expressed their fear by becoming hostile. Overcrowding soon became a problem as well, one that was intensified by the arrival of new urbanites from America's rural areas.

THINK THROUGH HISTORY
A. THEME **Cultural Diversity** *Why did immigrants tend to group together in the cities?*

MIGRATION FROM COUNTRY TO CITY

The rapid improvements in farming technology during the second half of the 19th century were good news for some farmers but bad news for others. Inventions such as the McCormick reaper and the steel plow made farming more efficient but meant that fewer laborers were needed to work the land. As use of the new equipment spread across the country, farms merged, and many rural people could not find jobs in agriculture. They left their land and agricultural way of life and made their way to cities to find whatever jobs they could.

THINK THROUGH HISTORY
B. Contrasting *How was the experience of moving to cities similar and different for African-American farm workers and other farm workers?*

Many of the Southern farmers who lost their jobs were African Americans. Other African Americans in the rural South also became aware of the opportunities in large cities. Between 1890 and 1910, about 200,000 African Americans moved north and west, to cities such as Chicago and Detroit, in an effort to escape racial violence, economic hardship, and political oppression. Many found conditions in the cities only somewhat better than those they had left behind. Because of racial prejudice and their inadequate education, they were often forced to take low-paying factory jobs or to work as domestic servants.

URBAN CULTURAL OPPORTUNITIES Although people moved to cities for economic reasons, cultural opportunities offered an additional attraction. In contrast to the relatively slow-paced life in both immigrants' native villages and American rural communities, life in a city was varied and exciting. Each city had a personality all its own. In New York City, you had an opportunity to see the first moving pictures. In Chicago, you could join your neighbors on an outing to the Columbian Exposition or to Buffalo Bill's Wild West Show. In

Immigrants and Urbanization **283**

Ethnic Enclaves in New York City, 1910

- ■ Austrian
- ■ German
- ■ Irish
- ■ Italian
- ■ Russian
- ■ Scandinavian

Light tint indicates at least 20% of population.
Darker tint indicates 40% of population or more.

Nonresidential
☐ No group with more than 20% of population
— Boundary between Brooklyn and Queens

BRONX

MANHATTAN

QUEENS

BROOKLYN

GEOGRAPHY SKILLBUILDER PLACE *What general pattern of settlement do you notice in this map of ethnic neighborhoods in New York City in 1910?*

Fire: Enemy of the City

THE GREAT CHICAGO FIRE
OCTOBER 8, 1871

- The fire burned for 29 hours.
- An estimated 300 people died.
- 100,000 were left homeless.
- More than 3 square miles of the central city was destroyed.
- Property loss was estimated at $200 million.
- 17,500 buildings were destroyed.

THE SAN FRANCISCO EARTHQUAKE
APRIL 18, 1906

- The quake lasted 28 seconds; fires burned for 4 days.
- An estimated 478 people died.
- 250,000 were left homeless.
- Fire swept through 5 square miles of the city.
- Property loss was estimated at $500 million.
- 28,000 buildings were destroyed.

Being a Strategic Reader
How to Use This
Reading Study Guide

The purpose of this *Reading Study Guide* is to help you read and understand your history textbook, *The Americans: Reconstruction through the 20th Century.* You can use this *Reading Study Guide* in two ways.

1. Use the *Reading Study Guide* side-by-side with your history book.

- Turn to the section that you are going to read in the textbook. Then, next to the book, put the pages from the *Reading Study Guide* that accompany that section. All of the heads in the *Reading Study Guide* match the heads in the textbook.
- Use the *Reading Study Guide* to help you read and organize the information in the textbook.

2. Use the *Reading Study Guide* to study for tests on the textbook.

- Reread the summary of every chapter.
- Review the definitions of the Terms and Names in the *Reading Study Guide*.
- Review the diagram of information that you filled out as you read the summaries.
- Review your answers to questions.

Strategy: Read the Terms and Names and the definition of each. The Terms and Names are in dark type in the section.
Try This: What are the definitions of "culture shock" and "melting pot"?

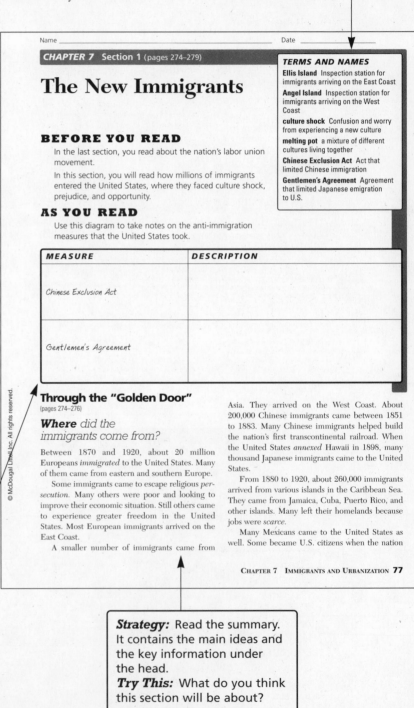

Name _____ Date _____

CHAPTER 7 Section 1 (pages 274–279)

The New Immigrants

BEFORE YOU READ
In the last section, you read about the nation's labor union movement.

In this section, you will read how millions of immigrants entered the United States, where they faced culture shock, prejudice, and opportunity.

AS YOU READ
Use this diagram to take notes on the anti-immigration measures that the United States took.

MEASURE	DESCRIPTION
Chinese Exclusion Act	
Gentlemen's Agreement	

TERMS AND NAMES
Ellis Island Inspection station for immigrants arriving on the East Coast
Angel Island Inspection station for immigrants arriving on the West Coast
culture shock Confusion and worry from experiencing a new culture
melting pot a mixture of different cultures living together
Chinese Exclusion Act Act that limited Chinese immigration
Gentlemen's Agreement Agreement that limited Japanese emigration to U.S.

Through the "Golden Door"
(pages 274–276)

Where did the immigrants come from?

Between 1870 and 1920, about 20 million Europeans *immigrated* to the United States. Many of them came from eastern and southern Europe.

Some immigrants came to escape religious *persecution.* Many others were poor and looking to improve their economic situation. Still others came to experience greater freedom in the United States. Most European immigrants arrived on the East Coast.

A smaller number of immigrants came from Asia. They arrived on the West Coast. About 200,000 Chinese immigrants came between 1851 to 1883. Many Chinese immigrants helped build the nation's first transcontinental railroad. When the United States *annexed* Hawaii in 1898, many thousand Japanese immigrants came to the United States.

From 1880 to 1920, about 260,000 immigrants arrived from various islands in the Caribbean Sea. They came from Jamaica, Cuba, Puerto Rico, and other islands. Many left their homelands because jobs were *scarce.*

Many Mexicans came to the United States as well. Some became U.S. citizens when the nation

CHAPTER 7 IMMIGRANTS AND URBANIZATION **77**

Strategy: Fill in the diagram as you read. The diagram will help you organize information in the section.
Try This: What is the purpose of this diagram?

Strategy: Read the summary. It contains the main ideas and the key information under the head.
Try This: What do you think this section will be about?

acquired Mexican territory in 1848 as a result of the Mexican War. About a million Mexicans arrived between 1910 to 1930 to escape *turmoil* in their country.

1. Name two regions of the world where immigrants to the U.S. came from.

_____

_____

Life in the New Land (pages 276–278)

How did immigrants cope in America?

Many immigrants traveled to the United States by steamship. On board the ship they shared a cramped, unclean space. Under these <u>conditions, disease spread quickly. As a result, some</u> immigrants died before they reached America.

Most European immigrants to the United States arrived in New York. There, they had to pass through an immigration station located on **Ellis Island** in New York Harbor. Officials at the station decided whether the immigrants could enter the country or had to return. Any immigrant with serious health problems or *contagious* disease was sent home. Inspectors also made sure that immigrants met the legal requirements for entering the United States.

Asian immigrants arriving on the West Coast went through **Angel Island** in San Francisco. The inspection process on Angel Island was more difficult than on Ellis Island.

Immigrants to the United States had to deal with **culture shock.** This was confusion and worry caused by experiencing a different culture. Many immigrants settled in communities with other immigrants from the same country. This made them feel more at home. They also formed organizations to help each other.

2. Name two ways immigrants dealt with culture shock.

_____

_____

Immigration Restrictions
(pages 278–279)

How did some Americans react to immigration?

By the turn of the century, some observers called America a **melting pot.** This term referred to the fact that many different cultures and races had blended in the United States.

However, this was not always the case. Many new immigrants refused to give up their culture to become part of American society.

Some Americans also preferred not to live in a melting pot. They did not like the idea of so many immigrants living in their country. The arrival of so many immigrants led to the growth of nativism. Nativism is an obvious preference for native-born Americans. Nativism gave rise to anti-immigrant groups. It also led to a demand for immigration restrictions.

On the West Coast, *prejudice* against Asians was first directed at the Chinese. During the depression of the 1870s, many Chinese immigrants agreed to work for low wages. Many American workers feared they would lose their jobs to the Chinese. As a result, labor groups pressured politicians to restrict Asian immigration. In 1882, Congress passed the **Chinese Exclusion Act.** This law banned all but a few Chinese immigrants. The ban was not lifted until 1943.

Americans showed prejudice against Japanese immigrants as well. In San Francisco, the local school board put all Chinese, Japanese, and Korean children in special Asian schools. This led to anti-American riots in Japan. President Theodore Roosevelt persuaded San Francisco officials to stop their separation policy. In exchange, Japan agreed to limit *emigration* to the United States under the **Gentlemen's Agreement** of 1907–1908.

3. Give two examples of anti-immigration measures in the U.S.

_____

_____

Strategy: When you see a word in italic type, read the definition in the Glossary at the end of the chapter.
Try This: What does *prejudice* mean? Look at the Glossary on the next page to find the definition.

Strategy: Answer the question at the end of each part.
Try This: Write an answer to Question 3.

Strategy: Underline main ideas and key information as you read.
Try This: Read the summary under the head "Life in the New Land." Underline information that you think is important. One important idea is already underlined.

How to Use This Reading Study Guide

At the end of every chapter in the *Reading Study Guide*, you will find a Glossary and a section called After You Read. The Glossary gives definitions of all the words in italic type in the chapter summaries.

After You Read is a two-page chapter review. Use After You Read to identify those parts of the chapter that you need to study more for the test on the chapter.

Name _____ Date _____

Glossary   *CHAPTER 7*   Immigration and Urbanization

annexed To incorporate territory into an existing country

contagious Spreading or tending to spread from one person to another

eligible Qualified to do something

emigration The act of leaving a country to settle in another

immigrate To enter and settle in a new country

persecution The act of oppressing or treating badly

prejudice A judgment formed without knowledge of the facts

salvation Deliverance from evil, the act of being saved

scarce Not often seen or found

turmoil Extreme unrest and commotion

unsanitary Dirty, unhealthy

AFTER YOU READ

Terms and Names

A. Write the letter of the name or term that best answers the question.

a. Social Gospel movement
b. Jane Addams
c. William Marcy Tweed
d. culture shock
e. political machine
f. patronage

_____ **1.** Which term refers to the confusion and worry that newly arrived immigrants experienced?

_____ **2.** Which term refers to a reform program that urged Christians to help improve the lives of the poor?

_____ **3.** Who was the founder of Chicago's Hull House?

_____ **4.** Who was one of the most powerful political bosses and the head of a New York City political machine?

_____ **5.** Which term refers to the giving of government jobs to people who had helped a candidate get elected?

B. Write the name or term that best completes each sentence.

Thomas Nast
Ellis Island
row house
Angel Island
kickback
Stalwart

1. Immigrants arriving on the Ea_____ the United States through _____

2. A _____ was _____ sharing side walls with other _____

3. A _____ is a _____

4. The cartoons of _____ Ring.

5. A _____ wa_____ patronage system.

Strategy: Review all of the Terms and Names before completing Parts A and B of After You Read.
Try This: Use the *Reading Study Guide* for Chapter 7 to answer Questions A 1-5.

Strategy: Review the chapter summaries before completing the Main Ideas questions. Write a complete sentence for every answer.
Try This: In your own words, what is Question 1 asking for?

AFTER YOU READ (cont.)   *CHAPTER 7* Immigration and Urbanization

Main Ideas

1. What difficulties did immigrants face in the United States?

_____

_____

2. What problems did rapid growth pose for cities?

_____

_____

_____

3. Why were immigrants such strong supporters of political machines?

_____

_____

_____

4. What problems did the patronage system create?

_____

_____

_____

5. Why did big business support high tariffs?

_____

_____

Thinking Critically

Answer the following questions on a separate sheet of paper.

1. Do you think America should be a melting pot? Why or why not?

2. Consider modern cities. What problems that existed at the turn of the 20th century have been fixed? Which do you think still exist?

Strategy: Write one or two paragraphs for every Think Critically question.
Try This: In your own words, what is Question 1 asking for?

CHAPTER 1 **Section 1** (pages 4–13)

The Americas, West Africa, and Europe

BEFORE YOU READ

In this section, you will learn about the people who lived in North America, West Africa, and Europe in the 1400s.

In the next section, you will see how these people came together in the Americas.

AS YOU READ

Use this diagram to take notes. These notes will help you remember what you learned about the lifestyles and beliefs of people in North America, Africa, and Europe.

PLACE	HOUSING, FOOD, AND SKILLS	SOCIAL ORGANIZATION	RELIGION AND VALUES
North America	Pueblos: adobe houses, farming		
West Africa			
Europe			

Ancient Cultures in the Americas (pages 4–5)

Who lived in the Americas first?

The first humans came to *the Americas* from Asia about 40,000 years ago. Over thousands of years, these people spread out across North and South America. They lived by hunting animals and gathering wild plants.

Between 10,000 and 5,000 years ago (800 to 3000 BC), people living in Mexico discovered a new way to get food. They began to raise plants or to farm. The practice of farming spread. Because people who farmed no longer had to search for plant foods, they could stay in one place. They could turn their attention to learning crafts and to building settled communities. In this way, farming made possible the growth of *civilizations*.

Beginning about 3,000 years ago (1000 BC), a number of rich and complex Native American civilizations developed. The **Aztecs** settled in Mexico in the 1200s. The **Anasazi** farmed the dry areas of the Southwest between AD 100 and 1300.

1. Who were the first people to live in the Americas?

Native American Societies of the 1400s (pages 6–8)

How did Native Americans live?

Native American people lived in many kinds of *environments*. For example, the **Pueblo** people lived in the dry Southwest (today's Arizona and New Mexico). They built *adobe* houses and grew corn and beans. In the forests of the Northeast (today's New York state), the **Iroquois** hunted, fished, and gathered fruits and nuts.

Trade routes across North America linked Native American groups that lived far apart. Trade allowed them to share both goods and ideas.

Native Americans did not buy and sell land. They treated the land as a *resource* for all groups to share. They felt that the world was filled with *spirits*. For instance, the spirit of a relative who had died might still serve as a guide to the living.

The family was the basic unit. Groups of families, or clans, got together for special events. By the time Europeans arrived in North America, Native American cultures were thousands of years old.

2. How did Native American people in different environments get their food?

_____

_____

West African Societies of the 1400s (pages 8–10)

What was life like in a West African kingdom?

Three powerful kingdoms with strong rulers played important roles in West Africa. **Songhai** controlled trade across the Sahara Desert. **Benin** was a powerful nation in the forests of the southern coast. In central Africa, the kingdom of the **Kongo** united smaller areas under one ruler.

Most West Africans lived with their families in small villages. They farmed, herded, hunted, and fished. The oldest people in the family had the most influence over the others.

Religious *rituals* were important in daily life. West Africans respected the spirits of living and non-living things. Many also believed in a single Creator.

By the 1400s, some West African leaders had accepted a new religion called Islam. **Islam** was founded by the prophet Muhammad in Arabia in 622. It taught that there is only one God, called Allah. Islam later spread among ordinary people.

The kingdoms of West Africa were connected to North Africa, Europe, and Asia by trade. Sailors and traders arrived from Portugal in the 1400s. Some Portuguese settled on islands off Africa. They started large farms, or plantations, to grow sugar cane. The Portuguese started the use of African slaves for field labor.

3. What were two ways of earning a living in a West African kingdom?

_____

European Societies of the 1400s (pages 10–13)

What was happening in Europe?

In European societies, everyone had a rank or position. Rulers and nobles owned the most land and were the most powerful. Leaders of the church, or *clergy*, were also important. At the bottom were the *peasants*, who worked in the fields. Most Europeans lived in small farming villages.

European society was beginning to change. Most people belonged to the Roman Catholic Church. In the early 1500s, *reformers* called for changes in the Church. Some of these reformers broke away and formed Protestant churches. This movement was called the **Reformation.**

People were looking for new sources of wealth. They developed new ways of doing business. One of these was **joint-stock companies.** In a joint-stock company people invested, or pooled, their money. The companies used the money for exploration or trade, and the *investors* shared in the *profits*.

Europeans also developed better ships and better ways to *navigate*. They were able to sail longer distances. All of these changes helped create an age of exploration.

4. What were two important changes in Europe?

_____

_____

Spanish North America

TERMS AND NAMES

Christopher Columbus Italian explorer who sailed to North America for Spain

Taino Native Americans who lived where Columbus first landed

Treaty of Tordesillas Agreement between Spain and Portugal to explore different lands

Columbian Exchange Trade across the Atlantic Ocean

conquistador Spanish explorer

Hernán Cortés Conquistador who defeated the Aztecs

New Spain Spanish colonies in Mexico and Central America

mestizo Person of mixed Spanish and Native American blood

encomienda Brutal Spanish system of using Native Americans for labor

New Mexico Spanish colonies in North America

BEFORE YOU READ

In the last section, you learned about the people living in North America, West Africa, and Europe.

In this section, you will learn about what happened when the Spanish came to North America from Europe.

AS YOU READ

Use this diagram to take notes. The notes will help you remember how the arrival of the Spanish affected people already living in the Americas.

PLACE	PEOPLE LIVING THERE	WHY THE SPANISH CAME THERE	WHAT THE SPANISH DID THERE
Hispaniola		seeking a trade route to Asia	
Mexico			
Southwest			

Columbus Crosses the Atlantic
(pages 14–17)

How did Columbus change people's lives?

Christopher Columbus was an Italian sailor. He believed he could find a new trade route to Asia by sailing west, across the Atlantic, instead of east. He asked the rulers of Spain to give him money and supplies. In exchange, he would claim new lands for Spain and *convert* the people he found to Christianity.

In 1492, Columbus sailed across the Atlantic. He landed on an island between North and South America, now called Hispaniola. He called the native people there **Taino,** from their word for "noble ones." He made three more voyages to the Americas, bringing soldiers, priests, and people to settle the land.

The arrival of the Spanish was a disaster for Native Americans. Many died from the harsh working conditions. Others caught diseases brought by Europeans. Because they had no resistance to these diseases, tens of thousands of Native

Americans died.

Because of the Native American deaths, the Spanish needed more laborers. So they began to bring Africans to the New World as slaves. From the 1250s to the 1800s, about 12 million Africans were taken to the Americas.

Many European countries wanted to claim American land for themselves. In 1494, Spain and Portugal signed the **Treaty of Tordesillas.** It divided the Western Hemisphere north to south. Spain could explore and start colonies in areas west of the line. Portugal could have lands to the east.

After Columbus, ships carried trade goods between the Americas and Europe. This ongoing transfer of goods came to be known as the **Columbian Exchange.**

1. How did Columbus's arrival in the Americas affect Native Americans, Africans, and Europeans?

_____

_____

_____

The Spanish Claim a New Empire (pages 17–19)

Why did Spain start colonies in the Americas?

After Columbus, many more Spanish explorers called **conquistadores** came to the Americas. They were looking for gold and silver.

The conquistador **Hernán Cortés** heard about a rich empire in Mexico. With the help of some native people, Cortés's army conquered the Aztecs and took their gold. Then the Aztecs rebelled. Finally, in 1521, the Spanish defeated the Aztecs again, partly because so many Aztecs had died of European diseases. The Spanish called their new colony **New Spain.**

Most of the Spanish who settled in the Americas were men. They often married Native American women. This created a large population of **mestizos,** people who were part Spanish and part Native American.

The Spanish forced native workers to labor under the *encomienda* system. Many workers were treated badly. Some died from overwork. In 1542, Spain ended the encomienda system because it was so brutal. Then Spanish settlers began to use African slaves.

Spain built a large empire in the Americas. It conquered the rich Native American empires of the Incas in South America and the Mayas in Central America and Mexico. Spain got large amounts of gold and silver from the *New World*. It became the richest and most powerful nation in Europe.

2. What was the main reason the Spanish claimed colonies in the New World?

_____

_____

Spain Explores the Southwest and West (pages 19–21)

Where did Spain send missionaries?

After founding New Spain, the Spanish sent explorers, *missionaries,* and settlers into North America. The colony of **New Mexico** extended throughout what is now the Southwestern United States. They founded the city of Sante Fe and traded with New Spain. Their aims were to convert the Pueblo peoples and to prevent other European nations from taking this land.

In 1528, the Spanish began to build *missions* in what is now Texas. In 1769, they founded a string of missions in California. They converted Native Americans and taught them European styles and ways. The Native Americans did the work of farming and building the mission buildings.

Some of the native people were angry at how they were treated by the Spanish. In 1680, the religious leader Popé led an uprising that drove the Spanish out of the area. It took the Spanish 14 years to get this area back.

3. Where did the Spanish missionaries found missions in North America?

_____

_____

CHAPTER 1   Section 3 (pages 22–32)

Early British Colonies

BEFORE YOU READ

In the last section, you learned how the Spanish claimed an empire in the Americas.

In this section, you will learn how the British came to North America and founded their own colonies.

AS YOU READ

Use this diagram to take notes. The notes will help you keep track of the colonies founded by the British in North America.

COLONY	WHO CAME?	WHY DID THEY COME?	WHAT PROBLEMS DID THEY FACE?	HOW DID THEY THEY SOLVE THEM?
Jamestown	English	wanted riches	nearly starved	
Massachusetts				
New Netherland				
Pennsylvania				

An English Settlement at Jamestown (pages 22–25)

What happened at Jamestown?

In 1607, English settlers founded **Jamestown, Virginia.** It was the first permanent English colony in the Americas. Its leader was **John Smith.**

Many colonists wanted to get rich quick by finding gold or furs. But Smith forced them to farm.

He also got help from the native Powhatan people. After Smith returned to England, the colonists almost starved. They were saved when more colonists and supplies arrived from England.

Then the colonists discovered they could sell tobacco in Europe for a big profit. They hired **indentured servants** to work on tobacco plantations. These workers traveled to America from Europe. They received food and a place to live. In exchange, they agreed to work on a plantation.

The Jamestown colony grew and needed more land for farming. The English settlers took Powhatan land, and the Powhatan fought back.

The settlers also fought among themselves. Poor farmers complained about being taxed and governed without being able to vote. But their rebellion failed.

1. What were two problems Jamestown faced?

Puritans Create a "New England" (pages 26–28)

Why did the Puritans come to America?

The **Puritans** were a religious group that wanted to *purify* the Church of England by removing some of the practices that were more like the Catholic Church. They had been punished in England. In 1620, a small group of Puritans came to North America and founded the colony of Plymouth.

In 1630, Puritans started the Massachusetts Bay Colony. Unlike the settlers in Jamestown, the Puritans were well prepared with people and supplies. **John Winthrop** was their first governor.

Puritans controlled the colony. They did not like dissent, or the expression of other points of view. Dissenters like Roger Williams and Anne Hutchinson both had to leave Massachusetts. They settled in what is now Rhode Island.

Native Americans helped the Puritans at first. As the colony grew, however, settlers began to take their lands. Native Americans died of European diseases. And the settlers wanted the Native Americans to accept Puritan laws and religion.

In 1675, **King Philip's War** began. A chief the English called King Philip led an alliance of Native Americans against the settlers. The brutal war lasted over a year, until the English finally won.

2. What did the Puritans want to find in America?

Settlement of the Middle Colonies (pages 28–30)

How were New Netherland and Pennsylvania alike?

Dutch settlers founded the colony of New Netherland in 1621. Their *religious tolerance* brought people of many faiths to New Amsterdam, the capital city. There were also many Africans, both free and enslaved.

The Dutch had friendly relations with the Native Americans. In 1644, England took over the colony and renamed it New York.

The colony of Pennsylvania was founded by **William Penn.** Penn was a **Quaker.** The ideals of this religious group were equality, cooperation, and religious tolerance. Pennsylvania gave land to all adult men and had a *representative assembly*. Penn also treated Native Americans fairly.

3. What two things did New Netherland and Pennsylvania have in common?

England and Its Colonies Prosper (pages 30–32)

How did the colonies thrive?

Trade was the main reason England wanted colonies. The theory of **mercantilism** said that a nation becomes rich and powerful two ways: (1) by getting gold and silver, and (2) by selling more goods than it buys.

England's American colonies provided *raw materials* to England. They also bought goods made in England. Under this system, both England and its colonies gained wealth. In 1651, England's *Parliament* passed the **Navigation Acts.** Their purpose was to control trade with the colonies.

By 1732, there were 13 English colonies. Governors appointed by the king headed most colonial governments. Only white men who owned land could vote. Colonial assemblies had the right to raise taxes and make laws.

4. How did England benefit from its colonies?

CHAPTER 1 Section 4 (pages 33–41)

The Colonies Come of Age

BEFORE YOU READ

In the last section, you learned how the British founded colonies in the Americas.

In this section, you will learn about the growth of those colonies in the North and South.

AS YOU READ

Use this diagram to take notes. These notes will help you remember how people lived in the colonies.

TERMS AND NAMES

middle passage The voyage that brought slaves to America

triangular trade The pattern of shipping trade across the Atlantic

Enlightenment Intellectual movement that started in Europe

Benjamin Franklin Philadelphia inventor, writer, and political leader

Great Awakening Religious revival movement in the colonies

Jonathan Edwards Forceful preacher in the Great Awakening

French and Indian War War that gave the British control of North America

William Pitt British leader in the French and Indian War

Pontiac Native American leader who fought the British

Proclamation of 1763 Law limiting the area of English settlement

REGION	ECONOMY	SOCIETY
The South	plantations growing a single cash crop use of slave labor	
The North		

A Plantation Economy Arises in the South (pages 33–35)

How did people farm in the South?

Colonists in the South created a society based on farming. A typical large Southern farm, or plantation, grew a single *cash crop*, such as tobacco or rice. Plantations often had their own warehouses and docks.

Most Southerners worked small farms. But the wealthy plantation owners, or *planters*, controlled the economy. They also controlled the social and political life of the South.

Planters used enslaved Africans as workers. Africans were brought to the Americas by a route across the Atlantic called the **middle passage.** This was one leg of the **triangular trade,** which had three main parts: (1) Merchants carried rum and other goods from New England to Africa; (2) they brought slaves from Africa to the West Indies, where they sold them for sugar and molasses; (3) finally, they sold those goods in New England.

Africans were brought to America on crowded ships. They were treated cruelly, and many died. Once in America, slaves tried to hold onto their African culture. Many resisted slavery, and some led revolts. These resulted in even harsher slave laws.

1. What were two main features of farming in the South?

_____

_____

Industry Grows in the North
(pages 35–36)

How did people earn a living in the North?

The economy of the North was based on small farms, *manufacturing,* and trade. Bustling port cities developed. Ship-building was important, and traders sailed all over the world. Merchants became wealthy and important. The Northern colonies attracted many immigrants from Europe.

Farms in the North usually produced several cash crops. They did not depend on slave labor. However, slavery and *racial prejudice* did exist in the North.

2. What are three kinds of work people did in the North?

_____

_____

The Enlightenment and the Great Awakening (pages 37–38)

What new ideas and beliefs spread in the colonies?

The **Enlightenment** was a philosophical movement that said you could use reason and science to find truth. It began in Europe and spread to the colonies. **Benjamin Franklin** was one of its leaders. He conducted scientific experiments and made several practical inventions.

The Enlightenment had two important effects: (1) its emphasis on science as a source of truth weakened the authority of the church, and (2) the idea that people have natural rights which governments must respect challenged the authority of the British rulers.

The **Great Awakening** was a series of religious *revivals* that spread through the colonies. **Jonathan Edwards** was one of its most powerful preachers. By awakening renewed religious feelings, the Great Awakening challenged the authority of existing churches. New Christian *denominations* became popular.

3. How did the Enlightenment and the Great Awakening change people's beliefs?

_____

_____

The French and Indian War
(pages 39–41)

What caused the French and Indian War?

Like Britain, France also had colonies in the Americas. France's vast empire included eastern Canada, the Great Lakes region, and the upper Mississippi River.

Most French settlers were fur traders or Catholic priests who wanted to convert the Native Americans. The French had better relations with the Native Americans than the English did.

The British and French fought over the western lands. In 1754, the **French and Indian War** began. At first, the British and the colonies were losing the war. Then the English king appointed **William Pitt** to the government. Under Pitt's leadership, the British began to win battles. After they took the city of Quebec, the British had won the war. In 1763, France gave up Canada and all of North America east of the Mississippi to Britain.

Native Americans did not like British settlers moving west onto their lands. Led by **Pontiac,** an Ottawa chief, they attacked British forts. The British purposely gave smallpox to Native Americans who came to discuss peace. The spreading disease weakened the Native American groups, and they surrendered.

To prevent further fighting, the British banned colonists from settling west of a line along the Appalachian Mountains. Many colonists were angered by this **Proclamation of 1763,** and continued to settle the area anyway.

4. What was the main cause of the war?

_____

_____

Glossary   CHAPTER 1 Exploration and the Colonial Era

adobe Sun-dried bricks

cash crop A crop grown for sale rather than for the farmer's use

civilization Society with highly developed culture, including arts, politics, writing, and science

clergy Religious leaders

convert To persuade someone to accept a particular religion

denomination A group of churches within one religion

environment Natural surroundings, including weather, plants, and animals

investor Person who contributes money to a project in the hope of making a profit

manufacturing Making goods such as clothes or tools

missionary Someone sent to convert others to a religion

missions Places where religious workers try to help local people and/or convert them.

navigate To plan and control the course of a ship

New World The Americas

Parliament The body that makes the British laws

peasants People who work in the fields for rich landowners

planters Landowners, usually of large farms or plantations

profit The money people receive above the amount they invest

purify To make pure or simplify

racial prejudice Dislike of people because of race

raw material Unprocessed natural resource such as timber or wool

reformers People who work to improve the way things are done

religious tolerance Equal treatment of all religious faiths

representative assembly A law-making body elected by the people

resource A natural source of something useful, like water

revivals Religious meetings where people renew commitment

ritual Repeated ceremony that gives meaning to events

spirit The soul or consciousness of a person

the Americas North, South, and Central America

AFTER YOU READ

Terms and Names

A. Write the letter of the name or term next to the statement that describes it best.

a. Anasazi

b. indentured servant

c. conquistador

d. Christopher Columbus

e. Puritan

f. Benjamin Franklin

_____ **1.** I am the Italian explorer who found the Americas instead of a westward route to Asia.

_____ **2.** I am a Spanish explorer and soldier.

_____ **3.** I am a member of an ancient Native American people of the Southwest.

_____ **4.** I am a colonial scientist and inventor.

_____ **5.** I am a member of a strict religious group that settled Massachusetts.

B. Circle the name or term that best completes each sentence.

1. Many people invested their money in _____ in order to finance colonial exploration.

   mercantilism   **Columbian Exchange**   **joint-stock company**

2. _____ is the colony founded by Cortés after he defeated the Aztecs.

   New Spain   **Jamestown**   **New Mexico**

3. The economic theory of _____ said that nations gain wealth by having colonies.

   mercantilism   **Columbian Exchange**   **joint-stock company**

4. The voyage that brought enslaved Africans to the New World was called the _____.

   middle passage   **Columbian Exchange**   **joint-stock company**

5. The _____ stressed reason and the scientific method.

   Columbian Exchange   **Enlightenment**   **mercantilism**

Main Ideas

1. How did the invention of farming lead to the development of civilizations?

   _____

2. What role did disease play in European colonization?

   _____

3. What are two things the Europeans and Native Americans fought over?

   _____

4. How did the colonies make England rich?

   _____

5. How did France lose its colonies in the Americas?

   _____

Thinking Critically

Answer the following questions on a separate sheet of paper.

1. Do you think the Enlightenment ideas are still important today? Give evidence for your opinion.

2. Compare and contrast how the Spanish created their empire in the New World with how the British settled their colonies.

CHAPTER 2 Section 1 (pages 48–55)

Colonial Resistance and Rebellion

BEFORE YOU READ

In the last section, you learned how the British and their American colonists pushed the French out of North America.

In this section, you will see how the American colonists rebelled against the British and formed a new nation—the United States of America.

AS YOU READ

Use the chart below to take notes on the increased tensions between Britain and the colonies.

BRITISH ACTIONS	COLONISTS' ACTIONS
Sugar Act	Became angry
Stamp Act	

TERMS AND NAMES

Sugar Act Law passed by Parliament to try to raise money

Stamp Act Law passed by Parliament to make colonists buy a stamp to place on many items such as wills and newspapers

Samuel Adams One of the founders of the Sons of Liberty

Boston Massacre Conflict between colonists and British soldiers in which four colonists were killed

Boston Tea Party Protest against increased tea prices in which colonists dumped British tea into Boston Harbor

King George III King of England during the American Revolution

John Locke English philosopher who believed people had natural rights to life, liberty, and property

Common Sense Pamphlet written by Thomas Paine that attacked monarchy

Thomas Jefferson Main author of the Declaration of Independence

Declaration of Independence Document that said the United States was an independent nation

The Colonies and Britain Grow Apart (pages 48–49)

Why were the colonists angry?

After winning the French and Indian War, Britain left troops in North America to protect the colonists from Native Americans. The colonists feared the troops could be used against them.

The British had spent a lot of money on the war. Britain wanted to raise money from the colonies to pay the cost of keeping troops there. In 1764, Parliament passed the **Sugar Act.** This act was meant to help Britain raise money by changing taxes.

Some colonists felt that Britain had no right to tax them because colonists were not represented in Parliament. They felt this violated their rights as

British citizens. Some colonists became angry at the British government.

1. What two things made the colonists angry at the British government?

_____

_____

The Colonies Organize to Resist Britain (pages 49–50)

Why did the colonists and the British fight over taxes?

The British Parliament passed the **Stamp Act** in 1765. It made the colonists buy and place stamps on many items. Angry colonists *boycotted* British goods in protest.

A secret group called the Sons of Liberty also protested. Colonial representatives held a Stamp Act Congress. They declared that Britain had no right to tax the colonies.

Parliament *repealed* the Stamp Act—and then passed other taxes on imports and on tea. **Samuel Adams** and other colonists protested again. There were riots. Britain sent more troops to Boston.

2. How did the colonists react to new taxes? What was the British response?

_____

_____

Tension Mounts in Massachusetts (pages 50–51)

Why did the colonists stay angry?

In 1770, some British soldiers fired on a mob of colonists. Several colonists were killed. Colonial leaders called the event the **Boston Massacre.**

For a while the situation relaxed. The British repealed all the taxes except the one on tea. In 1773, Britain gave a British company the right to all the trade in tea. Colonial merchants were angry at losing business. Colonists dressed as "Indians" dumped the British tea into Boston Harbor. This was called the **Boston Tea Party.**

To punish Massachusetts, Britain closed Boston Harbor and placed Boston under *martial law*. Other colonies supported Massachusetts and sent representatives to the First Continental Congress. They issued a declaration of colonial rights. They said that if Britain attacked, the colonies should fight back.

3. How did Britain try to punish Boston for its protests?

_____

_____

The Road to Revolution (pages 52–53)

How did the colonists prepare for war?

Some New England towns began to prepare for attack. *Minutemen* stored guns and ammunition. In 1775, the British marched to Lexington, Massachusetts, to seize these weapons. In the battle of Lexington and Concord, the colonists defeated the British.

The Second Continental Congress met. Some leaders urged independence, but others were not ready. They did form the Continental Army with George Washington in command. They were getting ready for war but hoping for peace.

The Congress sent **King George III** a peace offer, but he rejected it. Instead, the king declared that the colonies were in rebellion.

4. What actions did the colonies take to prepare for war?

_____

_____

The Patriots Declare Independence (pages 53–55)

What ideas supported rebellion?

More colonists began to object to British rule. Colonial leaders were influenced by the ideas of **John Locke.** Locke said that people have a right to life, liberty, and property. People form a *social contract*, or an agreement, with their government. If the government takes away the people's rights, the people can overthrow the government.

Thomas Paine argued for independence in his pamphlet **Common Sense.** Many people read it and agreed with his arguments.

The Second Continental Congress adopted the **Declaration of Independence** on July 4, 1776. **Thomas Jefferson** used some of Locke's ideas in the Declaration. He said the people's rights to life, liberty, and the pursuit of happiness cannot be taken away. Government gets its power from the people, and the people can remove a government that threatens their rights. Then he listed the ways the British had taken away the colonists' rights.

5. What ideas of John Locke did Thomas Jefferson put in the Declaration of Independence?

_____

_____

The War for Independence

BEFORE YOU READ

In the last section, you learned why the colonists rebelled against the British.

In this section, you will see how the Americans won the Revolutionary War and established a new nation.

AS YOU READ

Use the time line below to take notes on the important battles and other events of the Revolutionary War.

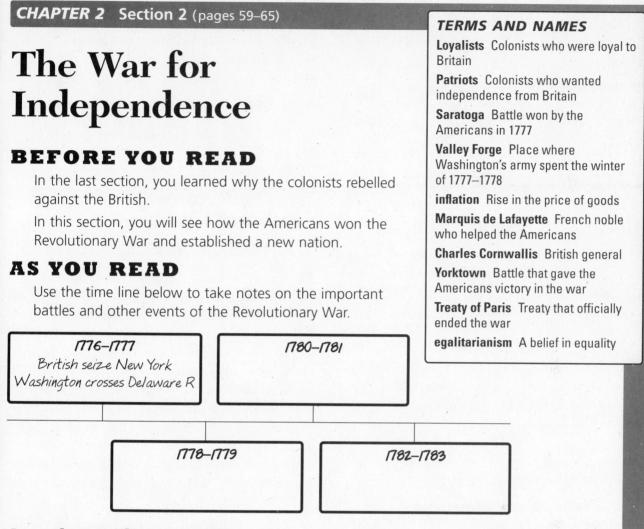

TERMS AND NAMES

Loyalists Colonists who were loyal to Britain

Patriots Colonists who wanted independence from Britain

Saratoga Battle won by the Americans in 1777

Valley Forge Place where Washington's army spent the winter of 1777–1778

inflation Rise in the price of goods

Marquis de Lafayette French noble who helped the Americans

Charles Cornwallis British general

Yorktown Battle that gave the Americans victory in the war

Treaty of Paris Treaty that officially ended the war

egalitarianism A belief in equality

1776–1777
British seize New York
Washington crosses Delaware R

1780–1781

1778–1779

1782–1783

Americans Choose Sides (pages 59–60)

Who were the Loyalists and Patriots?

Colonists were divided equally between Loyalists and Patriots. The Revolution was both a war for independence and a civil war.

Loyalists supported the British and were loyal to the king. Some felt that the British could protect their rights better than a new government could. Others did not want to be punished as rebels. Many went to British North America, or Canada.

Patriots wanted independence. Some wanted to be free of British rule. Others saw economic opportunity in a new nation.

Many African Americans joined the Patriots. Others fought on the British side because they were offered freedom from slavery. Most Native Americans supported the British.

1. Why did some colonists remain loyal to Britain?

_____

_____

The War Moves to the Middle States (pages 60–62)

What were the important battles?

In March 1776, the British army seized New York City. Their aim was to *isolate* New England. But on Christmas night of 1776, Washington crossed the Delaware River and took Trenton, New Jersey. He soon scored another victory. These wins gave Americans hope.

In the fall of 1777, the Americans won an important victory at **Saratoga,** New York. This win proved that American forces could defeat the British army. It convinced France to support the Americans.

Later, Washington's army suffered from cold and hunger during a winter at **Valley Forge,** Pennsylvania.

2. Why was the Battle of Saratoga important?

_____

_____

Life During the Revolution
(pages 62–63)

How did the war affect people?

The war touched all Americans. Congress printed money to pay American troops. The more money they printed, the less the money was worth. This caused **inflation,** which is a rise in the price of goods.

As men went to war, many women took their husbands' places running homes, farms, and businesses. Some women earned money washing and cooking for the troops. A few even went into battle.

Thousands of slaves escaped to freedom during the war. About 5,000 African Americans served in the Continental Army. Their courage and loyalty impressed many white Americans.

3. How did the war affect different groups of Americans?

_____

_____

Winning the War (pages 63–65)

Why did the Americans win?

In 1778, the Americans got help. The **Marquis de Lafayette,** a French nobleman, joined Washington. He helped make the American army an effective fighting force. The French also sent soldiers and their navy to help the Americans.

The British moved their war effort south. British general **Charles Cornwallis** moved his army to Yorktown, Virginia. Meanwhile, French military forces arrived in America. French and American forces surrounded the British at **Yorktown.** French ships defeated British naval

forces. Cornwallis could not get help. The British surrendered at Yorktown on October 19, 1783.

The **Treaty of Paris** was signed in 1783. Britain recognized the United States as a nation with borders from the Atlantic Ocean to the Mississippi River.

4. How did the French help the Americans win the war?

_____

_____

The War Becomes a Symbol of Liberty (page 65)

What did the Revolution mean?

The ideas that led to the Revolution influenced the new nation. The war also brought changes. Differences between rich and poor had not been important during the war. Military leaders had shown respect to their men. These changes caused a rise in **egalitarianism,** a belief in equality. It included the idea that people should be valued for ability and effort—not wealth or family.

This egalitarianism applied only to white males. The status of women, African Americans, and Native Americans did not change. They still did not have the rights that white male property-owners did.

5. Whom did the rise in egalitarianism apply to?

_____

_____

The Confederation and the Constitution

TERMS AND NAMES

republic A government in which the people elect representatives to govern

Articles of Confederation The first government of the United States

Northwest Ordinance of 1787 Law that organized the Northwest Territories

Shays's Rebellion Anti-tax protest by farmers

James Madison One of the leaders of the Constitutional Convention

checks and balances Powers given to separate branches of government to keep any one from getting too much power

ratification Official approval of the Constitution

Federalist Supporter of the new Constitution

Antifederalist Person opposed to ratification of the new Constitution

bill of rights Set of amendments passed to protect individual rights

BEFORE YOU READ

In the last section, you learned how the people of the United States won their independence.

In this section, you will read about the early years of the young nation.

AS YOU READ

Use the chart below to take notes on the characteristics of the government provided by the Articles of Confederation and the Constitution.

	CHARACTERISTICS
Articles of Confederation	Weak central government
Constitution	

Experimenting with Confederation (pages 68–69)

What was the Confederation?

Americans wanted a **republic**—a government in which the people elect representatives to govern. But the states were not eager to unite under a strong central government.

The Second Continental Congress wrote the **Articles of Confederation.** It gave much power to the states and little power to the *federal government*. This plan set up a Congress elected by the people. Each state had one vote in Congress.

The *Confederation* had some successes. One was the **Northwest Ordinance of 1787.** It organized the land west of the Appalachian Mountains into *territories*. It decided how new states would enter the union.

But the Confederation also had problems.

States with small populations had the same power as large states. Congress did not have the power to tax. The Articles could not be changed without the agreement of all states.

There were economic problems, too. Congress had borrowed large amounts of money during the war. To pay these debts, the states raised taxes. High taxes were a problem for many Americans.

1. What problems did the Confederation face?

_____

Drafting the Constitution
(pages 69–70)

Why did the delegates write a new Constitution?

Farmers were losing their land because they could not pay the high taxes. In 1787, a tax protest by farmers, which was called **Shays's Rebellion**, led to violence. The Massachusetts militia killed four protesters.

The weak national government could not solve the nation's problems. In 1787, 12 states sent *delegates* to Philadelphia to fix the Articles of Confederation. Instead, the delegates decided to form a whole new government. **James Madison,** a delegate from Virginia, was one of the leaders of the convention and kept a record of the debates. He is called the Father of the Constitution.

The delegates made compromises. They agreed on a legislature with two houses. Each state would have two members in the Senate, or upper house. In the House of Representatives, or lower house, representation would be based on a state's population. The Three-Fifths Compromise allowed states to count three-fifths of their slaves as part of their population.

2. **What three important decisions did delegates make at the convention?**

Creating a New Government
(pages 70–71)

Who had the power in the new Constitution?

Power was still divided between the national government and the states. But the central government was stronger than it was under the Articles.

The delegates agreed to a separation of powers. Congress, the legislative branch, would make the laws. The executive branch would carry out laws. The judicial branch would settle legal disputes. They created a system of **checks and balances** to prevent any branch from getting too much power. They also created a way of changing, or passing *amendments* to, the Constitution.

3. **How was power divided in the new Constitution?**

Ratifying the Constitution
(pages 71–74)

Would you vote to ratify the Constitution?

The convention decided that **ratification,** or official approval, of the Constitution would be in state conventions. Voters elected representatives to the conventions.

Federalists supported the new Constitution. They published essays called *The Federalist Papers* to explain and defend the Constitution. **Antifederalists** opposed the Constitution. They thought it gave the central government too much power. They wanted a **bill of rights,** a formal, written guarantee of people's rights and freedoms, like many states had. Federalists promised to add a Bill of Rights. Because of this promise, the required nine states ratified the Constitution in 1789.

The Bill of Rights consisted of ten amendments that guaranteed Americans rights such as freedom of religion, speech, and the press. They protected citizens from the threat of standing armies. They protected citizens against having their homes searched and property seized. They also protected the rights of people accused of crimes. Finally, they gave all powers that were not given to the federal government to the people and the states. The Bill of Rights was ratified in 1791.

4. **How did the Federalists and Antifederalists feel about the Constitution?**

Continuing Relevance of the Constitution (pages 74–75)

Why is the Constitution still important?

The Constitution has met the changing needs of Americans for over 200 years. That is because it is flexible.

The Constitution can be changed, or amended, when needed. But the amendment process is difficult. In over 200 years, there have been only 27 amendments to the Constitution.

5. **Why has the Constitution been able to meet the changing needs of the country for so long?**

Launching the New Nation

TERMS AND NAMES

Judiciary Act of 1789 Law that set up the national court system

cabinet Chief advisors of the president

Alexander Hamilton An early Federalist leader

Democratic-Republican Party led by Jefferson

two-party system Political system where two political parties compete for power

protective tariff Tax on imported goods to protect domestic business

John Jay Negotiated treaty with Britain over territory

XYZ Affair American anger over bribes demanded by French diplomats

Alien and Sedition Acts Laws that made it harder to become a citizen and created harsh punishments for people who criticize the government

nullification State effort to cancel a federal law

BEFORE YOU READ

In the last section, you learned how the new Constitution was created.

In this section, you will see how the new government acted.

AS YOU READ

Use the chart below to take notes on the leaders, beliefs and goals, and actions of the nation's first political parties.

	FEDERALISTS	ANTIFEDERALISTS
Leaders	Hamilton	
Beliefs/Goals	strong central government	
Actions		

Washington Heads the New Government (pages 78–80)

Why did Hamilton and Jefferson disagree?

George Washington was the first president of the United States. He and Congress set up the new government. The **Judiciary Act of 1789** set up a national court system.

Congress also set up three executive departments. The leaders Washington named to head these departments made up the first **cabinet**, or chief advisors of the president.

Secretary of the Treasury **Alexander Hamilton** wanted a strong central government. Secretary of State Thomas Jefferson wanted a weak central government.

Hamilton wanted to create a *national bank*. Jefferson opposed this. He and James Madison argued against Hamilton. Finally, they agreed to Hamilton's national bank. In exchange, the new capital of the nation was built in the South, in Washington, D.C.

1. What were the different views of government held by Hamilton and Jefferson?

_____

_____

The First Political Parties (pages 80–81)

What is a political party?

The differences between Hamilton and Jefferson led to the nation's first political parties. Federalists agreed with Hamilton. **Democratic-Republicans** agreed with Jefferson that state governments should be stronger.

The two groups developed into *political parties.* They were the basis for the **two-party system,** in which two political parties compete for power.

Congress passed two important taxes. One was a **protective tariff.** It placed a tax on goods imported from Europe. But Hamilton wanted more tax money. He pushed through a tax on whiskey. Whiskey was made by small farmers on the frontier. They were so angry about the tax that they attacked the tax collectors.

Hamilton wanted to show that the federal government could enforce the law on the frontier. The Whiskey Rebellion was put down by federal troops.

2. Who led the first political parties?

_____

_____

Foreign Affairs Trouble the Nation; Native Americans Resist White Settlers (pages 81–82)

What were America's earliest foreign policy problems?

In 1789 the French overthrew their monarchy. Then the French went to war against Britain. The United States had a *treaty* with France. Democratic-Republicans wanted to honor the treaty and support France. Federalists wanted to back the British. Washington decided on neutrality—to support neither side.

In 1795 Spain and the United States signed the Pinckney Treaty. Spain gave up claims to land east of the Mississippi. This treaty also paved the way for the westward expansion of the United States.

Settlers streamed into the Northwest Territory. This angered the Native Americans there. They continued to claim their tribal lands. Native Americans formed a confederacy that won some battles against American troops. In 1794 federal troops defeated the confederacy.

At the same time, **John Jay** negotiated a treaty with Britain. The British agreed to give up their forts in the Northwest Territory. Still, the British continued to bother American ships in the Caribbean.

3. How did the United States handle problems with France and Spain?

_____

_____

Adams Provokes Criticism
(pages 82–83)

Was John Adams a good president?

President Washington retired. Federalist John Adams was elected president. Thomas Jefferson, a Democratic-Republican, became vice-president.

France began to interfere with American shipping. Adams sent representatives to France. Three French officials demanded *bribes* from the Americans. This was called the **XYZ Affair.** Some Americans felt insulted and wanted war against France. But Adams settled the matter through *diplomacy.*

Adams thought the Democratic-Republicans and immigrants who supported them were dangerous. The Federalists supported the **Alien and Sedition Acts of 1798.** These acts made it harder to become an American citizen and created harsh punishment for people who criticized the government.

Democratic-Republicans opposed these laws. Kentucky and Virginia claimed that states could cancel laws that they thought were unconstitutional. This is called **nullification.**

4. How did Adams handle the fear of foreign influence at home?

_____

_____

Glossary — CHAPTER 2 Revolution and the Early Republic

amendment A formal change to the Constitution

boycotted Refused to buy certain goods

bribes Payments of money to persuade or influence

confederation A loose alliance of states

delegate A person given power to act for others; a representative to a convention

diplomacy Settling disagreements between nations by discussion and negotiation

federal government Form of government where a group of states share some powers but keep others

isolate To set apart from others

martial law Rule by the military

minutemen Ordinary citizens who could be ready to fight as soldiers "at a minute's notice"

national bank A bank funded by the federal government and wealthy investors to issue paper money and handle taxes

political parties Organizations that support candidates for office and try to control the government

social contract An agreement between citizens and the government

repealed Canceled

territories Areas of land owned and governed by the United States but that are not states

treaty A formal agreement between two or more nations

AFTER YOU READ

Terms and Names

A. Write the name or term that best completes each item. You will need to use one term twice.

Antifederalists   Democratic-Republicans   Federalists   Loyalists   Patriots

During the Revolutionary War, **1**_____ supported the British while

2_____ wanted independence.

People who wanted to ratify, or approve, the Constitution were called **3**_____.

Those who were against the Constitution were called **4**_____.

The political party that wanted a strong central government was the **5**_____. The

party that felt the states should have more power was the **6**_____.

B. Write the letter of the name or term next to the description that explains it best.

a. Articles of
   Confederation
b. checks and balances
c. *Common Sense*
d. Declaration of
   Independence
e. Alexander Hamilton
f. Thomas Jefferson
g. nullification
h. Shays's Rebellion
i. Stamp Act

_____ **1.** An anti-tax protest by farmers

_____ **2.** The idea that states can cancel laws they feel are unconstitutional

_____ **3.** A system to prevent one branch of government getting too much power over the other two

_____ **4.** Thomas Paine's pamphlet in support of independence

_____ **5.** Author of the Declaration of Independence and first Secretary of State

_____ **6.** Document establishing an independent United States

_____ **7.** A law that placed a tax on many items used by colonists

_____ **8.** A leading Federalist and first Secretary of the Treasury

_____ **9.** The first plan for governing the United States

AFTER YOU READ (cont.) *CHAPTER 2* Revolution and the Early Republic

Main Ideas

1. Who won the battles of Lexington and Concord?

_____

_____

2. How did the United States deal with Native Americans?

_____

_____

3. Why did the Patriots fight against Britain?

_____

_____

4. What was one success of the Articles of Confederation?

_____

_____

5. What two treaties helped settle American land claims east of the Mississippi River?

_____

_____

Thinking Critically

Answer the following questions on a separate sheet of paper.

1. By the time of the Revolutionary War, why did many colonists want independence from Britain?

2. How did the national, or central, government get stronger between independence and 1800? Write about either (a) the difference between the Articles of Confederation and the Constitution, or (b) actions taken under Presidents Washington and Adams.

THE LIVING CONSTITUTION   Section 1 (pages 88–93)

The Preamble and Article 1: The Legislature

TERMS AND NAMES
Preamble Introduction to the Constitution

Congress National legislature

House of Representatives Lower house of the national legislature

Senate Upper house of the national legislature

checks and balances Provisions of the Constitution that keep one branch of the government from controlling the other two branches

enumerated powers Powers specifically granted in the Constitution

implied powers Powers not specifically stated in the Constitution

elastic clause Clause in the Constitution that allows Congress to pass laws necessary to carry out its enumerated powers

BEFORE YOU READ

In the last section, you saw how the new government began to work under the Constitution.

In this section, you will learn about the Constitution itself—how the Preamble introduces the Constitution and explains its purpose and how Article 1 sets up the Congress.

AS YOU READ

Use the informal outline below to take notes on the Preamble and on the powers of Congress.

Preamble	shows legitimacy created by people who will be governed

Article 1 Congress
  House of Representatives
  Senate	

The Preamble: The Purpose of the Constitution (page 88)

What does the Preamble do?

The Preamble, or introduction, sets out to do two things. The first is to show the *legitimacy* of the new government, or its right to rule. The Preamble shows that this government is based on the agreement of those who are to be governed. It is the people themselves who have the power to create a government. That is why the Constitution begins with, "We the people of the United States . . . do ordain and establish this Constitution."

This statement also shows that the legitimacy of this government does not come from the states. Instead, it comes from the people. The Confederation was an agreement among the states, and the national government was too weak.

The second purpose of the Preamble is to state why this new government is being formed:

- to improve the structure of the government,
- to create justice and peace within the nation,
- to protect the nation from outside attack,
- to ensure the well-being of the people,
- to keep citizens and their descendants free.

1. What are the two purposes of the Preamble?

_____

_____

Congress: The House and the Senate Article 1 Sections 1–6

(pages 88–91)

How are the House and Senate different?

The *framers* of the Constitution set up **Congress** first. It was to be the legislature, or law-making branch of government. The framers saw the Congress as the central branch of government because it represents the people most directly.

Congress is made up of two houses. The **House of Representatives** is sometimes called "the House" or "the lower house." Its members are most responsible to the people who elect them because they serve for only two years. Then they must run for reelection. The number of representatives each state can send to the House is based on population. Thus, the House reflects the will of the majority of the people of the nation.

The **Senate** is sometimes called the "upper house." To make the government more stable, the framers made the Senate more removed from the will of the people. To do this, they had Senators chosen by state legislatures. (They are now elected directly by the voters in each state [Amendment 17]). Senators are elected for longer terms than House members, six-years.

Only one-third of the Senate is elected every two years. That also adds stability. Each state, regardless of population, has two Senators. This equal representation gives small states more power in the Senate than they have in the House.

Section 2.5 of Article 1 gives the House the power of *impeachment*. It can bring charges of mis-behavior in office against officials in other branches of government, including the president. When the House impeaches a federal official, the Senate tries the case. It takes a two-thirds vote of the Senate to convict the impeached person.

The power of impeachment means that the leg-islative and judicial branches can make sure that a president does not take too much power. It is part of the system of **checks and balances,** in which the Constitution prevents any branch from dominating the others.

2. What are two important differences between the House and the Senate?

Congressional Procedures and Powers Article 1 Sections 7–10

(pages 91–93)

What power does Congress have?

Section 7 of Article 1 explains how new laws are passed. A bill may be introduced in either the House or the Senate. But it must be approved by a majori-ty vote in both houses. To become a law, a bill needs the approval of the president. That is part of the sys-tem of checks and balances. It gives the president, who is elected by all of the people, a say in what becomes the law of the land. If the president does not sign, or approve, the bill, he is said to *veto* it. The bill can still become law if two-thirds of both houses vote to *override* the veto. This procedure ensures that the president does not have too much power.

Section 7 also states that all *bills* for raising money—such as taxes—must begin in the House of Representatives. That is the house most respon-sive to the people. The Senate may propose changes to the bill.

Section 8 lists particular powers of the Congress. They are often called the *federal* gov-ernment's **enumerated powers.** They include the power to tax, to borrow money, and to set up courts. Clauses 11–16 in Section 8 make sure that the civilians control the military. This is designed to prevent the armed forces from staging a *coup*, or seizing control of the government.

The 18th clause is different. It gives Congress the power to do what is "necessary and proper" to carry out its other powers. This is the basis of the **implied powers** of the federal government. It is called the **elastic clause** because it can be used to stretch, or expand, the government's power.

Section 9 tells what powers the federal govern-ment does *not* have. Clauses 2 and 3 say the gov-ernment cannot take away a citizen's right to a fair trial. Section 10 tells what powers the states do *not* have. It emphasizes that they cannot make treaties or war. Only a *sovereign* nation can do that.

3. How does Congress limit the power of the president and the military?

Articles 2 and 3:
The Executive and the Judiciary

BEFORE YOU READ

In the last section, you saw that the Preamble introduced the Constitution and that Article 1 dealt with the powers of Congress.

In this section, you will see that Article 2 covers the powers of the president and Article 3 lists the powers of the judiciary.

AS YOU READ

Continue to use the outline you began in the last section with the Preamble. Take notes on the powers of the executive and the judicial branches of government.

Article 2 The Executive	President is chief executive sees that laws are carried out

The Executive Article 2 (pages 94–96)

What are the powers of the president?

The president is the **chief executive**, or administrator of the nation. It is his or her responsibility to "take care that laws be faithfully executed," or carried out.

Section 1.2 sets up the **electoral college.** The president and vice-president are elected by electors chosen by the states. At first, this clause did not work well in practice. In 1800, when only one ballot was used to elect both president and vice-president, two candidates received the same number of votes. The election had to be settled by the House of Representatives. To prevent this from happening again, the Twelfth Amendment was passed in 1804. It calls for separate ballots for president and vice-president.

However, the electoral college is still important. Each state has as many electors as it has senators

and representatives in Congress. That is why presidential candidates work hard to "carry," or get the majority of the popular vote in, the largest states. The candidate that gets the majority of votes in a state gets all the electoral votes of that state.

Section 1.6 explains **succession:** what happens if a president dies in office or leaves office for another reason. It is important that everyone understands who will assume the power of the president. That prevents a struggle for power or a time when no one is in charge. It also makes sure that power will be transferred in a peaceful and orderly manner.

The president's salary cannot be changed during his or her term of office. In other words, the president cannot be punished or rewarded by payment for particular policies or official acts.

Section 2.1 makes the president commander-in-chief of the armed forces. This authority is another way to ensure civilian control of the military. It is also another example of checks and balances, because only Congress has the power to declare war. In practice, this authority has caused some problems. Since the president has the power to give orders to American military forces, some presidents have taken military action against the wishes of Congress and without a declaration of war.

Presidential appointments are another example of the separation of powers. The president can appoint ambassadors, justices of the Supreme Court, and other officials only "with the advice and consent of the Senate." In other words, the Senate must approve these appointments. The president can also make treaties, but these must also be approved by the Senate.

"Heads of departments" are mentioned in Section 2.1. These departments actually carry out the functions of the executive branch of government under the direction of the president. The heads of important departments make up the president's *cabinet*.

The framers included reporting to the Congress as one of the president's duties. This requirement has led to the president making a **State of the Union Address** once a year. It is a report to the other branches of government and to the people. Its subject is the condition, or state, of the nation. The address includes the president's plans and policies for the year.

1. **What are two examples of checks and balances found in Article 2?**

_____

_____

The Judiciary Article 3 (page 96)

What are the powers of the federal courts?

Article 3 sets up the judicial branch of the federal government. It establishes one **Supreme Court** but leaves the rest of the "inferior," or lower, federal courts to be set up by Congress. District courts and federal courts of appeal are now part of the regular federal court system. (States have their own court systems that deal with state laws.) Federal judges are appointed by the president with the approval of the Senate.

Judges serve "during good behavior." In other words, they are appointed for life, unless they are found guilty of misbehavior, or inappropriate conduct. The salary of a judge cannot be lowered while the judge is in office.

The federal courts have jurisdiction, or authority, only in certain kinds of cases. These are listed in Section 2. The Constitution gives the courts **judicial power**—the authority to decide cases involving disputes over the law or behavior of people. It does not specifically grant the Supreme Court the power of **judicial review**—the authority to decide whether a law is constitutional. The Supreme Court claimed this authority in the famous case of *Marbury* v *Madison* in 1803.

Clause 3 again protects citizens' rights to a trial by jury. (See Article 1, Section 9.) The framers' concern for this right is a result of the American colonists' experiences under British rule.

2. **What does the federal judiciary do?**

_____

_____

Articles 4–7: The States and the Federal Government; Amendments and Ratification

BEFORE YOU READ

In the last section, you saw how Articles 2 and 3 set forth the powers of the executive and judicial branches.

In this section, you will see how Articles 4–7 grant specific powers to the national and state governments. You will also learn how the Constitution assures the unity of the nation and the supremacy of the national government.

AS YOU READ

Continue your outline of the Constitution. Take notes on the relations among the states and between the states and the national government.

Relations among states	Must accept decisions that occur in other states

Relations Among States Article 4 (page 97)

Who has more power—the states or the national government?

Article 4 sets out many principles of the federal system. It describes the relations among the states. It also describes the relations between the national government and the states.

Sections 1 and 2 make it clear that the United States is one nation. The separate states must accept decisions, such as criminal convictions, that occur in other states. Section 2.2 allows for **extradition.** This means that if a person charged with a crime in one state flees to another state, he or she must be returned to the state where the crime was committed.

Section 2 also makes it clear that citizens of the United States are citizens of the whole nation.

They have the same rights and privileges of citizenship no matter which state they are in. However, slaves were not considered to be citizens and so did not have the rights of citizens.

Clause 3 provides for the return of runaway slaves to their masters, even if the slave escapes to another state. This shows that the Constitution recognized slavery as legitimate, even though the word "slave" is not used. When the Thirteenth Amendment abolished slavery in 1865, it effectively canceled this clause.

Section 3 describes the process for forming new states. It says that new states cannot be formed within any existing state without that state's approval. However, there is a case where something very close to that happened. During the Civil War, Virginia seceded, or separated, from the Union. However, the people of the western part of Virginia did not want to secede. They asked

Congress for permission to form the new state of West Virginia. They wanted West Virginia to be part of the Union. Congress agreed. After the Civil War, the legislature of Virginia gave its formal approval to the creation of West Virginia.

1. List two ways the framers made it clear that the United States is one nation, not a loose confederation of semi-independent states.

_____

_____

Amending and Ratifying the Constitution; The Supremacy of the National Government
(pages 98–99)

How can the Constitution be amended?

Article 5 sets up two ways of amending, or changing, the Constitution. In both cases, it takes more votes to **ratify,** or officially approve, than to propose an amendment. To propose an amendment takes two-thirds of Congress or two-thirds of state legislatures. To ratify takes three-fourths of state legislatures or state conventions.

The framers wanted it to be relatively easy to consider changes to the Constitution. Yet they wanted proposed changes to be carefully consid-

ered. They also wanted to be sure that Amendments had the full support of the nation. Therefore, it is more difficult to ratify an Amendment and make it into law than it is to propose, or suggest, it.

Article 6 makes the laws of the federal government, or national laws, the supreme law of the land. If a state law is in conflict with a national law, it is the national law which must be obeyed. States must then change their laws to agree with the national law. This article strengthens the national government. It again makes sure that the United States is one nation, not just a loose confederation of states.

Finally, Article 7 says that the Constitution was to go into effect as soon as nine states voted to accept it. It did not require agreement of all 13 states. The framers felt that it would be difficult to get all 13 states to agree right away. But they also felt that if nine states ratified, the others would follow. The Constitution was ratified on June 21, 1788, when the ninth state, New Hampshire, agreed. The last state, Rhode Island, finally ratified the Constitution in May of 1790. The first presidential election under the Constitution was to be in 1792.

2. Why is it harder to ratify an amendment than to propose it?

_____

_____

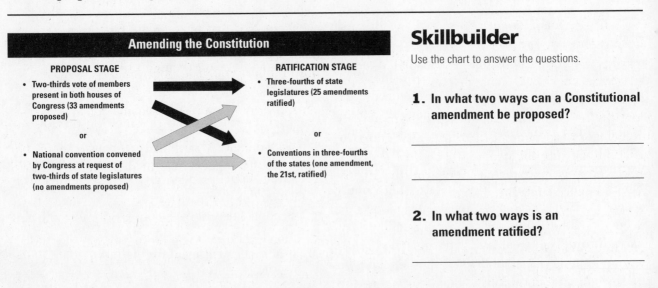

Amending the Constitution

PROPOSAL STAGE

- Two-thirds vote of members present in both houses of Congress (33 amendments proposed)

or

- National convention convened by Congress at request of two-thirds of state legislatures (no amendments proposed)

RATIFICATION STAGE

- Three-fourths of state legislatures (25 amendments ratified)

or

- Conventions in three-fourths of the states (one amendment, the 21st, ratified)

Skillbuilder
Use the chart to answer the questions.

1. In what two ways can a Constitutional amendment be proposed?

_____

_____

2. In what two ways is an amendment ratified?

_____

_____

The Bill of Rights and the Other Amendments

TERMS AND NAMES

Bill of Rights First ten Amendments

double jeopardy Being tried more than once for the same crime

due process of law All the procedures for fair treatment must be carried out whenever a citizen is accused of a crime

reserved powers Powers not specifically granted to the federal government or denied to the states belong to the states and the people

suffrage Right to vote

BEFORE YOU READ

In the last section, you saw the process of amending the Constitution.

In this section, you will learn about the Bill of Rights and the other Amendments.

AS YOU READ

Continue your outline. Take notes on how Amendments added to or changed the government of the United States.

Amendments 1-10 (The Bill of Rights)	First Amendment civil liberties
	   freedom of religion
	   freedom of speech

The Bill of Rights (pages 100–101)

What liberties are protected by the Bill of Rights?

The first ten Amendments are called the **Bill of Rights.** They were added to the Constitution in 1791. The supporters of the Constitution had to promise to include these protections of citizens' rights in order to get the states to ratify the Constitution. Some of these rights are the ones that the colonists had under British rule. The framers wanted to be sure the people still had these rights under the new government. Some are the rights that the colonists felt Britain had taken away from them. That was one reason why they fought the Revolutionary War.

Amendment 1 protects basic civil liberties. It prevents the government from interfering with citizens' freedom of religion, speech, and press. It says that citizens can gather together, or assemble, freely. Citizens also have the right to ask the government to redress, or correct, injustices. Because of this amendment, citizens can protest government action without fear of punishment.

Amendment 2 says the federal government cannot prevent states from having an armed militia. This was designed to make sure that states and citizens could protect themselves from the military power of a tyrannical government—as they did during the Revolution. The right of individual citizens to carry weapons has become controversial in modern times.

Amendment 3 says that citizens cannot be forced to let soldiers stay in their homes during peacetime. Amendment 4 extends the people's right to privacy. It is why a search warrant is required to look through a citizen's home or belongings. Such a warrant can be issued only if a judge decides that it is likely that evidence of a crime will be found. The warrant must state exactly what evidence the government is looking for.

Amendments 5 through 8 deal with the rights of citizens accused of crimes. Amendment 5 prevents

double jeopardy, or being tried more than once for the same crime. In other words, if a citizen is found not guilty in a trial, the government cannot keep bringing the case to trial until it gets a conviction. (Citizens found guilty do have the right of appeal, however.)

This amendment is also the basis for "pleading the Fifth." That is the slang term for a citizen's right to refuse to testify when that testimony might *incriminate* him/her. It also guarantees **due process of law.** That means that all of the procedures for fair treatment (including the rights mentioned here) must be carried out whenever a citizen is accused of a crime.

Amendment 6 guarantees the right to a "speedy and public trial." It is intended to protect citizens from being kept in jail (in a sense, punished) for long periods of time before they are even brought to trial. The right to know the charges and to have legal counsel also prevents citizens from having to defend themselves in court. This amendment also makes sure the public is informed of what is going on in their courts.

Amendment 9 guarantees that rights are not denied simply because they have not been mentioned in the Constitution. And Amendment 10 establishes the so-called **reserved powers.** It states that the powers that are not specifically given to the federal government—as long as they are not specifically denied to the states—belong to the states and to the people.

1. **Name two ways the Bill of Rights protects citizens accused of crimes.**

_____

_____

Amendments 11–27 (pages 102–107)

How have Amendments changed American society?

The amendments ratified after 1791 have had a variety of purposes. Some are quite technical, such as the legal question decided in Amendment 11. This amendment said that citizens of another state or a foreign country cannot sue a state in federal court unless the state agrees to it. Other amendments changed American society.

Amendments 13, 14, and 15 were a result of the Union victory in the Civil War. Amendment 13 (ratified in 1865) abolishes slavery. Amendment 14 (1868) grants citizenship to African Americans by saying that all persons born or *naturalized* in the United States are citizens. Amendment 15 (1870) protects the voting rights of citizens, particularly former enslaved persons.

However, it was not until 1964 that Amendment 24 made the poll tax illegal. Some Southern states used this tax to keep African Americans from voting. Because many blacks could not afford to pay the tax required at the *polls*, they could not exercise their right to vote.

Voting is the subject of several other Amendments. Amendment 17 provides for direct election of Senators by the people (rather than by state legislatures as described in Article 1). Amendment 19 grants **suffrage,** or the right to vote, to women. And Amendment 26 lowers the age at which citizens can vote to 18.

Amendment 18 is known as Prohibition. It prohibited, or banned, the manufacture, sale, or shipment of alcoholic beverages. It was an attempt to change American society that failed. It was repealed by Amendment 21.

Amendment 22 sets limits on the number of terms a president may serve. No person may be elected president more than twice. Franklin Roosevelt was the first and only president to be elected to more than two terms. He was elected to four. Many people felt that was too long to be president. Today, the idea of *term limits* for other federal offices has some supporters.

2. **How did Amendments 15, 19, 24, and 26 change American society?**

_____

_____

Glossary

bills Drafts of proposed laws presented for approval to the legislature

cabinet Official advisers appointed by a chief executive to head the executive departments of the government

coup Sudden overthrow of a government by a small group in positions of authority, such as military leaders

federal Relating to a political system in which authority is divided between a national government and its political subdivisions

framers Persons who wrote the U.S. Constitution

impeachment Judicial procedure whereby a government official is accused of wrongdoing and brought to trial before a legislative body

incriminate To cause to appear guilty of a crime

legitimacy Authority; in accordance with accepted standards

naturalized Granted full citizenship to one of foreign birth

override To declare null and void; to set aside

polls Voting places

sovereign Independent

term limits Legal restriction on how long a public official may serve

veto Power of a chief executive to reject a bill passed by the legislature and prevent it from becoming a law

AFTER YOU READ

Terms and Names

A. Write the letter of the name or term next to the description that explains it best.

a. Preamble
b. Senate
c. Supreme Court
d. Congress
e. chief executive
f. judicial power
g. House of Representatives

_____ **1.** The "lower" house of Congress whose membership is based on population

_____ **2.** The introduction to the Constitution

_____ **3.** The authority to decide cases involving disputes over law and behavior of people

_____ **4.** The legislative branch of government

_____ **5.** The "upper" house of Congress whose members are elected to six-year terms

_____ **6.** The president

_____ **7.** The highest federal court

B. Write the name or term that best completes each sentence.

enumerated powers	elastic clause	Bill of Rights	double jeopardy
succession	State of the Union	due process of law	suffrage

1. The Fifth Amendment protects citizens against _____, or being tried twice for the same crime.

2. Several Amendments expanded _____, or the right to vote.

3. The Amendments called the _____ protect the basic civil liberties of American citizens.

4. Particular powers of the Congress that are listed in Article 1 are often called the _____ of the federal government.

Name _____   Date _____

5. The clause giving Congress power to do whatever is "necessary and proper" to govern is called the

_____.

6. The Constitution describes _____, or who assumes the power of the presidency if the president dies in office.

7. _____, ensured by the Fifth Amendment, protects the rights of citizens accused of a crime.

8. The president uses the yearly _____ to report on the condition of the nation to the Congress and the people.

Main Ideas

1. Why are there more House members than Senate members?

_____

_____

2. How can the president lose his or her job before election time?

_____

_____

3. How are Supreme Court justices appointed?

_____

4. Why is judicial review, although not mentioned in the Constitution, an important activity for the Supreme Court?

_____

_____

5. What did the 26th amendment do?

_____

Thinking Critically

Answer the following questions on a separate sheet of paper.

1. How does the Constitution reflect the fear of making the country's leader too strong?

2. Why did the framers make it so difficult to amend the Constitution? Do you agree or disagree with their philosophy? Explain.

CHAPTER 3   Section 1 (pages 118–123)

The Jeffersonian Era

BEFORE YOU READ

In the last section, you saw how Washington and Adams led the young country.

In this section, you will learn about the presidencies of Jefferson, Madison, and Monroe.

AS YOU READ

Use the chart below to take notes on the major events that occurred during the presidencies of Jefferson, Madison, and Monroe.

TERMS AND NAMES

Jeffersonian republicanism The belief that a simple government, controlled by people, is best

Marbury v. Madison Court case that established the power of judicial review

John Marshall Chief Justice of the Supreme Court

judicial review The power of judges to declare a law unconstitutional

Louisiana Purchase Land bought from France in 1803

impressment Act of seizing sailors to work on ships

war hawks Those who favor war

Tecumseh Native American leader

James Monroe Fifth president

Monroe Doctrine Warning to European nations not to interfere in the Americas

PRESIDENT	EVENTS	EFFECT ON NATION
Jefferson	Marbury v. Madison	strengthened judicial branch of government
Madison		
Monroe		

Jefferson's Presidency (pages 118–121)

What kind of president was Jefferson?

The presidential election of 1800 was close and bitter. Thomas Jefferson and his followers accused President Adams of making the federal government too powerful. They said he put the people's liberties in danger.

Jefferson won the most popular votes. But a tie in the *electoral college* showed a problem. The 12th Amendment was passed to change the way presidents would be chosen.

As president, Jefferson got a chance to put his theory of **Jeffersonian republicanism** into practice. This was a belief that the people should control the government and that government should be simple and small.

John Marshall was Chief Justice of the Supreme Court. In the court case **Marbury v. Madison,** Marshall strengthened the power of the Court. The Supreme Court ruled a law passed by Congress to be *unconstitutional*. This power is called **judicial review.**

In 1803, Jefferson got the chance to buy land from France. He was not sure he had the

Constitutional power to do so, but he bought it anyway. The **Louisiana Purchase** stretched from the Mississippi River to the Rocky Mountains.

Jefferson sent Meriwether Lewis and William Clark to explore the new territory. The Lewis and Clark Expedition showed that people could travel across the continent. It paved the way for settlement of the West.

1. What are two ways in which Jefferson's presidency was important?

_____

_____

Madison and the War of 1812
(pages 121–122)

What brought the country to war?

Britain and France went to war. Both nations threatened American ships. The British also engaged in **impressment:** they seized American sailors and forced them to serve in the British navy.

American anger at Britain grew. Some leaders demanded war against Britain. These **war hawks** were led by John C. Calhoun and Henry Clay.

Meanwhile, a Native American confederacy led by **Tecumseh** fought settlers in the West. American troops defeated the confederacy in 1811. Then the Americans found out that the British had helped the Native Americans. There were more calls for war.

James Madison had become president in 1808. In 1812, he asked Congress to declare war on Britain. During the War of 1812, the British attacked Washington, D.C. President Madison had to flee the city. But General Andrew Jackson scored a victory for the Americans in the Battle of New Orleans. The Treaty of Ghent ended the war.

The War of 1812 had three important results:
- The anti-war Federalist Party died out.
- Americans began to develop their own industries.
- It showed that the United States was truly independent.

2. What were the two reasons United States went to war with Great Britain?

_____

_____

Nationalism Shapes Foreign Policy (pages 122–123)

What was the basis of Monroe's foreign policy?

National pride grew after the War of 1812. **James Monroe** was elected president in 1816. His Secretary of State was John Quincy Adams.

Foreign policy under Adams was based on nationalism: a belief that national interests as a whole should be more important than what one region wants. Adams settled some issues with Britain. He also convinced Spain to give Florida to the United States.

In 1823, President Monroe warned European nations not to interfere with any nation in the Americas. He said the United States would stay out of European affairs. This statement is called the **Monroe Doctrine.**

3. Name three things that marked Monroe's foreign policy.

_____

_____

Geography Skillbuilder
Use the map to answer the questions.

1. Where was the Louisiana Purchase?

_____

2. How does it compare in size to the rest of the United States before 1803?

_____

CHAPTER 3 Section 2 (pages 124–132)

The Age of Jackson

BEFORE YOU READ

In the last section, you learned about the presidencies of Jefferson, Madison, and Monroe.

In this section, you will learn about politics in the 1820s and 1830s.

AS YOU READ

Use the chart below to take notes on how the important events during the Age of Jackson helped unite or divide the nation.

American System	United nation: national bank, national currency, improved transportation
Missouri Compromise	
Nullification crisis	
Bank war	

TERMS AND NAMES

Henry Clay Speaker of the House of Representatives and political leader from Kentucky

American System Clay's plan for economic development

John C. Calhoun Vice-president and congressional leader from South Carolina

Missouri Compromise Agreement that temporarily settled the issue of slavery in the territories

Andrew Jackson Military hero and seventh president

Jacksonian democracy Political philosophy that puts its faith in the common people

John Quincy Adams Sixth president of the United States

Trail of Tears Path the Cherokee were forced to travel from Georgia to Indian Territory

Daniel Webster A Senate leader from Massachusetts

Martin Van Buren Eighth president

John Tyler Tenth president

Regional Economies Create Differences (pages 124–125)

What was the Industrial Revolution?

Manufacturing increased in the North. Production of goods moved from small workshops to large factories that used machines. This was the Industrial Revolution.

Farmers in the Northwest began to grow crops for sale. They bought goods made in Northern factories. In this *market economy*, farming and manufacturing supported each other.

In the South, the invention of the *cotton gin* increased cotton production and made large cotton plantations more profitable. More and more slaves were used to work on cotton plantations.

1. How did the Industrial Revolution affect each region?

_____

_____

Balancing Nationalism and Sectionalism (pages 126–127)

What held the nation together?

Speaker of the House **Henry Clay** created the **American System** to unify the nation. It included a protective tariff, a national bank, and internal improvements.

Most Northerners supported the tariff because it would help industry. Southerners did not want to pay the higher prices for goods. But Clay and **John C. Calhoun,** a Southerner, convinced Southern Congressmen to approve the tariff.

The nation built roads and canals. The Erie Canal linked the Great Lakes to the Atlantic Ocean.

In 1819, Missouri asked to enter the union. A crisis developed over whether the new state would have slavery or not. In the **Missouri Compromise** of 1820, Missouri was admitted as a slave state, and Maine was admitted as a *free state.* Also, slavery would be legal only south of a certain line.

2. What government actions helped to unify the nation?

_____

_____

Jackson's Path to the Presidency
(pages 127–128)

How did Jackson become president?

Andrew Jackson lost the 1824 presidential election to **John Quincy Adams.** Jackson's followers accused Adams of stealing the election.

In 1828, Jackson won the presidency by a *landslide.* Many states had passed laws that allowed more common people to vote.

Jackson's philosophy, called **Jacksonian democracy,** was based on faith in the common people. Jackson used the spoils system to fill many federal jobs. He gave jobs to friends and supporters.

3. What is the spoils system?

_____

_____

The Removal of Native Americans; Tariffs, States' Rights, and the National Bank
(pages 129–131)

What kind of president was Andrew Jackson?

In 1830, Congress passed the Indian Removal Act. It said that Native Americans must move west of the Mississippi River.

The Cherokee fought the act in court. The Supreme Court struck it down. Jackson refused to obey the court's ruling. In 1838, the Cherokee were forced to walk from Georgia to the new Indian Territory. A quarter of the Cherokee died on this **Trail of Tears.**

Southerners continued to object to tariffs. John C. Calhoun fought for *states' rights.* He argued that states could nullify federal laws that they felt were unconstitutional. In 1832, South Carolina tried to nullify a federal tariff. They also threatened to secede, or leave the union.

The Senate debated the issue. **Daniel Webster** of Massachusetts opposed efforts to nullify federal law. Later, Senator Robert Hayne of South Carolina defended *nullification.* Henry Clay worked out a compromise that kept South Carolina in the union.

President Jackson was against the second national bank. He took federal money out of the national bank and put it in other banks. The national bank went out of existence. Some people felt Jackson had too much power. They formed the Whig Party.

4. Name three major issues of Jackson's presidency.

_____

_____

Successors Deal with Jackson's Legacy (page 132)

What was the Panic of 1837?

Martin Van Buren was elected president in 1836. By 1837, many of the banks Jackson had put money in during the bank war had failed. This helped cause the Panic of 1837 and a *depression.*

In 1840, Van Buren lost to Whig candidate William Henry Harrison. Harrison died soon after, and his vice-president, **John Tyler,** became president.

5. How did Jackson's actions cause economic problems during Van Buren's presidency?

_____

_____

Name ______________________ Date ______________

CHAPTER 3 Section 3 (pages 133–141)

Manifest Destiny

TERMS AND NAMES

manifest destiny Belief that the United States would expand across the continent

Santa Fe Trail Trail from Missouri to Santa Fe, New Mexico

Oregon Trail Trail from Missouri to Oregon

Stephen F. Austin Most successful land agent in Texas

Texas Revolution Texas's war for independence from Mexico

the Alamo Site of a key battle in the Texas Revolution

Sam Houston First president of the Republic of Texas

James K. Polk 11th president

Bear Flag Republic Independent republic briefly declared in California

Treaty of Guadalupe Hidalgo Treaty ending the War with Mexico

BEFORE YOU READ

In the last section, you learned about politics in the 1820s and 1830s.

In this section, you will see how Americans continued to move westward and gained new territory through diplomacy and war.

AS YOU READ

Use the chart below to take notes on how each event added territory to the United States.

EVENT	CAUSES	EFFECTS
Treaty of Fort Laramie	Settlers wanted more land and to stop attacks by Native Americans.	U.S. promised not to settle in new Native American lands but broke promise.
Treaty with Britain		
War with Mexico		
Gadsden Purchase		

Settling the Frontier; Trails West

(page 133–135)

***Why** did Americans move west?*

Many Americans believed that God wanted the United States to expand across the continent. They felt that Americans were meant to control the West. This belief was called **manifest destiny.**

People went west for economic reasons. Many went in order to get cheap land. After the Panic of 1837, many Americans wanted a fresh start on the *frontier.*

Some Native Americans fought to keep their lands. The Treaty of Fort Laramie gave Native Americans control of much of the central plains. In return, Native Americans promised not to attack settlers. The United States also pledged that settlers would stay out of these Native American lands. The U.S. government did not honor this treaty.

Americans took several trails to the West. The **Santa Fe Trail** was a trade route between Independence, Missouri, and Santa Fe, New Mexico. The **Oregon Trail** stretched from Independence to Portland, Oregon.

The Mormons followed the Oregon trail to Utah. This religious group had been *persecuted* in the East. They settled on the edge of the Great Salt Lake.

In 1846, Britain and the United States agreed to split the Oregon territory. This established the current border between the United States and Canada.

1. **Give two reasons why Americans moved west.**

Texan Independence; The War with Mexico (pages 136–141)

Why did the United States go to war with Mexico?

In the 1820s Mexico encouraged Americans to settle in Texas. They offered land to settlers. They hoped these settlers would make the area more stable.

Stephen F. Austin, a *land agent,* set up a colony of American settlers in Texas. Soon Anglos, or English-speaking settlers, outnumbered Spanish-speaking Texans. There was conflict over cultural issues.

First, the Anglo settlers spoke English instead of Spanish. Second, the Anglos tended to be Protestant instead of Catholic. Third, many of the settlers were Southerners who brought their slaves with them. Mexico had outlawed slavery in 1829. They unsuccessfully tried to get the Texans to free their slaves.

Mexico tried to prevent more American settlers from coming to Texas, but the settlers came anyway. Austin asked Mexico for more self-government for Texas.

Instead, Mexican president Antonio López de Santa Anna arrested Austin. When Austin returned to Texas, he called for Texans to arm themselves. At the same time, Santa Anna led an army to San Antonio to force the Texans to obey Mexican law. The war that broke out became known as the **Texas Revolution.**

A small Texan force tried to defend **the Alamo,** a mission in San Antonio. When the Mexicans captured it, they killed all 187 of the Americans. "Remember the Alamo" became a rallying cry for Texas rebels. Under their commander **Sam Houston,** the Texans captured Santa Anna and won their independence.

Houston was elected president of the new Republic of Texas in 1836. But Texans wanted to join the United States. Some Northerners did not want another slave state. **James K. Polk** was elected president in 1844. He was a slaveholder and favored westward expansion. In 1845, Texas was admitted to the union.

The United States and Mexico had a dispute over the northern region of Mexico. President Polk sent the U.S. army to blockade the Rio Grande River.

War broke out between the United States and Mexico. New Mexico immediately asked to join the United States. American settlers in California declared their independence from Mexico. They set up the **Bear Flag Republic.** American troops won victory after victory.

The **Treaty of Guadalupe Hidalgo** gave almost half of Mexico's land to the United States. The United States bought more land from Mexico with the Gadsden Purchase in 1853. This set the current borders of the lower 48 states.

In 1848 gold was discovered in California. People streamed into California in the rush for gold. These "forty-niners" came from all over the United States as well as from foreign countries. California's population exploded. San Francisco became a boom town.

2. **Describe two causes of the War with Mexico.**

The Market Revolution

TERMS AND NAMES

the market revolution Economic changes where people buy and sell goods rather than make them themselves

free enterprise Economic system in which individuals and businesses control the means of production

entrepreneurs Businessmen

Samuel F. B. Morse Inventor of the telegraph

Lowell textile mills Early factories in Lowell, Massachusetts, where cloth was made

strike Work stoppages by workers

immigration Migration of people into the United States

Great Potato Famine Famine in Ireland in the 1840s

National Trades' Union Early national workers' organization

Commonwealth v. ***Hunt*** Court case supporting labor unions

BEFORE YOU READ

In the last section, you read about American expansion to the West.

In this section, you will learn about changes in the American economy.

AS YOU READ

Use the chart below to take notes on the market revolution. Use the boxes on the left to write about the causes of the market revolution. Write the effects of the market revolution in the boxes on the right.

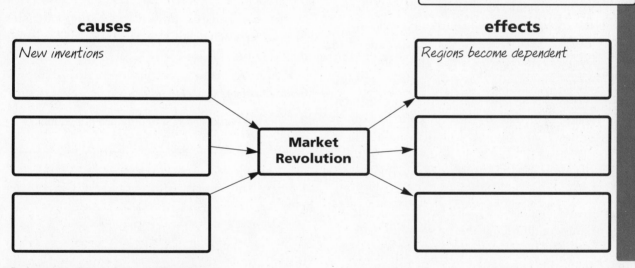

causes

New inventions

Market Revolution

effects

Regions become dependent

The Market Revolution (pages 144–146)

What was the market revolution?

There were great economic changes in the United States during the first half of the 19th century. In this **market revolution,** people began to buy and sell goods rather than making them for themselves. **Free enterprise,** an economic system in which private businesses and individuals control production, also expanded at this time.

Entrepreneurs, or businessmen, invested in new industries. New industries produced goods that made life more comfortable for ordinary people. New inventions improved manufacturing, transportation, and communication.

Samuel F. B. Morse invented the telegraph. It could send messages by wire in a few seconds. Steamboats, canals, and railroads helped improve transportation. Improved transportation linked North to South and East to West.

The different regions became dependent on each other because each region needed goods produced by other regions. The North became a center of *commerce* and manufacturing. Many people who wanted to farm moved to the Midwest. New inventions, such as the steel plow and the reaper, made farming easier. Midwestern crops were carried by canal and trains to markets in the East.

The South remained an *agricultural,* or farming, region. It still relied on cotton, tobacco, and rice. And it relied on slave labor to raise those crops.

1. **How did new inventions create a market revolution in the United States?**

_____

_____

Changing Workplaces (pages 147–148)

How did workplaces change?

The new market economy changed the way Americans worked. Work that had been done in the home or in small, local shops moved to factories. New machines allowed unskilled workers to make goods that skilled *artisans* once made. But these new workers had to work in the factory.

Thousands of people worked in the **Lowell textile mills.** These Massachusetts factories made cloth. The mills hired mostly young women because they could be paid less than men. These "mill girls" lived in boarding houses owned by the factory. At first, they felt lucky to have these jobs. Factory work paid better than other jobs for women—teaching, sewing, and being a servant.

Working conditions in the *textile mills* became worse in the 1830s. The workday was more than 12 hours. Factories were hot, noisy, and dirty. Many workers became ill.

2. **How did the new factories change how Americans worked?**

_____

_____

Workers Seek Better Conditions
(pages 148–149)

What did workers want?

Bad working conditions in factories led workers to organize. In 1834, the Lowell textile mills cut the wages of workers by 15 percent. The mill girls went on **strike**—they refused to work until they got their old rate of pay back. Public opinion was against the workers.

There were dozens of strikes for shorter hours or higher pay in the 1830s and 1840s. Employers won most of them because they could hire *strikebreakers,* new workers to replace strikers. Many strikebreakers were European immigrants.

European **immigration,** people moving into the United States, increased between 1830 and 1860. Irish immigrants fled the **Great Potato Famine.** In the 1840s, a disease killed most of the potato crop in Ireland. About 1 million Irish people starved. Over 1 million came to America. The Irish met prejudice in the United States.

Small trade unions began to band together in the 1830s. The **National Trades' Union** was formed in 1834. It represented a variety of trades. At first, the courts had declared strikes illegal. But in 1842, the Massachusetts Supreme Court supported the right of workers to strike in *Commonwealth* v. *Hunt.*

3. **Why did workers begin to organize into unions?**

_____

_____

CHAPTER 3 Section 5 (pages 152–157)

Reforming American Society

BEFORE YOU READ

In the last section, you learned about changes in the American economy.

In this section, you will read about reform movements in 19th-century America.

AS YOU READ

Use the chart below to take notes on the aims of the religious and reform movements of the early 19th century.

TOPIC	AIMS
Second Great Awakening	bring more people to God
Unitarianism	
Transcendentalism	
Abolition	
Women's rights	

TERMS AND NAMES

Second Great Awakening Widespread spiritual movement

Unitarians Religious movement that emphasized reason

Ralph Waldo Emerson Leading philosopher of the era

transcendentalism Philosophy that emphasized the truth to be found in nature and intuition

William Lloyd Garrison Abolitionist leader

Frederick Douglass Escaped slave who became a noted abolitionist leader

Nat Turner Leader of a violent slave rebellion

Elizabeth Cady Stanton Leader in the abolitionist and women's rights movements

Seneca Falls convention Convention held in 1848 to argue for women's rights

Sojourner Truth Former slave who became an abolitionist and women's rights activist

A Spiritual Awakening Inspires Reform (pages 152–153)

What was the Second Great Awakening?

The **Second Great Awakening** was a religious movement that relied on emotional sermons in revival meetings to awaken religious feelings. It stressed individual conversion to religion.

Preachers such as Charles Grandison Finney gave exciting sermons to get emotional responses from their audiences. These preachers gave their sermons at events called revival meetings.

The **Unitarian** movement was a spiritual movement that appealed to reason, not emotion. It started in New England. It attracted wealthy and educated people.

Transcendentalism attracted people who

wanted to reform society. It was founded by New England minister, writer, and philosopher **Ralph Waldo Emerson.** According to transcendentalism, people could find truth by looking at nature and within themselves. Transcendentalists believed in the dignity of the individual.

Many enslaved African Americans had become Christians. Many saw the Christian message as a promise of freedom. In the East, free blacks formed their own churches. These churches became political, educational, and social centers for African Americans.

1. How did the Second Great Awakening emphasize the importance of the individual?

_____

_____

Slavery and Abolition (pages 153–155)

Why did abolitionists oppose slavery?

During the 1830s, more and more whites began to speak out against slavery. One extreme *abolitionist* was **William Lloyd Garrison.** In his newspaper, *The Liberator*, Garrison called for immediate emancipation, or freeing of the slaves. Many people in both the North and the South thought that Garrison's ideas were too extreme.

Another important abolitionist was **Frederick Douglass.** He learned a trade while he was still enslaved. He also learned to read. Later, he escaped from slavery.

Douglass wrote and spoke powerfully in favor of freeing the slaves without violence. He founded an antislavery newspaper called *The North Star.*

By 1830 slavery was part of the Southern way of life. Most slaves worked hard under cruel conditions for wealthy plantation owners. Most white farmers were poor and did not have much better living conditions than some slaves.

White males and a few free blacks did, however, have freedom and the chance to improve themselves. Slaves were denied education and the most basic *civil rights.*

In 1831, a Virginia slave named **Nat Turner** led a violent slave rebellion. The rebels were captured and executed. The Turner rebellion frightened

white Southerners. They made restrictions on slaves even tighter. Some Southerners also began to defend slavery as a good thing.

2. Describe how three people fought against slavery in the 1830s.

_____

_____

Women and Reform (pages 156–157)

What did women reformers do?

Women were active in the 19th-century reform movements. Many women worked for abolition. Women also played key roles in the temperance movement, the effort to ban the drinking of alcohol.

Until 1820, American girls had little chance for education. Some female reformers opened schools of higher learning for girls. Emma Willard founded a secondary school in New York, and Mary Lyon started Mount Holyoke, which later became a college.

Some women addressed the issue of women's rights. **Elizabeth Cady Stanton** and Lucretia Mott had been abolitionists. In 1848, they organized a women's rights convention. The **Seneca Falls convention** supported many reforms. The most controversial one was women's suffrage, or the right to vote.

For the most part, African American women did not have a voice at that time. **Sojourner Truth,** however, made her voice heard. A former slave, Truth became famous for speaking out for both abolition and women's rights.

3. How did women work for reform in the 19th century?

_____

_____

Glossary   CHAPTER 3 The Growth of a Young Nation

abolitionist Someone working to end slavery

agricultural Farming

artisans Skilled workers who make products by hand

civil rights The rights belonging to someone because of citizenship

commerce The buying and selling of goods, especially on a large scale

cotton gin A machine for cleaning seeds from cotton

depression A period when economic activity declines

electoral college Delegates selected to vote directly for the president

free state A state where slavery was illegal

frontier A region at the edge of a settled area

land agent A seller of land

landslide A victory by a huge majority of votes

market economy An economic system based on different kinds of producers selling their goods to each other

nullification The belief that states could ignore federal laws they did not like

persecuted Treated badly because of their beliefs or background

states' rights A political idea that says federal power should be limited and states should keep power for themselves

strikebreakers People hired to replace striking workers

textile mills Factories that make cloth

unconstitutional In violation of the Constitution

AFTER YOU READ

Terms and Names

A. Fill in the blanks with the letter of the term that best completes the sentence.

a. Monroe Doctrine

b. Louisiana Purchase

c. judicial review

d. Trail of Tears

e. manifest destiny

f. Missouri Compromise

g. strike

h. market revolution

i. Jeffersonian republicanism

j. Nat Turner

1. _____ was the belief that the United States would control the West.

2. The _____ told European nations not to interfere in the Western Hemisphere.

3. The _____ allowed Missouri to enter the Union as a slave state and Maine to enter as a free state.

4. In the _____, Jefferson bought land from France.

5. In a _____, workers stop working in order to improve their working conditions.

6. The principle of _____ says that the Supreme Court can declare a law unconstitutional.

7. In the _____, people began to buy goods rather than make them for themselves.

8. The _____ was the path Native Americans were forced to travel from Georgia to the new Indian Territory.

9. _____ is a belief that the people should control the government and that small and simple government is best.

10. _____ led a slave rebellion that failed.

B. Write the letter of the name or term next to the description that explains it best.

a. Jacksonian democracy

b. Stephen F. Austin

c. Lowell textile mills

d. Frederick Douglass

e. Elizabeth Cady Stanton

_____ **1.** Worked for abolition and women's rights

_____ **2.** A Texas land agent and leader of Texans' fight for independence

_____ **3.** Factories where "mill girls" held strikes for better wages

_____ **4.** A former slave who became an important abolitionist

_____ **5.** A belief that common people should run the government

Main Ideas

1. What did the Treaty of Ghent do?

_____

2. What did President Jackson do about the national bank?

_____

3. What happened at the Alamo?

_____

4. Why did workers go on strike?

_____

5. What was the Second Great Awakening?

_____

Thinking Critically

Answer the following questions on a separate sheet of paper.

1. How did the Louisiana Purchase, manifest destiny, and the War with Mexico help the United States to expand westward?

2. How did the market revolution change the way people worked?

CHAPTER 4 Section 1 (pages 164–173)

The Divisive Politics of Slavery

TERMS AND NAMES

secession Decision by a state to leave the Union

Millard Fillmore 13th president

Underground Railroad Secret network of people who hid fugitive slaves who went north to freedom

Harriet Tubman Famous "conductor" on the Underground Railroad

Harriet Beecher Stowe Author of the antislavery novel *Uncle Tom's Cabin*

Franklin Pierce 14th president

James Buchanan 15th president

Dred Scott Slave who was briefly taken by his owner into free territory

Abraham Lincoln President during the Civil War

Jefferson Davis President of the Confederate States of America

BEFORE YOU READ

In the last section, you saw how some people began a movement to abolish slavery.

In this section, you will see how slavery divides the nation.

AS YOU READ

Use this time line to take your notes. Fill it in with important events that added to the hard feelings between North and South. Describe each event briefly.

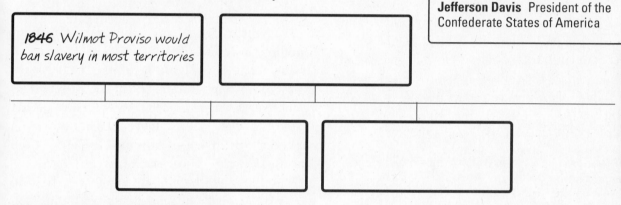

1846 Wilmot Proviso would ban slavery in most territories

Slavery in the Territories (pages 164–166)

How was a temporary slavery compromise reached?

North and South disagreed more and more over slavery in territories that wanted to become states. In 1846, Congress *debated* the Wilmot Proviso, a bill that would ban slavery in many territories. Northerners favored the bill. They felt that more slave states would give the South too much power in Congress. Southerners argued that slaves were property, protected by the Constitution. The Wilmot Proviso never passed.

In 1849, California asked to enter the Union as a free state. Southerners were angry because much of California was south of the Missouri Compromise line. President Zachary Taylor felt that states should decide for themselves whether to allow slavery. Southerners thought that any move to ban slavery was an attack on their way of life. They threatened **secession,** the decision by a state to leave the Union.

Henry Clay presented the Compromise of 1850. To please the North, it said that California would be admitted as a free state. For the South, it included the Fugitive Slave Act. This law requires Northerners to return *fugitive*, or escaped, slaves to their masters. The Compromise let some territories decide for themselves over slavery.

Congress argued over the Compromise of 1850 for months. When **Millard Fillmore** became president, he supported it. Finally the Compromise became law. But it did not settle the issue for long.

1. What were two features of the Compromise of 1850?

_____

_____

Protest, Resistance, and Violence
(pages 166–169)

How did people oppose slavery?

The Fugitive Slave Act provided harsh punishment for escaped slaves—and for anyone who helped them. Many Northerners were angry. Free African Americans and white *abolitionists* organized the **Underground Railroad.** This was a secret network of volunteers who hid fugitive slaves on their dangerous journey north to freedom. **Harriet Tubman**, an escaped slave, was a famous "conductor," or worker, on the Underground Railroad.

Meanwhile, a popular book helped many in the North see the fight to ban slavery as a moral struggle. **Harriet Beecher Stowe's** novel *Uncle Tom's Cabin* (1852) showed slavery's horrors. Southerners saw the book as an attack on their way of life.

In 1854, slavery in the territories became an issue again. The Kansas-Nebraska Act of 1854 split Nebraska into the territories of Nebraska and Kansas. Both could decide whether to allow slavery. Proslavery and antislavery people rushed into Kansas. Each side wanted to have enough people to decide the vote on slavery. After violence on both sides, the territory was nicknamed "Bleeding Kansas."

2. What were two ways in which people took actions against slavery?

_____

_____

The Birth of the Republican Party
(pages 169–170)

How did the slavery issue affect political parties?

The Whig Party split over the issue of slavery. That split left an easy victory for Democratic presidential candidate **Franklin Pierce** in 1852. Several new parties appeared in the North, including the Free Soil Party and the Know-Nothing Party. The Know-Nothings later also fell apart over slavery. The Republican Party was formed in 1854. It opposed slavery and the Kansas-Nebraska Act. The party took in people of many viewpoints. All that united them was the desire to keep slavery out of the territories. In the 1856 election, the first Republican presidential candidate came in a close second to Democrat **James Buchanan.**

3. What major political party was born out of the slavery issue?

_____

Slavery and Secession (pages 170–173)

What events widened the split between North and South?

Dred Scott was a slave who had been taken by his master into the free states of Illinois and Wisconsin for a time. Scott claimed that being in free states had made him a free man. In 1857, the Supreme Court ruled, in the Dred Scott case, that slaves were property protected by the Constitution. Southerners felt that this decision allowed slavery to be extended into the territories.

In 1858, Stephen Douglas ran for re-election to the Senate in Illinois. Republican **Abraham Lincoln** ran against him. They held a series of debates about slavery in the territories. Douglas was against slavery but favored popular sovereignty. This meant that the voters in each territory should decide whether to allow slavery. Lincoln called slavery "a vast moral evil." Douglas won the election, but the Lincoln-Douglas debates made Lincoln famous.

In 1859, a Northern white abolitionist tried to start a slave rebellion. John Brown and a few followers attacked a federal arsenal in Harper's Ferry, Virginia. They were captured and executed. Brown was praised in the North. Southerners were furious.

Republicans nominated Lincoln for president in 1860. The Democratic Party split into Northern and Southern branches. Lincoln won—without any electoral votes from the South. Southern reaction to Lincoln's election was dramatic. South Carolina *seceded* in December of 1860.

Southerners felt they had lost their political power in the United States. They feared an end to their whole way of life. By February 1861, seven Southern states had seceded. They formed the Confederate States of America, or Confederacy. They elected **Jefferson Davis** president.

4. What major event led to the secession of Southern states from the Union?

_____

CHAPTER 4 Section 2 (pages 176–183)

The Civil War Begins

TERMS AND NAMES

Fort Sumter Union fort in Charleston, South Carolina

Bull Run Battle won by the Confederates

Stonewall Jackson Confederate general

Ulysses S. Grant Union general

Robert E. Lee Confederate general

Antietam Union victory

Emancipation Proclamation Order issued by Lincoln freeing slaves behind Confederate lines

conscription Drafting of civilians to serve in the army

income tax Tax that takes a percentage of an individual's income

Clara Barton Union nurse

BEFORE YOU READ

In the last section, you saw how North and South came to war over slavery.

In this section, you will see that the Civil War became a long, bloody conflict.

AS YOU READ

Use this chart to take your notes. List the important military battles and political conflicts of the war and their effect on the North or South.

BATTLE/ POLITICAL ISSUE	EFFECT
Fort Sumter, 1861	Confederates take fort and begin Civil War

Union and Confederate Forces Clash (pages 176–178)

What were the advantages of the North and of the South?

The Civil War began in April 1861, when Confederate forces fired on **Fort Sumter** in Charleston, South Carolina. The fort was held by Union forces, but it was in Confederate territory. The Confederacy demanded that the Union surrender the fort. The Union refused. The Confederates attacked and took Fort Sumter.

Lincoln called for troops to fight to restore the Union. Four more Southern states seceded. Only four slave states remained in the Union. These were Maryland, Kentucky, Delaware, and Missouri.

The North had many advantages over the South. It had more people, more factories, more food production, and better railroads. The South's advantages were the demand for its cotton, better generals, and soldiers eager to defend their way of life. The North would have to conquer Southern territory to win.

The North had a three-part plan: 1) to blockade Southern ports to keep out supplies; 2) to split the Confederacy in two at the Mississippi; 3) to capture the Confederate capital of Richmond, Virginia.

The Confederates won the first battle of the war,

Bull Run, just 25 miles from Washington, D.C. The Southern general who stood firm and inspired his troops was nicknamed **Stonewall Jackson.**

In 1862, a Union army led by General **Ulysses S. Grant** captured Confederate forts in Tennessee. Both sides suffered terrible losses in the Union victory at Shiloh. Then the Union navy captured the port of New Orleans.

Also in 1862, the Union army marched toward Richmond. General **Robert E. Lee** successfully defended the Confederate capital. Then he marched toward Washington. He was defeated by Union forces at **Antietam,** Maryland, in the bloodiest clash of the war. Union troops did not chase Lee back into Virginia. If they had, they might have won the war then and there.

1. What four advantages did the North have over the South?

The Politics of War (pages 178–180)

What led Lincoln to issue the Emancipation Proclamation?

The South hoped that Britain would support them in the war. But Britain had a large supply of cotton. It needed to buy wheat and corn from the North. So the British remained *neutral.*

More and more people in the North felt that slavery should be abolished. At first, Lincoln did not feel he had the Constitutional right to end slavery where it already existed. But pressure to free the slaves increased. On January 1, 1863, Lincoln issued the **Emancipation Proclamation,** freeing all slaves behind Confederate lines. Lincoln's reasoning was that the slaves were enemy resources that contributed to the war effort. The Proclamation did not apply to slave states still in the Union.

In the North, the Emancipation Proclamation gave the war a high moral purpose. In the South, people became even more determined to fight to preserve their way of life. But there was *dissent* in both the North and South. Both presidents Davis and Lincoln expanded their presidential power to keep order and to put down dissent in time of war.

As the war went on, many soldiers were killed or wounded. Some *deserted.* Both sides turned to **conscription,** or the drafting of civilians to serve in

the army. In parts of the North, the *draft* led to riots.

2. What were two effects of the Emancipation Proclamation?

Life During Wartime (pages 181–183)

How did the war affect Northerners and Southerners?

The Civil War caused many changes in both North and South. In 1862, Congress allowed African Americans to serve in the Union Army. After the Emancipation Proclamation of 1863, many African Americans *enlisted.* By the end of the war, they were 10 percent of the Union army. African-American soldiers served in separate regiments. They were usually paid less than whites and suffered other kinds of *discrimination.*

As Union forces pushed deeper into the South, many slaves ran away. The decrease in its slave work force caused the South's economy to suffer. Prices rose. Food became scarce. In 1863, there were *bread riots* in Southern cities.

In the North, the war caused the economy to grow rapidly. Factories produced supplies needed by the army. But wages for factory workers did not keep up with prices. Some workers went on strike for higher wages.

To help pay for the war, Congress decided to collect the nation's first **income tax.** This tax takes a part of an individual's earned income.

Soldiers suffered and died not only from wounds they got in battles. They also suffered from poor army food, filthy conditions, and disease. Conditions in war prisons were even worse.

Early in the war, some Northern women and doctors founded a commission to improve sanitary conditions for soldiers. They set up hospital trains and ships. Over 3,000 women served as nurses. Some, like **Clara Barton,** went to the front lines. The Confederacy had many volunteer nurses, too.

3. How did the war affect the economies of both North and South?

CHAPTER 4 **Section 3** (pages 184–191)

The North Takes Charge

BEFORE YOU READ

In the last section, you saw the Civil War begin and the early battles fought.

In this section, you will see the South lose important battles and surrender. You will also see how the Civil War changed the nation in many ways.

AS YOU READ

Use the chart below to help you take notes on the effects of the Civil War on the nation. List the political, economic, and social changes.

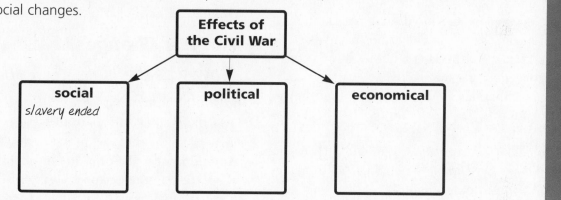

Effects of the Civil War → social (slavery ended) / political / economical

The Tide Turns (pages 184–186)

What battle turned the tide?

The South won several battles in 1863, but their famous general Stonewall Jackson died when he was shot accidentally by his own troops. That year General Robert E. Lee decided to invade the North. The Battle of **Gettysburg,** in Pennsylvania, turned the tide of the war. After three days of fierce fighting, Lee retreated to Virginia. He gave up any hope of invading the North.

The day after Gettysburg, General Grant captured **Vicksburg,** Mississippi, for the Union. When one more Mississippi River city fell, the Union controlled the river. The Confederacy was split in two.

In November of 1863, a cemetery was dedicated at Gettysburg. More than 50,000 soldiers had been lost on both sides at that battlefield. President

Lincoln delivered a short speech. The **Gettysburg Address** honored the dead and asked Americans to rededicate themselves to preserving the Union. Lincoln promised that "this government of the people, by the people, for the people" would survive.

1. How did Gettysburg change the war?

_____

_____

The Confederacy Wears Down
(pages 186–189)

How did Union forces wear down the South?

The losses at Gettysburg and Vicksburg caused Southern *morale* to drop. Many men had been lost in battle. The Confederate army was low on food, ammunition, and supplies. Soldiers began to desert. Some even joined the Union Army.

The South was exhausted and had few resources left. Some people called for peace. The Confederate Congress argued. President Jefferson Davis could not govern effectively.

Meanwhile, Lincoln made U.S. Grant commander of all Union armies. Grant gave **William Tecumseh Sherman** command of the military division of the Mississippi. Both generals believed they must fight not only the South's army and government but also the civilian population.

Grant fought Lee's army in Virginia. At the same time, Sherman's troops invaded Georgia. They marched across the state to the sea. They destroyed cities and farms as they went. Sherman did the same in South Carolina. Conditions became so bad for the South that by the time Sherman's troops reached North Carolina, they were giving food to the suffering Southerners.

Lincoln feared he would not be re-elected in 1864. Many Northerners felt the war had gone on too long and had caused too much destruction. But news of Sherman's victories helped Lincoln win a second term.

By March 1865, it was clear that the end of the Confederacy was near. President Davis fled Richmond. On April 9, Generals Lee and Grant met in **Appomattox,** Virginia, and arranged the Confederate surrender. Lincoln insisted the terms be generous. Confederate soldiers were allowed to go home, not taken prisoner. The Civil War was over.

2. Why did Lincoln fear he might not be reelected?

_____

_____

The War Changes the Nation
(pages 189–190)

How did the Civil War change the nation?

The Civil War changed the nation in many ways. After the war, no state ever threatened secession again. The federal government became much more powerful. During the war, it had passed conscrip-

tion and an income tax for the first time.

The war widened the economic gap between North and South. The Northern economy boomed as the region produced goods of many kinds. The Southern economy collapsed. The labor system of slavery was gone. Southern industry and railroads were destroyed. Many farms were also in ruins.

Nearly 10 percent of the nation's population had served in the military, leaving their jobs, farms, and families. About 360,000 Union soldiers and 260,000 Confederates had died.

The Civil War was also one of the first modern wars. It saw such "improvements" as hand grenades and land mines. The development of the ironclad ship led to the end of wooden warships.

3. What were two ways in which the Civil War changed the nation?

_____

_____

The War Changes Lives (pages 190–191)

How was the life of African Americans changed?

The situation of African Americans changed dramatically after the war. In 1865, the **Thirteenth Amendment** to the Constitution abolished slavery everywhere in the United States.

Only five days after Lee surrendered at Appomattox, President Lincoln was shot by a Southern *sympathizer.* Lincoln was at a play in Ford's Theater in Washington, D.C., when **John Wilkes Booth** shot him. He died the next day. Lincoln's body was carried by train from Washington to his hometown of Springfield, Illinois. Seven million people, or almost one-third of the Union population, turned out to pay their respects.

4. How was slavery finally abolished in the United States?

_____

_____

Reconstruction and Its Effects

BEFORE YOU READ

In the last section, you saw how the Union won the Civil War.

In this section, you will see that the federal government's efforts to rebuild Southern society after the war collapsed.

AS YOU READ

Use the chart below to take notes on the problems facing the South after the Civil War and the way people tried to solve those problems.

PROBLEM	SOLUTION
Former slaves have no land and no money	Freedman's Bureau provides food, clothing, hospitals, schools

---

TERMS AND NAMES

Reconstruction Period of rebuilding the nation after the Civil War

Andrew Johnson President after Lincoln's assassination

Fourteenth Amendment Gave African Americans citizenship

Fifteenth Amendment Banned states from denying African Americans the right to vote

scalawag White Southerners who joined the Republican Party

carpetbagger Northerners who moved to the South after the war

sharecropping System in which landowners gave a few acres of land to farm workers in return for a portion of their crops

tenant farming Renting land from landowners for cash

Ku Klux Klan A secret group of white Southerners who used violence to keep blacks from voting

Rutherford B. Hayes President who ended Reconstruction in 1877

The Politics of Reconstruction
(pages 192–194)

What was Reconstruction?

Reconstruction was the period of rebuilding the nation after the Civil War. It also refers to the process of bringing the Southern states back into the nation. It lasted from 1865 to 1877.

During the war, Lincoln made a plan for Reconstruction that was lenient, or easy, on the South. It included pardoning Confederates if they would swear *allegiance* to the Union. After Lincoln died, his vice-president, **Andrew Johnson,** became president. Johnson's plan was similar to Lincoln's.

However, Radical Republicans thought both plans were too easy on the South. They wanted to destroy the political power of former slave owners. They also wanted African Americans to be citizens with the right to vote.

Republicans in Congress won a struggle with the president to control Reconstruction. They had enough votes to pass a law creating the Freedman's Bureau. It gave food and clothing to former slaves and set up hospitals and schools. Congress also passed the Civil Rights Act of 1866. It said that states could not enact laws that discriminated against African Americans.

Congress then passed the **Fourteenth Amendment.** It gave African Americans citizenship. Johnson urged Southern states not to ratify it because they had no say in creating it. Congress responded with the Reconstruction Act of 1867. It said no state could re-enter the Union until it approved the Fourteenth Amendment and gave the vote to African-American men.

The fight between Congress and Johnson led Congress to look for a way to *impeach* the president. Johnson had removed a cabinet member. Congress said he did it illegally. Johnson was impeached, but he avoided conviction and removal from office by just one Senate vote.

In 1868, war hero Ulysses S. Grant was elected president. African-American votes in the South helped him win. Then, in 1870, the **Fifteenth Amendment** was ratified. It banned states from denying the vote to African Americans.

1. How did the Fourteenth and Fifteenth Amendments improve the lives of African Americans?

Reconstructing Society (pages 195–197)

Who held political power in the South?

By 1870, all former Confederate states were back in the Union. Their governments were run by Republicans. The South faced terrible economic conditions. Many men had died in the war. People had lost their investments. Farms were ruined. The state governments began *public works* programs to repair the physical damage. They also provided *social services.* They raised taxes to pay for these programs.

Three groups of Republicans had different goals. **Scalawags** were white Southerners. They were small farmers who did not want wealthy planters to regain power. **Carpetbaggers** were Northerners who had moved South. African Americans had voting rights for the first time. But many white Southerners resisted equality for African Americans.

During Reconstruction, many former slaves moved to the cities. With help, they organized schools and churches. Many African Americans voted, and some were elected to office.

2. Who now dominated the Republican Party in the South?

Changes in the Southern Economy (pages 198–199)

How did the economy in the South change after the war?

African Americans wanted to farm their own land. They had been promised "forty acres and a mule"

by General Sherman. Congress, though, did not honor this promise.

Meanwhile, Southern planters wanted to return to the plantation system. They tried to make sure African Americans could not own land. To survive, many former slaves became sharecroppers. **Sharecropping** is a system in which landowners give a few acres of land to their farm workers. The "croppers" keep a small portion of their crops and give the rest to the landowner.

Another system that allowed whites to control the labor of African Americans was **tenant farming.** Tenant farmers rented land from the landowners for cash.

3. Who had control of land and labor in the South?

The Collapse of Reconstruction
(pages 199–201)

What gains of Reconstruction were undone?

Many Southern whites did not like African Americans voting. Some formed secret groups such as the **Ku Klux Klan** that used violence to keep blacks from voting. Other whites refused to hire blacks who voted. Congress passed the Enforcement Acts to stop the violence. However, Congress also gave the vote to many former Confederates. As a result, Democrats began to regain power.

Meanwhile, corruption and scandals hurt the Republican Party. The Fourteenth and Fifteenth Amendments were weakened by decisions of the Supreme Court. As time passed, the nation lost interest in the problems of the South.

Rutherford B. Hayes became president in 1877. A deal between Republicans and Southern Democrats made his election possible. Republicans agreed to remove federal troops from the South to gain the support of white Democrats. Reconstruction was over. White Democrats again controlled the South.

4. How was Reconstruction undone?

Name _____ Date _____

abolitionists Persons who advocated doing away with slavery

allegiance Loyalty

bread riots The storming of bakeries and other food stores by hungry people in order to demand or steal food

debated Engaged in an argument by taking opposite points of view on an issue

deserted Ran away from or abandoned the army illegally

discrimination Unfair treatment of a person because of that person's racial, religious, ethnic, or other characteristics

dissent Difference of opinion; disagreement

draft Forced enrollment in the armed forces

enlisted Joined the armed forces

fugitive Runaway; escaped

impeach To remove a president from office by holding a trial in the Senate

morale The mood or spirits of a person or group of people

neutral Not supporting either side in a war

public works Construction projects, such as highways, paid for by the government for the benefit of the general public

seceded Formally withdrew from the Union

social services Services that help people improve their lives, such as schools

sympathizer One who supports a particular cause

AFTER YOU READ

Terms and Names

A. Fill in each blank with the name or term that best completes the paragraph.

Ulysses S. Grant   Robert E. Lee   Fort Sumter   Appomattox   Gettysburg   Bull Run

The Civil War began in 1861 when Confederate forces fired on **1**_____ in Charleston, South Carolina. Then, in the Battle of **2**_____, the South won an early victory only 25 miles from Washington, D.C. However, the tide turned at **3**_____, Pennsylvania. There, Confederate General **4**_____ was turned back from his attempt to invade the North. He finally surrendered to the Union commander **5**_____ at **6**_____, Virginia, in 1865.

B. Write the letter of the name or term next to the description that explains it best.

a. Harriet Beecher Stowe
b. Dred Scott
c. Thirteenth Amendment
d. Jefferson Davis
e. William Tecumseh Sherman
f. Ku Klux Klan
g. Underground Railroad
h. Abraham Lincoln
i. Emancipation Proclamation
j. Fifteenth Amendment

_____ **1.** President of the Confederacy

_____ **2.** Union general who destroyed Georgia in his march to the sea

_____ **3.** A slave who was denied freedom in a Supreme Court case

_____ **4.** Lincoln's freeing of all slaves behind Confederate lines

_____ **5.** A secret organization that used violence to prevent African Americans from voting

_____ **6.** The author of the antislavery novel *Uncle Tom's Cabin*

_____ **7.** Volunteers that helped slaves escape from the South

_____ **8.** Abolished slavery in the entire United States

_____ **9.** Extended the right to vote to African Americans

_____ **10.** President of the United States during the Civil War

Main Ideas

1. How did Abraham Lincoln and Stephen A. Douglas differ in their views on slavery?

_____

_____

2. What was the North's plan for winning the Civil War?

_____

_____

3. What were some signs that the South was exhausted after major battlefield losses in 1863?

_____

_____

4. How did emancipated slaves exercise their freedom?

_____

_____

5. How did Southern whites regain political power during Reconstruction?

_____

_____

Thinking Critically

Answer the following questions on a separate sheet of paper.

1. Suppose your state wanted to secede. What arguments would you make against it?

2. Did African Americans come through Reconstruction better or worse off? Explain.

CHAPTER 5 Section 1 (pages 214–221)

Native American Cultures in Crisis

BEFORE YOU READ

In the last section, you read about Reconstruction and its effects on the nation.

In this section, you will read how Americans began settling the West in the years following Reconstruction. This spelled disaster for Native Americans.

AS YOU READ

Use this diagram to take notes about the battles between Native Americans and settlers.

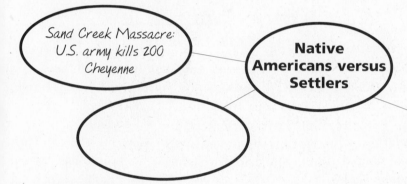

Sand Creek Massacre: U.S. army kills 200 Cheyenne

Native Americans versus Settlers

TERMS AND NAMES

Great Plains The grassland region of the United States

Homestead Act Act that offered free land to western settlers

exodusters African American settlers in the West

Sand Creek Massacre Mass killing of Cheyenne at Sand Creek, Colorado, by the U.S. army

Sitting Bull Leader of Hunkpapa Sioux

George A. Custer Colonel in U.S. Cavalry

assimilation Name of plan to make Native Americans part of white culture

Dawes Act Law that broke up Native American reservations

Ghost Dance Sioux ritual believed to chase away the whites

Battle of Wounded Knee U.S. massacre of Sioux at Wounded Knee Creek, South Dakota

The Culture of the Plains Indians (pages 214–215)

How did the Plains Indians live?

Native Americans lived on the **Great Plains,** the grasslands in the west-central portion of the United States. They followed a way of life that centered on the horse and buffalo. The horse allowed them to hunt more easily and to travel farther. The buffalo provided food, clothing, shelter, and other important items.

The Indians of the Great Plains lived in small extended family groups with ties to other groups that spoke the same language. The men hunted for food. The women helped butcher the *game* and prepare the buffalo hides that the men brought back to camp. Children learned the skills they would need as adults. They also learned proper behavior and culture through stories and *myths.*

1. What were the responsibilities of the different members of the tribe?

_____

_____

Settlers Push Westward (pages 215–216)

Why did Americans go west?

After the Civil War, thousands of white settlers moved to the Great Plains. They travelled there for a variety of reasons. Some were searching for gold. Others wanted to own land. Through the **Homestead Act,** Congress offered 160 acres of land free to anyone who would live on and farm it. In addition to whites, thousands of African Americans moved from the South to the West in a great *exodus.* They were known as **exodusters.**

2. For what two reasons did Americans settle the West?

The Government Restricts Native Americans; Bloody Battles Continue (pages 216–219)

Why did Indians and settlers fight each other?

Along the Great Plains, Native Americans and white settlers often clashed—mainly over land and resources. One of the more tragic clashes occurred in 1864. It happened in an area of the Colorado Territory known as Sand Creek Reserve. It was a *barren,* dry *reservation.* The Cheyenne lived there. They began raiding nearby settlements for supplies. In response, the army attacked and killed about 200 Cheyenne, mostly women and children. This incident became known as the **Sand Creek Massacre.**

More conflicts occurred along the border of what is now Wyoming and Montana. U.S. troops clashed with the Sioux over white settlements on the Sioux's hunting grounds. Some Sioux made peace with the government. Others, such as the Sioux leader **Sitting Bull,** continued to fight.

During the 1870s, gold was discovered in Sioux territory. The government offered to buy the land. When the Sioux refused, the army, which was led by **George A. Custer,** moved in. The two sides met at Little Bighorn River in 1876. The Sioux won decisively, killing Custer and all his soldiers. The army recovered, however. Within months it defeated the Sioux.

3. What were the reasons for the clashes between the U.S. government and the Sioux?

The Government Supports Assimilation (pages 219–220)

Why did assimilation fail?

As Indians and settlers fought, the country debated what to do about the Native Americans. Some called for a plan known as **assimilation.** In this plan, Native Americans would give up their beliefs and culture and become part of white culture.

To push assimilation, Congress passed the **Dawes Act** in 1887. The act broke up reservations and gave some of the land to each Native American family for farming. The plan, however, failed. Native Americans were cheated out of the best land. As a result, they had little success farming. Worse yet, by 1900, whites had killed nearly all the buffalo. Native Americans depended on the buffalo for their food, clothing, and shelter.

4. What were two reasons why assimilation failed?

The Battle of Wounded Knee (page 221)

What led to the Battle of Wounded Knee?

The Sioux were losing land and the buffalo. As a result, many Sioux turned to the **Ghost Dance.** This was a *ritual* they believed would bring the buffalo back and restore Sioux lands. The U.S. army was alarmed by the new movement. They attempted to arrest Sitting Bull, who had helped start the dance. During his arrest, a fight broke out and Sitting Bull was killed.

U.S. forces then rounded up about 350 Sioux and took them to a camp at Wounded Knee Creek in South Dakota. The army ordered the Sioux to give up all their weapons. One Native American refused and fired his rifle. The army fired back and killed about 300 unarmed Sioux. The **Battle of Wounded Knee** brought the Indian wars and the Native American era to an end.

5. What were the causes of the Battle of Wounded Knee?

The Growth of the Cattle Industry

BEFORE YOU READ

In the last section, you read how Native Americans and white settlers clashed over land in the American West.

In this section, you will read about the growth of the cattle industry and the life of the cowboy.

AS YOU READ

Use this diagram to organize the reasons for the rise and decline of the open range.

RISE	DECLINE
Americans' demand for beef grows	Too many herds destroy the grass

The Cattle Industry Becomes Big Business (pages 222–225)

What caused the cattle business to grow?

As the great herds of buffalo disappeared on the Great Plains, cattle herds took their place. After the Civil War, Americans' demand for beef grew. As a result, cattle ranching became big business from Texas to Kansas. Many cattle were **longhorns.** This breed was brought to the Americas by the Spanish. These were sturdy, long-horned, short-tempered animals that liked dry grasslands.

The men who tended to the cattle were known as cowboys. The cowboys' way of life was first developed by earlier Spanish ranchers in Mexico. Those ranchers influenced the American cowboys'

clothes, food, and vocabulary. American cowboys, however, added their own style.

Cowboys wore bandannas and special pointed-toe boots that fit inside their *stirrups.* The cowboys' six shooter was a gun that could fire six shots without reloading. It came to symbolize the Old West.

The cattle business did not really take off until railroads reached the Great Plains. Railroads linked the eastern and western parts of the country. They made it easier for ranchers to send their cattle to the cities.

1. What two factors helped the cattle business to grow?

_____

_____

_____

The Truth About Cowboys
(pages 225–226)

How did cowboys live?

Between 1866 and 1885, about 55,000 cowboys worked the plains. About 12 percent of these cowboys were Mexican. About 25 percent were African American.

A cowboy's life was difficult. Cowboys worked from 10 to 14 hours a day in all kinds of weather. They worked hard all spring and summer. In the winter, they lived off their savings or went from ranch to ranch and looked for odd jobs.

Famous cowboy figures like **James Butler "Wild Bill" Hickok** and **Martha Jane Cannary (Calamity Jane)** actually never dealt with cows. Hickok was the marshal of Abilene, Kansas. He was a violent man. He was killed during a poker game. Calamity Jane was an expert markswoman. Both also had been entertainers in Wild West shows. These shows, though, were not very much like life in the real West.

In the spring, cowboys rounded up their cattle and headed them out on the **long drive.** This was the journey from the plains to the shipping yards in Abilene, Kansas. From there, the cattle were loaded onto trains and shipped east. The long drive lasted about three months. During the trip, the cowboy slept on the ground and bathed in rivers. After delivering the cattle, cowboys celebrated in town. They then headed back to the ranch to collect their pay.

2. Cite at least two examples of how cowboys lived a rough life.

_____

_____

The End of the Cattle Frontier
(pages 226–227)

How did the open range come to an end?

Eventually, the era of the open range came to an end. Herds of cattle soon crowded the Great Plains and destroyed the grass. Then, a series of natural disasters struck. First, a *drought* hit the Great Plains in 1883. Another drought three years later turned much of the land into desert. The blazing heat was followed by the worst blizzard in American history. On one day, temperatures fell to 68 degrees below zero. Winds reached 60 miles per hour. Ranchers lost from 40 to 90 percent of their *livestock.*

After this disaster, most ranchers moved away from longhorns to breeds that would produce more meat per animal. Unlike the longhorns, many of these cattle had to be fed with hay. They also had to be cared for year-round. Ranchers wanted to keep their cattle from wandering or trampling their hay crops. As a result, they surrounded their land with a new invention called barbed wire. The use of barbed wire helped to end the era of the open range.

3. For what reasons did the era of the open range end?

_____

_____

Name _____ Date _____

Settling on the Great Plains

BEFORE YOU READ

In the last section, you read about the growth of the cattle industry and the life of cowboys.

In this section, you will read about life on the Great Plains for the men and women who settled there in search of land and prosperity.

AS YOU READ

Use this time line to make notes of the important events that shaped the settling of the Great Plains.

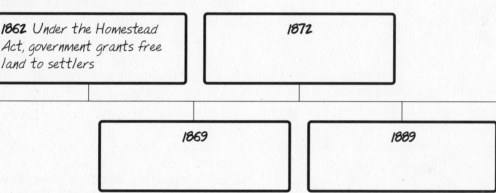

1862 Under the Homestead Act, government grants free land to settlers

1872

1869

1889

Settlers Flock Westward to Farm (pages 230–232)

How did the U.S. get people to go west?

More and more people migrated to the Great Plains with the building of the *transcontinental* railroads. From 1850 to 1871, the federal government gave huge tracts of land to companies ready to lay tracks through the West.

In 1867 the Central Pacific company began laying tracks east from Sacramento, California. Another railroad company, the Union Pacific, began laying tracks west from Omaha, Nebraska. Much of the work was done by Irish and Chinese immigrants. African Americans and Mexican Americans also did the back-breaking work. In 1869, the two routes met at Promontory, Utah. America's first transcontinental railroad was finished.

The railroad companies sold some of their land at low prices to settlers willing to farm it. Some companies even recruited people from Europe to settle on the land.

In addition, a growing number of people were responding to the Homestead Act of 1862. Under this law, the government offered 160 acres of free land to anyone who would farm it for five years. By 1900, the Great Plains was filled with more than 400,000 **homesteaders,** or settlers on this free land.

But the law did not always work as the government had planned. Only about 10 percent of the land was settled by the families for whom it was intended. Cattlemen and miners claimed much of the rest.

The government continued to pass other laws to encourage people to settle the West. Kansas' governor invited thousands of African Americans to settle in his state. In 1889, Oklahoma offered a major land giveaway. This led thousands of settlers to claim 2 million acres in less than 24 hours.

As more and more settlers gobbled up land in the West, the government took action to preserve some wilderness. In 1872, the government set aside land in Wyoming to create Yellowstone National Park. Millions of acres more were set aside later.

1. How did the government and the railroads encourage settlement of the West?

_____

_____

Settlers Meet the Challenges of the Plains (pages 232–234)

What was life like for settlers of the West?

From 1850 to 1900, the number of people living west of the Mississippi River grew from 1 percent of the nation's population to almost 30 percent. These new settlers had to endure many hardships.

The Great Plains did not have many trees. As a result, people built what became known as **soddys**. These homes were dug into the side of hills or made from sod. A soddy was warm in winter and cool in summer. However, it offered little light or air.

Homesteaders were largely *isolated* from one another. They had to make nearly everything they needed. Women worked in the fields alongside men. They also took care of the children, ran the house, and did the cooking and laundry.

Farming the Great Plains was difficult work. But several inventions helped make the task easier. The steel plow helped break up the prairie's tough soil. A new reaper cut wheat even faster.

The government also helped in the effort to improve farming techniques. The **Morrill Land Grant Acts** of 1862 and 1890 helped establish agricultural colleges. The government also established experiment stations on the Great Plains. Researchers there developed new types of crops as well as new growing techniques.

To buy much of the new farming machinery, farmers often went into *debt*. When crop prices fell, farmers ended up losing money. As a result, they had trouble repaying their loans. To make more money, they often had to raise more crops. This in turn led to the growth of **bonanza farms**. These were huge single-crop farms.

By 1900, the average farmer had nearly 150 acres under *cultivation*. However, when a drought hit the Plains between 1885 and 1890, many bonanza farms folded. They could not compete with the smaller farmers, who were more flexible in the crops they grew. The high price of shipping their crops also added to farmers' debt.

2. Name at least one social and economic hardship settlers faced.

_____

_____

A frontier family stands outside its home on the plains of Nebraska in 1889.
Credit: Nebraska State Historical Society, The Solomon D. Butcher Collection

Skillbuilder

Use the photograph to answer the questions.

1. What type of home does the family appear to live in?

_____

2. How does this photograph reinforce the geographical description of the Great Plains?

_____

CHAPTER 5 Section 4 (pages 235–239)

Farmers and the Populist Movement

BEFORE YOU READ

In the last section, you read about life for thousands of farmers trying to make a living on the Great Plains

In this section, you will read how these farmers organized and fought to improve their conditions.

AS YOU READ

Use this chart to take notes about the causes of the rise of the Populist Party and the effects the party had.

TERMS AND NAMES

Oliver Kelley Farmer who founded the Grange

Grange Organization that fought for farmers' rights

Populism Political movement that sought advancement for farmers and laborers

bimetallism backing money with silver and gold

William McKinley 1896 Republican presidential nominee

William Jennings Bryan 1896 Populist/Democratic presidential nominee

"Cross of Gold" speech Popular name of Bryan's convention speech supporting bimetallism

CAUSES	EFFECTS
farmers felt cheated	strong showing in the presidential election

Farmers Unite to Address Common Problems (pages 235–236)

How did farmers fight back?

By the 1800s, farmers were facing serious economic troubles. For one thing, the supply of money had gone down in the years following the Civil War. This made each dollar in circulation worth more. This was good news for consumers because their dollars bought more products. But it was bad news for farmers because they received less money for their crops.

The solution to the problem, farmers insisted, was to increase the money supply. This would decrease the value of the dollar. When money is "cheap," the prices of goods and services tend to

rise. Farmers urged the government to increase the the money supply. But the government refused.

Meanwhile, farmers continued to pay high prices to transport grain. Often they paid as much to ship their crops as they received for them. Many farmers were on the brink of ruin. The time, it seemed, had come for *reform*.

Many farmers joined together to push for reform. In 1867, a farmer named **Oliver Kelley** started an organization that became known as the **Grange**. Its original purpose was to provide a place for farm families to discuss social and educational issues. By the 1870s, however, Grange members spent most of their time and energy fighting the railroads.

The Grange gave rise to other organizations. They included the Farmers' Alliances. These organizations included teachers, preachers, and newspaper editors who sympathized with farmers. Alliance members traveled throughout the Great Plains. They educated farmers about a variety of issues, including how to obtain lower interest rates and ways to protest the railroads.

1. What steps did farmers take to address their concerns?

_____

_____

The Rise and Fall of Populism
(pages 236–239)

What did the Populist movement hope to achieve?

Alliance leaders realized that to make far-reaching changes, they needed political power. So in 1892, they created the Populist Party, or People's Party. This party was the beginning of **Populism.** This was a movement to gain more political and economic power for common people.

The Populist Party pushed for reforms to help farmers. It also called for reforms to make government more democratic. These reforms included direct election of senators and a secret ballot to stop cheating in voting.

Most Americans thought the populists' beliefs too radical. However, the party appealed to many struggling farmers and laborers. In 1892, the Populist presidential candidate won more than a million votes. That was almost 10 percent of the total vote. In the West, Populist candidates won numerous local elections. While not as strong as the two major parties, the Populist Party had become a political force.

Then, in 1893, the nation faced an economic crisis called the Panic of 1893. The causes of the panic started in the 1880s. During that decade, many companies and individuals had borrowed too much money. But starting in 1893, many of these companies went *bankrupt* because they were not making enough money to pay back their loans. Many people lost their jobs.

The panic continued into 1895. Then political parties began to choose candidates for the 1896 presidential election. One important issue was whether the country's paper money should be backed with both gold and silver.

Two groups of people debated this issue. One group wanted money to be backed only with gold. They were called "gold bugs." They thought that using only gold would make sure that every dollar had a high value.

The other group wanted to back the paper money with both gold and silver. This policy was known as **bimetallism.** This was a policy in which the government would give people either gold or silver in exchange for dollars or checks.

The group believed that bimetallism would make more dollars available. Prices of goods, including farm products, would rise. Wages would also rise. Common people would be able to make more money.

Republicans were "gold bugs." They elected **William McKinley** for president. The Democrats and the Populists both favored bimetallism. Both parties nominated **William Jennings Bryan.** At the Democratic convention, Bryan delivered an emotional speech, known as the **"Cross of Gold" speech,** in support of bimetallism.

But, on election day McKinley won. McKinley's election brought an end to Populism. But many of the reforms Populists wanted would be enacted in the 20th century.

2. Which groups did the Populists appeal to most?

_____

_____

Glossary
CHAPTER 5 Changes on the Western Frontier

bankrupt A condition in which a person or company cannot pay back debts

barren A lack of plant life

cultivate To prepare land for raising crops

debt The condition of owing something, such as money

drought A long period with no rain

exodus A departure, usually involving a large number of people

game A wild animal hunted for food or sport

isolated Separated from a group, alone

livestock Domestic animals, such as cattle, horses, or sheep, raised for home use or for profit

myth A traditional story dealing with supernatural beings, ancestors, or heroes

reform A change for the better; a correction of abuses

reservation An area of land set aside for Native Americans

ritual A ceremonial act

stirrup A loop or ring hung from either side of a horse's saddle to support the rider's foot

transcontinental Spanning or crossing a continent

AFTER YOU READ

Terms and Names

A. Write the letter of the term or name that matches the description.

a. exodusters
b. Populist Party
c. Homestead Act
d. longhorn
e. soddy
f. Democratic party

_____ **1.** A law that offered 160 acres of land free to anyone who would live on and farm it for five years

_____ **2.** The name given to African Americans who moved from the Reconstruction South to the Great Plains in the mid-1800s

_____ **3.** A type of cattle brought to the Americas by the Spanish

_____ **4.** A type of home made from prairie turf

_____ **5.** The political party that spoke for many farmers and laborers during the late 1800s

B. Write the name or term that best completes each sentence.

Populism
Grange
assimilation
bonanza farms
homesteaders
long drive

1. Under the policy of _____, Native Americans would give up their beliefs and culture and become part of white culture.

2. The _____ consisted of rounding up the cattle and leading them to the shipping yards in Abilene, Kansas.

3. Forced to grow more and more crops, many settlers built _____, huge, single-crop farms.

4. The _____ began as a social organization for farmers, but soon began to concentrate on battling the railroads.

5. _____, also known as the movement of the people, gave rise to the Populist Party.

AFTER YOU READ (cont.) *CHAPTER 5* Changes on the Western Frontier

Main Ideas

1. How effective was the Dawes Act in helping Native Americans become part of white culture?

_____

_____

2. What led to cattle becoming big business by the late 1800s?

_____

_____

3. Why does the life of cowboys seem less glamorous than the myths about them?

_____

_____

4. What economic problems confronted American farmers in the 1890s?

_____

_____

5. How would bimetallism help the economy, according to its supporters?

_____

_____

Thinking Critically

Answer the following questions on a separate sheet of paper.

1. Do you think that trying to assimilate Native Americans into white society was a good idea? Why or why not?

2. Explain why by the late 1800s there seemed to be two Americas—East and West.

The Expansion of Industry

BEFORE YOU READ

In the last section, you read about the growth of the Populist movement.

In this section, you will read how Americans used their natural resources and technological breakthroughs to begin building an industrialized society.

AS YOU READ

Use this diagram to take notes on the technological breakthroughs during the late 1800s and their impact on society.

TECHNOLOGICAL BREAKTHROUGH	IMPACT
electrical power	revolutionized business and daily life

Natural Resources Fuel Industrialization (pages 246–248)

What were America's important natural resources?

In the years after the Civil War, advances in technology began to change the nation. There were three causes of these advances: a large supply of natural resources, an explosion of inventions, and a growing city population that wanted the new products.

One of the more important natural resources was oil. In 1840 a Canadian *geologist* discovered that *kerosene* could be used to light lamps. Kerosene was produced from oil. This increased Americans' demand for oil.

In 1859, **Edwin L. Drake** used a steam engine to drill for oil. This technological breakthrough

helped start an oil boom. Oil-refining industries started in Cleveland and Pittsburgh. There, workers turned oil into kerosene.

Oil produced yet another product—gasoline. At first, gasoline was thrown away. However, when the automobile became popular, gasoline was in great demand.

In addition to oil, Americans discovered that their nation was rich in coal and iron. In 1887, explorers found large amounts of iron in Minnesota. At the same time, coal production increased from 33 million tons in 1870 to more than 250 million tons in 1900.

Iron is a strong metal. However, it is heavy and tends to break and rust. Researchers eventually removed the element carbon from iron. This produced a lighter, more flexible metal that does not rust. It became known as steel. The **Bessemer**

process, named after British manufacturer Henry Bessemer, provided a useful way to turn iron into steel.

Americans quickly found many uses for steel. The railroads, with their thousands of miles of track, bought large amounts of the new metal. Steel was also used to improve farm tools such as the plow and reaper. It also was used to make cans for *preserving* food. Engineers used steel to build bridges. One of the most remarkable bridges was the Brooklyn Bridge. It connected New York City and Brooklyn. Steel also was used to build skyscrapers, such as the Home Insurance Building in Chicago.

1. Name two ways Americans used steel.

Inventions Promote Change
(pages 248–249)

How did the new inventions change Americans' way of life?

Beginning in the late 1800s, inventors produced items that changed the way people lived and worked. In 1876 **Thomas Alva Edison** established the world's first research laboratory in Menlo Park, New Jersey. He used the lab to develop new inventions. Edison perfected an early light bulb there. He then worked to establish power plants to generate electricity.

Another inventor, George Westinghouse, developed ways to make electricity safer and less expensive.

The use of electricity changed America. By 1890, electricity ran machines such as fans and printing presses. Electricity soon became available in homes. This led to the invention of many appliances. Cities built electric streetcars. They made travel cheaper and easier.

In 1867, **Christopher Sholes** invented the typewriter. This led to dramatic changes in the workplace. Almost ten years later, in 1876, **Alexander Graham Bell** and Thomas Watson invented the telephone.

The wave of inventions during the late 1800s helped change Americans' daily life. More women began to work in offices. By 1910, women made up about 40 percent of the nation's office work force. In addition, work that had been done at home—such as sewing clothes—was now done in factories. Unfortunately, many factory employees worked long hours in unhealthy conditions.

Inventions had several positive effects. Machines allowed employees to work faster. This led to a shorter work week. As a result, people had more *leisure* time. In addition, citizens enjoyed new products such as phonographs, bicycles, and cameras.

2. Name two ways in which electricity changed people's life.

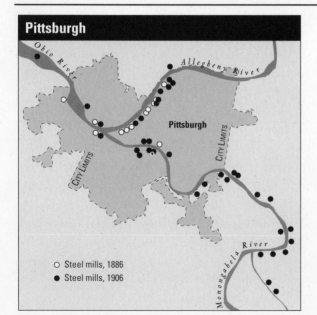

Geography Skillbuilder
Use the map to answer the questions.

1. Along what feature are all the mills located?

2. What does this map say about the steel industry during the late 1800s and early 1900s?

CHAPTER 6   Section 2 (pages 252–256)

The Age of the Railroads

BEFORE YOU READ

In the last section you read about how Americans used their natural resources and numerous inventions to begin transforming society.

In this section you will read about the growth of the nation's railroad industry and its effect on the nation.

AS YOU READ

Use this diagram to take notes on the effects of the rapid growth of railroads.

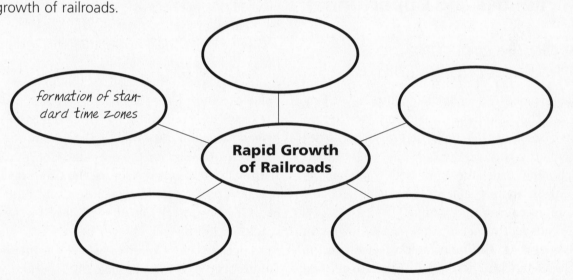

formation of standard time zones

Rapid Growth of Railroads

Railroads Span Time and Space
(pages 252–254)

Who built the railroads?

In 1869, the nation completed work on its first **transcontinental railroad**—a railroad that crossed the entire continent. In the years that followed, railroad tracks spread throughout the country. By 1890, more than 200,000 miles of rail lines zigzagged across the United States.

Railroads made long-distance travel a possibility for many Americans. However, building and running the railroads was difficult and dangerous work. Those who did most of the work were immigrants and poor Americans. Accidents and diseases affected thousands of railroad builders each year. By 1888, more than 2,000 workers had died. Another 20,000 workers had been injured.

The railroads paid workers very little. Working conditions were miserable as well. In 1866, for example, railroads hired Chinese immigrants to dig a tunnel through a *granite* mountain. For five months of that year, the Chinese lived and worked in camps surrounded by 40 feet of snow. Hundreds of people were buried by *avalanches*. Many others froze to death.

Railroads eventually linked the many different regions of the United States. However, railroad schedules proved hard to keep. This was because each community set its own times—based mainly on the movement of the sun. The time in Boston, for example, was almost 12 minutes later than the time in New York.

To fix this problem, officials devised a plan in 1870 to divide the earth into 24 time zones, one for each hour of the day. Under this plan, the United States would contain four time zones: Eastern, Central, Mountain, and Pacific. Everyone living in a particular zone would follow the same time. The railroad companies supported this plan. Many communities also supported it.

1. Name two ways in which life was difficult for railroad builders.

Opportunities and Opportunists
(pages 254–255)

How did the growth of the railroads affect the nation?

Railroads made it easier for people to travel long distances. They also helped many industries grow. The iron, steel, coal, lumber, and glass industries all grew partly because the railroads needed their products. Railroads also increased trade among cities, towns, and settlements. This allowed many communities to grow and prosper.

Railroads led to the creation of new towns. In 1880 **George M. Pullman** built a factory on the prairie outside Chicago. There, workers made the railroad sleeping cars he invented. As demand for his sleeping cars rose, Pullman built a large town to house the workers he needed. Pullman created quality housing for his workers. But he tried to control many aspects of their lives. Eventually, his workers rebelled.

The railroad industry offered people the chance to become rich. As a result, the industry attracted *corrupt* individuals.

One of the most well-known cases of corruption was the Crédit Mobilier scandal. In 1868, some officers of the Union Pacific railroad formed a construction company called **Crédit Mobilier.** They gave their company contracts to lay railroad track

at two to three times the actual cost. They kept all profits. To prevent government from interfering, they paid off members of Congress. Eventually, authorities uncovered the *scheme.*

2. What was one positive and negative effect of the growth of railroads?

The Grange and the Railroads
(pages 255–256)

Why did the farmers fight the railroads?

One group angered by corruption in the railroad industry were farmers. Farmers were upset with the railroads for a number of reasons. First, they claimed that railroads sold government land grants to businesses rather than to families. They also accused the railroads of setting high shipping prices to keep farmers in debt.

In response to these abuses, the Grangers took political action. They convinced some states to pass laws regulating railroad activity. The railroads challenged the states' rights to regulate them.

The battle reached the Supreme Court in 1877. In the case of **Munn v. Illinois,** the Court declared that government could regulate private industries in order to protect the public interest. The railroads had lost their fight.

A decade later, Congress passed the **Interstate Commerce Act.** The act gave the federal government even more power over the railroads. The railroads, however, continued to resist all government intervention.

Beginning in 1893, an economic depression struck the country. It affected numerous institutions—including the railroads. Many railroad companies failed. As a result, they were taken over by financial firms. By 1900, seven companies owned most of the nation's railways.

3. Give two reasons why farmers were upset with the railroad companies.

CHAPTER 6 Section 3 (pages 257–261)

Big Business Emerges

TERMS AND NAMES

Andrew Carnegie Scottish immigrant who became a giant in the steel industry

vertical integration Process in which a company buys out its suppliers

horizontal consolidation Process in which companies producing similar products merge

Social Darwinism Theory that taught only the strong survived

monopoly Situation in which one company controlled an entire industry

holding company Corporation that bought out the stock of other companies

John D. Rockefeller Head of Standard Oil Company

trust Corporation formed by separate companies

Sherman Antitrust Act Law that outlawed trusts

BEFORE YOU READ

In the last section, you read about the growth of the railroad industry in the United States.

In this section, you will read about the growth of big business in America and how economic power became concentrated in the hands of a few.

AS YOU READ

Use the diagram below to take notes on the business practices of Andrew Carnegie and John D. Rockefeller.

INDUSTRIALISTS	BUSINESS	METHODS
Carnegie	Steel	vertical integration, horizontal consolidation
Rockefeller		

Carnegie's Innovations (pages 257–258)

How did Carnegie take control of the steel industry?

Andrew Carnegie symbolized the growth of big business during the late 1800s. Carnegie was a Scottish *immigrant*. He made a fortune in the railroad business. Then he bought a steel company. From there, he set out to make his company the leader in the steel industry.

He attempted to control the entire steel industry. He did this mainly by **vertical integration.** Under this process, he bought the companies that supplied his *raw materials*, such as coal and iron. He also bought the railroad lines that transported his goods. This gave him total control over the quality and cost of his product.

Carnegie also attempted to buy out competing steel producers through a process known as **horizontal consolidation.** In this process, companies producing similar products *merge*. By 1900, Carnegie had gained control of both his suppliers and competitors. This allowed him to control nearly the entire steel industry.

1. Describe two ways in which Carnegie tried to control the steel industry.

_____

_____

_____

Social Darwinism and Business

(page 258)

What is the theory of Social Darwinism?

The success of people such as Carnegie led to an intellectual movement known as **Social Darwinism.** This movement grew from the ideas of the English biologist Charles Darwin. Darwin believed that some individuals succeed and pass their traits along to the next generation, while others do not. He claimed that this process weeded out weaker individuals and enabled the strongest to survive.

Darwin's theory appealed to the American business community. Businessmen argued that free competition in business would ensure survival of the strongest.

Social Darwinism also taught the importance of hard work and personal responsibility This appealed to ordinary Americans.

2. Why did Social Darwinism appeal to ordinary Americans?

_____

_____

Fewer Control More (pages 259–261)

How did so few get so much power?

Many businessmen did not totally support the idea of free competition. In fact, many *industrialists* tried to eliminate all competition that threatened the growth of their own business empires.

One way to eliminate competition was buy out all other companies in the industry. A firm that managed to buy out all its competitors could achieve a **monopoly,** or complete control over an industry.

Another way to create a monopoly was to set up a **holding company.** This was a corporation that did nothing but buy out the *stock* of other companies.

The Standard Oil Company used yet another method to establish a monopoly. **John D. Rockefeller,** the head of Standard Oil, took control of the oil industry by forming a **trust.** This was a system in which different companies agreed to work together as a large corporation. The companies then split the profits earned by the trust.

Critics of Rockefeller and the other industrialists labeled them robber barons. This was from the name of the feudal lords who owned huge estates in Europe during the Middle Ages. The industrialists, however, defended their great wealth. They emphasized that they gave much of their money back to society by donating to charities and other causes.

Eventually the government took a stand against the industrialists and their monopolies. In 1890, Congress passed the **Sherman Antitrust Act.** The act outlawed trusts. However, the courts refused to support the law. As a result, business monopolies continued.

3. Describe at least two ways in which a company could create a monopoly.

_____

_____

Business Boom Bypasses the South (page 261)

Why was there no industrial growth in the South?

The industrial boom of the late 1800s occurred mainly in the North. In the South, industrial growth was much slower.

Several factors contributed to the South's slow economic growth. First, the region had not yet recovered from the Civil War. Second, many Southerners refused to *invest* their money in businesses in the South after the war. Third, most Southerners who tried to start businesses had difficulty overcoming economic obstacles. Finally, Southern businesses could not compete with Northern companies—which were already well established.

4. Name two reasons why the South did not experience a business boom.

_____

_____

CHAPTER 6 Section 4 (pages 262–269)

Workers of the Nation Unite

BEFORE YOU READ

In the last section, you read about the growth of big business in America.

In this section, you will read about how workers united to improve conditions in the nation's growing industries.

AS YOU READ

Use the time line below to take notes of the major events in labor activism between 1866 and 1911.

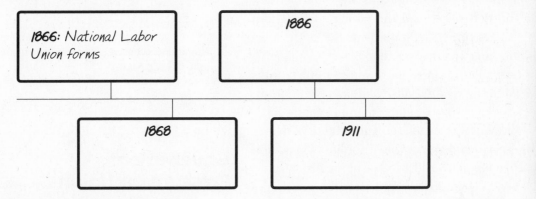

1866: National Labor Union forms

1886

1868

1911

Workers Are Exploited; Labor Unions Emerge (pages 262–264)

What did unions want?

Workers in the nation's industries led a rough life. They labored long hours in dangerous conditions for low pay.

Workers had no choice but to put up with the horrible conditions. Incomes were so low that all family members had to work. This included women and children. Many children worked from dawn to dusk. This left no time or energy for school. Many child laborers suffered from hunger and exhaustion.

To improve their conditions, workers began to form labor unions. A labor union is a group of employees working together. Things that workers wanted included safer working conditions and higher wages. The National Labor Union formed

in 1866. It was made up of about 300 local unions in 13 states. This union persuaded the government to adopt an eight-hour workday in government offices. The National Labor Union formed its own political party—the Labor Reform Party. The party ran its own candidate in the 1872 presidential election.

The Knights of Labor formed in 1868. It was another large union. This union was open to all workers, regardless of race, *gender*, or type of skill. The Knights of Labor pushed for an eight-hour day in numerous industries. It also demanded equal pay for women.

1. Name two things unions wanted.

_____

_____

Union Movements Diverge; Strikes Turn Violent (pages 264–268)

Why did some unions support socialism?

As the union movement spread, two major types of unions emerged. In 1886, trade and craft unions formed the **American Federation of Labor (AFL).** It was led by **Samuel Gompers.** This union focused on **collective bargaining,** or group negotiations, to reach agreements between workers and employers. Another union leader, **Eugene V. Debs,** formed the American Railway Union (ARU). This union was opened to both skilled and unskilled laborers.

Debs and other labor leaders believed that the problems workers faced were due in part to the American economic system. They believed that the idea of private ownership and free competition made the rich richer and the poor poorer. These labor leaders turned to **socialism.** Socialism is an economic and political system based on government control of business and property. It also calls for distributing wealth equally among everyone. In 1905, a radical group of union members and socialists in the West organized the **Industrial Workers of the World (IWW),** or the Wobblies. This union welcomed women and African Americans.

In order to improve their conditions, workers often went on strike. A strike occurs when laborers refuse to work.

In May 1886, about 1,200 people gathered in Chicago's Haymarket Square. They had come to protest the killing of a striker by police the day before. The meeting turned into a riotous battle between police and workers. As a result of the Haymarket violence, the public began to turn against the labor movement.

However, this did not stop workers from striking. In 1892, workers shut down the Carnegie Steel Plant in Pennsylvania. A battle followed that left several people dead. The owners hired **scabs,** or replacement workers, to keep the plant open. Eventually the strikers had to give in.

In 1894, a strike at the Pullman railcar company resulted in *bloodshed.* Federal troops restored order. Many of the workers lost their jobs.

2. For what reason did socialism appeal to some unions?

_____

_____

Women in the Labor Movement (pages 268–269)

What role did women play?

Women were barred from many unions. However, they helped in the fight to improve labor conditions. **Mary Harris "Mother" Jones** helped organize mine workers. Pauline Newman helped organize clothing workers.

In 1911, a fire broke out in the Triangle Shirtwaist Factory—a clothing factory in New York City. Almost 150 women workers died, in part because they had been locked inside. The public was outraged. As a result, New York passed several labor reform laws.

3. Name two women labor organizers and the unions they helped lead.

_____

_____

Government Pressure on Unions (page 269)

How did big business battle the unions?

Despite some gains, union members faced growing opposition from industrialists and the federal government. Business leaders took a number of steps to prevent workers from organizing. They banned union meetings or fired union workers.

Business leaders also got help from the federal government. When workers went on strike, employers would claim that the strike hurt interstate trade. As a result, the government would force the workers to return to their jobs.

4. Name at least two ways big business tried to break up unions.

_____

_____

Name _____ Date _____

avalanche A large snowfall down a mountainside	**immigrant** One who leaves a country to settle in another	**merge** To join together
bloodshed The shedding of blood, violence	**industrialist** A leader in a business or industry	**preserve** To protect from injury
corrupt Immoral or dishonest	**invest** To put money towards something in the hope of future profit	**raw materials** Unprocessed natural products
gender Relating to the sexes		**scheme** A plan, usually secret
geologist Someone who studies the origin, history, and structure of the earth	**kerosene** A thin oil used as a fuel	**stock** A share of ownership in a company
granite A type of rock	**leisure** Freedom from duties or responsibilities	

AFTER YOU READ

Terms and Names

A. If the statement is true, write "true" on the line. If it is false, change the underlined word or words to make it true.

1. _____ The <u>Bessemer process</u> was a useful way of turning iron into steel.

2. _____ <u>Edwin L. Drake</u> invented the telephone.

3. _____ The <u>Interstate Commerce Act</u> increased the federal government's power over the railroads.

4. _____ A business firm that controls all the competition in an industry holds a <u>trust</u> over the industry.

5. _____ In the late 1800s some unions looked to <u>collective bargaining</u> to reach agreements between workers and employers.

B. Write the letter of the name or term that matches the description.

a. Andrew Carnegie
b. Knights of Labor
c. *Munn* v. *Illinois*
d. Industrial Workers of the World
e. Thomas Alva Edison
f. Mary Harris "Mother" Jones

_____ **1.** Developed the light bulb and a research laboratory in Menlo Park, New Jersey

_____ **2.** The court ruling that won states the right to regulate the railroads

_____ **3.** Millionaire businessman who gained control of the steel industry

_____ **4.** Union organized by a group of radical union members and social-ists.

_____ **5.** Activist who helped lead the United Mine Workers of America

AFTER YOU READ (continued)   *CHAPTER* 6 A New Industrial Age

Main Ideas

1. In what ways did natural resources and inventions help change the nation in the years after the Civil War?

_____

_____

_____

2. How did the growth of the railroad industry affect the development of other industries?

_____

_____

_____

3. Why were industrialists known as robber barons?

_____

_____

_____

4. Why did the South industrialize more slowly than the North did?

_____

_____

_____

5. How was the union movement successful? How was its success limited?

_____

_____

_____

Think Critically

Answer the following questions on a separate sheet of paper.

1. Which invention do you consider more important, the telephone or electricity? Explain.

2. Do you think workers today can benefit from unions? Why or why not?

CHAPTER 7 Section 1 (pages 274–279)

The New Immigrants

BEFORE YOU READ

In the last section, you read about the nation's labor union movement.

In this section, you will read how millions of immigrants entered the United States, where they faced culture shock, prejudice, and opportunity.

AS YOU READ

Use this diagram to take notes on the anti-immigration measures that the United States took.

MEASURE	DESCRIPTION
Chinese Exclusion Act	
Gentlemen's Agreement	

Through the "Golden Door"
(pages 274–276)

Where did the immigrants come from?

Between 1870 and 1920, about 20 million Europeans *immigrated* to the United States. Many of them came from eastern and southern Europe.

Some immigrants came to escape religious *persecution*. Many others were poor and looking to improve their economic situation. Still others came to experience greater freedom in the United States. Most European immigrants arrived on the East Coast.

A smaller number of immigrants came from Asia. They arrived on the West Coast. About 200,000 Chinese immigrants came between 1851 to 1883. Many Chinese immigrants helped build the nation's first transcontinental railroad. When the United States *annexed* Hawaii in 1898, many thousand Japanese immigrants came to the United States.

From 1880 to 1920, about 260,000 immigrants arrived from various islands in the Caribbean Sea. They came from Jamaica, Cuba, Puerto Rico, and other islands. Many left their homelands because jobs were *scarce*.

Many Mexicans came to the United States as well. Some became U.S. citizens when the nation acquired Mexican territory in 1848 as a result of the Mexican War. About a million Mexicans arrived between 1910 to 1930 to escape *turmoil* in their country.

1. **Name two regions of the world where immigrants to the U.S. came from.**

_____

_____

Life in the New Land (pages 276–278)

How did immigrants cope in America?

Many immigrants traveled to the United States by steamship. On board the ship they shared a cramped, unclean space. Under these conditions, disease spread quickly. As a result, some immigrants died before they reached America.

Most European immigrants to the United States arrived in New York. There, they had to pass through an immigration station located on **Ellis Island** in New York Harbor. Officials at the station decided whether the immigrants could enter the country or had to return. Any immigrant with serious health problems or *contagious* disease was sent home. Inspectors also made sure that immigrants met the legal requirements for entering the United States.

Asian immigrants arriving on the West Coast went through **Angel Island** in San Francisco. The inspection process on Angel Island was more difficult than on Ellis Island.

Immigrants to the United States had to deal with **culture shock.** This was confusion and worry caused by experiencing a different culture. Many immigrants settled in communities with other immigrants from the same country. This made them feel more at home. They also formed organizations to help each other.

2. **Name two ways immigrants dealt with culture shock.**

_____

_____

Immigration Restrictions
(pages 278–279)

How did some Americans react to immigration?

By the turn of the century, some observers called America a **melting pot.** This term referred to the fact that many different cultures and races had blended in the United States.

However, this was not always the case. Many new immigrants refused to give up their culture to become part of American society.

Some Americans also preferred not to live in a melting pot. They did not like the idea of so many immigrants living in their country. The arrival of so many immigrants led to the growth of nativism. Nativism is an obvious preference for native-born Americans. Nativism gave rise to anti-immigrant groups. It also led to a demand for immigration restrictions.

On the West Coast, *prejudice* against Asians was first directed at the Chinese. During the depression of the 1870s, many Chinese immigrants agreed to work for low wages. Many American workers feared they would lose their jobs to the Chinese. As a result, labor groups pressured politicians to restrict Asian immigration. In 1882, Congress passed the **Chinese Exclusion Act.** This law banned all but a few Chinese immigrants. The ban was not lifted until 1943.

Americans showed prejudice against Japanese immigrants as well. In San Francisco, the local school board put all Chinese, Japanese, and Korean children in special Asian schools. This led to anti-American riots in Japan. President Theodore Roosevelt persuaded San Francisco officials to stop their separation policy. In exchange, Japan agreed to limit *emigration* to the United States under the **Gentlemen's Agreement** of 1907–1908.

3. **Give two examples of anti-immigration measures in the U.S.**

_____

_____

CHAPTER 7 Section 2 (pages 282–287)

The Problems of Urbanization

TERMS AND NAMES

urbanization The growth of cities

Americanization movement Program to teach American culture to immigrants

row house Home that shared side walls with other similar homes

dumbbell tenement Apartment building shaped like a barbell

Social Gospel movement Movement that urged people to help the poor

settlement house Community center that addressed problems in slum neighborhoods

Jane Addams Social reformer who helped the poor

BEFORE YOU READ

In the last section, you read about the arrival of millions of immigrants to America's shores.

In this section, you will read how the arrival of so many immigrants caused cities' populations to swell—and their problems to increase.

AS YOU READ

Use this diagram to take notes on the problems that residents faced in America's rapidly growing cities.

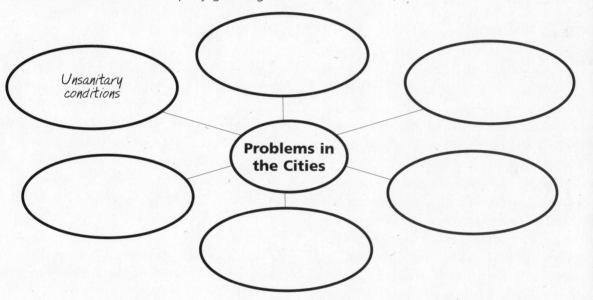

Urban Opportunities (pages 282–284)

Why did people move to the cities?

Many of the nation's new immigrants settled in the cities in the early 1900s. They came there to find jobs in the cities' growing factories and businesses. Immigrants settled mainly in cities in the Northeast and Midwest. The result was rapid **urbanization,** or growth of cities, in those regions.

By 1910, immigrants made up more than half of the populations of 18 major American cities. Many immigrants settled in neighborhoods with others from the same country or even from the same village.

Newcomers to the United States learned about their new country through an education program known as the **Americanization movement.** Under this program, schools taught immigrants English, and American history and government. These subjects helped immigrants become citizens.

Immigrants were not the only people who settled in the cities around the turn of the century. On the nation's farms, new machines replaced workers. As a result, many workers in the rural areas lost their jobs. Unemployed farm workers soon moved to cities to find jobs.

Many of the Southern farmers who lost their jobs were African Americans. Between 1890 and 1910 about 200,000 African Americans moved from the South to cities in the North. They hoped to escape economic hardship and racial violence. However, many found prejudice and low wages in the North.

The cities offered people many economic opportunities. They also provided numerous cultural attractions. Cities offered people entertainment such as moving pictures, Wild West shows, and baseball games.

1. Name two groups that settled in the cities.

_____

_____

Urban Problems (pages 284–286)

What problems did city dwellers face?

City populations grew rapidly. This led to many problems. One major problem was a shortage in housing. New types of housing allowed many people to live in a small amount of space. One type was the **row house.** This was a single-family dwelling that shared side walls with other similar houses.

Newcomers to the city also moved into single-family houses. Sometimes three or four families lived there. These houses became overcrowded and *unsanitary.*

Some cities tried to improve housing conditions. New York City passed a law requiring building owners to improve plumbing and air flow. As a result, landlords began building **dumbbell tenements.** These were long, narrow, five-or six-story buildings shaped like barbells. They contained air shafts for better air flow. Because garbage at the building was not picked up often, people began to dump it down the air shafts. This attracted rats. Soon these dumbbell tenements became worse places to live than the single-family houses.

The growing population of cities also created transportation problems. Planners developed new transit systems to carry large numbers of people. They included the electric streetcar and the electric subway.

Cities also faced the problem of supplying enough clean, safe water to everyone. Removing garbage and waste was yet another problem. In addition, cities struggled to control fires as well as crime.

2. Name two problems that city residents faced.

_____

_____

Reformers Mobilize (page 286–287)

How did reformers help the poor?

A number of social reformers worked to improve life in the cities. One early reform program was the **Social Gospel movement.** Leaders of this movement preached that people reached *salvation* by helping the poor. Many reformers responded to the movement's call. They established **settlement houses.** These were community centers located in slum neighborhoods. Workers there provided help and friendship to immigrants and the poor.

Many of these houses were run by middle-class, college-educated women. The settlement houses also offered schooling, nursing, and other kinds of help.

One of the more well-known social reformers of this time was **Jane Addams**. She helped establish Hull House. This was a settlement house that helped the poor of Chicago.

3. Name two things a settlement house provided for the poor.

_____

_____

CHAPTER 7 Section 3 (pages 288–290)

The Emergence of the Political Machine

TERMS AND NAMES

political machine A group that controlled a political party

graft Illegal use of political influence for personal gain

kickback Illegal payment of a portion of one's earnings to someone else

Tammany Hall A powerful political machine in New York

Tweed Ring Group of corrupt politicians led by Boss Tweed

Thomas Nast Political cartoonist who ridiculed Boss Tweed

BEFORE YOU READ

In the last section, you read about the problems that residents faced in America's growing cities.

In this section, you will read about the people and organizations that controlled the nation's major cities.

AS YOU READ

Use this diagram to take notes on things, both good and bad, related to political machines.

GOOD	BAD
Jobs	Kickbacks

Political Machines Run the Cities
(pages 288–289)

How did political machines control the cities?

During the late 1800s, many cities were run by a **political machine.** This was an organized group that controlled the activities of a political party in a city. The machine offered services to voters and businesses in exchange for political or financial support.

The city boss controlled the political machine—and city government. Bosses controlled many city jobs. These included jobs in the police, fire, and sanitation departments. Bosses also controlled the city agencies that granted licenses to businesses.

They controlled the money used to pay for large construction projects.

Bosses used more than money to control the cities. When they solved problems for voters, it strengthened voters' loyalty. This helped bosses gain more influence.

Immigrants were the bosses' biggest supporters. Many bosses were themselves immigrants who had worked their way up in politics. Bosses could speak to the immigrants in their own language. They understood immigrants' concerns and problems. The political machines helped immigrants find places to live and got them jobs. In return, the immigrants provided what the political bosses needed most—votes.

1. Name two ways in which political machines held power.

_____

_____

_____

Municipal Graft and Scandal
(pages 289–290)

How were the political bosses corrupt?

Political machines provided city dwellers with vital services. But as they gained power, many political bosses became greedy and corrupt. They became rich through **graft.** This was the illegal use of political influence for personal gain.

Some bosses used illegal ways to win elections. They filled the list of *eligible* voters with the names of dogs, children, and people who had died. They then used those names to cast as many votes as were needed to win.

A political machine had many opportunities for corruption. After hiring a person to work on a city construction project, a machine could ask the worker to turn in a bill that was higher than the actual cost of the work. The workers then "kicked back" a part of the earnings to the machine. These illegal payments were known as **kickbacks.** They made many political bosses very wealthy.

Another way that politicians made money was by doing favors for businesses in return for cash. They also accepted bribes to allow illegal activities, such as gambling. The police rarely interfered because the bosses often controlled the police departments.

One of the most powerful political bosses was William Marcy Tweed. He became the head of **Tammany Hall,** New York City's most powerful Democratic political machine. The **Tweed Ring** was a group of corrupt politicians led by Boss Tweed. They took in as much as $200 million from kickbacks and bribes between 1869 and 1871.

Thomas Nast, a political cartoonist, made fun of Tweed in various newspapers. Eventually, the public grew outraged by Tweed's corrupt practices. Authorities broke up the Tweed Ring in 1871. Tweed and many of his followers were convicted of various crimes and sentenced to prison.

2. Describe two forms of corruption practiced by political bosses.

_____

_____

_____

A corrupt 19th-century political boss.
Credit: Corbis-Bettmann

Skillbuilder
Use the cartoon to answer the questions.

1. What does the political boss shown here appear to be doing?

_____

_____

2. What has he "cut through" to get to the money?

_____

_____

Politics in the Gilded Age

BEFORE YOU READ

In the last section, you read about political machines and their corruption.

In this section, you will read about how reformers tried to end corruption.

AS YOU READ

Use this diagram to take notes on the achievements of these presidents regarding patronage and tariffs.

TERMS AND NAMES

patronage The giving of government jobs to supporters

civil service The entire government administration

Rutherford B. Hayes 19th president of the United States

Stalwarts Politicians who supported the patronage system

James A. Garfield 20th president of the United States

Chester A. Arthur 21st President of the United States

Pendleton Act Act that implemented merit system in civil service hiring

Grover Cleveland 22nd and 24th president of the United States

Benjamin Harrison 23rd president of the United States

PRESIDENT	ACHIEVEMENTS
Chester Arthur	Pendleton Act—reformed civil service
Grover Cleveland	
Benjamin Harrison	
William McKinley	

Civil Service Replaces Patronage
(pages 291–292)

How was the civil service system reformed?

The late 1800s was known as the Gilded Age in America. This term refers to a time when the nation appeared wealthy and strong. But beneath this surface, the nation faced corruption and widening gap between rich and poor. During this time, reformers tried to rid some of the corruption in federal government.

For many decades, presidents had complained about the problem of **patronage.** This is the giving of government jobs to people who had helped a candidate get elected. Patronage was based on the belief that the winning administration deserved to employ whomever it wanted. As a result of patronage, many unqualified workers were hired. Others used their positions for personal gain.

Reformers wanted to end the patronage system. They called for a merit system. Under the merit system, jobs in **civil service**—government administration—would go to the most qualified people. It would not matter what their political views were.

President **Rutherford B. Hayes** attempted to reform civil service. This angered some members of his own party. Hayes decided not to run for reelection in 1880. As a result, the Republicans had to decide on a new presidential candidate.

The party quickly divided over the issue of patronage hiring. On one side were the **Stalwarts.** These Republicans opposed changes in the patronage system. On the other side were the reformers. They supported changing the system. The party eventually settled on an independent candidate, **James A. Garfield.**

Garfield won the presidential election. However, he turned out to have ties to the reformers. Shortly after being elected he was assassinated by a Stalwart.

Garfield's vice-president, **Chester A. Arthur,** succeeded him. Despite being known as a Stalwart, Arthur turned reformer when he became president. He pushed through a civil service reform bill known as the **Pendleton Act** of 1883. This act created a civil service commission to give government jobs based on merit, not politics. The Pendleton Act helped reform the civil service.

However, the Pendleton Act had mixed results. More qualified workers did fill government positions. But because politicians had no jobs to offer, they had trouble seeking money from supporters. As a result, some politicians turned to wealthy leaders for financial support. This only strengthened the ties between government and business.

1. Describe two effects of the Pendleton Act.

_____

Efforts to Regulate Tariffs Fail
(page 293)

What happened to tariffs?

Political reformers in the late 1800s also addressed the issue of tariffs. A tariff is a tax placed on goods coming into or going out of a country. Most Americans believed that tariffs were necessary to protect U.S. industries from foreign competition. But tariffs did cause prices to rise. The question was how high tariffs should be.

In 1884, Democrat **Grover Cleveland** won the presidential election. He tried to lower tariffs. But Congress refused to support him. In 1888, Cleveland ran for reelection on a low-tariff platform. His opponent was **Benjamin Harrison.** Harrison's campaign was funded by large businesses. These businesses wanted tariffs even higher than they were.

Harrison won the election. As president, Harrison passed the McKinley Tariff Act of 1890. This act raised tariffs to their highest level ever.

In 1892, Grover Cleveland was elected president again. He supported legislation to lower the McKinley Tariff Act. However, he refused to sign the bill because it called for an income tax. The bill became law in 1894 without the president's signature. As a result, tariffs decreased. In 1896, William McKinley was elected president. He raised tariffs once again.

2. Which two presidents raised tariffs?

_____

Skillbuilder
Use the picture to answer the questions.

1. What two classes are represented here?

_____

_____

2. How does this image represent the Gilded Age?

_____

_____

A luxurious apartment house towers over a nearby shantytown in New York City in 1889. Credit: The Granger Collection, New York

Glossary   CHAPTER 7 Immigration and Urbanization

annexed To incorporate territory into an existing country

contagious Spreading or tending to spread from one person to another

eligible Qualified to do something

emigration The act of leaving a country to settle in another

immigrate To enter and settle in a new country

persecution The act of oppressing or treating badly

prejudice A judgment formed without knowledge of the facts

salvation Deliverance from evil, the act of being saved

scarce Not often seen or found

turmoil Extreme unrest and commotion

unsanitary Dirty, unhealthy

AFTER YOU READ

Terms and Names

A. Write the letter of the name or term that best answers the question.

a. Social Gospel movement
b. Jane Addams
c. William Marcy Tweed
d. culture shock
e. political machine
f. patronage

_____ **1.** Which term refers to the confusion and worry that newly arrived immigrants experienced?

_____ **2.** Which term refers to a reform program that urged Christians to help improve the lives of the poor?

_____ **3.** Who was the founder of Chicago's Hull House?

_____ **4.** Who was one of the most powerful political bosses and the head of a New York City political machine?

_____ **5.** Which term refers to the giving of government jobs to people who had helped a candidate get elected?

B. Write the name or term that best completes each sentence.

Thomas Nast
Ellis Island
row house
Angel Island
kickback
Stalwart

1. Immigrants arriving on the East Coast in the late 1800s gained entry into the United States through _____.

2. A _____ was a new type of housing that saved space by sharing side walls with other buildings.

3. A _____ is a type of illegal payment.

4. The cartoons of _____ helped to bring down the Tweed Ring.

5. A _____ was a person who was against change in the patronage system.

Name _____   Date _____

Main Ideas

1. What difficulties did immigrants face in the United States?

_____

_____

2. What problems did rapid growth pose for cities?

_____

_____

3. Why were immigrants such strong supporters of political machines?

_____

_____

4. What problems did the patronage system create?

_____

_____

5. Why did big business support high tariffs?

_____

_____

Thinking Critically

Answer the following questions on a separate sheet of paper.

1. Do you think America should be a melting pot? Why or why not?

2. Consider modern cities. What problems that existed at the turn of the 20th century have been fixed? Which do you think still exist?

CHAPTER 8 Section 1 (pages 298–302)

Science and Urban Life

BEFORE YOU READ

In the last section, you read about politics during the Guilded Age.

In this section, you will read about how technology improved life in the cities and dramatically changed the world of communications.

AS YOU READ

Use this diagram to take notes on the new technology that helped transform communications

TERMS AND NAMES

Louis Sullivan Early leader of architecture

Frederick Law Olmsted Developer of Central Park

Central Park Large park located in middle of New York City

Daniel Burnham Chicago architect

Orville and Wilbur Wright Brothers who flew the first airplane

web-perfecting press Machine that printed on both sides of a paper roll

Linotype machine Machine that made typesetting easier

George Eastman Inventor of the camera

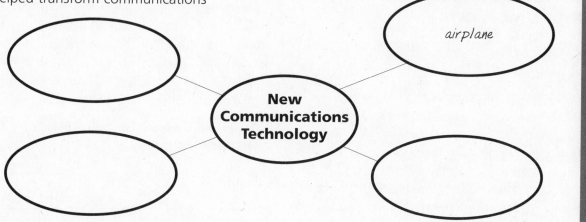

airplane

New Communications Technology

Technology and City Life
(pages 298–301)

How did cities cope with their growing populations?

By 1900, millions of Americans had settled in the nation's cities. To *accommodate* their growing populations, cities had to rely on technology. One example of this was the development of the skyscraper. Skyscrapers are tall buildings that allow people to live many floors above ground. As a result, skyscrapers save space.

Two factors allowed architects to design taller buildings: the invention of elevators, and the development of steel. One of the early skyscraper architects was **Louis Sullivan.** In 1890, he designed the ten-story Wainwright building in St. Louis.

Skyscrapers allowed cities to grow upward. Changes in transportation helped cities spread outward. In 1888, Richmond, Virginia, became the first American city to use electric-powered streetcars. Soon other cities installed electric streetcars. By the turn of the century, electric streetcars carried people from their homes in outlying neighborhoods to downtown stores, offices, and factories. People could now live in one part of a city and work in another.

To avoid overcrowding on streets, a few large cities moved their streetcars above street level. This created elevated or "el" trains. Other cities built subways by moving rail lines underground. Steel bridges joined sections of cities across rivers.

City planners also tried to make cities more livable by creating parks and *recreational* areas. Journalist and farmer **Frederick Law Olmsted** led the movement for planned city parks. In 1858, he and an architect drew up plans for **Central Park** in New York. The finished park included boating and tennis facilities, a zoo, and bicycle paths. All of these were placed in a natural setting.

In Chicago, architect **Daniel Burnham** designed a plan that would change a swampy region near Lake Michigan into a recreational area. His plan resulted in *elegant* parks and sandy beaches along Chicago's Lake Michigan shores.

1. Name two technological advances that helped make cities more livable.

_____

_____

New Technologies Transform Communications (pages 301–302)

How did technology transform communications?

Technology also improved the field of communications. One such example was the development of the airplane. Two brothers, **Orville and Wilbur Wright,** built the first airplane. Their first successful flight occurred in 1903 at Kitty Hawk, North Carolina. It covered 120 feet and lasted 12 seconds.

People paid little attention to the Wright brothers' achievement. By 1908, however, the govern-

ment took an interest in the new technology. By 1920, the United States had established the first transcontinental airmail service.

As the number of people who could read increased, publishers sought to print more books, magazines, and newspapers. Technological advances in printing helped make this possible. Chemists eventually discovered that wood *pulp* could be used to make paper. As a result, American paper mills began to make huge amounts of cheap paper.

Improved printing presses also played a role. The **web-perfecting press,** for example, printed on both sides of a paper role, instead of just one. This allowed for newspapers and magazines to be printed more quickly and easily.

Typing also became easier with the invention of the **Linotype machine.** The process of chemical *engraving* allowed printers to reproduce paintings and photographs cheaply and accurately. As a result, illustrations filled newspapers and magazines.

In 1888 **George Eastman** invented his Kodak camera. This provided millions of Americans with an easy way to take pictures. The camera also changed news reporting. Reporters could now photograph events as they occurred.

2. Name two inventions that helped change the world of communications.

_____

_____

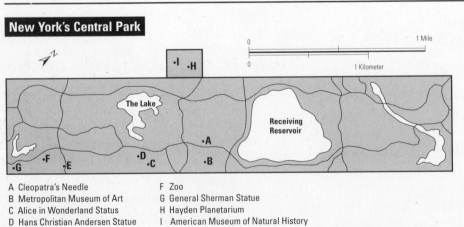

New York's Central Park

0 ——————————————— 1 Mile

0 ——————————————— 1 Kilometer

The Lake

•I •H

•A

•D
•F •C
•G •E •B

Receiving Reservoir

A Cleopatra's Needle
B Metropolitan Museum of Art
C Alice in Wonderland Status
D Hans Christian Andersen Statue
E Children's Zoo
F Zoo
G General Sherman Statue
H Hayden Planetarium
I American Museum of Natural History

Skillbuilder

Use the image to answer the questions.

1. Roughly how long is Central Park? How wide? (Do not include the small section with locations H and I.)

_____

2. Categorize the types of attractions found in the park.

_____

Education and Culture

TERMS AND NAMES

W. E. B. Du Bois First African American Ph.D.

Booker T. Washington Prominent African-American scholar

Thomas Eakins Popular American artist

Mark Twain Popular American novelist

BEFORE YOU READ

In the last section, you read about how technology transformed cities and the world of communications.

In this section, you will read about the growth of public education in America.

AS YOU READ

Use this diagram to take notes on the changes made to America's educational institutions during the late 19th and early 20th centuries.

INSTITUTION	CHANGES
elementary school	mandatory school attendance
high school	
college	

Expanding Public Education; Education for Immigrants
(pages 303–305)

How did education change in the late 1800s?

During the late 1800s, reformers tried to improve public education. At that time, most children in the United States received little education. Many children did not even attend school. Those who did left after only four years.

Eventually, the situation began to improve. Between 1865 and 1895, 31 states passed laws requiring children from 8 to 14 to attend school for at least three months out of every year. By 1900, almost three-quarters of American children between those ages attended school. Schools taught reading, writing, and arithmetic.

By the turn of the century, the number of schools had increased greatly. The number of kindergartens grew from 200 in 1880 to 3,000 in 1900. The number of high schools increased even more. In 1878 there were 800 high schools in the United States. By 1898 that number had grown to 5,500.

The high-school *curriculum* also expanded. It included courses in science, civics, home economics, history, and literature. Many people realized that the new industrial age needed people who had technical and managerial skills. As a result, high schools also included courses such as drafting and bookkeeping. This prepared students for industrial and office jobs.

The growth of public education mainly affected the nation's white communities. During the late

1880s only 34 percent of African-American children attended elementary school. Fewer than one percent attended high school.

Unlike African Americans, immigrants attended schools in large numbers. Some immigrant parents hoped that school would "Americanize" their children.

Many adult immigrants also went to school. They attended night classes to learn American culture and English. Some employers offered daytime programs to Americanize their workers.

1. Provide two examples of how public education changed in the late 1800s.

_____

_____

Expanding Higher Education
(pages 305–307)

What changes did colleges make?

At the turn of the century, only about 2 percent of Americans attended college. Most college students came from middle-class or wealthy families. Colleges prepared well-to-do young men for successful careers in business.

Between 1880 and 1900, more than 150 new colleges were founded in the United States. From 1880 to 1920, the number of students enrolled in college *quadrupled.*

During this time, colleges added more subjects. Before, many universities had taught only classical subjects such as Greek and Latin. Now they began teaching more modern subjects. These included engineering, science, and economics. Universities also began teaching specialized subjects. They included medicine, architecture, and law.

A few colleges offered higher education for African Americans. In 1895, **W. E. B. Du Bois** became the first African American to receive a Ph.D. **Booker T. Washington** was another African-American college graduate. He believed that racism would end once African Americans were educated and could contribute to the American economy.

Washington established the Tuskegee Normal and Industrial Institute in Alabama. The goal of the school was to enable African Americans to teach and to do agricultural, domestic, or mechanical work.

2. Name two ways in which colleges changed during the late 1800s.

_____

_____

Education Influences Culture
(pages 307–308)

What painting and writing styles appealed to Americans?

As more Americans became educated in the late 1800s, their taste for culture grew. Art galleries and museums spread. Many Americans became interested in the works of American artists such as **Thomas Eakins.** The works of Eakins and other artists of the time showed realistic scenes of life.

Americans enjoyed viewing realistic scenes of city life and working-class people. Art galleries also showed the work of European artists. Eventually, abstract art also became popular. This new form of art showed unrealistic scenes.

Many cities also began to build public libraries. By 1900, there were thousands of free public libraries in the United States. During this time many people enjoyed reading novels that presented a realistic picture of American life. The works of writer **Mark Twain** realistically presented life along the Mississippi River. Other popular authors were Theodore Dreiser, Stephen Crane, and Jack London.

Other Americans preferred to read light fiction. These usually were adventure tales. Often, these books were sold for only ten cents. Thus, they became known as "dime novels."

3. Name a style of painting and writing that appealed to Americans.

_____

_____

Segregation and Discrimination

BEFORE YOU READ

In the last section, you read about improvements made to public education around the turn of the century.

In this section, you will read about how life for African Americans and other nonwhites remained one of hardship and discrimination.

AS YOU READ

Use this diagram to take notes on the discrimination against African Americans at the turn of the century.

TERMS AND NAMES

literacy test Test given to voters to determine whether they could read

poll tax Money one had to pay in order to vote

grandfather clause Clause that allowed poor, uneducated whites to vote

Jim Crow laws Laws that helped keep whites and blacks separate

segregation The word used to describe racial separation

Plessy* v. *Ferguson Court case that upheld the Jim Crow laws

Ida B. Wells African-American reformer who tried to end lynching

debt peonage A system in which a person is forced to work to pay off debts

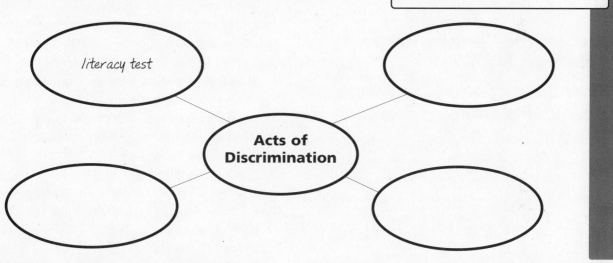

African Americans Fight Legal Discrimination (pages 309–311)

How were African Americans kept from voting?

For about 10 years after Reconstruction, African Americans in the South voted and held political office. By 1900, however, all Southern states had set up new voting restrictions. These restrictions were meant to keep blacks from voting.

For example, some states required voters to be able to read. To determine this, officials gave each voter a **literacy test.** They often gave African Americans more difficult tests. The officials giving

the test could pass or fail people as they wished.

Another voting requirement was the **poll tax.** This was a tax that one had to be pay to enter a voting booth. African Americans and poor whites often did not have the money to pay the tax. So they were unable to vote.

Several Southern states wanted to make sure that whites who could not read or pay a poll tax still could vote. So they added a **grandfather clause** to their constitutions. This clause stated that any person could vote if their father or grandfather was qualified to vote before January 1, 1867. This date was important because before that time freed slaves did not have the right to vote. Therefore, the grandfather clause did not allow African Americans to vote. Some Americans challenged the literacy test and poll tax laws. But the Supreme Court allowed the laws to stand.

The Southern states also passed **Jim Crow laws.** These laws separated whites and blacks in private and public places. Separating people on the basis of race became known as **segregation.** Racial segregation developed in such places as schools, hospitals, and transportation systems throughout the South.

Eventually a legal challenge to segregation reached the U.S. Supreme Court. However, in the case **Plessy v. Ferguson** the Supreme Court ruled that separating the races in public places was legal.

1. Name two ways that Southern states restricted the voting rights of African Americans.

Turn-of-the-Century Race Relations (pages 311–312)

How did social customs restrict African Americans?

In addition to laws, customs also restricted the rights of African Americans. African Americans had to show respect to whites, including children. These customs often *belittled* and humiliated African Americans. For example, blacks had to yield the sidewalk to whites. Black men always had to remove their hats for whites.

African Americans who did not follow these customs could face severe punishment. Often, African Americans accused of failing to perform the customs were lynched—hanged without trial. African American reformer **Ida B. Wells** worked to end lynching.

African Americans in the North also faced *discrimination.* They lived in segregated neighborhoods. They also faced discrimination in the workplace.

African American reformers debated over how to address racial discrimination. Booker T. Washington argued that blacks should not insist on full legal equality—which whites would never allow. Instead, he argued, blacks should concentrate on gaining economic power. Other African Americans, like W. E. B. Du Bois, demanded legal equality right away.

2. Name two ways blacks had to show respect to whites.

Discrimination in the West
(pages 312–313)

What other groups faced discrimination in America?

African Americans were not the only ones who faced discrimination at the turn of the century. Mexican Americans faced similar treatment. In the 1880s and 1890s, railroad companies hired many Mexicans to build new rail lines in the Southwest. Railroad managers hired Mexicans because they were used to the Southwest's hot, dry climate. Managers also felt they could pay Mexicans less than members of other ethnic groups.

Mexicans also played an important role in the Southwest's mining and farming industries. Raising crops such as grapes, lettuce, and citrus fruits required large amounts of labor. Mexicans provided much of this farm work.

Landowners often forced Mexicans to work to repay debts. This system was called **debt peonage.** The Supreme Court ruled against this system in 1911. The Court called it a *violation* of the Thirteenth Amendment.

The Chinese also faced discrimination in America. Many Chinese immigrants worked for the railroads in the West. They also worked in shoe factories and woolen mills.

Many white workers feared losing their jobs to Chinese workers. As a result, strong opposition to Chinese immigration developed. Congress responded in 1882 by passing the Chinese Exclusion Act. It banned Chinese immigration to America.

3. Name two groups that faced discrimination in the West.

CHAPTER 8 Section 4 (pages 314–321)

Dawn of Mass Culture

TERMS AND NAMES

vaudeville Performances that included song, dance, and comedy

ragtime music that combined African American and European sounds

Joseph Pulitzer Publisher of the *World* newspaper

William Randolph Hearst Publisher of the *New York Morning Journal*

department store Large store that sold a variety of goods

mail-order catalog Book from which consumers could buy goods

rural free delivery System that brought packages directly to homes

BEFORE YOU READ

In the last section, you read about how African Americans and other nonwhites continued to suffer racial discrimination at the turn of the century.

In this section, you will read about how Americans developed new forms of entertainment and ways to spend their money.

AS YOU READ

Use this diagram to take notes on how these people helped transform American culture.

PEOPLE	ACHIEVEMENTS
Pulitzer/Hearst	Created sensational newspapers
D.W. Griffith	
F.W. Woolworth	

American Leisure (pages 314–317)

How did Americans spend their free time?

The use of machines allowed workers at the turn of the century to do their jobs faster. This led to a shorter workweek. As a result, Americans had more leisure time.

Americans found new ways to use that time. Many city dwellers enjoyed trips to amusement parks. There, rides such as the roller coaster and the Ferris wheel thrilled people.

Another recreational activity that became popular at the turn of the century was bicycling. This activity entertained both men and women. Many Americans also grew fond of playing tennis. The first tennis match was held in 1874.

Those Americans who did not wish to exercise watched professional sports. Boxing became popular in the late 1800s. Baseball also became a well-loved spectator sport. The National League was formed in 1876 and the American League in 1901. African-American baseball players were not allowed to play in either league. As a result, they formed their own clubs—the Negro National League and the Negro American League.

Several kinds of snack foods also became popular. Americans turned to brand-name snacks such as a Hershey chocolate bar and drinks such as a Coca-Cola or a Pepsi-Cola.

1. Name two activities that were popular in the United States at the turn of the century.

_____

_____

Going to the Show (pages 317–318)

What were some popular forms of entertainment in America?

Americans also favored a variety of artistic entertainment. Many people enjoyed the theater. Many people also enjoyed **vaudeville.** These performances included song, dance, and comedy acts. Another popular attraction was the circus.

The most popular form of music at the time was **ragtime.** This music blended African-American and European sounds.

A new art form emerged on the American scene around the turn of the century: the motion picture. The first movies were rather simple and ran for only about 10 minutes. Then, in 1914, D. W. Griffith's film *Birth of a Nation* paved the way for more *sophisticated* movie making.

The film dealt with the Reconstruction. It was about three hours long. In addition, it used bold new techniques, such as close-ups and fade-outs, and blockbuster scenes. However, many people criticized the movie's content. They claimed the film portrayed African Americans in a racist way.

2. Name two forms of entertainment that appealed to Americans.

_____

_____

Mass Circulation Newspapers
(page 319)

How did newspapers attract more readers?

Newspapers also entertained Americans. Many publishers changed their newspapers in order to attract more readers. They filled their pages with *sensational* headlines. They also devised promotional stunts. In 1889, for example, the *New York World* sent a reporter around the world to copy the fictional character in Jules Verne's novel *Around the World in Eighty Days.*

Some publishers used other techniques. **Joseph Pulitzer,** the owner of the *World,* introduced a large Sunday edition. It included comics, sports coverage, and women's news. Pulitzer presented news in a sensational way to beat his main competitor, **William Randolph Hearst.** Hearst owned the *New York Morning Journal.* Hearst tried to outdo Pulitzer by publishing *exaggerated* and even made-up stories. By 1898, both publishers were selling more than one million copies each day.

3. Name two ways in which publishers tried to sell more newspapers.

_____

_____

New Ways to Sell Goods (pages 319–321)

How did Americans shop?

Americans at the turn of the century also began to change the way they shopped. As cities grew, shopping centers emerged. These structures made many kinds of stores available in one area.

Another new development was the **department store.** This type of store offered consumers a wide range of goods to buy. Chain stores—groups of stores owned by the same person—also started in the late 1800s. F. W. Woolworth's "five-and-dime store" and chain grocery stores became popular. These types of stores offered consumers brand names and low-cost sales.

As shopping became more popular, so too did advertising. Companies filled magazines and newspapers with ads for their products. Advertisers also placed their products on barns, houses, and billboards.

In the late 1800s Montgomery Ward and Sears Roebuck introduced **mail-order catalogs.** These books brought department store items to those who lived outside of the cities. Each company's catalog contained a description of its goods. The company mailed its catalog to farmers and small town residents. These people then could order goods from the catalog. By 1910, about 10 million Americans shopped by mail.

The United States Post Office increased mail-order business by starting a **rural free delivery** system. This brought packages directly to every home.

4. Name two developments in the ways goods were sold.

_____

_____

Glossary — CHAPTER 8 Life at the Turn of the Century

accommodate To provide for

belittle To make someone feel small and unimportant

curriculum All of the courses of studies offered by a school

discrimination To judge someone differently based on certain factors, including race

elegant Refined and graceful, tasteful

engrave To print from a block or plate

exaggerated That which goes beyond the truth or reality

pulp A soft, moist shapeless mass

quadrupled Increased by four times

recreational Having to do with activities away from work, play

sensational Intended to stir curiosity or interest

sophisticated Complex or complicated, refined

violation The act of breaking a law or regulation

AFTER YOU READ

Terms and Names

A. Write the letter of the term that best answers the question.

a. Booker T. Washington
b. George Eastman
c. vaudeville
d. segregation
e. Linotype machine
f. W. E. B. Du Bois

_____ **1.** Who invented the Kodak camera?

_____ **2.** Which term refers to the machine that made the process of setting type more efficiently?

_____ **3.** Who is the African American who founded Tuskegee Normal and Industrial Institute in an effort to enable African Americans to teach and to do agricultural or mechanical work?

_____ **4.** Which term refers to the system of separating people on the basis of race?

_____ **5.** Which term refers to a popular type of live performance that included song, dance, and comedy?

B. If the statement is true, write "true" on the line. If it is false, make it true by changing the underlined word or words and placing the new word on the line.

_____ **1.** Elevator and steel supports helped to make skyscrapers possible.

_____ **2.** Booker T. Washington became the first African American to earn a Ph.D.

_____ **3.** Jim Crow laws were added to the constitutions of several Southern states to allow white people who could not pass a literacy test or pay a poll tax to vote anyway.

_____ **4.** In *Plessy* v. *Ferguson,* the Supreme Court ruled in favor of the separation of the races in public facilities.

_____ **5.** Montgomery Ward and Sears Roebuck created what became known as "five-and-dime stores."

AFTER YOU READ (cont.)　　CHAPTER 8　Life at the Turn of the Century

Main Ideas

1. How did the methods of communications improve around the turn of the 20th century?

_____

_____

2. How did college and high school change around the turn of the century?

_____

_____

_____

3. How were the works of Thomas Eakins and Mark Twain similar?

_____

_____

_____

4. How did Southern states restrict African Americans politically? Socially?

_____

_____

_____

5. What leisure activities flourished in the late 19th and early 20th centuries?

_____

_____

_____

Thinking Critically

Answer the following questions on a separate sheet of paper.

1. Why might someone argue that the federal government played a key role in making African Americans second-class citizens?

2. Consider how you spend your leisure time. Explain how it is similar as well as different from how people spent it at the turn of the century.

CHAPTER 9   Section 1 (pages 330–336)

The Origins of Progressivism

BEFORE YOU READ

In the last section, you read about popular culture at the turn of the century.

In this section, you will learn about the social reforms that made up the progressive movement.

AS YOU READ

Use this web diagram to take notes. Fill it in with names of the organizations and people who campaigned for the four types of reform. The notes will help you remember what you learned about the progressive movement.

TERMS AND NAMES

progressive movement Social reform movement in the early 20th century

Florence Kelley Social reformer

prohibition Making the sale or use of alcohol illegal

muckraker Writer who exposes wrongdoing

scientific management Using scientific ideas to make work more efficient

Robert M. LaFollette Progressive Wisconsin governor and senator

initiative A way for people to propose laws directly

referendum A way for people to approve changes in laws by a vote

recall A vote on whether to remove a public official from office

Seventeenth Amendment Amendment providing for senators to be elected directly

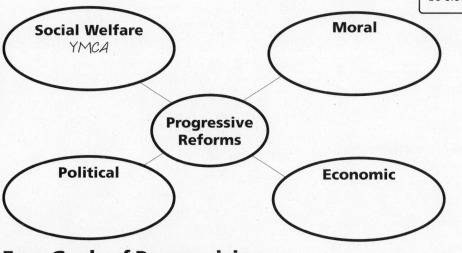

Four Goals of Progressivism

(pages 330–333)

What did reformers want?

As the 1900s opened, reformers pushed for a number of changes. Together their efforts built the **progressive movement.** The progressive movement had four major goals: (1) to protect social welfare, (2) to promote moral improvement, (3) to create economic reform, and (4) to promote efficiency.

Reformers tried to promote social welfare by easing the problems of city life. The YMCA built libraries and exercise rooms. The Salvation Army fed poor people in the cities and cared for children in nurseries. *Settlement houses* helped families. One reformer, **Florence Kelley,** helped to win the passage of the Illinois Factory Act in 1893. The law prohibited child labor and limited women's working hours. The law became a model for other states.

Reformers promoted moral reform by working for **prohibition**—the banning of alcoholic drinks. Many of these reformers, called prohibitionists, were members of the Woman's Christian Temperance Union (WCTU). The well-organized union became the largest women's group the country had ever seen.

Reformers tried to make economic changes by pointing out the great *inequality* between the rich and the poor. They pushed for better treatment of workers. *Journalists* called **muckrakers** wrote stories about corruption and unfair practices in business.

To help make businesses more *efficient* and *profitable,* some reformers promoted the idea of **scientific management.** The idea was to apply scientific ideas to make each task simpler. One outcome was the *assembly line.*

1. **How did reformers try to make businesses more efficient and profitable?**

Cleaning Up Government
(pages 333–334)

How did progressives change city governments?

Progressives also reformed politics. City governments were sometimes corrupt. For instance, they might be run by *party bosses* who gave jobs to their friends and bribed people to vote for them. One answer to this problem was a new system of city government called the commission system.

In the commission system a group of experts runs the city. Each expert takes charge of a different city department. By 1917, about 500 cities had commission forms of city government.

Another reform idea was the council-manager form of government. By 1925, nearly 250 cities had managers. These managers were appointed by councils elected by the people.

Some cities had progressive mayors. They improved cities without changing their system of government. They put in such reforms as fairer tax systems and lower public transportation fares.

2. **How did the commission system help clean up city government?**

Reform at the State Level
(pages 334–336)

How did state laws change?

Reformers also worked at the state level. Many states had progressive governors. These states passed laws to *regulate* railroads, mines, telephone companies, and other large businesses.

Robert M. La Follette, as governor of Wisconsin, led the way in regulating big business. His reforms of the railway industry (1) changed the way the railroad companies were taxed, (2) set limits on the rates they could charge, and (3) cut out many unfair practices.

Progressives also worked to improve conditions in the workplace and to end the employment of children. Factories hired children because children could do the same unskilled work as adults for less money. Often wages were so low that every member of the family needed to work.

Progressive reformers did not get a federal law to ban child labor. They did, however, get state legislatures to ban child labor. States also set maximum hours for all workers.

Progressives also won some reforms from the Supreme Court. In the case of *Muller* v. *Oregon,* the Court decided that a state could legally limit the working hours of women. In 1917, the Supreme Court upheld a ten-hour workday for men.

Democratic reforms at the state level gave voters more power. Oregon was the first to adopt the secret ballot, giving voters privacy. Three other reforms were important: (1) **initiative** gives voters themselves the right to propose a law, (2) voters could accept or reject the initiative by a direct vote on the initiative, called a **referendum,** and (3), voters got the right of **recall,** which meant they could force a government official to face another election.

Wisconsin became the first state to use the direct primary. This meant that voters, instead of political machines, would choose candidates for public office through a special popular election. The direct primary led to the passage of the **Seventeenth Amendment** to the Constitution. This amendment called for senators to be elected directly by the people instead of by state lawmakers.

3. **What are three ways progressive reforms helped ordinary people?**

Women in Public Life

BEFORE YOU READ

In the last section, you read about the progressive movement.

In this section, you will learn about the new, active roles women were taking in the workplace and in politics.

AS YOU READ

Use this diagram to take notes. Fill it in with details about women and their work in the four settings shown. The notes will help you remember what you learned about women's work in the late 1800s.

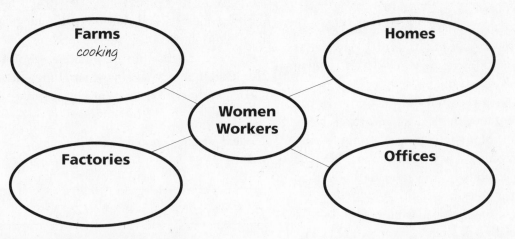

TERMS AND NAMES
Maria Mitchell Well-known teacher of science at Vassar College, one of the new colleges for women
NACW National Association of Colored Women; founded in 1896 to improve living and working conditions for African-American women
suffrage The right to vote; a major goal of women reformers
NAWSA National American Woman Suffrage Association; founded in 1890 to help women win the right to vote
Susan B. Anthony Leader of the woman suffrage movement, who helped to define the movement's goals and beliefs and to lead its actions

Women in the Work Force
(pages 337–338)

What jobs did women do?

Before the Civil War, most married women worked at home. They cared for their families and did not have paid jobs. By the end of the 19th century, however, many women had to work outside the home in order to earn money.

Farm women continued to work as they always had. They did the cooking, cleaning, sewing, and child rearing. They helped with the crops and animals.

Many women became domestic workers—cooking, cleaning, and washing for other people.

Unmarried immigrant women did domestic work. Many middle-class homes in the Northeast, for instance, hired young Irish women as domestic workers. Married immigrant women added to the family income by taking in *piecework* or by caring for *boarders* at home.

By 1890, about 1 million African-American women held jobs. Of those, about 46 percent were domestic workers.

One quarter of the women who worked outside the home worked in factories. Women usually held the least skilled positions. They also received the lowest pay. Even when women did the same work as men, they received only about half as much money.

Business was growing. More and more women worked in offices as typists, *stenographers,* and bookkeepers. Many women became teachers. More women attended high school to train for these jobs. In addition, new business schools prepared women for office jobs.

1. What are three jobs that women often held?

_____

_____

Women's Leadership in Reform
(pages 338–340)

What reforms did women want?

Middle- and upper-class women sometimes joined women's clubs. By 1910, nearly 800,000 women belonged to clubs. Some of these groups turned to reform.

Graduates of the new women's colleges often became active in public life. Vassar College accepted its first students in 1865. **Maria Mitchell** was an *astronomer* who became one of the college's greatest teachers. Now marriage no longer seemed to be a woman's only choice.

Because women were not allowed to vote or run for public office, they worked for reforms outside the government. Many fought against unsafe conditions in factories. They worked for housing reform, improvements in education, and new food and drug laws.

In 1896, African-American women founded the National Association of Colored Women (**NACW**). This organization helped by creating nurseries, reading rooms, and kindergartens.

Women also wanted to improve their political strength by winning the right to vote, or **suffrage.** By 1890 these women, called suffragists, had united in the National American Woman Suffrage Association (**NAWSA**).

The leaders of the suffrage movement tried to win the vote three ways: (1) first, they tried to convince state legislatures to give women the right to vote; (2) second, they tested the Fourteenth Amendment to see whether it already granted them the vote, and (3) third, they pushed for a national constitutional amendment.

The suffragists were successful in winning the right to vote in several states. Further efforts failed, however.

The Fourteenth Amendment said that states could not deny the vote to men who were citizens. States who did so would lose their seats in Congress. **Susan B. Anthony** and other leaders in the suffrage movement argued that women should be allowed vote because they are citizens too. The Supreme Court ruled that that did not guarantee them the right to vote.

Women pushed for an amendment to the Constitution that would give them the right to vote. The amendment was repeatedly rejected by the Senate.

2. What are three ways in which women tried to win the vote?

_____

_____

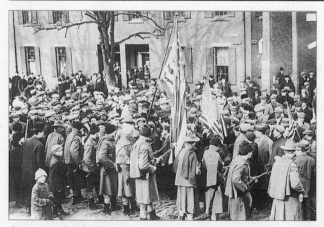

Angry crowds confront the militia at the Lawrence mill workers' strike in 1912. Credit: Corbis-Bettmann

Skillbuilder
Use the photograph to answer these questions.

1. Name the two sides confronting each other.

_____

_____

2. Cite one example of what you think workers might strike over.

_____

_____

Teddy Roosevelt's Square Deal

BEFORE YOU READ

In the last section, you read about women who worked for reforms in their communities and for the right to vote.

In this section, you will learn about President Theodore Roosevelt's success in promoting reforms at the national level.

AS YOU READ

Use this diagram to take notes. Read the list of problem areas on the left and fill in the columns to give examples of how these problems were solved.

TERMS AND NAMES

Upton Sinclair Novelist who exposed social problems

The Jungle Novel by Upton Sinclair describing meatpacking

Theodore Roosevelt President from 1901 to 1909

Square Deal President Roosevelt's program of progressive reforms

Meat Inspection Act Law reforming meatpacking conditions, 1906

Pure Food and Drug Act Law to stop the sale of unclean food and drugs, 1906

conservation The planned management of natural resources

NAACP National Association for the Advancement of Colored People, founded in 1909 to work for racial equality

PROBLEM AREAS	EXAMPLES	SOLUTIONS
Strikes	1902, Pennsylvania coal miners	
Trusts		
Meat processing		
The environment		

A Rough-Riding President

(pages 341–342)

What was Roosevelt like?

Theodore Roosevelt became president in 1901. He was bold, ambitious, and full of energy. He had been active in sports and politics. In the Spanish–American–Cuban War he led a fighting unit called the Rough Riders. His personality made him a popular president.

Roosevelt used his popularity to get his programs passed. He wanted to see that the common people received what he called a **Square Deal.** This term referred to a program of progressive reforms sponsored by his administration.

1. How did Roosevelt's personality shape his presidency?

_____

_____

Using Federal Power (pages 342–344)

How did Roosevelt handle big business?

President Roosevelt used the power of the government to help solve the nation's problems.

In 1902, about 140,000 coal miners in Pennsylvania went on strike. The mine owners refused to *negotiate* with them. President Roosevelt called both sides to the White House to talk. He threatened to have the government take over the mines. The two sides agreed to have an *arbitration* commission help settle their differences. The commission succeeded in reaching a compromise. From then on, the federal government would often step in to help settle a strike.

Roosevelt also used the power of his government to deal with the problem of trusts. Trusts were large companies that had control over their markets. Trusts, or monopolies, first drove smaller companies out by lowering their own prices. Then when the smaller companies were gone, the trusts could raise their prices. They no longer had any competition.

By 1900, trusts controlled about 80 percent of U.S. industries. Roosevelt supported big business, but he also wanted to stop trusts that harmed people. He had the government sue harmful trusts under the Sherman Antitrust Act of 1890. In all, Roosevelt filed 44 *antitrust* suits. He was called a trustbuster.

In 1887, the Interstate Commerce Commission (ICC) had been set up to regulate the railroad industry. It had not been effective. Roosevelt pushed through laws that made it stronger. The results were fairer shipping rates and less corruption.

2. How did Roosevelt use the power of the federal government to change business practices?

Protecting Citizens and the Environment (pages 344–346)

What did Roosevelt do for public health and the environment?

In 1906, **Upton Sinclair** published a novel called *The Jungle,* describing filthy conditions in the meatpacking industry. Roosevelt pushed for passage of the **Meat Inspection Act.** This law, passed in 1906, called for strict cleanliness requirements for meatpackers. It created a program of federal meat inspection.

Also in 1906, Congress passed the **Pure Food and Drug Act.** This law (1) regulated what manufacturers could put into foods and drugs and (2) said that these products must be labeled honestly. For instance, it stopped manufacturers from adding dangerous chemicals to foods to preserve them. It also stopped them from making false claims about medicines.

Before Roosevelt became president, the federal government had paid little attention to the nation's natural resources. Roosevelt supported the **conservation** of land. He believed that wilderness areas should be preserved and used wisely for the common good. He set aside land to use for its water and mineral resources. He established wildlife sanctuaries—places where animals would be safe from humans—and national parks.

3. What are two ways that Roosevelt helped to make people's lives safer and healthier?

Roosevelt and Civil Rights
(pages 346–347)

What did Roosevelt do for African Americans?

Roosevelt supported individual African Americans like Booker T. Washington. But he did not help African Americans in general. In 1909, black leaders, including W. E. B. Du Bois, founded the National Association for the Advancement of Colored People **(NAACP).** The organization pushed for civil rights and racial equality. The progressive movement, however, continued to focus on the needs of middle-class whites.

4. What action did the NAACP take?

CHAPTER 9 Section 4 (pages 350–353)

Progressivism Under Taft

BEFORE YOU READ

In the last section, you read about the reforms of Teddy Roosevelt's presidency.

In this section, you will learn about the reforms and political problems of the next president, William Howard Taft.

AS YOU READ

Use this diagram to take notes. Fill in the boxes with causes of Taft's problems in office. The notes will help you remember what you learned about Taft's presidency.

TERMS AND NAMES

William Howard Taft President from 1909 to 1913, successor to Roosevelt

Payne-Aldrich Tariff Bill meant to lower tariffs on imported goods

Gifford Pinchot Head of the U.S. Forest Service under Roosevelt, who believed that it was possible to make use of natural resources while conserving them

Bull Moose Party Nickname for the new Progressive Party, which was formed to support Roosevelt in the election of 1912

Woodrow Wilson Winner of the 1912 presidential election

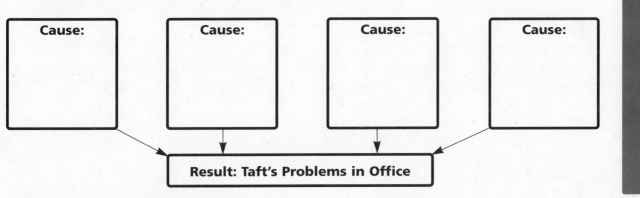

Cause: | Cause: | Cause: | Cause:

Result: Taft's Problems in Office

Taft Becomes President (pages 350–351)

Why did Taft have problems?

President Roosevelt promised not to run for another *term.* Instead, he wanted **William Howard Taft** to become president. Taft had been Roosevelt's secretary of war, and Roosevelt felt Taft would carry out his policies. Taft was elected in 1909, and he did continue many of the progressive programs. In fact, he busted more than twice as many trusts as Roosevelt had. However, Taft was not as effective as Roosevelt had been. He had many problems in office.

His first problem came over *tariffs.* Taft wanted to lower tariffs. He supported the Payne bill, which was passed in the House. However, the Senate passed a weakened version of the bill, the **Payne-Aldrich Tariff.** The revised bill did not

lower tariffs much at all. The progressives in Taft's own Republican Party were annoyed.

Another problem for Taft arose over conservation. *Conservationists* like **Gifford Pinchot,** the head of the U.S. Forest Service, believed that wilderness areas could be managed for public enjoyment as well as private development. This meant, for instance, that someone could make a profit by logging land that belonged to the federal government. This was called a multi-use land program.

Taft appointed Richard A. Ballinger as secretary of the interior. Ballinger did not want to keep so much federal land in reserve. He wanted to free up land for forestry and mining. He wanted to sell some land for private uses. When he did these things, Pinchot complained. Pinchot accused him of misusing the natural resources for *commercial* interests. As a result of Pinchot's criticism, Taft felt he had to fire him from the U.S. Forest Service.

1. In what two areas did Taft have problems?

_____

_____

The Republican Party Splits
(pages 351–352)

Why did the Republican Party split?

The Republican Party had two wings: (1) the progressives, who wanted change and (2) the conservatives, who did not want reform. Taft was not able to hold the two wings of his party together.

The two groups disagreed over Taft's support of political boss Joseph Cannon. Cannon was Speaker of the House of Representatives, and he ran the House his own way. He appointed people to committee positions who weren't the next in line. He even made himself the head of the Committee on Rules. This gave him the power to control what bills Congress would take up. As a result, under Cannon, the House often did not even vote on progressive bills.

The Republican party split over how to handle Cannon. This gave the Democrats a chance to take over the House in the 1910 _midterm_ elections. Democrats had control of the House for the first time in almost 20 years.

By 1912, Teddy Roosevelt had decided to run for a third term as president, after all. Taft had an advantage because he was already in office. The Republican Party nominated Taft, but Roosevelt's supporters broke off and formed the Progressive Party. This third party was also called the **Bull Moose Party**. It ran on a _platform_ of reform. The Democrats were in a stronger position now that the Republicans were split. They nominated the reform governor of New Jersey, Woodrow Wilson.

2. Who formed the Bull Moose Party?

_____

_____

The Election of 1912 (pages 352–353)

Who won the election of 1912?

The 1912 election offered Americans four main choices: Wilson, Taft, Roosevelt, and the socialist Eugene V. Debs.

Wilson campaigned on a progressive platform, called the New Freedom. He wanted stronger antitrust legislation, banking reform, and lower tariffs.

Both Roosevelt and Wilson wanted to give the government a stronger role in the economy. But they differed over strategies, that is, how to do that. Roosevelt supported government supervision of big business. Wilson opposed all business monopolies, or trusts. Debs went even further. He wanted the government to distribute national wealth more equally among the people.

Wilson won the 1912 election. He also brought in a Democratic majority in Congress. In all, about 75 percent of the vote went to the candidates who favored economic reform—Wilson, Roosevelt, and Debs. Because so many people supported reform, Wilson had more power to carry out his reforms once in office.

3. What did Wilson have in common with Roosevelt? With Debs?

_____

_____

CHAPTER 9   Section 5 (pages 354–359)

Wilson's New Freedom

BEFORE YOU READ

In the last section, you read about the problems Taft faced as president.

In this section, you will learn how Woodrow Wilson managed to get some parts of his progressive platform passed but had to give up others.

AS YOU READ

Use this time line to take notes. Fill in the boxes with key events during Wilson's first term.

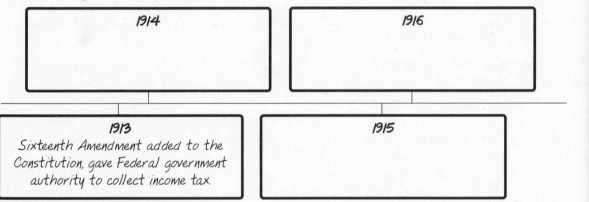

1914

1916

1913
Sixteenth Amendment added to the Constitution, gave Federal government authority to collect income tax.

1915

Progressive Reform Under Wilson (pages 354–356)

What reforms did Wilson support?

Woodrow Wilson grew up in a religious family in the South. He began his career as a lawyer and then became a college professor, university president, and finally state governor. As governor of New Jersey, he worked for many progressive causes. When he was elected president, he pushed for a reform program called the New Freedom.

Under Wilson, Congress passed two antitrust measures. The first was the **Clayton Antitrust Act** of 1914. This law had several important effects. The law (1) made it more difficult for monopolies to form, (2) said that the people who ran a company could be held personally responsible if the com-

pany violated the law, and (3) ruled that labor unions and farm organizations were not themselves to be considered trusts. This made strikes, peaceful picketing, and *boycotts* legal.

The second antitrust measure was the Federal Trade Act of 1914, which set up the **Federal Trade Commission (FTC).** This agency had the power to investigate businesses for the government. The FTC became very active during Wilson's administration. It issued nearly 400 orders telling companies to stop breaking the law.

Wilson also worked to lower tariffs. He believed that high tariffs encouraged monopolies. By raising the cost of imported goods, they cut competition against American goods. He supported the Underwood Tariff of 1913, which lowered tariffs for the first time since the Civil War.

With less money coming in from tariffs, however, the government needed another source of money. It turned to an income tax. This tax on people's earnings was created by the Sixteenth Amendment to the Constitution, which was ratified by the states in 1913. The tax gave to the federal government a small percentage of all workers' income and business profits.

After reforming tariffs, Wilson turned his attention to the banking system. It was difficult for people far from banking centers to obtain credit. The new **Federal Reserve System** solved this problem by dividing the country into 12 districts, each with a federal reserve bank. This system controlled the money supply and made credit more easily available. Setting up the federal reserve was one of Wilson's most important reforms.

1. What were three areas that Wilson reformed?

Voting Rights for Women
(pages 356–358)

How did women get the vote?

At the same time Wilson was pushing for reforms, women continued to push for voting rights. By 1912, only five states had given suffrage to women. But several things were happening that gave the suffrage movement hope.

For one thing, more young, college-educated women joined the movement. They held rallies and campaigned door-to-door. A few women were influenced by the suffrage movement in England. British suffragists used more *militant* tactics. For instance, they would heckle government officials—that is, shout annoying questions and comments at them. American women tried these tactics.

In 1900 **Carrie Chapman Catt** became president of the National American Woman Suffrage Association (NAWSA). Suffragists Lucy Burns and Alice Paul grew impatient with the methods of NAWSA and formed their own more radical organization—the National Woman's Party. They demonstrated at the 1917 convention of the Democratic Party and picketed the White House.

President Wilson, however, did not respond. He remained cool to their campaign.

Some of the picketers went to jail and even started a hunger strike. But it took World War I to bring women the vote. A great number of women became active in supporting the war effort. Women ran committees, rolled bandages, and sold liberty bonds in order to raise funds for the war. Once they were active in public life, women felt more strongly than ever that they should have the right to vote. At last, in 1919 Congress passed the **Nineteenth Amendment.** This amendment giving women the vote was ratified by the states the next year.

2. How did the British suffragists influence American suffragists?

The Limits of Progressivism
(pages 358–359)

Did Wilson support civil rights?

Like Roosevelt and Taft, Wilson backed away from civil rights. During the 1912 campaign he won the support of the NAACP by promising to treat blacks equally. He also promised to speak out against lynching, that is, mob killings of blacks. However, once he was president Wilson opposed federal laws against lynching. This was because he felt that states, rather than the federal government, had the right to make such laws.

Another blow for those who wanted *integration* of blacks and whites was Wilson's appointment of his cabinet. Wilson chose cabinet members who extended segregation, or separate facilities for blacks and whites. African Americans who had voted for Wilson felt betrayed.

3. Why did African Americans feel betrayed by President Wilson?

Glossary
CHAPTER 9   The Progressive Era

antitrust Against monopolies

arbitration Process of having a third party make a decision when two sides can't settle an argument

assembly line An efficient way of putting together a product in which each worker does a different specific task

astronomer Scientist who studies stars, planets, and outer space

boarders People who pay to live and eat at another person's house

boycott Protest in which people refuse to buy a certain product

commercial Aimed at making a profit

conservationist Person who favors using natural resources carefully

efficient Done with the least possible effort and expense

inequality Unfair difference in the way people are treated

integration Mixing racial groups

journalist News writer

midterm The election halfway between two presidential elections

militant Aggressive, hostile, and bold

negotiate To try to reach an agreement by talking

party boss Person who controls a political party

piecework Work, such as sewing, that is paid for by the piece rather than by the hour

platform Official statement of political beliefs

profitable Earning a profit, for instance, selling something for more than it costs to make

regulate To set rules for

settlement house A center where poor people can get help

stenographer Office worker who takes notes in shorthand

tariff Tax charged on goods coming into the country

term Length of time an official is elected to serve

AFTER YOU READ

Terms and Names

A. Write the letter of the best description or definition of word.

_____ **1.** Recall is
- **a.** a bill initiated by citizens
- **b.** a vote on an initiative
- **c.** a vote to remove a public official
- **d.** a law making alcohol illegal

_____ **2.** Suffrage means the
- **a.** separation of races
- **b.** denial of the right to vote
- **c.** illegal sale of alcohol
- **d.** right to vote

_____ **3.** The Clayton Antitrust Law
- **a.** stopped the sale of spoiled foods
- **b.** created federal meat inspection
- **c.** weakened monopolies
- **d.** preserved wilderness areas

_____ **4.** The Nineteenth Amendment
- **a.** established the FTC
- **b.** recognized woman's suffrage
- **c.** made monopolies illegal
- **d.** decentralized private banking

B. Write the letter of the name or term that matches the description.

a. NAACP

b. Bull Moose Party

c. Payne-Aldrich Tariff

d. prohibition

e. NACW

_____ **1.** A cause taken up by the Women's Christian Temperance Union

_____ **2.** An organization of African-American women

_____ **3.** An organization started by prominent African-American and white reformers to promote civil rights for African-Americans

_____ **4.** Weakened bill that got Taft in trouble with the progressives

_____ **5.** Supporters of Roosevelt who broke away from the Republican Party

AFTER YOU READ (continued)   **CHAPTER 9** The Progressive Era

Main Ideas

1. What were the four major goals of the progressive movement?

_____

_____

2. Name two women's organizations and describe their mission.

_____

_____

3. How did the novel *The Jungle* lead to changes in American laws governing meatpacking?

_____

_____

4. Why was Roosevelt's handling of the 1902 coal strike important?

_____

_____

5. How did the Clayton Antitrust Act benefit labor?

_____

_____

Thinking Critically

Answer the following questions on a separate sheet of paper.

1. How did Theodore Roosevelt expand the role of the Federal government?

2. How might you characterize most African Americans' view of the progressive era? Why?

CHAPTER 10 Section 1 (pages 364–367)

Imperialism and America

BEFORE YOU READ

In the last section, you read about Woodrow Wilson.

In this section, you will learn how economic activity led to political and military involvement overseas.

AS YOU READ

Use this web diagram to take notes. Fill it in with details about the causes of U.S. imperialism.

TERMS AND NAMES

Queen Liliuokalani The Hawaiian queen who was forced out of power by a revolution started by American business interests

imperialism The practice of strong countries taking economic, political, and military power over weaker countries

Alfred T. Mahan American imperialist and admiral who urged the United States to build up its navy and take colonies overseas

Sanford B. Dole American businessman who became president of the new government of Hawaii after the queen was pushed out

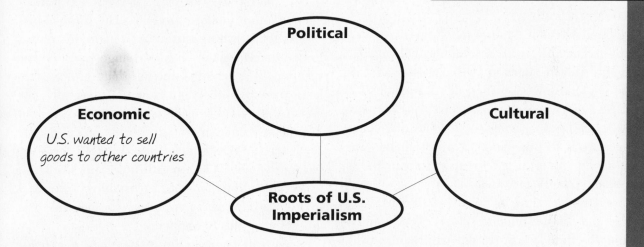

Political

Economic

U.S. wanted to sell goods to other countries

Cultural

Roots of U.S. Imperialism

Global Imperialism (pages 364–365)

What was imperialism?

By the 1880s, many Americans thought the United States should extend its influence overseas. This would mean adopting a policy of imperialism. **Imperialism** was the practice of stronger nations extending their economic, political, and military strength over weaker countries. European nations had done this for a long time.

Imperialism was a trend around the world. Seven European nations, for instance, divided up Africa into colonies for themselves. They did this to take the raw materials that Africa offered and to sell their own goods in African markets. By the early 1900s, only two African countries remained independent.

The British founded a huge empire in Africa, Asia, and the Pacific. Under Queen Victoria (1837–1901), the British empire included one quarter of the world's land and people.

1. What did strong countries gain from imperialism?

_____

_____

American Imperialism (pages 365–366)

Why did Americans support imperialism?

Most Americans came to support the idea of American imperialism. They did this for three main reasons: (1) economic competition with other industrial nations, (2) military competition from other countries, and (3) a lack of concern for the (mostly nonwhite) people who lived in the countries being taken over.

The economic root of imperialism grew from a few simple facts. Farms and factories had become more productive because of advances in *technology*. That meant the United States could produce more goods than Americans could buy. It wanted to sell these goods to other countries. It also wanted raw materials from other countries to supply its factories.

The United States also wanted to achieve a favorable balance of trade. This meant the country wanted to sell to other countries more than they bought from other countries.

The second root of American imperialism was a desire for military strength. This strength was needed in part to protect the economic interests of the country abroad.

Admiral **Alfred T. Mahan** spoke out for expanding the military. He made several major points. He urged the United States to (1) build a strong U.S. navy to defend shipping lanes, or trade routes; (2) establish bases where the ships could take on more fuel; (3) build a canal across the *Isthmus* of Panama so that goods did not have to travel all the way around South America; and (4) make colonies out of Hawaii and other Pacific Islands.

The United States followed Admiral Mahan's advice and began building ships. The country became the third largest naval power in the world.

The third root of American imperialism was a belief that the people of the United States were better than the people of other countries. This *racist* belief came from people's pride in their Anglo-Saxon (Northern European) heritage. People sometimes felt they had a duty to spread their culture and Christian religion among other people.

Many other Americans were against imperialism. They believed that it was morally wrong for the United States to take over other countries. They also felt that colonies would cost too much.

2. What were three reasons Americans supported imperialism?

_____

_____

The United States Takes Hawaii
(pages 366–367)

How did the Hawaiian Islands become a U.S. territory?

The Hawaiian Islands, in the Pacific Ocean, had been important to the United States since the 1790s. Merchants had stopped there on their way to China and India. In the 1820s, American missionaries founded Christian schools and churches on the islands.

A number of Americans had established sugar plantations in Hawaii. In the mid-1800s these large farms accounted for about three-quarters of the wealth in the islands. Plantation owners brought thousands of laborers to Hawaii from Japan, Portugal, and China. This weakened the influence of the native Hawaiians. By 1900, the foreign laborers outnumbered the Hawaiians three to one.

In 1887, white business leaders in Hawaii forced the Hawaiian king to change Hawaii's constitution. The change meant that only wealthy landowners had the right to vote. It basically gave control of the Hawaiian government to the American businessmen.

When the Hawaiian king died in 1891, his sister became queen. **Queen Liliuokalani** wanted a new constitution that would give voting power back to ordinary Hawaiians. American business interests did not want this to happen.

American business groups organized a revolt against the queen. The U.S. ambassador John L. Stevens helped them. The planters took control of the island. They established a temporary government and made American businessman **Sanford B. Dole** the president.

Stevens urged the U.S. government to *annex* the Hawaiian Islands. President Grover Cleveland refused to take over the islands unless a majority of Hawaiians favored that. In 1897, however, William McKinley became president. He favored annexation. In 1898, Hawaii became a U.S. *territory*.

3. How did Hawaiians lose control of their islands?

_____

_____

CHAPTER 10 Section 2 (pages 370–374)

The Spanish–American–Cuban War

TERMS AND NAMES

José Martí Political activist who worked for Cuban independence

Valeriano Weyler General sent from Spain to Cuba to restore order in 1896

yellow journalism Reporting in newspapers and magazines that exaggerates the news in order to make it more exciting

U.S.S. *Maine* U.S. warship that exploded in a Cuban harbor in 1898

George Dewey U.S. naval commander who led the American attack on the Philippines

Rough Riders Fighting unit led by Theodore Roosevelt in Cuba

San Juan Hill Location of an important American land victory in Cuba

BEFORE YOU READ

In the last section, you learned how the United States became an imperialist power and took over the Hawaiian Islands.

In this section, you will learn how the United States became involved in Cuba and fought a war with Spain.

AS YOU READ

Use this time line to take notes. In each box, write what happened on that date.

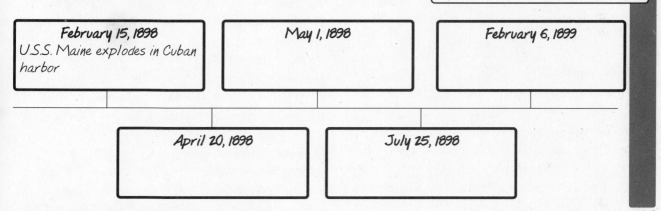

February 15, 1898
U.S.S. Maine explodes in Cuban harbor

May 1, 1898

February 6, 1899

April 20, 1898

July 25, 1898

American Interest in Cuba
(pages 370–371)

What happened when Cuba rebelled against Spain?

Between 1868 and 1878, Cubans fought their first war for independence from Spain. The rebels did not win, but they did force Spain to *abolish* slavery in 1886. After that, United States *capitalists* invested heavily in sugar cane plantations in Cuba.

Sugar was the most important product of Cuba. The United States was the main market for the sugar. As long the United States did not charge a tariff on Cuban sugar, the Cuban economy thrived. But the Cuban economy collapsed in 1894 when a tariff on sugar was imposed.

In 1895, Cubans began a second war for independence. The rebellion was led by **José Martí.** He was a Cuban poet and journalist who had been living *in exile* in New York. The rebels wanted the United States to join their cause.

American opinion was mixed. Some wanted to support Spain in order to keep their investments safe. Others wanted to help the Cuban people win their freedom from Spain just as the United States had won its independence from England.

1. How did Cuba's two wars for independence affect American business interests?

_____

_____

_____

The Threat of War Escalates
(pages 371–372)

Why did Americans become angry with Spain?

In 1896, Spain sent an army to Cuba to restore order. The army was led by General **Valeriano Weyler.** Weyler rounded up the entire rural population of central and western Cuba. He kept 300,000 people as prisoners in concentration camps. That way they could not help the rebels. Many of them died of hunger and disease.

This story was widely reported in the United States. Rival newspapers in New York made the terrible events sound even worse. They exaggerated the *brutality* of the story in order to attract readers. These sensational stories became known as **yellow journalism**—reporting that exaggerates the news in order to make it more exciting.

William McKinley became president in 1897. At that time, many Americans wanted the United States to help the rebels against Spain. McKinley tried to find a peaceful solution to the crisis. His efforts had several positive results. Spain sent General Weyler home, changed the concentration camp policy, and gave Cuba limited self-government.

Then two events made Americans very angry at Spain. The first was the publication of a letter that insulted the American president. The de Lôme letter was written by a Spanish *diplomat*. It criticized McKinley for being weak. Although some Americans agreed that the president was weak, they did not want to hear this criticism from a Spanish official.

Only a few days after the letter was published, something worse happened. The battleship **U.S.S. Maine** was stationed in Cuba to protect American lives and property. On February 15, 1898, the ship exploded. The ship sank, and 260 officers and crew on board died. The cause of the explosion was not known. However, newspapers blamed Spain. Americans cried for war.

2. What two events led Americans to call for war against Spain?

_____

_____

_____

War Breaks Out
(pages 372–374)

Where and when did the fighting take place?

On April 20, 1898, the United States went to war with Spain. The first battle took place in the Philippines. The Philippines had been a Spanish colony for 300 years. They had rebelled many times. In 1896, they began another rebellion.

On May 1, 1898 the American naval commander **George Dewey** sailed into Manila Bay in the Philippines. His ships destroyed the Spanish fleet there. In the next two months, U.S. soldiers fought on the side of the *Filipino* rebels. The Spanish surrendered to the United States in August.

In Cuba, the American navy blocked off the harbor of Santiago de Cuba. Spanish ships could not leave. Then American troops landed on the island in June 1898.

One unit of volunteer soldiers was called the **Rough Riders.** Theodore Roosevelt was one of their leaders. They helped win the important battle of **San Juan Hill.** American newspapers made Roosevelt a hero.

When the Spanish ships tried to leave the harbor, their fleet was destroyed. This led the Spanish to surrender on July 25.

Spain quickly agreed to a peace treaty. The treaty granted Cuba its independence. Spain gave Puerto Rico and the Pacific island of Guam to the United States. The United States paid Spain $20 million for the annexation of the Philippine Islands. The Senate approved the treaty on February 6, 1899.

3. What three territories did the United States get from the war with Spain?

_____

_____

Acquiring New Lands

BEFORE YOU READ

In the last section, you learned how the United States and Spain fought over Cuba and the Philippines.

In this section, you will read how the United States continued its imperialism.

AS YOU READ

Use this diagram to take notes. Fill in the boxes to describe the relationships between the United States and Puerto Rico, Cuba, the Philippines, and China.

COUNTRY	AMERICAN ACTIONS	RESPONSES TO ACTIONS
Puerto Rico	sent military forces to Puerto Rico in 1898	
Cuba		
The Philippines		
China		

U.S. Involvement in Puerto Rico
(pages 375–376)

How did Puerto Ricans feel about U.S. control?

Puerto Rico had become an American territory as a result of the Spanish–American–Cuban War. American forces landed in Puerto Rico in July 1898. The commanding officer declared that the Americans were there to protect the Puerto Ricans. But other U.S. military officials insulted the Puerto Ricans. They spoke of them as children

and set limits on their personal freedom. Many Puerto Ricans began to resent the military government.

The United States kept strict control over the people and their government. In 1917, however, Congress made Puerto Ricans U.S. citizens.

1. Why did some Puerto Ricans resent U.S. control of their government?

_____

_____

Cuba Becomes a Protectorate
(pages 376–377)

How did the United States keep control over Cuba?

Cuba was officially independent after the war. The U.S. army, however, remained in Cuba for four years. It punished Cubans who did not like this American *occupation.*

In 1900 the new Cuban government wrote a constitution. The United States insisted they add the **Platt Amendment.** The amendment limited Cuba's rights in dealing with other countries. It gave the United States special privileges, including the right to intervene to preserve order.

Cuba became a U.S. **protectorate,** a country whose affairs are partially controlled by a stronger power. The United States insisted on these rights because of its economic interests in Cuba.

2. What did the United States do to protect business interests in Cuba?

Filipinos Rebel (pages 377–378)

Why did the Filipinos rebel against the United States?

Filipinos had been fighting for independence for years. They were angry that the United States had annexed their islands. Rebel leader **Emilio Aguinaldo** believed that the United States had promised independence. He felt that the United States had betrayed the Filipinos after helping them win independence.

In 1899, Aguinaldo started a rebellion, which lasted three years. After winning that war, the United States set up a government similar to the one it had set up in Cuba.

3. Why did Aguinaldo feel betrayed by the United States?

China and the Open Door Policy
(pages 378–380)

What were U.S. interests in China?

By 1899, many countries had economic interests in China. The United States wanted to be able to trade with China. The Secretary of State, **John Hay,** sent a statement of this policy to the other countries. His policy statements were called the **Open Door notes.** They called for China's ports to remain open and for China to remain independent. No country would have special trading rights. The other countries agreed.

In 1900, a secret society in China started a rebellion. They were protesting the influence of Western countries in China. Troops from many countries including the United States fought against the rebels, or Boxers. After the **Boxer Rebellion** was defeated, the United States issued more Open Door notes to make sure other countries did not make colonies out of China.

4. Why did Secretary of State John Hay issue the Open Door notes?

The Impact of U.S. Territorial Gains (pages 380–381)

How did American's feel about U.S. imperialism?

President William McKinley was reelected in 1900. His opponent had been an anti-imperialist, William Jennings Bryan. The outcome of the election suggests that most Americans disagreed with Bryan. Imperialism was popular.

Americans began to learn about the Philippines. One way they learned was through international expositions. In these fairs, Filipinos were shown to be capable but backwards. Such attitudes helped Americans to justify their control over the Philippines.

Other Americans, like writer Mark Twain, did not feel good about imperialism. They felt that it was unfair for one country to dominate another.

5. What did McKinley's reelection show about American attitudes toward imperialism?

America as a World Power

BEFORE YOU READ

In the last section, you learned about the growth of American imperialism.

In this section, you will learn how Roosevelt and Wilson used American military and economic power.

AS YOU READ

Use this diagram to take notes. Fill in the boxes as you read about Roosevelt's and Wilson's use of American power.

TERMS AND NAMES

Panama Canal A channel across Central America, between the Atlantic and Pacific Oceans, opened in 1914

Roosevelt Corollary Roosevelt's 1904 extension of the Monroe Doctrine, stating that the United States has the right to protect its economic interests in South and Central America by using military force

dollar diplomacy The policy of intervening in other countries to protect U.S. business interests

Francisco "Pancho" Villa Mexican revolutionary

John J. Pershing U.S. general who led troops to capture Villa

USING AMERICAN POWER	
Roosevelt	**Wilson**
Mediated settlement in Russo-Japanese War	

Teddy Roosevelt and the World
(pages 382–385)

How did Roosevelt use American power?

In 1901, President McKinley was assassinated, and Theodore Roosevelt became president. Roosevelt continued the policies of imperialism. He first used U.S. influence to help settle the Russo-Japanese War.

The war began in 1904. Both Russia and Japan wanted to control Korea. Japan captured Korea and also invaded Manchuria, which was controlled by Russia.

Then Japan wanted to stop the fighting. The Japanese asked President Roosevelt to *mediate* the conflict. In 1905 representatives of Russia and Japan met. Roosevelt used his personal charm to help them *negotiate* a compromise. They signed a

treaty, and Roosevelt received the 1906 Nobel Peace Prize for his efforts.

Roosevelt also used his influence to help build the **Panama Canal.** The idea of a canal connecting the Atlantic and Pacific Oceans had been discussed for some time. Such a canal would cut travel time for military and commercial ships. Ships would no longer have to go all the way around South America in order to get from one ocean to the other.

The narrow Isthmus of Panama was a logical place to cut a canal. Political problems stood in the way, however. Panama was a province of Colombia. When Colombia did not agree to the canal, the United States helped Panama to rebel against Colombia. Panama became independent. Then the United States got Panama's permission to build the canal.

Construction of the Panama Canal was one of the world's greatest *engineering* accomplishments. Work began in 1904 and took 10 years. In 1913, there were 43,400 workers on the project. The work was hard and dangerous.

On August 15, 1914, the canal opened for business. It was a success from the start. More than 1,000 ships passed through during its first year. However, relations between the United States and Latin America had been damaged by the takeover of Panama.

President Roosevelt wanted the United States to be the major power in the Caribbean and Central America. He declared his policy in a message to Congress in 1904. His statement was called the **Roosevelt Corollary.** A corollary is a logical result of another statement, in this case the Monroe Doctrine of 1823. That doctrine had said the United States would not allow European influence in the Western Hemisphere. Roosevelt now said that the United States had the right to intervene in Latin American countries to protect U.S. business interests.

In 1911, President Taft used this policy in Nicaragua. A rebellion had left the country in debt. Taft arranged for U.S. bankers to loan Nicaragua money. In exchange, American business took control of the railroads and banks in the country. They also collected Nicaragua's custom duties.

Nicaraguans did not like this arrangement. They rebelled. The United States then sent troops to Nicaragua to preserve the peace. Those who did not like this kind of *intervention* called it **dollar diplomacy.**

1. **What are two ways Roosevelt used U.S. power in other countries?**

_____

_____

_____

Woodrow Wilson's Missionary Diplomacy (pages 385–387)

Why did President Wilson send troops to Mexico?

President Woodrow Wilson took a step beyond Presidents Monroe and Roosevelt by adding a *moral* tone to Latin American policy. He said that the United States *must* act in certain circumstances.

This so-called "missionary diplomacy" meant that the United States could not officially *recognize* governments that were *oppressive*, undemocratic, or opposed to U.S. business interests. The new doctrine put pressure on countries to have democratic governments. A revolution in Mexico tested this policy.

In 1910, Mexican peasants and workers rebelled against their military dictator. Two new governments followed, the second headed by General Victoriano Huerta.

Wilson refused to support the Huerta government because it came to power through violence.

Wilson sent in troops. When a new leader, Venustiano Carranza, took power in Mexico, Wilson withdrew the troops.

Mexico remained in *turmoil*. **Francisco "Pancho" Villa** and others led revolts against Carranza. Some of Villa's followers killed Americans. The United States wanted to capture Villa.

Finally the Mexican government gave permission to send in troops. Wilson sent General **John J. Pershing** with 15,000 soldiers. A year later, Villa was still free. Wilson then stationed 150,000 National Guardsmen along the border.

Mexicans were angered by the U.S. invasion. In 1916, U.S. troops fought with Carranza's army. In 1917, Wilson withdrew U.S. troops. At that time, he was facing possible war in Europe.

Finally, Mexico adopted a constitution. The Mexicans regained control of their own resources and put limits on foreign investment. American intervention in Mexico showed how far the United States was willing to go to protect its economic interests.

2. **What were two reasons Wilson sent troops to Mexico?**

_____

_____

_____

Name _____ Date _____

abolish Put an end to

annex Add to a country as a territory or protectorate

brutality Cruelty

capitalist A person who invests money in business

diplomat A person sent to another country as a representative

engineering Applying science and mathematics to practical problems

Filipino A native or inhabitant of the Philippines

in exile Not allowed to live in one's own country

intervention To interfere in the affairs of another country

isthmus A narrow strip of land

mediate To help two sides negotiate, as a peacemaker

moral Based on a judgment of right and wrong

negotiate To try to reach an agreement by talking

occupation The act of taking over and holding a place

oppressive Cruel, harsh

racist Based on the prejudice that one race is better than another

recognize To accept officially that a government has the right to be in power

technology Practical devices and machines invented by science

territory Area under the control of a country as a colonial possession

turmoil Confusion and upset

AFTER YOU READ

Terms and Names

A. Write the letter of the name that best matches each description.

a. Francisco "Pancho" Villa

b. Alfred T. Mahan

c. Theodore Roosevelt

d. Woodrow Wilson

e. John Hay

f. José Martí

_____ **1.** U.S. naval officer who supported imperialism

_____ **2.** Cuban poet and journalist who launched a revolution

_____ **3.** Secretary of state who issued the Open Door notes

_____ **4.** President who used missionary diplomacy

_____ **5.** Mexican revolutionary leader American troops tried to capture

B. Fill in the blank with the letter of the name or term that best completes each sentence.

a. Rough Riders

b. the Philippines

c. Sanford B. Dole

d. Roosevelt Corollary

e. Platt Amendment

f. U.S.S. *Maine*

g. San Juan Hill

h. Boxer Rebellion

i. Panama

j. Emilio Aguinaldo

1. American business groups created a government in Hawaii with _____ as president.

2. The United States declared war on Spain, soon after the _____ exploded in a Cuban harbor.

3. After the Spanish–American–Cuban War, the United States paid Spain $20 million to annex _____.

4. The _____ gave the United States broad rights in the affairs of Cuba.

5. The Filipino rebel leader _____ believed that the United States had betrayed his people.

6. The United States helped to start a revolution in _____ in order to get land for a canal.

7. The battle of _____ in Cuba helped the United States defeat Spain.

8. A Chinese secret society led the _____ to protest Western influence in their country.

9. The _____ stated that the United States could intervene in Latin American countries.

10. _____ was the nickname of Theodore Roosevelt's cavalry unit.

Main Ideas

1. What benefits did countries get from practicing imperialism?

_____

_____

2. How were Americans divided about Cuban independence?

_____

_____

3. What sparked the Boxer Rebellion in 1900 and how was it crushed?

_____

_____

4. How did the Roosevelt Corollary lead to dollar diplomacy?

_____

_____

5. How did President Wilson justify his invasion of Mexico?

_____

_____

Thinking Critically

Answer the following questions on a separate sheet of paper.

1. Which of Admiral Mahan's goals for becoming a world power do you consider most important? Why?

2. Do you think it was right for the United States to get involved in the affairs of Columbia, Nicaragua, and Mexico? Why or why not?

World War I Begins

BEFORE YOU READ

In the last section, you learned how Presidents Roosevelt and Wilson used American power around the world.

In this section, you will read how war broke out in Europe while the United States tried to remain neutral.

AS YOU READ

Use this diagram to take notes. Fill it in with events that speeded up or slowed down the entrance of the United States into the war. The notes will help you remember the beginnings of World War I.

THE U.S. ENTRANCE INTO WORLD WAR I	
What Speeded It Up?	**What Slowed It Down?**
Many Americans sympathized with the Allies	

Long-Term Causes of World War I
(pages 394–396)

What conditions led to war?

Four main factors led to the outbreak of World War I in Europe. The first was nationalism—the belief that the interests of a single country were more important than cooperation among countries. This led to competition.

The second cause was imperialism. Countries tried to increase the power and influence around the world. This led to conflicts among them.

The third main cause was militarism.

Militarism meant building up armies, navies, and other armed forces. It also meant using them as a tool for negotiating with other countries.

The fourth cause was the alliance system. Some countries in Europe had made treaties promising to defend each other. These mutual-defense treaties placed European countries in two main groups. The **Allies** were made up of France, Great Britain, and Russia. The **Central Powers** were Germany, Austria-Hungary, and the Ottoman Empire.

1. Name two causes of World War I.

_____

An Assassination Leads to War

(page 396)

What sparked the war?

In 1914, **Archduke Franz Ferdinand** was assassinated. He had been the *heir* to the throne of Austria-Hungary. His killer was a Serb who wanted to unite all Serbs (including those in Austria-Hungary) under one government. This touched off an action to punish Serbia.

The war could not stay small, however. The alliance system pulled one nation after another into the conflict. If a nation had sworn to protect another nation, it had to declare war on that nation's enemies. Germany and Austria-Hungary were facing France, Great Britain, and Russia.

2. Why did the assassination lead to fighting?

The Fighting Starts (pages 396–398)

Where did the fighting begin?

Germany began by invading Belgium. It planned to overrun France and then to attack Russia. The British and French could not save Belgium. They did, however, manage to stop Germany's advance.

By the spring of 1915, two lines of deep trenches had developed in France. Germans occupied one line. The Allies occupied the other line. Between the two lines lay **"no man's land."** The soldiers would climb out of their trenches and try to overrun enemy lines. They did this while facing machine-gun fire and poison gas.

This bloody **trench warfare** continued for more than three years. Soldiers sometimes fought and died to gain only a few yards. Neither side gained territory, but more than one million soldiers died.

3. Why did the fighting take place in France?

American Neutrality (pages 398–399)

How did Americans feel?

In the United States, public opinion about the war was strong but divided. Many *naturalized* U.S. cit-

izens still had ties to the countries they came from. Many immigrants from Germany, for example, sympathized with Germany.

Socialists saw the war as an imperialist struggle between German and English businessmen. *Pacifists* believed that all wars were bad. They urged the United States to set an example for peace. Many other Americans simply did not want to send their sons to war.

Americans tended to sympathize with Great Britain and France. They shared a common language and heritage with Britain. They were horrified at Germany's brutal attack on Belgium. And they had strong economic ties with the Allies.

4. What were three things that influenced Americans' feelings about the war?

The United States Enters the War (pages 399–401)

Why did the U.S. join the war?

The war affected American shipping. Great Britain set up a *blockade* along the German coast to keep goods from getting through. American ships would not challenge Britain's blockade.

Then Germany began to attack ships going to Great Britain. Some Americans died in these attacks. A German U-boat, or submarine, sank the British passenger ship **Lusitania.** Many more Americans died.

War was finally declared after two more incidents. The first was the **Zimmermann note.** British agents *intercepted* a telegram that proposed an alliance between Germany and Mexico against the United States. The second incident was the sinking of four unarmed American merchant ships. President Wilson asked Congress to declare war on Germany. It did so on April 6, 1917.

5. What are three important incidents that led the United States to declare war?

American Power Tips the Balance

BEFORE YOU READ

In the last section, you learned how the United States was drawn into the war.

In this section, you will read how Americans prepared to fight and how they helped the Allies to win.

AS YOU READ

Use this web diagram to take notes. Fill it in with problems the United States faced as it entered the war.

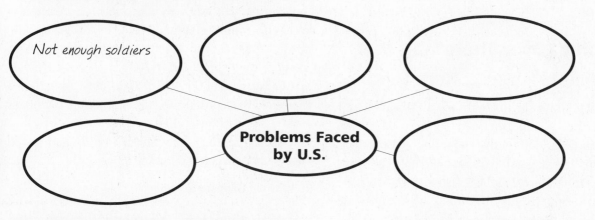

American Military Mobilization
(pages 402–403)

How did the U.S. prepare for war?

The United States first needed to build up its armed forces. When war was declared, only about 200,000 men were in service. To solve this problem, Congress passed the **Selective Service Act.** It required men to register with the government so that some of them could be selected for military service. This process—called the draft—quickly put about 3 million men in uniform.

Women were not drafted. The army would not let them join. But the navy accepted women in *noncombat* positions. Woman served as nurses, secretaries, and telephone operators.

Many African Americans served in the military. They were placed in separate units, usually under the leadership of white officers. But some blacks

were trained as officers. Blacks were among the first to receive the French military honor of the Croix de Guerre.

1. How did the United States build up its armed forces?

_____

_____

American Success in Combat
(pages 403–406)

How did the United States help?

First, the United States needed to get its troops to Europe. It began to build ships. The government also took over ships built for other purposes.

The United States also needed to reduce the loss of ships to German submarine attacks. The

United States and Britain began to use the **convoy system.** In this system, merchant ships traveled in a large group guarded by naval vessels.

At first, American soldiers served as replacements for men killed or wounded in Allied armies. Then Americans fought as an independent force.

One of America's greatest war heroes, **Alvin York,** fought the Germans in France. When the war came, York had wanted to be *excused* from the draft. He was a **conscientious objector,** that is, a person who opposes war on moral grounds. The draft board denied his request to be excused.

York served with great personal bravery. He was promoted to sergeant and became a popular *celebrity* in the United States.

2. How did the United States help the Allies?

_____

_____

Fighting "Over There" (pages 406–407)
What new weapons were used?

New weapons made the fighting in World War I very destructive. One such weapon was a German cannon that could fire a shell 75 miles. Another was the zeppelin—a gas-filled airship that Germans used to drop bombs on English cities. Machine guns were also introduced. And the first large-scale use of poison gas took place in April 1915.

The two most *innovative* weapons were the tank and the airplane. Fighting with these weapons

was called **mechanized warfare.** Such warfare depended on machines powered by gasoline and diesel engines.

One hero in air combat was **Eddie Rickenbacker.** He fought in 134 air battles and shot down 26 enemy planes.

Conditions in the trenches were miserable. Soldiers got many diseases and medical treatments were limited.

3. Name two new weapons used in the war.

_____

_____

The Collapse of Germany
(pages 407–408)
Why did Germany surrender?

German *morale* was very low. German sailors and soldiers began to give up. The German leader, the kaiser, left his throne. The Germans had been worn down.

On November 11, 1918, Germany agreed to a cease-fire that ended the war. The other countries in the Central Powers had already surrendered.

The toll of the war was massive. It had lasted four years and taken 26 million lives.

4. Why did Germany surrender?

_____

_____

World War I Casualties

Russia
9,300,000

Germany
7,209,413

France
6,220,800

Austria-Hungary
4,650,200

Great Britain
3,428,535

United States
325,236

Skillbuilder
Use the chart to answer these questions.

1. Which nation suffered the most casualties?

_____

_____

2. How does the chart reflect America's late entry into the war?

_____

_____

CHAPTER 11 Section 3 (pages 409–416)

The War at Home

TERMS AND NAMES

Bernard M. Baruch Leader of the War Industries Board

War Industries Board (WIB) Agency to improve efficiency in war-related industries

George Creel Head of the Committee on Public Information (CPI), the government's propaganda agency

Espionage and Sedition Acts Laws that enacted harsh penalties against anyone opposing U.S. participation in World War I

Great Migration Movement of many African Americans to northern cities from the South in the early 1900s

BEFORE YOU READ

In the last section, you learned how the United States fought in World War I.

In this section, you will read about how the war changed American society at home.

AS YOU READ

Use this diagram to take notes. Fill it in with ways in which Americans at home supported the war effort.

GROUP OR INDIVIDUAL	CONTRIBUTIONS TO THE WAR EFFORT
War Industries Board	

Congress Gives Power to Wilson
(pages 409–411)

How did business and government work together?

To fight the war, the United States needed the help of industry. The economy had to change from making *consumer goods* to making weapons and war supplies. Congress gave President Wilson direct control over much of the economy. He had the power to fix prices and to regulate war-related industries.

Wilson named **Bernard M. Baruch** to head the **War Industries Board** (WIB). This agency helped boost industrial production by 20 percent. Other federal agencies also regulated the economy

for the war effort. The Railroad Administration controlled the nation's railroads. The Fuel Administration watched over the use of coal, gasoline, and heating oil.

Wages in some industries went up. But workers in other jobs lost money because of inflation. As a result, many workers joined unions. Wilson established the National War Labor Board. This agency worked to settle disputes between management and labor. It also helped to improve working conditions.

Another new agency, the Food Administration, was established to help produce and conserve food supplies. It encouraged people to grow their own food. It taught them to eat differently. Americans were able to send more food to the Allies.

1. How did the government handle labor disputes in wartime?

_____

_____

Selling the War (pages 411–412)

How did the government win over public opinion?

The government needed to raise money for the war. They did this by increasing several kinds of taxes and by selling war bonds. Thousands of volunteers sold the bonds. Famous people spoke at rallies to promote the sales. Newspapers and billboards carried advertisements free of charge.

To popularize the war, the government created the Committee on Public Information (CPI). It was the nation's first *propaganda* agency. The agency was headed by **George Creel.** He had been a muckraking journalist. He used artists and advertising people to create thousands of posters, paintings, and cartoons to promote the war. He distributed pamphlets in many languages.

2. How did the U.S. government pay for the war?

_____

_____

Attacks on Civil Liberties

(pages 412–414)

How did the war affect civil liberties?

The war brought out anti-immigrant feelings. Immigrants from Germany were often targeted for attack. Americans with German-sounding names lost their jobs. Orchestras refused to play German music. Some towns with German names changed them.

Congress passed the **Espionage and Sedition Acts** to punish people who did not support the war effort. People could not interfere with the draft or *obstruct* the sale of war bonds. They could not even speak against the war effort.

These laws violated the spirit of the First Amendment, which guarantees freedom of speech.

The law led to 6,000 arrests and 1,500 convictions for antiwar activities. If a newspaper or magazine criticized the war, it could lose its mailing privileges.

The chief targets of the Espionage and Sedition Acts were socialists and union leaders. Labor leader Eugene V. Debs was jailed for making a speech about the economic causes of the war. The Industrial Workers of the World urged workers to strike. This was considered an antiwar activity, and they received jail sentences.

3. How did the Espionage and Sedition Acts contradict the First Amendment?

_____

_____

Social Changes During the War

(pages 414–416)

How did the war affect women and blacks?

The war brought many social changes for African Americans and women.

African-American leaders were divided over the war. W. E. B. Du Bois believed that helping the war effort would help the fight for equality. Others believed that blacks should not help a government that did not support equality for everyone.

The war sped up the **Great Migration.** This was the movement of thousands of African Americans from the South to cities of the North. They wanted to escape racial discrimination. They also wanted to find jobs in Northern industries.

American women played new roles during the war. They did jobs that had previously been done only by men. They worked as truck drivers, cooks, dockworkers, and builders. Women volunteered in the Red Cross and sold war bonds.

Women's activities made them more visible. They were not paid the same as men. But, soon after the war, the Congress finally passed an amendment giving them the right to vote.

4. How did women's roles change during the war?

_____

_____

CHAPTER 11 Section 4 (pages 417–421)

Wilson Fights for Peace

TERMS AND NAMES

Fourteen Points Wilson's plan for world peace following World War I

League of Nations An international peace-keeping organization proposed by Wilson and founded in 1920

Treaty of Versailles The 1919 treaty that ended World War I

reparations Payments made by defeated countries after a war

war-guilt clause Part of the Treaty of Versailles in which Germany took responsibility for the war

Henry Cabot Lodge Conservative senator who wanted to keep the United States out of the League of Nations

BEFORE YOU READ

In the last section, you learned how the war in Europe changed life at home.

In this section, you will read about the treaty that ended the war and Wilson's proposal for a League of Nations.

AS YOU READ

Use this diagram to take notes. Fill it in with details about the Treaty of Versailles. The notes will help you remember the consequences of World War I.

TREATY OF VERSAILLES	
Provisions	**Weaknesses**
Established 9 new nations	

Wilson at Versailles (pages 417–418)

What were Wilson's plans for peace?

President Wilson presented his plan for world peace to Congress in January 1918. The plan was called his **Fourteen Points.**

The first five points suggested ways that wars could be avoided. They state that (1) countries should not make secret treaties with one another, (2) freedom of the seas should be maintained, (3) tariffs should be lowered to promote free trade, (4) countries should reduce their arms, and (5) the interests of the colonial people should be considered.

The next eight points suggested new national boundaries. Wilson believed in self-determination: different ethnic groups should be able to decide for themselves what nation they would belong to.

The fourteenth point called for a **League of Nations.** This international organization would address problems between countries before they led to war.

Wilson met with leaders of Italy, France, and Great Britain to discuss the terms of peace. These leaders had won the war, and they wanted to punish Germany. Wilson had to give up most of his Fourteen Points. The one he insisted on was the League of Nations.

1. What did Wilson's first first five points address?

_____

_____

Treaty of Versailles (pages 418–421)

What did the treaty say?

On June 28, 1919, the leaders of the Allies and the Central Powers met at the Palace of Versailles in France. They were to sign the **Treaty of Versailles.**

The treaty created new national boundaries by (1) establishing nine new nations, including Poland, Czechoslovakia, and Yugoslavia; (2) shifting the boundaries of other nations; and (3) carving out parts of the Ottoman Empire to create colonies in the Middle East for Great Britain and France.

The treaty took away Germany's army and navy. It forced Germany to pay **reparations,** or war damages, to the winners. In addition, the treaty contained a **war-guilt clause.** Germany had to admit that it was responsible for causing the war.

The Treaty of Versailles had three basic weaknesses. The first was its harsh treatment of Germany. Germany was humiliated. Germany was not the only country that had also been militaristic, yet Germany alone was punished. And, Germany would not be able to pay the huge reparations.

The second weakness was that the Soviet Union (formerly Russia) lost more territory than Germany did. Russia had been one of the Allies, and had suffered more *casualties* than any other country. The Soviet Union was determined to get its territories back.

The third weakness concerned colonies. The treaty did not recognize the claims of colonies for self-determination. In Southeast Asia, for instance, a movement for independence had developed in what is now Vietnam. Those who favored independence proposed a constitutional government. The treaty ignored their request. As a consequence, the Vietnamese later fought the French and then the United States.

Wilson brought the treaty back to the United States for approval. He found several groups opposed it. Some thought the treaty too harsh. Others thought it favored the imperialists. Some ethnic groups objected to the treaty because of the way it treated their homelands.

The main opposition to the treaty was over the League of Nations. The League was only one of Wilson's Fourteen Points that was included in the treaty. Conservative senators, headed by **Henry Cabot Lodge,** opposed joining the League. They did not like the idea of working with other countries to take economic and military action against aggression. They wanted the treaty to include the constitutional right of Congress to declare war.

Wilson refused to compromise on the League. He would not accept amendments proposed by Republican leaders. As a result, the Senate failed to ratify the treaty. The United States never entered the League of Nations. It finally signed a separate treaty with Germany in 1921, when Wilson was no longer president.

2. Name two weaknesses of the treaty.

_____

_____

The Legacy of the War (page 421)

What led to Hitler's rise in Germany?

The kaiser's government had *censored* the news. They had not told the German people that the war was going badly. As a result, many Germans were surprised when they lost. They were upset at the harsh treatment they received under the Treaty of Versailles.

Economic conditions were especially bad in Germany. A severe depression started in 1923, and millions of workers lost their jobs. Inflation made the mark—Germany's money—nearly worthless. People needed bundles of marks to buy groceries.

In this atmosphere, Adolf Hitler came to power. Many Germans were looking for scapegoats, that is, other people to blame for their problems. Hitler blamed their problems on Jews and socialists in the government. Hitler and his Nazi Party won control of the German government in 1933. Hitler's policies led directly to World War II.

3. Why were the German people surprised when they lost the war?

_____

_____

Glossary   *CHAPTER 11* The First World War

blockade The blocking of a harbor or shipping lanes by hostile ships

casualties People killed or wounded

celebrity Famous person

censor To keep some news out of the papers

consumer goods Things made for household use

excused Allowed to avoid serving in the armed forces

heir Person who is next in line to receive a title

innovative Introducing something new and different

intercepted Stopped before it was delivered

morale State of spirit, cheerfulness

naturalized Naturalized citizens are those who come to a country from somewhere else and become citizens—as compared with people

who are citizens of a country because they are born there

noncombat Not fighting

obstruct Get in the way of

pacifist Someone who opposes war and violence

propaganda Biased information that is spread to promote a particular cause

AFTER YOU READ

Terms and Names

A. Write the letter of the name or term that matches the description.

a. Allies

b. George Creel

c. conscientious objector

d. Henry Cabot Lodge

e. Central Powers

_____ **1.** The alliance, in 1914, that was made up of Germany, Austria-Hungary, and the Ottoman Empire

_____ **2.** The alliance, in 1914, that was made up of France, Great Britain, and Russia

_____ **3.** A person who opposes warfare on moral grounds

_____ **4.** The muckraking journalist who led the Committee on Public Information

_____ **5.** A conservative United States senator who strongly opposed the Treaty of Versailles

B. If the statement is true, write "true" on the line. If it is false, write the word or words that would replace the underlined words to make it true.

_____ **1.** The assassination of <u>Archduke Franz Ferdinand</u> sparked the beginning of World War I.

_____ **2.** <u>Alvin York</u> shot down at least 26 enemy planes and was America's leading ace pilot in the war.

_____ **3.** The use of the tank and the airplane as weapons in World War I was the beginning of <u>mechanized warfare</u>.

_____ **4.** Under the <u>National War Labor Board</u>, the nation's main wartime regulatory body, industrial production in the United States increased by about 20 percent.

_____ **5.** The <u>first</u> point in Wilson's Fourteen Points called for the establishment of a League of Nations.

AFTER YOU READ (continued)   *CHAPTER 11* The First World War

Main Ideas

1. What were the long-term causes of World War I?

_____

_____

2. What acts brought the United States into the war?

_____

_____

3. How did the U.S. government sell the war to the nation?

_____

_____

4. What events during the war undermined Americans' civil liberties?

_____

_____

5. Why did the U.S. Senate reject the Treaty of Versailles?

_____

_____

Thinking Critically

Answer the following questions on a separate sheet of paper.

1. What do you think would have happened if the United States had not entered the war on the side of the Allies?

2. How did the Treaty of Versailles make conditions ripe for the rise of Hitler in Germany?

CHAPTER 12   Section 1 (pages 430–435)

Americans Struggle with Postwar Issues

BEFORE YOU READ

In the last section, you read about the end of the First World War.

In this section, you will see how Americans adjusted to the end of the war.

AS YOU READ

Use the chart below to take notes on the results of the Red Scare and labor strikes.

RED SCARE	LABOR STRIKES
Civil rights violated	Coolidge used force to put down Boston police strike

Revolution Abroad and Reaction at Home (pages 430–433)

Why did Americans fear communism?

After World War I, Americans wanted to return to "normalcy." This meant normal, typical, stable daily life. They were tired of the problems of war. They were also tired of the demands of reform. This desire had three results:

- Isolationism: pulling away from world affairs
- Nativism: a suspicion of foreign-born people
- Political conservatism: opposition to progressive reform

People saw **communism** as a threat to normalcy. Communism is an economic and political system that supports government control over property to create equality. Some communists said there should be only one political party: the Communist party. Communists came to power in Russia through violent revolution.

World War I created economic and political problems in Russia. In 1917, the Russian *czar*, or emperor, stepped down. Later, a group of revolutionaries called Bolsheviks took power. Their leader was Vladimir I. Lenin. They established the world's first communist state.

This new government called for worldwide revolution. Communist leaders wanted workers to seize political and economic power. They wanted to overthrow *capitalism*.

In the United States, about 70,000 people joined the Communist Party. This was a tiny percentage of the population. Still, the ideas of the communists, or "Reds," frightened many people. A fear of communism, known as the "Red Scare," swept the nation.

Attorney General **A. Mitchell Palmer** decided to take action against communism. He set up a new agency in the Justice Department. (It later became the Federal Bureau of Investigation.) Palmer sent his agents to arrest communists and *socialists*. He also attacked **anarchists,** people who opposed any and all forms of government.

Palmer's agents trampled on the civil rights of many people in the United States. Many *radicals* were sent out of the country without trial. But Palmer found no evidence of a plot to overthrow the government.

Many Americans suffered because of *abuses of power* during the Red Scare. One case involved two Italian immigrants, Nicola Sacco and Bartolomeo Vanzetti. **Sacco and Vanzetti** were arrested for robbery and murder in Massachusetts. They admitted they were anarchists. But they denied committing any crime. The case against them was weak. But they were convicted anyway. Many people protested the conviction. They believed it was based on a fear of foreigners. Sacco and Vanzetti were executed in 1927.

Some Americans used the Red Scare as an excuse to act against any people who were different from themselves. The Ku Klux Klan revived. This secret organization had threatened African Americans during Reconstruction.

Now the Klan turned against blacks, Jews, Roman Catholics, immigrants, and union leaders. They resented advances made by blacks, immigrants, and unions. They used violence to keep these groups "in their place." Klan membership rose to more than four million. The Klan briefly gained political power in several states.

1. Describe one cause and one effect of the Red Scare.

_____

_____

A Time of Labor Unrest (pages 433–435)

What were the three major strikes of 1919?

Strikes were not allowed during World War I because they might have hurt the war effort. But in 1919 three important strikes occurred.

Boston police officers went on strike for a *living wage.* The *cost of living* had doubled since their last raise. Massachusetts governor **Calvin Coolidge** used force to put down the strike.

A strike by steelworkers began at U.S. Steel Corporation. It led to violence. Workers demanded the right to join unions. Force was used to put down the strike. In 1923 a church group revealed the harsh conditions in steel mills. Public opinion turned against the steel companies. The steel companies gave workers an eight-hour day. But the steelworkers still had no union.

A more successful strike was led by **John L. Lewis,** the president of the United Mine Workers. When Lewis's workers closed the coal mines, President Wilson tried to help to settle the dispute between the miners and mine owners. The miners got higher wages, but they did not get shorter hours.

In 1925, A. Philip Randolph founded the Brotherhood of Sleeping Car Porters, an African-American union of railroad workers. But few blacks belonged to other unions. In the 1920s, unions were not generally successful. Membership dropped from about 5 million to about 3.5 million workers.

2. Describe the three important labor strikes of 1919.

_____

_____

"Normalcy" and Isolationism

BEFORE YOU READ

In the last section, you learned about some of the issues Americans faced following World War I.

In this section, you will read about President Harding and the issues his administration faced at home and abroad.

AS YOU READ

Make a chart like the one below and fill it in with the major events of Harding's presidency. Take notes on the effects of each event.

EVENT	NOTES
Washington conference	reduced arms

A Return to "Normalcy"
(pages 436–438)

How did Harding handle foreign affairs?

In 1920 the Republicans nominated **Warren G. Harding** for president. He was a pleasant man. But he had little ability.

Harding promised to return normalcy to the nation. He wanted America to return to simpler days, like the prewar days. He and his *running mate* Calvin Coolidge won the election easily.

Harding worked for world peace. In 1921, he led a conference in Washington, D.C., that produced a historic agreement. Five major naval powers agreed to destroy some of their ships. For the first time,

nations agreed to *disarm*, or reduce their weapons. Then, in 1929, long after Harding left office, 64 nations signed the **Kellogg-Briand Pact.** By signing the Pact, these nations said they would give up war as national policy.

The United States was becoming more **isolationist.** Americans wanted to stay out of world affairs. But the United States still wanted France and Britain to repay the money they had borrowed during World War I.

Those two nations had suffered during the war. Their economies were too weak for them to repay the loans. To make matters worse, Congress passed the **Fordney-McCumber Tariff** in 1922. This tariff protected American business from foreign competition. But the tariff made it impossible for Britain and France to sell their goods in the United States.

France and Britain put pressure on Germany to pay its promised *reparations.* Germany's economy had been destroyed. It could not make the payments. So the United States loaned Germany money to pay reparations. Then France and Britain paid their U.S. loans.

1. Name one step Harding took to achieve world peace.

_____

_____

Limiting Immigration (pages 438–439)

Why did nativism rise?

The fact that many immigrants had been involved in postwar labor strikes led to nativism. Nativism is anti-immigrant feeling. Many Americans thought immigrants were revolutionaries and communists. Americans also did not want immigrants competing for better-paying jobs.

Racist ideas led to anti-immigrant feeling, too. Many Americans disliked Eastern Europeans, Jews, and Catholics.

As a result of anti-immigrant feeling, Congress passed the Emergency Quota Act of 1921. It established a **quota system.** This set a limit on how many immigrants from each country could enter the United States each year. In 1924 a new quota limited immigrants from Eastern and Southern Europe. These people were mostly Jewish and Roman Catholic.

The 1924 law also banned immigration from Japan. This insulted the Japanese. None of these laws applied to people from the Western Hemisphere. Canadians and Mexicans still entered the United States in large numbers.

2. What three things caused anti-immigrant feeling?

_____

_____

Scandal Hits Harding's Administration (pages 439–440)

How did scandal hurt Harding's administration?

Some of Harding's cabinet appointments were excellent. But others caused problems. Three good members of his cabinet were **Charles Evans Hughes,** Herbert Hoover, and Andrew Mellon. Hughes was secretary of state. He later became Chief Justice of the Supreme Court. The talented Herbert Hoover became secretary of commerce. Secretary of the Treasury Andrew Mellon reduced the *national debt* by about a third.

Other cabinet appointments caused problems. Some were part of the so-called **Ohio gang.** These were the president's poker-playing buddies from back home.

Some of his corrupt friends used their offices to become rich. They took *bribes* in return for official decisions to benefit their friends. One of these people was **Albert B. Fall,** Harding's secretary of the interior.

The worst case of corruption was the **Teapot Dome scandal.** It involved pieces of land called Teapot Dome and Elk Hills. This land was owned by the government. It held large reserves of oil. Fall secretly leased the land to two oil companies. He received money and property in return.

Harding was not charged with corruption himself. He suddenly died in 1923, and Calvin Coolidge became president. Coolidge was then elected president in 1924.

3. What does the Teapot Dome scandal tell about President Harding?

_____

_____

CHAPTER 12 Section 3 (pages 441–445)

The Business of America

TERMS AND NAMES

urban sprawl The outward expansion of cities

installment plan An easy way to borrow money to buy goods

BEFORE YOU READ

In the last section, you read about Harding's presidency.

In this section, you will read about the economy of the 1920s.

AS YOU READ

In the chart below, use the boxes on the left to take notes on the changes in business and technology in the 1920s. Use the boxes on the right to show some of the effects of these changes.

CHANGES	EFFECT
Standard of living goes up	Pro-business attitude

America's Standard of Living Soars (pages 441–444)

What were the successes of American business?

American business helped make the nation prosperous in the 1920s. The *standard of living* went up. There was a pro-business spirit. President Coolidge said, "The business of America is business." He wanted to keep taxes down and profits up. His goal was to keep government out of business and to let private enterprise succeed on its own.

The automobile business was one of the most successful. The automobile changed the American landscape. New roads and highways were built. Gas stations appeared. Rural families became less isolated. Young people and women who could drive became more independent. Cars also made it possible for people to live farther from their jobs. This led to **urban sprawl,** as cities spread out in all directions.

Cities in Ohio and Michigan grew as major centers of automobile manufacturing. States that produced oil such as California and Texas also prospered.

The automobile also became a *status symbol.* Everyone wanted to have one. By the late 1920s, about 80 percent of all the cars in the world were in the United States.

The airline industry also grew. Planes carried the nation's mail. Passenger service began.

Another major change was the spread of electricity. In the 1920s electric power stretched beyond big cities to the *suburbs*. Still, farms lacked electricity.

Americans began to use all kinds of electrical appliances. Radios, washing machines, and vacuum cleaners became popular. These appliances made housework easier. One result was more leisure time for families. Another effect was to increase the number of women working outside the home.

More consumer goods appeared on the market. Businesses used advertising to sell these goods. Ads didn't just give information about the product. Now, they used *psychology*. They tried to use people's desire for youth, beauty, and popularity to sell products. Things that once were luxuries became necessities. Some brand names became known nationwide.

Businesspeople formed organizations to do charity work. They also formed organizations to promote business.

1. How did the success of American business change American life?

_____

_____

A Superficial Prosperity (pages 444–445)

What hidden problems did the economy have?

Most Americans had confidence in the prosperity of the 1920s. The *national income* rose from $58 billion in 1921 to $83 billion in 1929. Most businesses seemed to make fortunes. The stock market reached new heights. But this prosperity hid two big problems.

First, business was not as healthy as it seemed. As workers produced more goods, businesses grew. Large businesses bought up, or merged with, smaller ones. But as businesses grew, business managers made much more money than workers did. Also, mining companies, railroads, and farms were not doing well.

Second, *consumer debt* rose to high levels. Businesses needed to sell all the goods they were now producing. So they encouraged customers to buy on the **installment plan.** This was a form of borrowing. Customers could make low payments over a period of time. That way people could afford to buy more. Banks provided money at low *interest rates.* Advertising also pushed the idea of buying on credit. Average Americans were spending more money than they actually had.

2. Describe two economic problems hidden by the business boom of the 1920s.

_____

_____

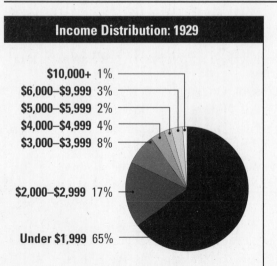

Income Distribution: 1929

$10,000+ 1%
$6,000–$9,999 3%
$5,000–$5,999 2%
$4,000–$4,999 4%
$3,000–$3,999 8%

$2,000–$2,999 17%

Under $1,999 65%

Source: *Historical Statistics of the United States: Colonial Times to 1970.*

Skillbuilder

Use the chart to answer these questions.

1. What percentage of Americans earned more than $5000 in 1929?

_____

_____

2. How much money did most Americans earn in 1929?

_____

_____

Glossary | CHAPTER 12 Politics of the Roaring Twenties

abuses of power Efforts by officials to use their offices in corrupt ways

bribes Money or property given to an official in order to get that person to do something dishonest or illegal

capitalism An economic system based on private ownership of property

consumer debt Money people owe to banks or stores for goods they have purchased

cost of living The average cost of the basic necessities of life

czar Emperor of Russia

disarm To reduce weapons

interest rate The charge for a loan

living wage Wage needed to keep a person or family out of poverty

national debt The money the government owes from borrowing or issuing bonds

national income The total amount of money earned by individuals and businesses in one nation

psychology Study of the way people think

radicals People in favor of revolutionary change

reparations Payments to make up for damages

running mate The candidate running for a lower political office on the same ticket with another candidate of the same party

socialists People who believe in an economic system based on government control over the economy and on equal distribution of wealth

standard of living A level of comfort measured by the things people could afford to buy

status symbol Something that shows that its owner is a person of high rank

suburbs The residential area around a major city

AFTER YOU READ

Terms and Names

A. Write the letter of the name or term next to the description that explains it best.

a. A. Mitchell Palmer
b. Calvin Coolidge
c. John L. Lewis
d. Sacco and Vanzetti
e. Warren G. Harding

_____ **1.** This president of the United Mine Workers led a successful strike.

_____ **2.** These radicals were executed for murder, probably as a result of the Red Scare.

_____ **3.** This President of the United States suffered from scandal.

_____ **4.** This attorney general sent agents to arrest communists and other radicals.

_____ **5.** This American president said, "The business of America is business."

B. Write the name or term that best completes each sentence.

Fordney-McCumber Tariff   quota system   Kellogg-Briand Pact   communism   installment plan

1. Congress passed the _____ to protect American business, but it prevented Britain and France from selling their products in the United States.

2. During the 1920s, many Americans feared _____, an economic and political system based on state ownership of property.

3. People who couldn't afford to pay the whole price of a car could buy it on the _____ and make small payments over time.

4. Fear of foreign influences and racism led to a _____ that limited immigration from Eastern and Southern Europe.

5. Nations that signed the _____._____ agreed not to use war as part of their national policy.

AFTER YOU READ (cont.) *CHAPTER 12* **Politics of the Roaring Twenties**

Main Ideas

1. How did the Sacco and Vanzetti case reflect the fears of many Americans?

_____

_____

2. Why were strikes risky for workers in the 1920s?

_____

_____

3. What was the main goal of the quota system?

_____

_____

4. Who was most closely linked to the Teapot Dome scandal?

_____

_____

5. What new methods did advertisers use in the 1920s?

_____

_____

Thinking Critically

Answer the following questions on a separate sheet of paper.

1. How are isolationism and nativism related? In the 1920s, what actions did Americans take that reveal their distrust of others?

2. What were signs of American business success in the 1920s? What were some signs that the economic situation might not be as good as it seemed?

Name _____ Date _____

Changing Ways of Life

TERMS AND NAMES

speakeasy Hidden saloons and nightclubs that illegally sold liquor

bootlegger Smugglers who brought alcohol in from Canada and the Caribbean

fundamentalism Religious movement based on the belief that everything written in the Bible was literally true

Clarence Darrow Famous trial lawyer

Scopes trial Trial of John Scopes for teaching evolution

BEFORE YOU READ

In the last section, you learned about American business in the 1920s.

In this section, you will read about new lifestyles and values that emerged in the 1920s.

AS YOU READ

Make a chart like the one below and fill it in. Take notes on the effects of Americans moving from rural areas to the cities.

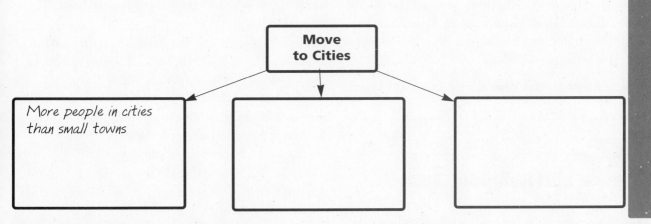

Move to Cities

More people in cities than small towns

Rural and Urban Differences

(pages 452–456)

What was Prohibition?

The 1920 *census* showed a change in America. For the first time, more Americans lived in large towns and cities than in small towns and on farms.

The values that most Americans had grown up with were small-town values. They included conservative social standards, hard work, thriftiness, and close families. People knew their neighbors and followed the teachings of their churches.

By the 1920s, *urbanization*, or the movement of Americans from rural areas to the cities, had increased. New York, Chicago, and Philadelphia had become huge cities. There were over 65 cities with more than 100,000 people. Two million people

a year left their farms and small towns for the cities.

Urban values began to dominate the nation. Life in big cities was different from in small towns. People with different backgrounds came into contact with one another.

City people were more open to new ideas in art, science, and politics. They went out at night. They were more tolerant of drinking and gambling. Life was fast-paced. Sometimes it was impersonal and lonely. Many people who were new to city life found it hard to adjust.

One clash between small-town values and city values occurred over *Prohibition*. Prohibition was the ban on alcoholic beverages set forth in the Eighteenth Amendment. It took effect in 1920. Most support for Prohibition came from religious rural white Protestants.

Even though it was the law, the effort to stop drinking was doomed. The government did not have enough officers to enforce it. People made their own alcohol illegally.

In cities, even respectable middle-class people flocked to **speakeasies.** These were hidden saloons and nightclubs that served liquor illegally.

People also bought liquor from **bootleggers,** or smugglers who brought it in from Canada and the Caribbean. Bootleggers created a chain of corruption by bribing police officers and judges.

Prohibition caused a general disrespect for the law. It also caused a great deal of money to flow out of lawful businesses and into organized crime. Underworld gangs took control of the illegal liquor business. The most famous gang was headed by Chicago's Al Capone. Chicago became known for bloody gang killings.

This rise in crime and violence led many people to demand the repeal of Prohibition. By the middle of the decade, only 19 percent of Americans supported it. Prohibition was repealed by the Twenty-first Amendment in 1933.

1. How did Prohibition affect the nation?

_____

_____

Science and Religion Clash

(pages 456–457)

What was the Scopes Trial?

During the 1920s, the nation saw the rise of Christian **fundamentalism.** This religious movement was based on the belief that everything written in the Bible was literally true, or true in all the details. Fundamentalists rejected the growing trust in science that most Americans had. They were also against the religious faiths of other people, especially immigrants.

These beliefs led fundamentalists to reject Charles Darwin's *theory of evolution.* According to that theory, plant and animal species had developed over millions of years.

Fundamentalists believed that the Bible was correct in stating that the world and all its plants and animals were created by God in six days. They did not want evolution taught in schools.

Fundamentalist preachers drew large crowds to religious revivals, especially in the South and West. Fundamentalists also gained political power. In 1925, Tennessee passed a law making it a crime to teach evolution.

Many people opposed this law. The American Civil Liberties Union (ACLU) promised to defend in court any teacher who would challenge the law.

John Scopes, a young biology teacher from Dayton, Tennessee, challenged the law. He openly taught about evolution. He was arrested, and his case went to trial. The ACLU hired **Clarence Darrow,** the most famous trial lawyer in the nation, to defend Scopes. William Jennings Bryan was the prosecutor.

Scopes was guilty because he broke the law. But the trial was really about evolution. It was also about religion in schools. Reporters came from all over the world to cover the **Scopes trial.** Huge crowds gathered.

The highlight of the trial was when William Jennings Bryan took the stand. Darrow questioned Bryan until Bryan said that while the earth was made in six days, they were "not six days of 24 hours." Bryan was admitting that the Bible could be interpreted in different ways.

Even so, Scopes was found guilty. His conviction was later overturned by the state Supreme Court. But the ban on teaching evolution remained a law in Tennessee.

2. How did fundamentalist beliefs lead to the Scopes trial?

_____

_____

CHAPTER 13 Section 2 (pages 458–461)

The Twenties Woman

TERMS AND NAMES

flapper Young woman who embraced the new fashions and values of the 1920s

double standard Set of principles granting one group more freedom than another group

BEFORE YOU READ

In the last section, you read about some lifestyle changes in the 1920s.

In this section, you will learn how women's lives changed during the 1920s.

AS YOU READ

Use the web below to take notes on the changes women experienced in the 1920s.

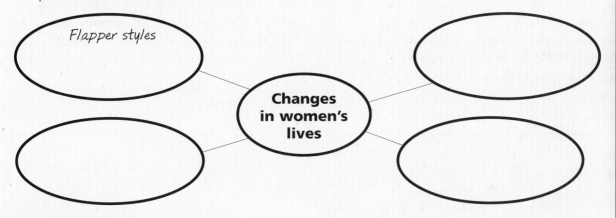

Young Women Change the Rules (pages 458–459)

What was a flapper?

In some ways, the spirit of the twenties was a reaction to World War I. Many young soldiers had witnessed horrible events in Europe. This led them to rebel against traditional values. They wanted to enjoy life while they could.

Young women also wanted to take part in the rebellious, pleasure-loving life of the twenties. Many of them demanded the same freedom as men.

The new urban culture also influenced many women. Their symbol was the **flapper.** She was an *emancipated* young woman. She held new independent attitudes and liked the sophisticated new fashions of the day.

She wore make-up, short skirts, short hair, and more jewelry than would have been proper only a few years before. She often smoked cigarettes and drank alcohol in public. She went dancing to new, exciting music.

Other attitudes changed, too. Many young men and women began to see marriage as more of an equal partnership.

At the same time, churches and schools protested the new values. The majority of women were not flappers. Many people felt torn between the old values and the new ones.

One result of this clash between old values and the image of the flapper was the **double standard.** This was a set of principles or values generally accepted by society. One American double standard allowed men to have greater sexual freedom than women. Women still had to observe stricter standards of behavior than men did.

1. How did the flapper represent the spirit of the twenties?

_____

_____

_____

Women Shed Old Roles at Home and at Work (pages 460–461)

How did women's roles change?

Many women had gone to work outside the home during World War I. This trend continued in the twenties. But their opportunities had changed after the war. Men returned from the war and took back traditional "men's jobs." Women moved back into the "women's professions" of teaching, nursing, and social work.

Big business provided another role for women: clerical work. Millions of women became secretaries. Many others became salesclerks in stores. Many women also worked on *assembly lines* in factories. By 1930, 10 million women had paid jobs outside the home. This was almost one-fourth of the American work force.

Women did not find equality in the workplace. Few women rose to jobs in management. Women earned less than men. Men regarded women as temporary workers whose real job was at home keeping house and raising children. In the twenties, patterns of *discrimination* against women in the business world continued.

Family life changed, too. Families had fewer children. Electrical appliances made housework easier. Many items that had been made at home—from clothing to bread—could now be bought ready-made in stores.

Public agencies took over some family responsibilities, too. They provided services for the elderly and the sick. Nevertheless, most women remained homemakers. Some women had to work and also run their homes. It was hard for them to combine these roles.

In the 1920s, marriages were more often based on romantic love than arranged by families. Children were no longer part of the work force. They spent their days in school and other activities with their peers, or people of their own age. *Peer pressure* began to be an important influence on teens' behavior. This reflected the conflict between traditional attitudes and modern ways of thinking.

2. Describe two changes in women's roles in the workplace.

_____

_____

_____

_____

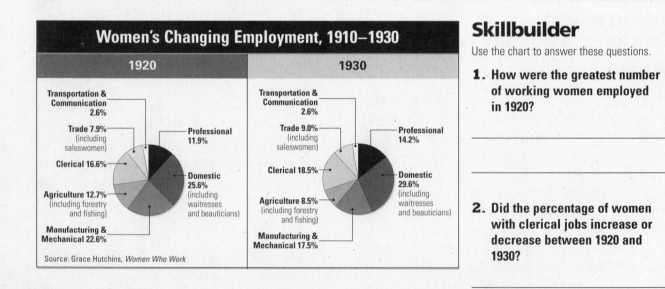

Women's Changing Employment, 1910–1930

1920

Transportation & Communication 2.6%
Trade 7.9% (including saleswomen)
Clerical 16.6%
Agriculture 12.7% (including forestry and fishing)
Manufacturing & Mechanical 22.6%
Professional 11.9%
Domestic 25.6% (including waitresses and beauticians)

1930

Transportation & Communication 2.6%
Trade 9.0% (including saleswomen)
Clerical 18.5%
Agriculture 8.5% (including forestry and fishing)
Manufacturing & Mechanical 17.5%
Professional 14.2%
Domestic 29.6% (including waitresses and beauticians)

Source: Grace Hutchins, *Women Who Work*

Skillbuilder

Use the chart to answer these questions.

1. How were the greatest number of working women employed in 1920?

_____

_____

2. Did the percentage of women with clerical jobs increase or decrease between 1920 and 1930?

_____

_____

CHAPTER 13 Section 3 (pages 464–469)

Education and Popular Culture

TERMS AND NAMES

Babe Ruth Star baseball player

Gertrude Ederle First woman to swim the English Channel

Charles A. Lindbergh First person to fly solo across the Atlantic

George Gershwin Composer

Georgia O'Keeffe Artist

Sinclair Lewis Novelist

F. Scott Fitzgerald Novelist

Edna St. Vincent Millay Poet

Ernest Hemingway Novelist

BEFORE YOU READ

In the last section, you learned about women in the 1920s.

In this section, you will read about education and popular culture during the 1920s.

AS YOU READ

Use the web below to take notes on the factors that helped create American popular culture in the 1920s.

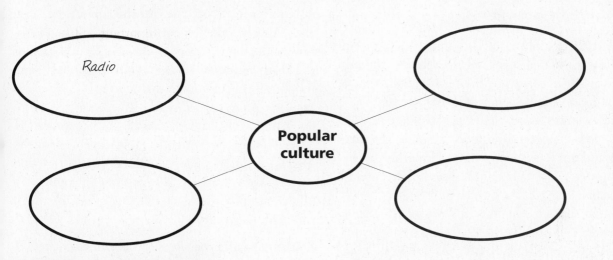

Schools and the Mass Media Shape Culture (pages 464–466)

How did popular culture change in America?

America was becoming more prosperous. Business and industry required a more educated work force. These two factors caused a huge increase in the number of students going to high school. In 1914, only 1 million American students went to high school after elementary school. In 1926, the number was 4 million.

Schools changed as they grew. Before the 1920s, high schools were mostly for students who were going on to college. In the twenties, high schools had a wide range of students. Schools offered vocational, or work-related, training for industrial jobs. It also offered home economics courses for future homemakers.

High schools also taught many children of immigrants. Many of these students did not speak English. Even so, the nation's schools were successful in teaching large numbers of Americans to read.

As a result of increased *literacy*, more people read newspapers than before. *Tabloid* newspapers with sensational stories became popular. But so did stories from big-city newspapers that now appeared all over the country.

National magazines were also popular. Some of them delivered the news. Other magazines published fiction and articles.

The most powerful of the *mass media* was radio. Radio networks with stations in many cities were formed in the twenties. The networks did research to find out what people wanted to hear—and gave it to them. Radio networks created something new in America: the shared national experience of hearing things as they happened. By 1930, 40 percent of American households had radios.

1. What was an effect of increased literacy in the United States?

_____

_____

America Chases New Heroes and Old Dreams (pages 466–469)

Who were the American heroes in the 1920s?

In the 1920s, Americans had more money and more free time than ever before. *Fads*, including puzzles and games, swept the nation. People also spent a great deal of money at sports events.

The twenties were called the Golden Age of Sports. Many talented athletes set new records. These athletes were portrayed as superheroes by the media. They became heroes to many Americans.

One of the most famous athletes of the 1920s was baseball's **Babe Ruth.** The Yankee slugger hit a record 60 home runs in 1927. There were great African-American baseball players too, such as Satchel Paige and Josh Gibson.

Americans also followed boxing, college football, tennis, and golf. **Gertrude Ederle** became famous as the first women to swim across the *English Channel.*

Charles A. Lindbergh thrilled the nation by becoming the first person to fly solo across the Atlantic Ocean.

By 1925, movie-making was the nation's fourth-largest industry. Hollywood was America's movie capital. It produced silent films with such stars as Charlie Chaplin, Clara Bow, and Rudolph Valentino.

In 1927, *The Jazz Singer* appeared. It was the first motion picture with sound. "Talkies" made the movies even more popular. Movies, like magazines and radio, helped create a national culture.

Many artists contributed to a flowering of American culture. Playwright Eugene O'Neill won a Nobel Prize for his plays. Composers **George Gershwin** and Aaron Copland wrote music that combined popular American music with classical forms.

American painters recorded the America they saw and felt. Edward Hopper painted the loneliness of American life. **Georgia O'Keeffe** showed the grandeur of New York City. She later became famous for her paintings of the Southwest.

Many gifted American writers criticized American society. **Sinclair Lewis** was the first American to win a Nobel Prize for Literature. His novels *Main Street* and *Babbitt* made fun of middle-class America's *conformity* and *materialism.*

Novelist **F. Scott Fitzgerald** coined the term "Jazz Age" to describe the twenties. His books showed the negative side of the age. But the poems of **Edna Vincent Millay** celebrated youth and freedom from traditional restrictions.

Some Americans disliked American culture so much they went to live abroad. Many gathered in Paris. The writer Gertrude Stein called them the Lost Generation. They included Fitzgerald and **Ernest Hemingway.** Hemingway introduced a tough, simple style of writing that changed American literature.

2. Describe the accomplishments of two American heroes in the twenties.

_____

_____

The Harlem Renaissance

BEFORE YOU READ

In the last section, you read about popular culture in the 1920s.

In this section, you will learn about the Harlem Renaissance.

AS YOU READ

Use the chart below to take notes on how African-American artists expressed themselves in the 1920s.

TERMS AND NAMES

Zora Neale Hurston Anthropologist and author

James Weldon Johnson Poet and civil rights leader

Marcus Garvey Black nationalist leader

Harlem Renaissance African-American artistic movement

Claude McKay Poet

Langston Hughes Poet

Paul Robeson Athlete, singer, and civil-rights leader

Louis Armstrong Jazz musician

Duke Ellington Jazz musician

Bessie Smith Blues singer

James Weldon Johnson	Author, lawyer, led antilynching effort

African-American Voices in the 1920s (pages 470–472)

How did African-Americans approach civil rights in the 1920s?

Between 1910 and 1920, hundreds of thousands of African Americans had moved from the South to the big cities of the North. This was called the *Great Migration.* It was a response to racial violence and economic discrimination against blacks in the South. By 1929, 40 percent of African Americans lived in cities. As a result, racial tensions increased in Northern cities. There were race riots.

The National Association for the Advancement of Colored People (NAACP) worked to end violence against African Americans. W. E. B. Du Bois led a peaceful protest against racial violence.

The NAACP also fought to get laws against *lynching* passed by Congress. **James Weldon Johnson,** a poet and lawyer, led that fight. While no law against lynching was passed in the twenties, the number of lynchings gradually dropped.

Marcus Garvey voiced a message of black pride that appealed to many African Americans. Garvey thought that African Americans should build a separate society. He formed a black nationalist group called the Universal Negro Improvement Association (UNIA).

Garvey promoted black-owned businesses. He also urged African Americans to return to Africa to set up an independent nation.

1. How did the NAACP and Marcus Garvey's followers respond to racial discrimination?

The Harlem Renaissance Flowers in New York (pages 472–475)

What was the Harlem Renaissance?

In the 1920s, many African Americans moved to Harlem, a section of New York City. So did blacks from the West Indies, Cuba, Puerto Rico, and Haiti. Harlem became the world's largest black urban community.

This neighborhood was also the birthplace of the **Harlem Renaissance.** This literary and artistic movement celebrated African-American culture.

Above all, the Harlem Renaissance was a literary movement. It was led by well-educated middle-class blacks. They took pride in their African heritage and their people's *folklore*. They also wrote about the problems of being black in a white culture. An important collection of works by Harlem Renaissance writers, *The New Negro*, was published by Alain Locke in 1925.

The Harlem Renaissance produced many outstanding poets, including Jean Toomer and Countee Cullen. **Claude McKay** wrote about the pain of prejudice. He urged African Americans to resist discrimination.

The most famous Harlem Renaissance poet was **Langston Hughes.** In the 1920s, he wrote about the daily lives of working-class blacks. He wove the tempos of jazz and the blues into his poems.

Zora Neale Hurston was the most famous female writer of the Harlem Renaissance. She collected the folklore of poor Southern blacks. Hurston also wrote novels, short stories, and poems.

Music and drama were important parts of the Harlem Renaissance, too. Some African-American performers became popular with white audiences. **Paul Robeson** became an important actor and singer. In 1924 he starred in Eugene O'Neill's play *The Emperor Jones* and in Shakespeare's *Othello*.

Jazz became more popular in the twenties. Early in the 20th century, musicians in New Orleans blended ragtime and blues into the new sound of jazz. Musicians from New Orleans traveled North, and they brought jazz with them. The most important and influential jazz musician was **Louis Armstrong.**

Many whites came to Harlem to hear jazz in night clubs. Edward Kennedy **"Duke" Ellington** led an orchestra there. He was a jazz pianist and one of the nation's greatest composers.

The outstanding singer of the time was **Bessie Smith.** Some black musicians chose to live and perform in Europe. Josephine Baker became a famous dancer, singer, and comedy star in Paris.

2. Describe the contributions of one artist of the Harlem Renaissance.

This photo shows Louis Armstrong with King Oliver's Creole Jazz Band in the 1920s. Credit: Culver Pictures

Skillbuilder

1. What does this photograph of Louis Armstrong's band tell you about the 1920s?

2. How do pictures of popular bands today compare with this picture?

Glossary   *CHAPTER 13* The Roaring Life of the 1920s

assembly line An arrangement of workers and machines in which a product is put together as it passes from one worker to another

census An official, government count of citizens, including where they live

conformity Being like everyone else

discrimination The act of limiting the opportunities of a certain group

emancipated Freed from restraint or from limits on thought and behavior

English Channel Narrow body of water between Britain and France

fad A fashion that is very popular for a short period of time

folklore The traditional myths and tales of a people

Great Migration Movement of African Americans from the South to the North in the early 20th century

literacy The ability to read and write

lynching An execution without due process of law, especially a hanging by a mob

mass media Means of communication that reach a large audience

materialism Placing great value on money and possessions

peer pressure The influence of a person's friends to be like everyone else

Prohibition Outlawing of alcoholic beverages

tabloid A small newspaper that often focuses on sensational stories

urbanization The movement of Americans from rural areas to cities

theory of evolution The theory that modern plant and animal life developed slowly over millions of years

AFTER YOU READ

A. Write the name or term in each blank that best completes the meaning of the paragraph.

Babe Ruth
Duke Ellington
speakeasy
flapper
bootlegger

What was life like in the twenties? On a Saturday night in a big city, a young woman might stand in front of her mirror admiring her new short hairstyle and new short dress. This **1**_____ might then go out on a date with a young man. They might go to a **2**_____ where they could drink illegal liquor. (The liquor was probably bought from a **3**_____ who smuggled it into the country.) And they might go to the Cotton Club in Harlem to listen to the jazz orchestra of **4**_____. Perhaps on a second date they might plan to go to a Yankee game to see **5**_____ hit a home run. Or they might decide to listen to the game on the radio.

B. Write the letter of the name or term next to the description that explains it best.

a. Harlem Renaissance
b. fundamentalism
c. Scopes trial
d. Marcus Garvey
e. James Weldon Johnson

_____ **1.** A Tennessee court case about teaching evolution in the public schools

_____ **2.** An African-American literary and artistic movement of the 1920s

_____ **3.** A religious movement based on the belief that everything in the Bible is literally true

_____ **4.** An African-American leader who promoted black pride and black nationalism

_____ **5.** A leader of the NAACP who worked for anti-lynching laws

AFTER YOU READ (continued) *CHAPTER 13* The Roaring Life of the 1920s

Main Ideas

1. Name two consequences of the Scopes trial.

_____

_____

2. What did the typical flapper look like?

_____

_____

3. Describe three heroes of the 1920s.

_____

_____

4. What caused the Great Migration?

_____

_____

5. What was the Harlem Renaissance?

_____

_____

Thinking Critically

Answer the following questions on a separate piece of paper.

1. How did the 1920s change the lives and expectations of women and African Americans?

2. The 1920s included changes in values, lifestyles, and popular culture. How did some people try to hold onto older, more conservative values?

The Nation's Sick Economy

BEFORE YOU READ

In the last section, you learned about the issues African Americans faced in the 1920s.

In this section, you will read about the economic problems that led to the Great Depression.

AS YOU READ

Use the chart below to take notes about the economic situation each group faced in the late 1920s.

<table>
<tr><td>**Farmers**</td><td>*Income declined*</td></tr>
<tr><td>**Industry**</td><td></td></tr>
<tr><td>**Consumers**</td><td></td></tr>
</table>

TERMS AND NAMES

price support Law that keeps prices above a set level

credit Short-term loans to buy goods with promises to pay later

Alfred E. Smith Democratic presidential candidate in 1928

speculation Investments in high-risk ventures

buying on margin Buying stock by paying only a portion of the full cost up-front with promises to pay the rest later

Black Tuesday October 29, 1929, the day the stock market crashed

Great Depression Period of bad economic times in the United States that lasted from 1929 to 1941

Dow Jones Industrial Average Index of stock prices of select companies

Hawley-Smoot Tariff Act Law that raised taxes on imports and worsened the Depression

Economic Troubles on the Horizon (pages 482–484)

Why was the nation's economy sick in the late 1920s?

During the 1920s, the economy boomed. But there were economic problems under the surface. Industries, such as clothing, steel-making, and mining, were hardly making a profit.

Many industries had been successful in the early 1920s. But by the late 1920s, they were losing money. These industries included auto manufacturing, construction, and consumer goods.

The biggest problems were in farming. After the war, the demand for food dropped and farmers suffered. Farmers' incomes went down. Many could not make the *mortgage* payments on their farms. As a result, many farmers lost their land.

Congress tried to help farmers by passing **price supports.** With price supports, the government would not allow food prices to fall below a certain level. But Calvin Coolidge vetoed the bill. Farmers' incomes continued to drop.

Consumer spending declined for several reasons:
• Farmers had less money to spend.
• Many consumers were paying off their debts. During the 1920s, they had spent more money than they earned. They did this by buying goods on **credit,** promising to pay for them later.
• People's wages went up more slowly than the price of goods. This meant they could not afford to buy all the things they wanted.

At the time of the 1928 presidential election,

most voters were not aware of these economic problems. The Republican candidate, Herbert Hoover, talked about the years of prosperity under Republican presidents Harding and Coolidge. He won easily over the Democratic candidate, **Alfred E. Smith.**

1. What problems did farmers face in the 1920s?

The Stock Market Comes Tumbling Down (pages 485–488)

What caused the Great Depression?

Many Americans were having money problems. Even so, prices of stocks on the stock market continued to go up. People bought stocks in the hope of becoming rich. Some tried **speculation,** making risky investments in the hope of quick profits.

Because they were sure that stock prices would continue to rise quickly, many people were **buying on margin.** This meant that they borrowed most of the money to buy the stock.

But there was a major problem with buying on margin. If the person had to sell the stock at a lower price, he or she might not be able to pay off the loan. So if stock prices fell, there would be big economic trouble.

Stock prices did begin to fall in September 1929. On Tuesday, October 29, 1929, prices fell so sharply that people said the stock market had "crashed." That day became known as **Black Tuesday.**

People panicked and tried to sell their stocks quickly. But sometimes no one else was willing to buy them.

The great stock market crash of 1929 marked the beginning of the **Great Depression.** This period of bad economic times when many people were out of work lasted from 1929 to 1941.

The stock market crash did not cause the Depression, but it did make it worse. Among the main causes of the Depression were:

- out-of-date equipment in many industries;
- the economic problems of farmers;
- the overuse of credit;

- too few people had too much of the nation's wealth, leaving many other people poor.

Americans could hardly believe that there would be an economic disaster in the United States. President Hoover told the American people that the economy would recover on its own. But the **Dow Jones Industrial Average**—the average price of several representative stocks—continued to drop.

2. Why was the stock market crash of 1929 important?

Financial Collapse (pages 488–489)

How did the stock market crash affect businesses?

After the stock market crashed, many people panicked and took their money out of banks. Many banks were forced to close. When the banks failed, other depositors lost the savings they had in the banks.

Businesses also began to close. Millions of Americans lost their jobs. Workers who kept their jobs experienced pay cuts or reduced hours.

The Depression spread around the world. Germany was still paying war reparations. Other European countries were struggling with debts from the war. With Americans unable to buy their goods now, European economies suffered even more.

The situation became worse when Congress passed the **Hawley-Smoot Tariff Act.** Congress hoped that higher tariffs would push Americans to buy goods made in the United States. The result would be to help American industry. Instead, when the United States charged more to bring goods in, imports from Europe declined. Then Europeans had even less money to spend on U.S. goods, and American industry suffered.

3. Why did many banks fail after the stock market crashed?

CHAPTER 14 Section 2 (pages 490–494)

Hardship and Suffering During the Depression

BEFORE YOU READ

In the last section, you learned about the start of the Great Depression.

In this section, you will read about the hardships caused by the Depression.

AS YOU READ

Use the web below to take notes about the problems people faced during the Depression.

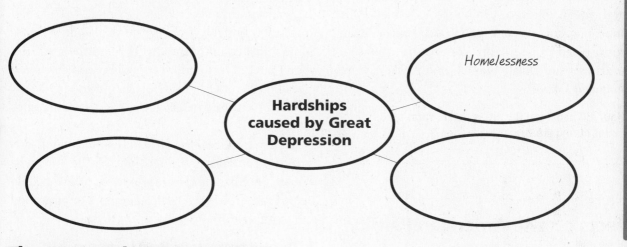

TERMS AND NAMES

Dust Bowl Area of the Great Plains made worthless for farming by drought and dust storms in the 1930s

shantytown A neighborhood where people live in shacks

soup kitchen Place where free food is served to the needy

bread line A line of people waiting for free food

direct relief Money or food given directly from the government to the needy

The Depression Devastates People's Lives (pages 490–492)

How did the Depression affect people in cities and on farms?

The Depression brought suffering and hardship to many Americans. The hard economic times ruined many lives. Millions of people lost their jobs. Some went hungry or became homeless. Those who could not meet their housing payments were thrown out of their homes.

Cities across the country were full of these homeless people. Some slept in parks and wrapped themselves up in newspapers to keep warm. Others built **shantytowns,** where they lived in little shacks they made out of scrap material. Those who could not afford to buy food stood in **bread lines** to receive free food. Some ate in **soup kitchens,** where charities served meals to the needy.

African Americans and *Latino Americans* who lived in the cities had a very hard time. They had a higher unemployment rate than whites. If they did have work, they were paid less than white workers.

There was even violence directed against African Americans and Latinos. Angry whites who had lost their jobs did not want to compete against these minority groups for the few jobs that were left. They sometimes attacked African Americans. They demanded that Latino Americans be sent back to the countries they came from.

The Depression hurt people in rural areas, too. Food prices continued to go down as the Depression deepened. Farmers earned less and less. Many farm families could not meet their mortgage payments. More and more of them lost their farms. From 1929 to 1932, about 400,000 farmers lost their land.

To make matters worse, a long *drought* hit *the Great Plains*. There was little rain from Texas to North Dakota. Much of this area had been grassland that farmers broke up with their plows in order to grow crops.

The soil was now *exhausted* from over-farming. The grass that had once held the soil in place was gone. When powerful winds swept across the Great Plains, the soil simply blew away. This dry area of blowing soil was called the **Dust Bowl.** Huge dust storms covered the plains and blew dust as far away as the East Coast.

The southern plains—from western Kansas to northern Texas—were hit the hardest. Many Oklahoma farmers packed up their belongings and started for California to look for work. They became migrant workers, people who move from place to place to pick crops. Because so many of them came from Oklahoma, migrant workers were often called Okies.

1. How did people in the cities and in rural areas suffer during the Great Depression?

_____

_____

Effects on the American Family
(pages 492–494)

How did the Depression affect families?

The Depression put a heavy strain on family life. Many families pulled together during the hard times. They shared what they earned. Instead of going out for entertainment, parents and children often stayed home. They played board games or listened to the radio.

But some families broke apart under the strain of poverty and unemployment. Many men felt ashamed because they had lost their jobs. Some of them simply left their families. There were large numbers of men wandering the country looking for work.

Women tried to find work, too. But they were usually paid less than men. Many people complained that employers should not hire women. They thought that men should have the jobs instead. These people argued that men were the ones who supported families, so it was more important for them to have jobs.

Children suffered terribly from poverty and the break-up of families. Many children had poor *diets* and no health care. Their parents could not afford to buy healthy food or to pay doctor bills. Many children became sick because of a lack of vitamins.

During the early years of the Great Depression, the federal government did not give **direct relief**—cash or food directly to poor people. Charities and some city governments struggled to help. But they could not provide enough relief to keep people out of poverty.

Because so many people were out of work, cities and states collected less tax money. They had to cut their budgets for programs like child welfare. Some cities could not afford to keep their schools open for a full term. Many school boards shortened the school year. Other schools simply closed. Many children went to work to try to help their families survive.

While the Great Depression caused much suffering, it sometimes brought out the best in individuals, families, and communities. Many people shared resources with their neighbors or gave food and clothing to the needy.

2. Describe two ways the Great Depression affected families.

_____

_____

CHAPTER 14 Section 3 (pages 495–499)

Hoover Struggles with the Depression

TERMS AND NAMES

Herbert Hoover 31st president

Boulder Dam Dam on the Colorado River built during the Depression to create jobs

Federal Home Loan Bank Act Law passed in 1931 to reduce mortgage rates to save farmers from foreclosure

Reconstruction Finance Corporation Agency established in 1932 to provide emergency relief to large businesses, insurance companies, and banks

Bonus Army Unemployed World War I veterans who marched to Washington to demand their war bonuses

BEFORE YOU READ

In the last section, you read about how the Depression affected common people.

In this section, you will learn how President Hoover tried to stop the Depression.

AS YOU READ

Use the chart below to take notes about the actions President Hoover took to end the Depression.

ACTIONS	
Boulder Dam	Public works project to put people to work

Hoover Tries to Reassure the Nation (pages 495–497)

What did Hoover think the government should do?

Economic slowdowns occur regularly. Over time, economies go through cycles. There are times of economic growth and prosperity. They are followed by slumps when the economy slows down. In the 1930s, many experts believed that it was best not to interfere with these *economic cycles*. They argued that slumps would end on their own and good times would return.

At first, President **Herbert Hoover** believed that the Great Depression was just another slow-down that would end on its own. His advisors thought that it was best to do nothing. The economy would heal itself. Hoover believed the government should take some action. But he also believed

that government should be careful not to take too much power.

According to Hoover, there were two important things government should do. He believed that government should help different groups work together to improve the economy. For example, Hoover thought government should help managers and workers find solutions to their problems. But he did not think government should decide on the solution.

Hoover also believed that the government should encourage private groups to help the needy. He thought that charities—not government—should give food and shelter to people who were poor or out of work. Hoover felt that government could guide these private relief efforts. But he did not think government should give direct aid to poor people.

Hoover met with bankers, businessmen, and

labor leaders. He urged them to work together to help improve the economy. He asked employers not to fire workers or to lower their pay. He asked labor leaders not to ask for higher pay or to strike.

Ordinary people became more frustrated with the situation. Some farmers threw away food or stopped growing it rather than sell it a low price. People called the shantytowns "Hoovervilles."

1. What did Hoover think government should do in bad economic times?

_____

_____

Hoover Takes Action (pages 497–499)

What did Hoover do?

Hoover stuck to his principles. He did not offer direct aid to the poor. But he did worry about the suffering of large numbers of the American people. He took some steps to use the government to improve the economy.

One important step was a program of major *public works*. These included projects to build roads, bridges, and dams. These projects were funded by the government. They provided jobs to many unemployed workers. One important public-works project was **Boulder Dam.**

Another program tried to raise the prices farmers received for their crops. Hoover also urged bankers to join a credit organization. It gave loans to banks that were in danger of failing.

By 1932, the economy had not improved. Congress passed the **Federal Home Loan Bank Act.** This law lowered mortgage rates. Congress hoped that low mortgage rates would help farmers change the terms of their mortgages. This would help protect their farms from *foreclosure*.

Hoover also created the **Reconstruction Finance Corporation.** The RFC provided money for projects to create jobs.

Hoover became less popular with the public. His popularity fell even more in 1932 when World War I veterans came to the *capital*. These veterans had been promised bonuses to make up for their poor wartime pay. Congress was about to vote on a bill to give the veterans their bonuses so they wouldn't have to wait for their money.

Thousands of veterans and their families came to Washington. This so-called **Bonus Army** set up tents to live in near the *Capitol* building. At first, Hoover helped the veterans by sending them food. But after the bonus was voted down in Congress, Hoover told the veterans to leave. About 2,000 stayed. Hoover ordered the army to remove them. The sight of U.S. Army troops using tear gas on American citizens outraged many people.

2. What actions did Hoover take to improve the economy?

_____

_____

_____

Skillbuilder

Use the cartoon to answer these questions.

1. What does this cartoon suggest most Americans felt about Hoover and the Depression?

_____

_____

2. Do you think that view of Hoover is justified?

_____

_____

In this cartoon, a circle of Americans all point their fingers at President Hoover. Credit: Reprinted from the Albany *Evening News,* June 7, 1931, with permission of the *Times Union,* Albany, New York

Glossary

capital The city of Washington, D.C., is the capital of the United States

Capitol The building in Washington, D.C., where Congress meets

diet The food people eat

drought A long period of unusually low rainfall

economic cycles Periods of good times, or prosperity, alternating with periods of economic hard times

exhausted Used up, worn out

foreclosure The taking of mortgaged property by the lender because the borrower cannot make the payments on the loan

the Great Plains A large flat area of the west-central United States originally covered by a type of grass that does not need much rain and that has strong roots which hold the soil in place

Latino Americans Americans whose families originally came from Spanish-speaking areas

mortgage The payments made to pay back the loan used to buy a house or land

public works Projects run by the government

AFTER YOU READ

Terms and Names

A. Fill in each blank with the letter of the name or term that best completes the paragraph.

a. bread lines

b. Bonus Army

c. Great Depression

d. shantytowns

e. soup kitchens

The **1**_____ was the worst economic crisis in U.S. history. People suffered terribly during it. Groups of homeless people built **2**_____ where they lived in shacks made of scrap metal. People who could not afford to buy food stood in **3**_____ to receive free meals in **4**_____ where charities provided meals for the needy. A group of World War I veterans called the **5**_____ marched to Washington to try to get their war bonuses immediately. But they were forced to leave the Capitol.

B. Write the letter of the term that best completes the sentence.

a. Black Tuesday

b. Dust Bowl

c. Hawley–Smoot Tariff Act

d. Herbert Hoover

e. price supports

1. On _____ stock prices fell so sharply that people said the stock market "crashed."

2. Congress passed the _____ that raised taxes on imports to help industry. Instead, it hurt American industry.

3. Farmers on the Great Plains faced a terrible drought that created the _____.

4. _____ believed that the government should do something to stop the Depression. But he did not want the government to take too much power.

5. Congress passed _____ to help protect farmers from falling prices.

AFTER YOU READ (continued) *CHAPTER 14* The Great Depression Begins

Main Ideas

1. Describe two weaknesses in the economy in the 1920s.

_____

_____

_____

2. How did the Hawley-Smoot Tariff affect the economy?

_____

_____

_____

3. How did the Depression create shantytowns, soup kitchens, and bread lines?

_____

_____

_____

4. What did Hoover do about the Bonus Army?

_____

_____

_____

5. How did Hoover try to use the government to end the Depression?

_____

_____

_____

Thinking Critically

Answer the following questions on a separate piece of paper.

1. Describe two causes and two effects of the Great Depression.

2. What did President Hoover do to end the Depression?

A New Deal Fights the Depression

BEFORE YOU READ

In the last section, you read about Herbert Hoover's reaction to the Great Depression.

In this section, you will learn about Franklin Delano Roosevelt's programs to fight the Depression.

AS YOU READ

Use the chart below to take notes on the problems Roosevelt faced at the beginning of his presidency and how he tried to solve them.

TERMS AND NAMES

Franklin Delano Roosevelt 32nd president

New Deal Franklin Roosevelt's programs to end the Depression

Glass-Steagall Banking Act of 1933 Law that created insurance for bank deposits

Federal Securities Act Law to regulate stock information

Agricultural Adjustment Act Programs to help farmers

Civilian Conservation Corps Program to employ young men in work projects

National Industrial Recovery Act Programs to help industry

Huey Long Political leader from Louisiana who criticized the New Deal

PROBLEM	SOLUTION
Bank failures	bank holiday Emergency Banking Relief Act

New Deal Actions (pages 504–506)

What were the goals of the New Deal?

By the end of 1932, Americans were ready for a change. Democratic candidate **Franklin Delano Roosevelt**—often called FDR—beat Hoover in the presidential election of 1932 by a landslide. Democrats also won large majorities in the House and Senate.

Roosevelt and his advisors planned programs to end the Depression. These programs became known as the **New Deal.** It had three goals: relief for the needy, economic recovery, and financial reform.

Congress quickly passed many important laws.

These laws expanded the federal government's role in the nation's economy.

Roosevelt declared a "bank holiday." He closed the banks to prevent more bank failures. Then Congress passed the Emergency Banking Relief Act, which allowed healthy banks to reopen. This restored public confidence in banks. So did the **Glass-Steagall Banking Act of 1933.** It established the Federal Deposit Insurance Corporation (FDIC), which protects the savings people put in banks. Congress also passed the **Federal Securities Act.** This law made companies give accurate information in its stock offerings. Later, Congress created the Securities and Exchange Commission (SEC) to *regulate* stock markets.

FDR spoke directly to the American people in

radio talks called "fireside chats." He explained the New Deal measures and asked for public support. These chats did a lot to restore the nation's confidence.

1. Describe the three goals of the New Deal.

_____

_____

Helping the American People
(pages 506–508)

Who did the New Deal help?

Roosevelt worked to help farmers and other workers. The **Agricultural Adjustment Act** (AAA) helped to raise crop prices by lowering production.

The New Deal included programs that gave relief through work projects and cash payments. The **Civilian Conservation Corps** (CCC) put young men to work building roads and planting trees. The Federal Emergency Relief Administration (FERA) provided direct relief of food, clothing, and cash to the needy.

The **National Industrial Recovery Act** (NIRA) set codes of fair practice for industries. It also guaranteed the workers' right to organize unions. The NIRA set up the National Recovery Administration (NRA) to stop the trend of wage cuts, falling prices, and *layoffs.*

Other New Deal programs helped promote regional development. The Tennessee Valley Authority (TVA) built dams in the Tennessee River valley. These projects created thousands of jobs, provided flood control, and brought electricity to the region.

2. How did the New Deal provide help to different groups of Americans?

_____

_____

The New Deal Comes Under Attack (pages 508–510)

Who criticized the New Deal?

The New Deal did much to restore public confidence. But some people criticized it. Some liberals said it did not do enough to help the poor. Conservative critics said it gave the federal government too much control over agriculture and business.

The Supreme Court found two important parts of the New Deal unconstitutional. The Court struck down the NIRA and the AAA. This upset Roosevelt. He proposed a bill to allow him to appoint more new Supreme Court justices.

Critics claimed that Roosevelt was trying to "pack the Court" with justices who supported him. Protest over this proposal cost Roosevelt support. But as justices resigned from the Court, Roosevelt was able to appoint seven new justices. Court decisions began to favor the New Deal.

Three critics of Roosevelt were particularly important. Father Charles Coughlin was a Roman Catholic priest. He used his popular radio sermons to criticize Roosevelt. His anti-Jewish views eventually cost him support.

Dr. Francis Townsend proposed a *pension plan* to give monthly payments to the elderly. Many elderly voters liked Townsend's plan.

The most serious challenge to the New Deal came from Senator **Huey Long** of Louisiana. He was an early supporter of the New Deal. But he wanted to become president himself. Long proposed a program called Share Our Wealth. In 1935, at the height of his popularity, Long was assassinated.

3. List two critics of the New Deal and describe their arguments.

_____

_____

CHAPTER 15 Section 2 (pages 511–516)

The Second New Deal Takes Hold

TERMS AND NAMES

Eleanor Roosevelt Wife of FDR

Works Progress Administration New Deal jobs program

National Youth Administration Program to provide aid and jobs to young people

Wagner Act Law to protect workers' rights

Social Security Act Program that provided aid to people with disabilities and pensions for retired workers

BEFORE YOU READ

In the last section, you read about the early days of the New Deal.

In this section, you will learn about the Second New Deal.

AS YOU READ

Use the web below to take notes on the major programs of the Second New Deal.

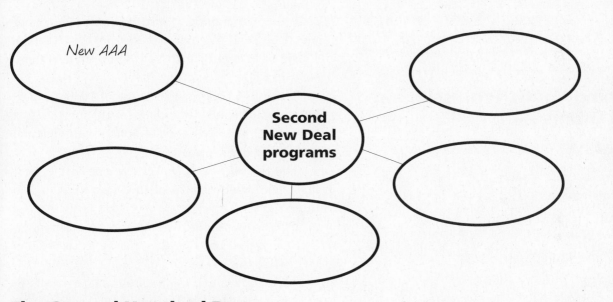

The Second Hundred Days
(pages 511–512)

What did voters think about the New Deal?

The economy improved in the first two years of Roosevelt's presidency. But it did not improve much. Still, the New Deal was very popular. Democrats increased their majority in Congress in the *midterm elections* of 1934.

FDR launched a second wave of reforms—sometimes called the Second New Deal. These were programs designed to help poor people. The president's wife, **Eleanor Roosevelt,** traveled around the country. She reported to the president

on the suffering of the poor. She spoke up for women and minorities.

The 1936 election was an overwhelming victory for Roosevelt, the Democrats, and the New Deal. It also marked the first time most African Americans voted Democratic. And it was the first time that labor unions supported a single candidate. They supported Roosevelt.

1. What did the elections of 1934 and 1936 tell about the New Deal?

_____

_____

_____

Helping Farmers (pages 512–513)

How did the Second New Deal help farmers?

Things were still tough for farmers in the mid 1930s. The first AAA had helped some farmers before it was struck down by the Supreme Court.

Now Congress passed new laws to replace the first AAA. One program paid farmers to use *soil conservation* measures in managing their land. The new AAA was passed without the tax that had made the first one unconstitutional.

Other laws helped sharecroppers and tenant farmers. They provided loans to help farmers buy land. New laws also helped migrant workers by providing better housing for them.

2. **What action did the Second New Deal take to help farmers?**

_____

_____

Helping Youth, Professionals, and Others (pages 513–514)

What were the WPA and NYA?

A new agency called the **Works Progress Administration** (WPA) set out to create jobs as quickly as possible. The WPA used millions of workers to build airports, roads, libraries, schools, and hospitals. Sewing groups made clothes for the needy.

Some people criticized the WPA as a **make-work program** that created useless jobs just to give people a paycheck. But the WPA created works of lasting value. And it gave working people a sense of hope and dignity along with their paychecks.

The WPA also employed teachers, writers, artists, actors, and musicians. And it made special efforts to help women, minorities, and the young.

The **National Youth Administration** (NYA) provided aid and part-time jobs to many high school and college students. This allowed them to get an education even in tough economic times.

3. **How did the WPA and NYA help people?**

_____

_____

Labor and Other Reforms
(pages 514–516)

How did the Second New Deal help workers?

The Second New Deal created important reforms for labor. Congress passed the National Labor Relations Act to replace the NIRA, which the Supreme Court struck down. This law is often called the **Wagner Act.**

The Wagner Act supported workers' right to *collective bargaining*. It also banned unfair labor practices. The Wagner Act set up the National Labor Relations Board (NLRB) to enforce these reforms.

The Fair Labor Standards Act of 1938 set maximum hours and a *minimum wage* for the first time. It set a workweek of 44 hours. It also banned child labor in factories.

The **Social Security Act** was one of the most important achievements of the New Deal. It had three parts:

- Old-age insurance—payments to elderly people based on what they paid into the system while they were working
- Unemployment compensation—payments to workers who lost their jobs
- Aid to the disabled and families with children—this helped people who could not be expected to work

The Second New Deal also extended electricity to rural areas through the Rural Electrification Administration (REA).

4. **How did the Second New Deal try to protect workers?**

_____

_____

The New Deal Affects Many Groups

TERMS AND NAMES

Frances Perkins Secretary of Labor

Mary McLeod Bethune Head of the Office of Minority Affairs in the NYA

John Collier Commissioner on Indian Affairs

New Deal Coalition Voters from different groups that supported the Democratic Party because of the New Deal

Congress of Industrial Organizations Labor union

BEFORE YOU READ

In the last section, you read about the Second New Deal.

In this section, you will learn about some of the effects of the New Deal.

AS YOU READ

Use the chart below to take notes on how the New Deal affected the groups listed in the chart.

GROUP	EFFECT OF NEW DEAL
women	First women in cabinet
African Americans	
Mexican Americans	
Native Americans	

New Opportunities for Women
(pages 517–518)

How did the New Deal affect women?

Women made some important gains during the New Deal. More women were appointed to important federal jobs.

Frances Perkins became the first female cabinet member. She was Secretary of Labor. Perkins helped create the Social Security system. Roosevelt also appointed women as federal judges. Roosevelt hoped that these appointments would make him more popular among women voters.

Many New Deal agencies did not discriminate in hiring. This gave women more opportunities. But some government agencies and many businesses did not hire as many women as men. For example, the Civilian Conservation Corps hired men only. And women were almost always paid less than men. For instance, the National Recovery Administration set lower wage levels for women than for men.

1. **Describe two ways that the New Deal expanded and limited opportunities for women.**

_____

_____

_____

New Opportunities for African Americans (pages 518–519)

How did the New Deal affect African Americans?

President Roosevelt gave a number of African Americans a voice in government. **Mary McLeod Bethune** was an educator who became head of the Minority Affairs Office of the National Youth Administration.

She worked to ensure that the NYA hired some African Americans. Bethune also helped organize the "Black Cabinet." This was a group of influential African Americans that advised Roosevelt on racial issues.

However, President Roosevelt did not push for full civil rights for African Americans. He was afraid of losing the support of white Southerners.

2. What gains did African Americans make during the New Deal?

_____

_____

Mexican-American Fortunes; Native American Gains (page 520)

What gains did Mexican Americans and Native Americans make?

Mexican Americans tended to support the New Deal. But they received few benefits from New Deal programs. Many were farm workers who were not covered by federal laws. Some New Deal agencies discriminated against them.

Native Americans got support from the New Deal. In 1933, Roosevelt made **John Collier** commissioner on Indian affairs. He was a strong supporter of Native American rights. Collier helped pass the Indian Reorganization Act. This law strengthened Native American land claims.

3. How did Mexican Americans and Native Americans fare under the New Deal?

_____

_____

A New Deal Coalition (pages 520–522)

Who supported the New Deal?

Roosevelt got votes from Southern whites, city people, African Americans, and workers who belonged to unions. Together these groups of voters formed a *coalition* that supported FDR. It became known as the **New Deal Coalition.**

Labor unions made gains in the 1930s. New Deal laws made it easier for workers to form unions and to bargain with employers. Union membership soared from 3 million to 8 million.

Divisions emerged between labor unions. The American Federation of Labor (AFL) was made up of mostly *crafts unions*, such as plumbers or carpenters. Other unions wanted to represent workers in a whole industry, such as the automobile industry. These unions broke away to form the **Congress of Industrial Organizations** (CIO).

Labor employed a new kind of strike in the 1930s—a sit-down strike. In a sit-down strike, workers did not leave their workplace. They remained inside but refused to work. That prevented factory owners from using strikebreakers or scabs to get the work done.

Some strikes led to violence. On Memorial Day, 1937, police killed ten people during a steel strike in Chicago. The National Labor Relations Board stepped in. It forced the steel company to negotiate with the union. This helped labor gain strength.

The Democratic Party got a great deal of support from people living in cities. Powerful city political organizations helped build this support. So did New Deal programs that helped the urban poor. Roosevelt also appealed to people of many ethnic groups. He appointed people of urban-immigrant backgrounds to important government jobs.

4. What was the New Deal Coalition?

_____

_____

CHAPTER 15 Section 4 (pages 523–528)

Society and Culture

TERMS AND NAMES

Gone with the Wind Popular movie

Orson Welles Actor, director, and filmmaker

Grant Wood Artist

Richard Wright Author

The Grapes of Wrath Novel by John Steinbeck

BEFORE YOU READ

In the last section, you learned about the New Deal Coalition.

In this section, you will learn about American culture during the Depression.

AS YOU READ

Use the chart below to take notes on radio, the movies, literature, and the arts during the Depression.

Movies	Popular escape inexpensive
Radio	
Literature	
Arts	

The Lure of Motion Pictures and Radio (pages 523–525)

What did Americans do for fun during the Depression?

The 1930s were a golden age for the radio and film industries in spite of the hard economic times. Movie tickets were not expensive. Movies provided an escape from the problems of Depression life. About two-thirds of Americans went to a movie once a week.

Hollywood studios made a wide variety of movies and created many new movie stars. Films starring the dancing partners Fred Astaire and Ginger Rogers portrayed a glamorous world of romance and good times.

Gone with the Wind with Clark Gable and Vivien Leigh was one of the most popular films of the 1930s. It showed a romantic version of the South during the Civil War. *The Wizard of Oz* starring Judy Garland also provided escape for Depression-era audiences. So did the wacky comedies of the Marx brothers.

Other kinds of films were popular during the Depression. Gangster films showed a dark, dangerous urban America. They featured "tough guy" characters. James Cagney and Edward G. Robinson became famous in these movies.

Frank Capra made a different type of movie. In his movies, honest, kind-hearted people won out over greedy people.

Radio showed the democratic spirit of the times. There were radios in nearly 90 percent of American homes. Most American families listened to their favorite radio shows together. The radio offered inexpensive entertainment. There were comedy and variety shows, news programs, soap operas, and children's shows. There were also excellent dramas and mysteries.

Radio made people like Bob Hope, Jack Benny, and George Burns and Gracie Allen stars long before they had success on television. In order to reach the greatest number of people, President Roosevelt went on the radio during his famous fireside chats.

The most famous radio broadcast was by **Orson Welles.** He was an actor, director, and filmmaker. His fictional radio show "The War of the Worlds" was so realistic that it convinced many Americans that Martians had landed in New Jersey. It showed the power of radio at a time when many Americans got their news that way.

1. What was the appeal of movies and radio during the Depression?

_____

_____

Art and Literature in Depression America (pages 525–528)

How did the New Deal help artists?

The art and literature of the Depression was more serious and sober than radio and movies. Many artists used realism to show the hardships of Depression life. Some criticized American society. Others praised the strength of character and the democratic values of the American people.

Some people believed that the government should not play any role in funding arts projects. But New Deal officials believed the arts were important for the nation. They created several programs to put artists to work.

The Federal Arts Project was part of the WPA. It paid artists to create posters, murals, and other works of art for public places. Artists such as Thomas Hart Benton and **Grant Wood** painted rural midwestern subjects. Wood's *American Gothic* is a famous portrait of a serious-looking man and woman standing in front of their farmhouse.

The Federal Theater Project was another part of the WPA. It helped support American playwrights. It also brought live drama to many communities around the country.

The Federal Writers' Project funded writers. Saul Bellow was one of these writers. He later won a Pulitzer Prize. **Richard Wright** was an African-American writer. He received financial help while writing *Native Son.* This novel shows the problems racism caused for a young African-American man.

John Steinbeck also got help from the FWP. His novel ***The Grapes of Wrath*** is one of the most famous books about the Depression. It shows the problems faced by Oklahoma farmers who were forced from their homes during the Dust Bowl. They became migrant workers. They made it to California, but their hardships continued.

Another famous book of the Depression was by the writer James Agee and the photographer Walker Evans. *Let Us Now Praise Famous Men* showed the dignity of Alabama sharecroppers in the face of hardship. The play *Our Town* by Thornton Wilder captured the warmth and beauty of small-town life. William Saroyan's play *The Time of Your Life* took a tender look at urban characters.

2. Describe two New Deal programs that supported the arts.

_____

_____

CHAPTER 15 Section 5 (pages 529–533)

The Impact of the New Deal

BEFORE YOU READ

In the last section, you learned about American culture during the Depression.

In this section, you will read about the legacy of the New Deal.

AS YOU READ

Use the chart below to take notes on the lasting effects of the New Deal.

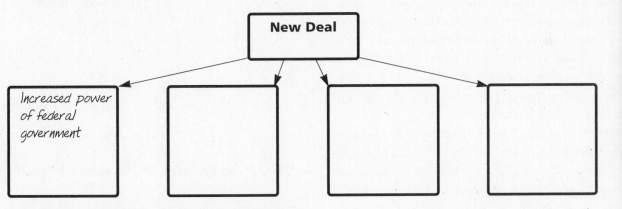

New Deal

Increased power of federal government

New Deal Reforms That Endure
(pages 529–532)

What do critics say about the New Deal?

By the end of the 1930s, the economy had improved somewhat. Industrial production had reached 1929 levels. Unemployment was still high. But it was much lower than during the worst days of the Depression. Congress urged Roosevelt to cut back on New Deal programs. Roosevelt did, and the economy slid back a bit. Still, Roosevelt did not start another phase of the New Deal.

One reason FDR did not launch another New Deal was that he did not want any more **deficit spending.** That is when the government spends more money than it takes in. Roosevelt was also more and more worried about events in Europe, particularly the rise of Hitler.

People still disagree over whether the New Deal was good or bad for the country. Conservative critics say that the New Deal made the government too big and too powerful. They say that it got in the way of free enterprise. They feel that government should not be so involved in the economy. They also say that the New Deal programs made people not want to work.

Liberal critics say that the New Deal did not go far enough. They think it should have done more to change the economy. They think that Roosevelt should have done more to end the differences in wealth between the rich and the poor.

Supporters of the New Deal say that it was well balanced between saving capitalism and reforming it. They point to many lasting benefits of the New Deal.

The New Deal expanded the power of the fed-

TERMS AND NAMES

deficit spending Spending more money than comes in

National Labor Relations Board Agency to regulate business

parity An equal or fair amount

Securities and Exchange Commission Agency to regulate stock markets

Federal Deposit Insurance Corporation Insurance for savings

Tennessee Valley Authority Regional work project of lasting value

eral government. It gave the government a greater role in shaping the economy. It also relieved the suffering of millions of people during the darkest years of the Depression. To do so, the federal government went into debt. The federal deficit rose. But the huge increase in government spending caused by World War II drove the deficit way up—and ended the Depression.

Many New Deal policies have had lasting effects. One was the protection of workers' rights. New Deal laws set standards for wages and hours. It also banned child labor and protected the right of workers to organize. The **National Labor Relations Board** still *mediates* labor disputes today.

The New Deal was also involved in farming. The New Deal helped to control the supply of crops. It also regulated the demand for goods. It allowed farmers to store their crops until prices reached **parity**—a price equal to what farmers had been paid between 1910 and 1919. It provided price supports to help farmers. The policy of price supports continued into the 1990s.

New Deal programs also protect people who put their savings into banks or who invest in the stock market. The **Securities and Exchange Commission** (SEC) still regulates the sale of stocks and bonds. The **Federal Deposit Insurance Corporation** (FDIC) still insures people's savings.

1. How did some liberals and conservatives criticize the New Deal?

_____

_____

Continuing Benefits (pages 532–533)

How did the New Deal make the economy more stable?

New Deal reforms had lasting effects. They helped make the economy more stable. The nation has had economic downturns. But none have been as bad as the Great Depression. And people's savings are insured.

One of the most important and lasting benefits of the New Deal is the Social Security system. It provides old-age insurance and unemployment benefits. It also helps families with dependent children and the disabled. For the first time the federal government took responsibility for the welfare of its citizens.

The New Deal also helped the environment. Roosevelt was very interested in protecting the nation's natural resources. New Deal policies promoted soil conservation to prevent a repeat of the Dust Bowl. The **Tennessee Valley Authority** helped prevent floods and provided electricity. And New Deal programs also added to the national park system. They set up areas to protect wildlife. However, the TVA did contribute to pollution through *strip mining*.

2. What are two continuing benefits of the New Deal?

_____

_____

_____

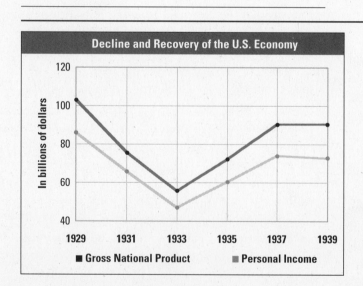

Decline and Recovery of the U.S. Economy

In billions of dollars — 1929, 1931, 1933, 1935, 1937, 1939

■ Gross National Product ■ Personal Income

Skillbuilder

Use the chart to answer these questions.

1. Which year according to the chart was the worst year of the Depression?

_____

_____

2. In which year in the 1930s was the economy the strongest?

_____

_____

Glossary

coalition An alliance of groups supporting a political party or cause

collective bargaining Negotiations between organized workers and their employer to decide wages and work rules

crafts unions Labor organizations made up of skilled workers who do a particular kind of job, no matter what industry they work in

layoffs The firing or temporary suspension of employees, especially because of lack of work

make-work program A program that creates useless jobs just to give workers a paycheck

mediate To resolve or settle differences by working with all the conflicting parties

midterm elections Congressional elections held in years when there is no presidential election

minimum wage The lowest wage that law will allow a worker to be paid

pension plan A plan that provides for money to be paid as a retirement benefit

regulate To set rules for an industry

soil conservation Ways to keep the soil fertile and prevent it from blowing away

strip mining Mining that removes the topsoil of large areas of land

AFTER YOU READ

A. Write the name or term that best completes each sentence on the blank.

Civilian Conservation Corps

New Deal

Franklin Delano Roosevelt

The Grapes of Wrath

Tennessee Valley Authority

Social Security Act

Works Progress
    Administration

Wagner Act

Federal Deposit Insurance
    Corporation

Richard Wright

1. _____ became president in 1933.

2. FDR's programs to end the Depression were called the _____ .

3. The president and Congress created the _____ to insure people's bank accounts.

4. A program supported by FDR to put people to work, the _____ hired young men to plant trees and build roads.

5. The _____ hired people to build schools and hospitals, and it employed artists, writers, and actors.

6. The _____ protected workers' rights to collective bargaining and banned unfair labor practices.

7. One of the most important laws was the _____. It set up a system of old-age insurance, unemployment insurance, and aid to people unable to work.

8. Another part of the New Deal was the _____, which prevented flooding and brought electricity to a large area.

9. John Steinbeck's novel _____ tells the story of Oklahoma farmers during the Depression.

10. The novel *Native Son* by _____ describes the difficulties faced by a young African-American man.

Name _____   Date _____

B Write the name or term after the description that explains it best.

Eleanor Roosevelt

New Deal Coalition

Orson Welles

deficit spending

Congress of Industrial
  Organizations

1. Groups of voters including Southern whites, urban voters, African Americans, and labor who supported FDR

2. The creator of a radio broadcast that convinced many Americans that Martians had landed in New Jersey

3. The act of a government paying out more money than it is taking in

4. An organization of industrial labor unions started in the 1930s

5. The wife of the president, who fought for equality for women and minorities

Main Ideas

1. What were the three goals of the New Deal?

_____

_____

2. Describe two reasons that people opposed the New Deal.

_____

_____

3. What did the Wagner Act do to help workers?

_____

_____

4. Why were movies popular during the Depression?

_____

_____

5. List three New Deal programs that still exist today.

_____

_____

Thinking Critically

Answer the following questions on a separate sheet of paper.

1. How did the New Deal help people during the Depression?

2. How did the New Deal make lasting changes in American government?

Dictators Threaten World Peace

BEFORE YOU READ

In the last section, you saw the effects of the New Deal reforms in the United States during the Great Depression.

In this section, you will see how economic and political conditions in Europe and Asia in the 1930s gave rise to expansionist totalitarian states.

AS YOU READ

Take notes on the chart below. Fill it in with the beliefs and goals of these dictators and on what they did to reach their goals.

TERMS AND NAMES

Joseph Stalin Communist dictator of the Soviet Union

totalitarian Government that has complete control over its citizens and puts down all opposition

Benito Mussolini Fascist dictator of Italy

fascism Political system based on a strong, centralized government headed by a dictator

Nazism Fascist political philosophy of Germany under Nazi dictator Hitler

Adolf Hitler Nazi dictator of Germany

Neutrality Acts Laws passed by Congress to ban the sale of arms or loans to nations at war

---

DICTATOR / NATION	BELIEFS AND GOALS	ACTIONS
Stalin/Soviet Union	communism, stamp out free enterprise	

Nationalism Threatens Europe and Asia (pages 542–546)

How did dictators take power in Europe and Asia?

World War 1 had ended with the Treaty of Versailles. President Woodrow Wilson had hoped that that treaty would create a "just and secure peace." He had also hoped that it would make the world "safe for democracy." It did neither.

Germans resented being blamed for starting World War I. They also were upset about losing territory they thought of as German. The Soviet Union resented the new nations created out of what had been Russian territory.

The new democracies formed after the war suffered huge economic and social problems. But they were given no help. Many of these democratic governments were weak. They collapsed, and dictators seized power.

In the Soviet Union, **Joseph Stalin** came to power in 1924. He was a ruthless leader who let nothing stand in his way. Stalin focused on creating a model communist state. He wanted to stamp out private enterprise. He did away with private farms and created collectives, or huge state-owned farms. The state also took over industry. Stalin made the Soviet Union into a leading industrial power.

But he also made it into a police state. Anyone who criticized him or his policies was arrested by the secret police. Some were executed. Others were sent to forced-labor camps. Stalin created a **totalitarian** government—a government with complete control over its citizens. Individuals have no rights, and the government puts down all opposition.

At the same time, **Benito Mussolini** was creating a totalitarian state in Italy. His political movement was called **fascism.** It was based on a strong, centralized government headed by a dictator. Fascism grew out of extreme nationalism. Mussolini, called *Il Duce,* or the leader, was known for his efficiency in running all aspects of Italian life. But he did not want the government to own farms and factories. Fascism was actually anti-communist.

In Germany, another fascist party came to power. Its political philosophy was called **Nazism.** The Nazis were led by **Adolf Hitler.** Hitler hoped to unite all German-speaking people into a new German empire, or Reich. He believed that Germans—especially blond, blue-eyed "Aryans"— were the master race. According to Hitler, Aryans were meant to have power over all "inferior races," such as Jews and nonwhites. Hitler believed Germany needed to expand—to gain territory—so that the German people could thrive.

Nazism combined extreme nationalism, racism, and expansionism. It appealed to unemployed, desperate, and resentful Germans during the Great Depression. In the 1932 elections, the Nazi Party gained power. Hitler became *chancellor.* He did away with the *Weimar Republic* and set up the Third Reich, or third German empire.

Meanwhile, in Asia, military leaders had taken over Japan. They believed that Japan needed more land and resources. Japan attacked Manchuria, a province of China, in 1931. The League of Nations protested, but Japan left the League and kept Manchuria.

The League's failure to stop Japan made Hitler and Mussolini bolder. Hitler sent troops into the Rhineland and rebuilt the German army. These acts broke the Versailles Treaty. Mussolini captured the African nation of Ethiopia. Haile Selassie, the *ousted* leader of Ethiopia, asked the League for help. When the League did nothing, he said, "It is us today. It will be you tomorrow."

1. **What four major countries fell to totalitarian dictatorships in the 1930's?**

_____

_____

The United States Responds Cautiously (pages 546–547)

How did the United States respond to the rise of dictators?

Most Americans wanted the United States to stay out of foreign conflicts. Many people thought that the United States had made a mistake in getting involved in World War I. Anti-war rallies were held. *Isolationism* became more popular.

Congress passed the **Neutrality Acts.** These laws banned loans or arms sale to nations at war. Because of the Spanish Civil War, the Neutrality Acts included those involved in civil wars.

In Spain, the fascist general Francisco Franco was trying to overthrow the elected government. Many American volunteers went to Spain to fight the fascists. These volunteers felt that Spain was the place to stop fascism and defend democracy. The governments of the Western democracies sent only food and clothing to democratic forces in Spain. Hitler and Mussolini supported Franco with troops and weapons. When Franco won in 1939, Europe had another totalitarian government.

When Japan invaded China again in 1937, Roosevelt spoke out against isolationism. He felt that peace-loving nations should take a stand against lawless nations. In spite of the Neutrality Acts, Roosevelt continued to send aid to China.

2. **How did the United States react to the rise of expansionist dictatorships in Europe and Asia?**

_____

_____

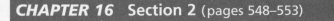

CHAPTER 16 **Section 2** (pages 548–553)

War in Europe

TERMS AND NAMES

Neville Chamberlain Prime minister of Great Britain before World War II

Winston Churchill Prime minister of Great Britain during World War II

appeasement Trying to pacify an aggressor in order to keep the peace

nonaggression pact Agreement between Germany and Russia not to fight each other

blitzkrieg Lightning war strategy used by Germany against Poland

Charles de Gaulle Head of the French government in exile in England

BEFORE YOU READ

In the last section, you saw how dictatorships rose in Europe and Asia in the 1930s.

In this section, you will see how the expansionist policies of Hitler led to World War II in Europe.

AS YOU READ

Fill in the time line below with the major events in Hitler's and Stalin's attempts to expand their territory.

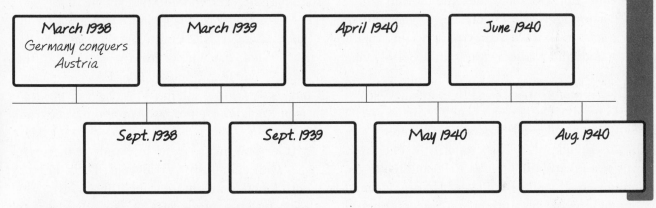

| March 1938 Germany conquers Austria | March 1939 | April 1940 | June 1940 |
| Sept. 1938 | Sept. 1939 | May 1940 | Aug. 1940 |

Austria and Czechoslovakia Fall
(pages 548–550)

How did Britain and France react to Hitler's aggression?

Hitler decided that the new living space the German people needed would come from nearby nations. He would annex, or add, Austria and Czechoslovakia. And he was willing to use force to do it.

Hitler bullied the Austrian chancellor into agreeing to bring Austrian Nazis into his government. When the Austrian leader changed his mind, Hitler became furious. In March 1938, German troops marched into Austria. They met no opposition. Germany announced an Anschluss, or "union" with Austria.

Then Hitler claimed that the Czechs were mistreating German-speaking people in an area called

the Sudetenland. He massed troops on the border. France and Britain promised to defend Czechoslovakia. Their leaders met with Hitler in Munich, Germany. Hitler promised that the Sudetenland would be his "last territorial demand." France, Britain, and Germany signed the Munich Pact in September 1938. It gave the Sudetenland to Germany.

Neville Chamberlain was the British prime minister who signed the Munich Pact. He called it "peace with honor." Another British leader, **Winston Churchill,** disagreed. He called the Pact dishonorable **appeasement.** That means giving up your principles in order to *pacify* an *aggressor.* Churchill predicted that appeasement would eventually lead to war.

The German Offensive Begins
(pages 550–552)

What did Britain and France do about Nazi and Soviet aggression?

Hitler did not keep the promise he made at Munich. In March of 1939, he conquered the rest of Czechoslovakia.

Then Hitler began to claim that Germans living in Poland were being persecuted. Many people thought Hitler would never attack Poland. They thought he would be afraid that the Soviet Union, on Poland's eastern border, would then fight Germany. But Germany and the Soviet Union signed a **nonaggression pact,** an agreement not to fight each other. In a secret part of this treaty, Hitler and Stalin also agreed to divide Poland between them.

On September 1, 1939, Hitler launched World War II by attacking Poland. The Germans used a new strategy called a **blitzkrieg,** or lightning war. They used tanks and planes to take the enemy by surprise and crush them quickly. Poland fell to the Germans in a month. Britain and France declared war on Germany. Meanwhile, the Soviets attacked Poland from the east, and grabbed some of its territory.

For the next few months, not much happened. This was called the "phony war." French and British troops gathered on the French border. German troops also waited.

Meanwhile, Stalin seized regions that the Soviet Union had lost in World War I. He took the Baltic states in September and October of 1939. Finland resisted, and was conquered only after fierce fighting in March 1940.

In April, Hitler launched surprise invasions of Denmark and Norway. Then in May, he quickly took the Netherlands, Belgium, and Luxembourg. This war was very real indeed.

France and Britain Fight On
(pages 552–553)

How did Hitler's attacks on France and on Britain turn out?

Germany attacked France in May 1940—but not where the Allies expected. It cut off Allied forces in the north. The British sent all kinds of boats—from fishing vessels to yachts—to bring nearly 340,000 British, French, and other Allied troops safely across the English Channel.

Meanwhile, Italy joined the war on the side of Germany. The Italians attacked France from the south. France surrendered quickly, in June 1940. The Germans *occupied* the northern part of France while a Nazi-controlled *puppet government*, called the Vichy government, ruled the southern part of France. The French general **Charles de Gaulle** set up a French *government in exile* in England. He promised to free France from the Nazis.

Hitler now made plans to invade Britain. He began with air raids over England. The Germans bombed London night after night in August 1940. The British air force (RAF) defended Britain against these attacks. They used a new technology called radar, and shot down hundreds of German planes. This air war was called the Battle of Britain. The new prime minister, Winston Churchill, rallied the spirits of the British people and declared that Britain would never surrender. Hitler gave up the idea of invading Britain.

3. What happened to Hitler's plans for conquering France and Britain?

The Holocaust

TERMS AND NAMES

Holocaust Systematic murder of 11 million Jews and other people in Europe by the Nazis

Kristallnacht Name given the night of November 9, 1938, when Nazis in Germany attacked Jews, their businesses, and their synagogues

genocide Deliberate and systematic killing of an entire people

concentration camp Prison camps operated by the Nazis where Jews and others were starved while doing slave labor or murdered

BEFORE YOU READ

In the last section, you saw how Hitler began World War II.

In this section, you will see how Hitler put his plan of Aryan domination into place by killing Jews and other groups he considered inferior.

AS YOU READ

Take notes on the chart below. Fill it in with the attitudes and actions that led to the Holocaust.

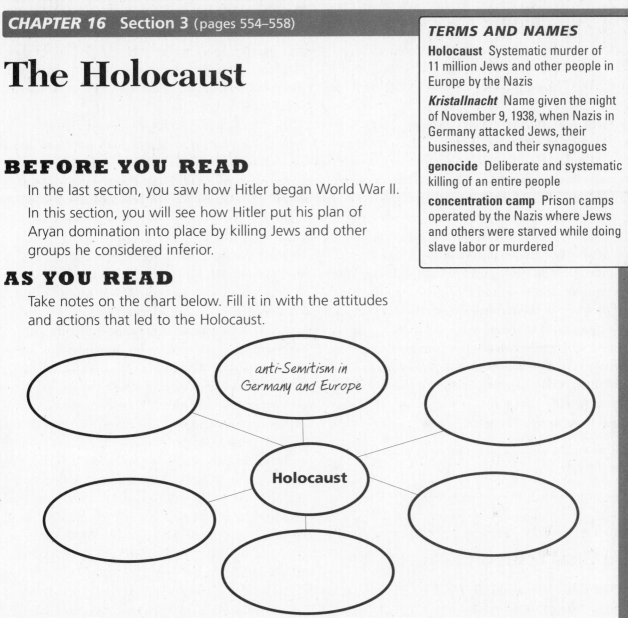

anti-Semitism in Germany and Europe

Holocaust

The Persecution Begins (pages 554–555)

How did the persecution of the Jews begin in Germany?

Part of Hitler's plan for Germany was to make the country racially pure. In 1933, just three months after taking power, Hitler ordered all non-Aryans out of government jobs. Then Hitler began an organized persecution of non-Aryans, particularly of Jews. This resulted in the **Holocaust**—the systematic murder of over 11 million people across Europe. Over half of the murdered people were Jews.

Anti-Semitism, or hatred of Jews, had a long history in Germany and in other parts of Europe.

For a long time, Germans had used Jews as a scapegoat, someone to blame for their own failures and frustrations. Therefore, when Hitler blamed Jews for Germany's defeat in World War I, many Germans agreed. When Hitler blamed the Jews for Germany's economic problems, many Germans supported him.

Persecution of Jews increased under Hitler. In 1935, new laws took away Jews' civil rights and their property. Jews were forced to wear yellow stars of David on their clothing.

On November 9, 1938, organized, violent persecution began with ***Kristallnacht.*** (*Kristallnacht* is a German word meaning "crystal night," or night of broken glass.) Gangs of Nazi *storm troopers* attacked Jewish homes, businesses, and *synagogues* across Germany. The streets were littered with broken glass. Then the Nazis blamed Jews for the destruction. Many Jews were arrested; others were fined.

Many Jews started to flee Germany. Nazis were in favor of this, but other nations did not want to accept the Jewish refugees. Some refugees, including Albert Einstein and Thomas Mann, were allowed into the United States. But the United States would not change its immigration quotas. This was partly due to American anti-Semitism. It was also because many Americans feared competition for the few jobs available during the Depression.

Once war broke out in Europe, Americans said they feared that refugees would be "enemy agents." The Coast Guard even turned away a ship carrying refugees who had *emigration papers* for the United States. Three-quarters of those passengers were killed by the Nazis after the ship was forced to return to Europe.

1. How did the world react to Germany's persecution of the Jews?

_____

_____

The Final Solution (pages 555–558)

How did the Nazis try to kill off the Jews and others?

After *Kristallnacht*, the Nazis took a new approach. They adopted the "final solution" to what they called "the Jewish problem." Jews healthy enough to work were sent to slave labor camps. The rest were sent to extermination camps—places where they would be murdered. This horrifying plan amounted to **genocide,** the deliberate and systematic killing of an entire people.

The final solution was based on the belief that the Aryans were a superior people. All others were *Untermeschen* (the German word for "subhuman"), inferior people who should work for the master race or be killed. The Nazis arrested their political opponents—Communists, Socialists, and others. They rounded up and killed Gypsies, Jehovah's Witnesses, homosexuals, the mentally and physically handicapped, and others who did not fit their standard of the master race. As the Nazis conquered other nations, they added Poles, Russians, and others to their list.

But their main target remained the Jews. In Poland, the Nazis rounded up and shot many Jews. Other Jews were forced to live in ghettoes, crowded Jewish sections of cities where they were left to starve. Most were sent to **concentration camps,** where they suffered hunger, illness, overwork, torture, and death.

Even the early concentration camps did not kill Jews fast enough for the Nazis. In 1941, they built six death camps in Poland. These camps had gas chambers that could kill 6,000 people a day. Prisoners were gassed or shot. Some died in horrible "medical experiments." Their bodies were often burned in huge ovens called crematoriums.

Six million Jews died in death camps and Nazi *massacres*. Some Jews, however, were saved. Ordinary people sometimes risked their own lives to hide Jews or to help them escape. The small nation of Denmark was remarkable in protecting its Jewish population. When the Nazis demanded that Jews wear yellow stars of David, the king of Denmark declared that he and his family would also wear the stars. Many other Danes did too. They also helped most Danish Jews escape to neutral Sweden.

Some Jews even survived the concentration camps. Elie Wiesel, who won the Nobel Peace Prize in 1986, is a survivor of Auschwitz. He has written memorably about his concentration camp experiences and the need to prevent such genocide from ever happening again.

2. What was the Nazi's "final solution" and how was it carried out?

_____

_____

CHAPTER 16 Section 4 (pages 559–565)

America Moves Toward War

BEFORE YOU READ

In the last section, you saw how Hitler's plan to make Germany racially pure killed millions of people.

In this section, you will see how the United States moved closer to entering the war against the Nazis.

AS YOU READ

Take notes on the time line below. Fill it in with the events in each year that brought the United States to war.

> **TERMS AND NAMES**
>
> **Axis powers** Germany, Italy, and Japan
>
> **Lend-Lease Act** Law that allowed lending or leasing arms to any nation "whose defense was vital to the United States"
>
> **Atlantic Charter** British and American statement of goals for fighting World War II
>
> **Allies** Group of nations, including the United States, Britain, and the Soviet Union, who opposed the Axis powers
>
> **Hideki Tojo** Prime minister of Japan during World War II

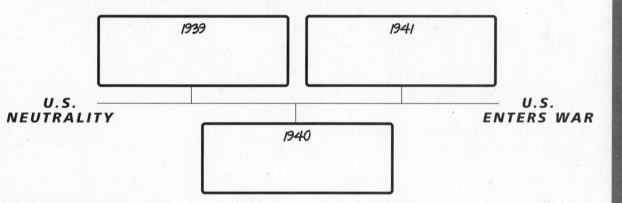

```
                1939                         1941

U.S.                                                    U.S.
NEUTRALITY  ────────────────────────────────  ENTERS WAR

                          1940
```

The United States Musters Its Forces (pages 559–560)

How did the United States try to stay out of war but be prepared?

According to the Neutrality Acts, the United States could not enter the war in Europe. However, President Roosevelt asked for a change in the Acts. He suggested a cash-and-carry provision. Such a provision would allow Britain and France to buy and transport American arms. Congress passed this new Neutrality Act in November 1939.

In 1940, Germany, Italy, and Japan signed a mutual defense treaty. They became the **Axis powers.** The treaty meant that if the United States went to war against any one of them, all three would fight. That would put America at war on two *fronts*: in Europe and in Asia. Nevertheless,

Roosevelt gave the British "all aid short of war" to help them fight Hitler.

Roosevelt assured the nation that the United States would stay out of war. But he prepared for war. After years of isolationism, America's military forces were weak. Congress increased spending for national defense. It passed the nation's first *peacetime draft* in September 1940.

Roosevelt broke the tradition of a two-term presidency. He ran for re-election in 1940. The Democrats' *party platform* said the United States will not fight in foreign wars. Roosevelt insisted on adding "except if attacked." He won the election.

1. How did the United States slowly move toward war?

_____

_____

_____

"The Great Arsenal of Democracy" (pages 560–562)

Why did the United States change its policy of neutrality?

After the election, Roosevelt spoke to the American people. He said that the United States could not stand by and let Hitler conquer the world. America would become "the great *arsenal* of democracy." At that time, Britain could no longer pay for arms and supplies. Roosevelt suggested lending or leasing arms to any nation "whose defense was vital to the United States." Isolationists bitterly opposed his policy. But Congress passed the **Lend-Lease Act** in March 1941.

Meanwhile, Germany invaded its former ally, the Soviet Union. The United States gave lend-lease support to the Soviets as well as to Britain.

Nazi submarines called U-boats attacked and sank ships carrying arms across the Atlantic to Germany's enemies. In June 1941, Roosevelt ordered the U.S. Navy to protect lend-lease ships. He also gave American warships permission to attack German U-boats in self-defense.

2. **Name two ways in which the United States became the "arsenal of democracy."**

_____

_____

Planning for War (pages 562–563)

How did the United States move toward war?

In August 1941, Roosevelt met secretly with British Prime Minister Winston Churchill. Roosevelt did not actually commit the United States to war. But he and Churchill did sign the **Atlantic Charter.** That was a statement of the goals for fighting World War II. These goals included protecting peoples' rights to choose their own form of government and building a secure peace.

Later, 26 nations signed a similar agreement. These nations, called the **Allies,** were united in fighting Germany, Italy, and Japan.

On September 4, 1941, a German U-boat fired on an American *merchant ship*. President Roosevelt ordered the U.S. Navy to fire on German ships on sight. U-boats responded by sinking several American ships, and American seamen were killed. In a very close vote, the Senate finally allowed the arming of merchant ships. Roosevelt knew he did not yet have enough public support to declare war.

3. **What events moved the United States closer to war?**

_____

_____

Japan Attacks the United States (pages 563–565)

What brought the United States into conflict with Japan?

In Japan, expansionists had long dreamed of creating a huge empire. Japan was now acting on this dream. It began seizing Asian territory held as colonies by European nations. The United States also owned islands in the Pacific.

When Japan invaded Indochina, the United States cut off trade with Japan. Japan needed American oil to run its *war machine*. The new prime minister of Japan was a *militant* general named **Hideki Tojo.** He started peace talks with the United States, but he also prepared for war.

The United States broke Japan's secret communications code. The Americans knew Japan was preparing for a military strike. But they did not know when or where the strike would be.

On December 7, 1941—during the peace talks—Japan attacked the main U.S. naval base at Pearl Harbor in Hawaii. The Japanese crippled the U.S. Pacific fleet in one blow. Planes and ships were destroyed. Over 2,400 people were killed.

Roosevelt was grim. He did not want to fight a war on two fronts. He had expected to enter the war in Europe, not to fight in Asia, too. Roosevelt described the "unprovoked and dastardly attack on American soil." He called December 7, 1941, "a day that will live in infamy."

Roosevelt asked Congress for a declaration of war against Japan. Congress quickly agreed. Then Italy and Germany declared war on the United States.

4. **What event caused the American declaration of war against Japan?**

_____

Name _____ Date _____

Glossary

CHAPTER 16 World War Looms

aggressor One who starts violence, a war, or an invasion

arsenal Supplier of ammunition, arms, and other war materials

chancellor Prime minister; leader of the government

emigration papers Official documents giving permission to enter a nation

front Area of contact between combating forces; battlefront

government in exile Government that has had to flee to a foreign country because its own territory has been conquered and occupied

isolationism Policy of opposing political and economic involvement with other countries

massacre Savage killing of many victims

merchant ship Ship used for trade

militant Aggressive; fighting or warring

ousted Removed by force

occupy Seize and maintain control over by force

pacify Ease the anger of; soothe

party platform Statement of the goals and policies of a political party, usually written at the party's nominating convention

peacetime draft Forced enrollment of certain persons into the armed forces when there is not a war

puppet government Government with no real power of its own that is controlled by another nation

storm troopers Special German soldiers trained to carry out sudden attacks or assaults

synagogues Jewish houses of worship

war machine Machinery necessary to wage war, including production of weapons, transport, and military vehicles

Weimar Republic Democratic government of Germany set up after World War I

AFTER YOU READ

Terms and Names

A. Write the letter of the name next to the description that fits it best.

a. Adolf Hitler
b. Joseph Stalin
c. Benito Mussolini
d. Winston Churchill
e. Charles de Gaulle
f. Hideki Tojo

_____ **1.** British prime minister who opposed appeasement

_____ **2.** Italian fascist dictator who formed an alliance with Hitler

_____ **3.** Nazi dictator who believed the Germans were a master race

_____ **4.** French general who set up a government-in-exile when France fell

_____ **5.** Militant general who became prime minister of Japan and planned the attack on Pearl Harbor

_____ **6.** Soviet dictator who signed a nonaggression pact with Hitler and had his own expansionist ideas

B. Circle the name or term that best completes each sentence.

1. _____ is the deliberate and systematic killing of an entire people.
appeasement   fascism   genocide

2. A _____ is a "lightning war" of quick, crushing surprise attacks.
Holocaust   blitzkrieg   fascism

3. When Germany, Italy, and Japan formed an alliance, they became known as the _____.
Allies   Holocaust   Axis powers

4. In the _____, the Nazis systematically murdered over 11 million Jews and others.
blitzkrieg   Holocaust   appeasement

5. _____ is a form of very nationalistic totalitarian government with a strong dictator.
fascism   genocide   blitzkrieg

6. The _____ included Britain, France, the United States, and others fighting the Axis.
Lend-Lease Act   Allies   Holocaust

7. The policy of _____ at Munich allowed Germany to annex part of Czechoslovakia.
Lend-Lease Act   appeasement   blitzkrieg

8. The racist, nationalistic, expansionist philosophy of Hitler's Germany was called _____.
appeasement   Nazism   genocide

9. The Nazis rounded up Jews and other people they felt were inferior and sent them to _____.
Axis powers   concentration camps   blitzkrieg

Main Ideas

1. What are the characteristics of a totalitarian state?

_____

2. What was the outcome of Britain's and France's policy of appeasement?

_____

3. What groups did the Nazis deem unfit to belong to the Aryan "master race"?

_____

4. How did the United States give aid to nations resisting Hitler?

_____

Thinking Critically

Answer the following questions on a separate sheet of paper.

1. How did the expansionist ideas of Hitler, Stalin, and Tojo lead to World War II?

2. World War II has been called "the good war" because it was fought to rid the world of brutal and dangerous dictatorships. Explain why people think of it this way.

CHAPTER 17 Section 1 (pages 570–577)

Mobilization on the Home Front

TERMS AND NAMES

George Marshall Army chief of staff during World War II

A. Philip Randolph Important African-American labor leader

Nisei Japanese Americans born in the United States

Office of Price Administration (OPA) Agency of the federal government that fought inflation

War Production Board (WPB) Government agency that decided which companies would make war materials and how to distribute raw materials

rationing Restricting the amount of food and other goods people may buy during wartime to assure adequate supplies for the military

BEFORE YOU READ

In the last section, you learned the reasons why the United States entered World War II.

In this section, you will learn how Americans joined in the war effort.

AS YOU READ

Use the web diagram below to take notes on the changes on the American home front during World War II.

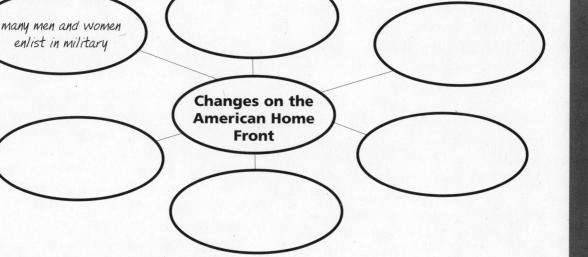

Americans Join the War Effort
(page 570–572)

How did Americans react to Pearl Harbor?

The Japanese had expected Americans to react with fear and despair to the attack on Pearl Harbor. Instead, Americans reacted with rage. "Remember Pearl Harbor" became a rallying cry. Five million men volunteered for military service.

But fighting a war on two fronts—in Europe and in the Pacific—required huge numbers of soldiers. Another ten million men were drafted. New

soldiers received eight weeks of basic training. Then they were officially "GIs," a nickname coming from the term "Government Issue."

To free more men for combat, Army Chief of Staff General **George Marshall** suggested using women for noncombat military tasks. Congress created the Women's Auxiliary Army Corps (WAAC) in 1942. About 25,000 women served in the military. They did not receive the same pay or benefits as men.

Men and women from minority groups also served in World War II. They included Mexican Americans, Asian Americans, and Native Americans.

Some African Americans had mixed feelings about defending a country where they were often segregated and denied the basic rights of citizenship. But they also knew they would be worse off under any of the Axis powers. More than a million African Americans served, but in racially segregated units. These units were not even allowed into combat until the last year of the war.

1. How did women and minorities join in the war effort?

_____

_____

Life on the Home Front (pages 572–574)

What changes took place in American life?

The nation's factories quickly switched to war production. Automobile factories made planes and tanks. Pencil-makers turned out bomb parts. Shipyards and defense plants expanded. They produced warships with amazing speed.

About 18 million workers kept these war industries going. Some 6 million new factory workers were women. At first, industry did not want to hire women. Men feared women would not be able to handle the heavy work. Once women proved they could do the work, factories hired them. But they paid women only 60 percent as much as men.

Before the war, most defense contractors had refused to hire African Americans. **A. Philip Randolph,** the president of the Brotherhood of Sleeping Car Porters, was an important African-American labor leader. He threatened to have African Americans march on Washington to demand an end to this discrimination. Roosevelt feared such a march. He issued an *executive order* banning discrimination in defense industries.

The government hired scientists to develop new weapons and medicines. They made improvements in radar and *sonar,* and in "miracle drugs" like penicillin. The government also set up the Manhattan Project, which developed the atomic bomb.

Even Hollywood contributed to the war effort with patriotic films. They also made escapist romances and comedies. Public hunger for news of the war made magazines and radio more popular.

2. How did the war change life at home?

_____

_____

The Federal Government Takes Control (pages 574–577)

How did the federal government get involved in the economy?

To make the war effort go smoothly, the federal government became more involved in people's lives.

After Pearl Harbor, many Americans feared that people of Japanese descent could be helping Japan. There was panic and prejudice on the West Coast. Starting in February 1942, the U. S. government rounded up 110,000 Japanese Americans. They were put in *internment camps* far from the West Coast. There they were essentially prisoners. About two-thirds of those interned were **Nisei.** These were Japanese Americans who had been born in the United States and were thus American citizens. No one ever found evidence of disloyalty among Japanese Americans.

The federal government was also worried about economic issues. Congress wanted to prevent the high inflation that had occurred during World War I. Congress set up the **Office of Price Administration.** It successfully fought inflation by "freezing," or not increasing, prices on most goods. Congress also raised taxes. The **War Production Board** decided which companies would make war materials and how to distribute raw materials.

The OPA also set up a system of **rationing.** Families were issued coupons to be used for buying scarce items, such as meat and gasoline. Most Americans cooperated with the rationing system. They also bought *war bonds* and collected goods, such as tin cans and paper, that could be recycled, or reused, for the war effort.

3. How did the federal government regulate American life during the war?

_____

_____

Name _____ Date _____

The War for Europe and North Africa

TERMS AND NAMES

Dwight D. Eisenhower American general

D-Day Allied invasion to liberate Europe

George Patton American general

Harry S. Truman 33rd president of the United States

Battle of the Bulge German counteroffensive in December 1944

V-E Day Victory in Europe Day, May 8, 1945

BEFORE YOU READ

In the last section, you saw how the American involvement in World War II affected life on the home front.

In this section, you will see how the United States, Britain, and the Soviet Union combined to defeat Germany and its partners in Europe.

AS YOU READ

Take notes on the time line below. Fill it in with events that led to the defeat of Germany.

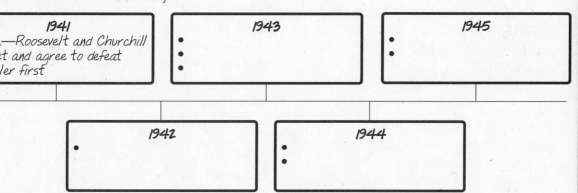

1941
- Dec.—Roosevelt and Churchill meet and agree to defeat Hitler first

1943
- •
- •
- •

1945
- •
- •

1942
- •

1944
- •
- •

The United States and Britain Join Forces (pages 578–580)

What were the goals of the American and British alliance?

In late December 1941, a few weeks after Pearl Harbor, President Roosevelt met with British Prime Minister Winston Churchill. They planned their war strategy. They agreed that the first thing to do was to defeat Hitler's Germany. They also agreed to accept only *unconditional surrender* from the Axis powers. They felt that complete victory was necessary to protect human rights. Roosevelt and Churchill began a lasting friendship and a strong alliance between America and Britain.

After war was declared, German U-boats increased attacks on American ships in the Atlantic. Many American ships were sunk. The Allies organized convoys, or groups for shared protection. Warships and airplanes escorted the convoys. They used *sonar* and radar to find and destroy many German submarines.

The United States also started building ships at a rapid pace. Soon there were more Allied cargo ships, or Liberty ships, being made than being sunk. By mid-1943, the tide of the Battle of the Atlantic had turned in favor of the Allies.

1. What was the Battle of the Atlantic, and how did the Allies win it?

_____

_____

_____

The Eastern Front and the Mediterranean (pages 580–582)

What happened in the Soviet Union, North Africa, and Italy?

By the summer of 1943, the Allies were winning on land as well as on the sea.

The German invasion of the Soviet Union had begun in 1941. When it stalled early in 1942, Hitler changed his tactics. He moved to capture Soviet oil fields and to take the industrial city of Stalingrad. The Germans bombed Stalingrad until almost the whole city was on fire.

But Stalin refused to give up. In three months of horrible hand-to-hand combat, the Germans took most of Stalingrad. Then the Soviets counter-attacked. They trapped a large German force just as winter came. The Germans froze and starved. In February 1943, the few German soldiers who were still alive surrendered. The Battle of Stalingrad was a turning point. From then on, Soviet forces moved steadily west towards Germany.

Meanwhile, in November 1942, the Allies invaded North Africa. North Africa at the time was controlled by the Axis. American forces led by General **Dwight D. Eisenhower** defeated German troops under General Erwin Rommel. The Germans surrendered in May 1943.

Next, in July 1943, the Allies invaded Italy. They captured Sicily. The war-weary Italian king stripped Prime Minister Mussolini of power and had him arrested. But then Hitler seized Italy. It took 18 long and bloody months of fighting for the Allies to drive the Germans out of Italy. They were helped by Italian partisans, members of underground resistance movements fighting the Nazis. When these partisans found Mussolini, they shot him and hung his body in a city square.

2. How were the Allies victorious in the Soviet Union, North Africa, and Italy?

_____

_____

The Allies Liberate Europe (pages 582–585)

Why did the Allies invade Normandy?

The Americans and British had been building a huge invasion force for two years. It was designed to *liberate* Europe. June 6, 1944, was **D-Day**—the day the Allies crossed the English Channel and landed in Normandy, France. This invasion was the largest land-sea-air operation in history.

British, American, and Canadian forces landed on the beaches of Normandy. They met fierce German resistance, and many were killed. But they took the beaches. Over 1 million Allied troops landed in France, and began to advance. American General **George Patton** and his Third Army liberated Paris in August. By September, the Allies had liberated other European nations and had entered Germany itself.

In the United States, Roosevelt won reelection to a fourth term as president. He had a new running mate—**Harry S. Truman.**

To the Allies' surprise, Hitler began a counter-attack in December. At first, the Germans cut deeply into Allied lines. After a month of fierce fighting, the Allies pushed the Germans back. The Germans had lost so many men and weapons in this **Battle of the Bulge** that they could only retreat.

Meanwhile, the Soviets pushed through Poland toward Germany. The Soviets were the first to liberate death camps and to describe the unbelievable horrors they saw there. By April 25, the Soviets were in Berlin. Hitler responded to certain defeat by shooting himself.

On May 8, 1945, General Eisenhower accepted the unconditional surrender of Nazi Germany. That became known as **V-E Day**—Victory in Europe Day.

3. How did the Allies liberate Europe and defeat Germany?

_____

_____

The War in the Pacific

BEFORE YOU READ

In the last section, you saw how the Allies won victory in Europe.

In this section, you will see how the Allies defeat Japan in the Pacific.

AS YOU READ

Use the diagram below and list the key military and diplomatic actions of the last years of the war. Tell why they were important.

TERMS AND NAMES

Douglas MacArthur American commander in the Philippines

Chester Nimitz Commander of American naval forces in the Pacific

kamikaze Japanese suicide plane

Manhattan Project Secret project to develop the atomic bomb

J. Robert Oppenheimer Scientist who led the Manhattan Project

Hiroshima City that was the site of the first atomic-bomb drop in Japan

Nagasaki Japanese city that was the site of the second atomic-bomb drop

Yalta Conference Meeting of Truman, Churchill, and Stalin in 1945

United Nations (UN) International organization formed in 1945

Nuremberg Trials Tribunal that tried Nazi leaders for war crimes

MILITARY/DIPLOMATIC ACTION	IMPORTANCE
U.S. withdraws from Philippines	Japan begins conquering Pacific islands

The Allies Stem the Japanese Tide (pages 586–589)

What were the important battles in the Pacific?

After Pearl Harbor, the Japanese conquered large parts of Asia and many Pacific islands. Outnumbered American and Filipino troops commanded by General **Douglas MacArthur** tried to defend the Philippines. MacArthur was ordered to leave, and the Philippines fell in April 1942.

Many ships had been sunk at Pearl Harbor. But the United States still had submarines and aircraft carriers. In April, American planes bombed Tokyo. This lifted American spirits. In May, an American and Australian fleet prevented Japan from taking Australia. In June, the Americans won an important victory. Admiral **Chester Nimitz,** commander of the outnumbered American naval forces in the Pacific, successfully defended Midway Island. The Japanese lost so many ships that people said the Americans had "avenged Pearl Harbor."

American forces, led by General MacArthur, now went island-hopping towards Japan. They avoided islands that were well defended by the Japanese. Airfields were built on captured islands. Planes could then bomb Japanese supply lines.

American marines stormed the island of Guadalcanal in August 1942. This marked Japan's first defeat on land. In October 1944, Americans landed on the island of Leyte in the Philippines. The Japanese launched **kamikaze** raids. In these suicide-plane attacks, Japanese pilots crashed their planes into Allied ships supporting the invasion. Still, Japan lost so many ships in the Battle of Leyte Gulf that the Japanese Navy was essentially knocked out of the war.

Finally, the Americans took the island of Iwo Jima in March 1945. This extremely bloody battle gave the United States a base to launch heavy bombers that could reach Japan itself.

1. Why was the Battle of Leyte Gulf so important?

The Atomic Bomb Ends the War (pages 589–592)

Why did the United States use the atomic bomb?

As American forces neared Japan in March 1945, President Roosevelt died. Vice-President Harry S. Truman became president.

A fierce battle raged over the island of Okinawa. It was Japan's last defensive *outpost.* The Americans finally won on June 22, 1945, but it cost 7,600 American lives. Japan lost 110,000 men. The Allies feared the human cost of invading Japan.

President Truman was told about the **Manhattan Project.** This was the secret development of the atomic bomb led by **J. Robert Oppenheimer.** On July 16, 1945, the first atomic bomb was tested. It was even more powerful than predicted. Many scientists felt it would be immoral to drop the bomb on Japan. Others said it would shorten the war and save lives. It would also give the United States an advantage over the Soviets after the war. Truman decided to use the bomb.

On August 6, 1945, an atomic bomb was dropped on **Hiroshima,** Japan. Almost every building collapsed into dust. But Japan did not surrender. A sec-

ond bomb was dropped on **Nagasaki,** killing 200,000. Emperor Hirohito was horrified. Japan surrendered September 2, 1945. The war was over.

2. Why did Truman decide to use the atomic bomb?

Rebuilding Begins (pages 592–593)

How did the Allies try to shape the postwar world?

In February 1945, Roosevelt had met with Churchill and Stalin. At this **Yalta Conference,** they had discussed the postwar world. They had agreed to create a new international organization based on the Atlantic Charter. Stalin agreed to this **United Nations (UN)** and to free elections in nations occupied by the Soviets. In exchange, he was given islands off Japan.

The UN was established in April 1945. The General Assembly was made up of all 126 member nations. The 11-member Security Council had the real power. The five wartime allies had permanent seats on the Council. Each could veto any Council action. The other seats rotated among member nations. It was hoped that the UN would be more effective than the League of Nations.

Truman, Churchill, and Stalin met at Potsdam. They divided Germany into four zones. Each was to be occupied by one of the Allies—the United States, Britain, France, and the Soviet Union. The capital of Berlin was divided the same way.

The **Nuremberg Trials,** an international *tribunal,* was held to try Nazi leaders. For the first time, a nation's leaders were held legally responsible for their wartime acts. They were tried for starting the war; for acts against the customs of war, such as killing prisoners; and for the murder and enslavement of civilians.

American forces, headed by General MacArthur, occupied Japan for six years. First, Japanese officials were put on trial for war crimes. Then, the Americans helped Japan set up a free-market economic system and create a new democratic constitution.

3. How did the Yalta and Potsdam conferences shape the postwar world?

CHAPTER 17 Section 4 (pages 596–601)

The Impact of the War

TERMS AND NAMES

GI Bill of Rights Law passed by Congress to help servicemen readjust to civilian life

James Farmer Civil rights leader who founded the Congress of Racial Equality

Congress of Racial Equality (CORE) Interracial organization formed to fight discrimination

Japanese American Citizens League (JACL) Civil rights group formed by Japanese Americans

BEFORE YOU READ

In the last section, you saw how the Allies prepared for the postwar world.

In this section, you will see how the war had changed the United States.

AS YOU READ

Use the chart below to take notes on the advances and problems in the economy and in civil rights during the war.

	ADVANCES	PROBLEMS
Economy	More jobs Better pay	Housing shortage
Civil Rights: • African Americans		
• Mexican Americans		
• Japanese Americans		

Opportunity and Adjustment
(pages 596–598)

How did the war create opportunities at home?

World War II was a time of opportunity for many Americans. The economy boomed. There were plenty of jobs. Wages rose. Farmers also did well. There was good weather, and crop production increased. Farm income tripled. Many farmers could pay off their mortgages.

Women had many job opportunities during the war. The share of women in the work force rose to 35 percent. (They lost some of these jobs when the men returned from military service.) Women also did a wide range of jobs and entered professions that had not been open to them before the war.

Many Americans relocated—picked up and moved. They moved to where there were defense jobs. States with military bases or defense plants saw huge gains in population. Some city populations grew by one third. The result was a housing shortage. Even though workers had the money to pay, there was no housing to rent. There were also food shortages in some areas.

People also had to adjust to new family situations. Many fathers were in the armed forces, so women had to work and raise children on their own. Many children were put in day care. Teenagers were often left on their own. When fathers returned from the war, there usually was a difficult time of re-adjustment.

The war also caused a boom in marriages. Many couples married before the men went overseas. But when the men returned after years of military service, many of these marriages failed. The divorce rate increased.

In 1944, Congress passed the **GI Bill of Rights.** It was designed to help servicemen readjust to civilian life. This bill paid for veterans to attend college or technical school. Over half the returning soldiers took advantage of this opportunity. It also gave federal loan guarantees to veterans buying homes or farms or starting businesses. The GI Bill gave many people opportunities they otherwise would never have had.

1. What opportunities did the war create at home?

_____

_____

Discrimination and Reaction
(pages 598–601)

How did the war affect minority groups?

For African Americans, World War II was a kind of turning point. They continued to be placed in all-black military units. They also were sent to segregated training camps in the South. There, some African Americans from the North experienced civilian *segregation* for the first time.

However, civil rights organizations put pressure on the military to allow African American units into combat. When these soldiers and airmen finally got their chance, they fought bravely and won many medals.

On the *home front,* many African Americans left the South and moved to the West Coast. There they found skilled jobs that paid well. But they also found prejudice. In 1942, civil rights leader **James Farmer** formed a new interracial organization to fight discrimination. It was called the **Congress of Racial Equality (CORE).**

African Americans also moved into the crowded cities of the North. Tension among the races grew. In 1943 it led to *race riots.* The worst one was in Detroit, where over 30 people were killed. President Roosevelt had to send federal troops to restore order. In response, many communities formed committees to improve race relations.

Mexican Americans also served in segregated military units during the war. And they also suffered prejudice at home. The worst race riots directed at Mexican Americans occurred in 1943 in Los Angeles.

Japanese Americans suffered the most. Their homes, businesses, and possessions were taken away from them when they were sent to internment camps. There, they tried to keep their dignity in the face of injustice and hardship.

Many young Japanese-American men volunteered for military service. They wanted to prove their loyalty to the United States. The military formed all-Nisei units, which served bravely. The famous 442nd was the most decorated combat unit of the war. When the 442nd returned home, President Truman said, "You fought not only the enemy. You fought prejudice—and you won."

But Japanese Americans were not done fighting prejudice. The **Japanese American Citizens League (JACL)** asked both Congress and the Supreme Court for justice. In 1944, the Supreme Court ruled that the internment of Japanese Americans had been justified for "military necessity." Nevertheless, over the years, Congress passed bills to compensate, or pay back, those who had been interned for the loss of their property. Finally, in 1990, cash payments were sent to all former internees. In a letter, President Bush said the nation "recognized the injustice done to Japanese Americans during World War II."

2. How did World War II affect African Americans, Mexican Americans, and Japanese Americans?

_____

_____

Glossary   CHAPTER 17   The United States in World War II

executive order Order issued by the president to any part of the executive branch of government

home front Civilian population or the civilian activities of a country at war

internment camp Area where people are kept under guard, especially during wartime

liberate Set free from oppression or foreign control

outpost Fortified area away from a main settlement, used to prevent an attack on the main settlement

race riots Riots caused by racial hatred or dissension

segregation Legal practice of separating the races (in schools, housing, etc.), especially to discriminate against people of color in a mostly white society

sonar System using underwater sound waves to detect submerged objects

tribunal Court of justice

unconditional surrender Giving up to an enemy without any demands or requests

war bonds Certificates of debt issued by a government—the government uses the money to pay for a war and pays the investor at a certain future date

AFTER YOU READ

Terms and Names

A. Circle the phrase that best completes each sentence.

1. The Battle of the Bulge was _____.

an Allied campaign in North Africa   a battle against Japan in the Pacific

the final German counterattack in Europe

2. On D-Day, the Allies _____.

landed in Normandy to liberate Europe   defeated Japan   defeated Germany

3. The Manhattan Project _____.

sent Japanese Americans to internment camps   planned the Allies' strategy   developed the atomic bomb

4. In the Nuremberg Trials, the Nazis _____.

were tried for war crimes and crimes against humanity   starved and froze outside of a Soviet city

destroyed Jewish businesses

5. The GI Bill of Rights _____.

desegregated the armed forces   paid for veterans to go to college   allowed women to serve in the military

6. Rationing was _____.

the scientific process of developing the atomic bomb   a way of allotting scarce products, like meat and gasoline

the percentage of women allowed to work in defense industries

7. Hiroshima was _____.

the Japanese city on which the first atomic bomb was dropped   the emperor of Japan

an internment camp in the United States

AFTER YOU READ (cont.) *CHAPTER 17* The United States in World War II

B. Write the letter of the name or term next to the description that explains it best

a. A. Philip Randolph

b. Harry S. Truman

c. Nisei

d. Dwight David Eisenhower

e. Douglas MacArthur

f. V-E Day

g. Congress of Racial Equality

h. *kamikaze*

_____ **1.** Japanese Americans born in the United States

_____ **2.** The day Nazi Germany surrendered to the Allies

_____ **3.** An important African-American labor leader

_____ **4.** The American general who liberated the Philippines and supervised the occupation of Japan

_____ **5.** The American general who commanded the D-Day invasion and received Germany's surrender

_____ **6.** Japanese suicide-plane air raids

_____ **7.** An organization formed to fight discrimination

_____ **8.** The vice-president who became president when Roosevelt died

Main Ideas

1. How did the federal government's actions affect civilian life during World War II?

_____

_____

2. How did the Battle of the Bulge signal that the end of World War II in Europe was near?

_____

_____

3. What was the result of dropping atomic bombs on Hiroshima and Nagasaki?

_____

_____

4. What events showed racial tension in the United States during World War II?

_____

_____

Thinking Critically

Answer the following questions on a separate sheet of paper.

1. What social and economic changes in American society arose from World War II?

2. Answer one of the following:

(**a**) How did the Allies defeat Germany in Europe?

(**b**) How did the United States defeat Japan in the Pacific?

CHAPTER 18 **Section 1** (pages 606–612)

Origins of the Cold War

BEFORE YOU READ

In the last section, you saw the social and economic changes that would reshape postwar America.

In this section, you will see how the Allied coalition that won the war fell apart and the United States and the Soviet Union came into conflict.

AS YOU READ

Fill in the chart below with notes on U.S. actions and Soviet actions that contributed to the beginning of the Cold War.

SOVIET ACTIONS	U.S. ACTIONS
Stalin sets up satellite nations	

Former Allies Clash (pages 606–608)

What caused Soviet-American problems?

The United States and the Soviet Union were wartime allies. But there had been trouble between them for some time. A major reason was that they had opposing political and economic systems. In addition, the Soviets were angry that the United States had taken so many years to officially recognize their Communist government. Americans were upset that Stalin had signed a treaty with Hitler before World War II. Still, at the end of the war, people hoped that the United Nations would help

bring a time of peace. Instead, the UN became a place where the two *superpowers* competed and tried to influence other nations.

Meanwhile, Roosevelt had died. Harry S. Truman had become president. Truman was a plain, self-educated man. But he had honesty, self-confidence, and a willingness to make tough decisions.

Truman met with the British and Soviet leaders at the Potsdam Conference in July 1945. He reminded Stalin of his promise to allow free elections in Eastern Europe. But Stalin would not listen to Truman. Soviet troops occupied Eastern Europe. There was little *the West* could do.

1. What were three issues that led to hard feelings between the Soviet Union and the United States?

_____

Tension Mounts (pages 608–609)

What did Stalin and Truman want for postwar Europe?

Truman and Stalin disagreed over the future of Europe. Truman wanted strong democratic nations. He wanted the United States to be able to buy raw materials in Eastern Europe. He also wanted Eastern European markets for American products.

Stalin wished to spread communism. He also wanted to control Eastern Europe to prevent another invasion of Soviet territory. He wanted to use the resources of Germany and Eastern Europe to rebuild his war-torn nation. Stalin also felt that war between the Soviet Union and the West could not be avoided.

Stalin set up Communist governments in the European nations occupied by Soviet troops. They became **satellite nations,** countries that depended on and were dominated by the Soviet Union. The United States answered with a policy of **containment.** This was an effort to block Soviet influence by making alliances and supporting weaker nations.

In 1946, Winston Churchill described "an iron curtain" coming down across Europe. It separated the nations in the "Soviet sphere" from the capitalist democracies of the West.

2. How did Truman's and Stalin's plans differ?

_____

Cold War in Europe (pages 610–611)

What were the Truman Doctrine and the Marshall Plan?

The conflicting aims of the United States and the Soviet Union led to the **Cold War.** This was a state of hostility between these superpowers, but one without military action. Each tried to spread its political and economic influence worldwide.

Truman's first test of containment was when Greece and Turkey needed economic and military aid in 1947. In the **Truman Doctrine,** the president argued that aid should be sent to any nation trying to stop Communists from taking over.

Congress agreed. Aid was sent to Turkey and Greece.

Western Europe was also in terrible economic shape. Factories and fields had been destroyed. A terrible winter in 1946–1947 increased hardship. Secretary of State George Marshall wanted to send aid to nations that cooperated with American economic goals. Then Soviet troops took over Czechoslovakia in 1949. Congress saw the need for strong, stable governments to resist communism. It approved the **Marshall Plan.** The plan was a great success in rebuilding Western Europe and halting the spread of communism.

3. How did the United States begin to send aid to nations fighting communism?

_____

Superpowers Struggle Over Germany (pages 611–612)

How did the Soviets and the West disagree over Germany?

East and West also disagreed over Germany. Stalin wanted to keep it weak and divided. The Western allies thought Europe would be more stable if Germany were united and productive. Britain, France, and the United States combined their occupied zones into the nation of West Germany.

Berlin was also divided into four occupied zones. But it was located in Soviet-controlled East Germany. The Soviets cut off all transportation to West Berlin. West Berlin was the name given the zones occupied by Britain, France, and the United States. The Soviets said they would hold the city *hostage* until the West gave up the idea of German *reunification.* Instead, the United States and Britain started the **Berlin Airlift.** For 327 days, planes brought food and supplies to West Berlin. Finally, the Soviets gave up the blockade.

The blockade made the West worry about Soviet aggression. The United States and Canada joined with ten European nations in a defensive military alliance called the **North Atlantic Treaty Organization (NATO).** Members agreed that an attack on one was an attack on all.

4. What led to the Berlin blockade?

_____

CHAPTER 18 Section 2 (pages 613–618)

The Cold War Heats Up

TERMS AND NAMES

Mao Zedong Leader of the Communist forces in China

Chiang Kai-shek Leader of the Nationalist forces in China

Taiwan (Formosa) Island off the coast of China

38th parallel Imaginary line that divides Korea at 38 degrees north latitude

Korean War War begun when North Korea invaded South Korea in 1950

BEFORE YOU READ

In the last section, you read about postwar Europe.

In this section, you will read about the postwar in Asia.

AS YOU READ

Fill in the time line below with the major events of the Communist takeover in China and the Korean War.

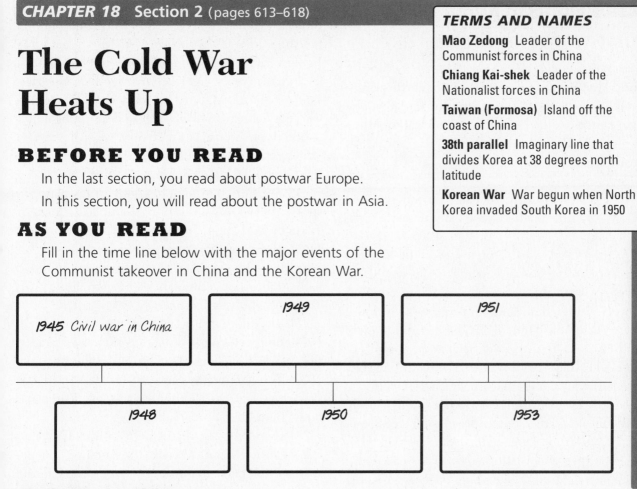

1945 Civil war in China   1949   1951

1948   1950   1953

Civil War in China (pages 613–615)

How did the Communists gain control of China?

World War II had interrupted a civil war in China. The two sides joined to fight the Japanese. **Mao Zedong** led the Communist forces in the North. The Nationalist forces of **Chiang Kai-shek** fought the Japanese in the south. After the war ended in 1945, the Communists and Nationalists went back to fighting each other for control of China.

The United States backed the Nationalists because they were anti-Communist. But Chiang often acted like a dictator. His government was wasteful, ineffective, and corrupt. He overtaxed the Chinese people even during times of *famine*. He did not have the support of the people.

Mao won the support of the Chinese *peasants*. He distributed land to them and reduced rents. He had an experienced army with high morale.

President Truman refused to send American troops to help the Nationalists fight communism. But he did send aid. Even so, in 1949, Chiang and his forces had to flee to **Taiwan (Formosa),** an island off the coast of China. China was now Communist. Containment in China had failed!

American conservatives said that the United States had "lost" China because not enough had been done to help the Nationalists. Truman's followers said that the Communist success was because Chiang could not win the support of the Chinese people. Conservatives claimed that the U.S. government was filled with Communist agents. American fear of communism began to burn out of control.

1. How did Communists gain control of China?

_____

_____

_____

Koreans Go To War; The United States Fights in Korea (pages 615–618)

What caused the Korean War?

Japan had ruled Korea since 1910. At the end of World War II, Japanese forces in the north surrendered to the Soviets. In the south, the Japanese surrendered to the Americans. Two nations then developed. They were separated by the **38th parallel,** an imaginary line that divides Korea at 38 degrees north *latitude.*

In 1948 South Korea became an independent nation. North Korea became a Communist nation. Each claimed the right to rule all of Korea.

In June 1950, North Korea started the **Korean War** by invading South Korea. Truman was afraid another Asian nation was about to fall to communism. He ordered air and naval support for South Korea. Then the United Nations agreed to help South Korea. Troops from 16 nations—most of them American—were sent to South Korea. They were led by General Douglas MacArthur.

North Korean troops moved steadily south. They conquered the South Korean capital of Seoul. Then MacArthur launched a counterattack. His forces trapped about half the North Korean Army, which surrendered. MacArthur's success in Korea made him a national hero.

UN and South Korean forces advanced toward the 38th parallel. If they crossed it, the war would become an *offensive* rather than a *defensive* one. In October 1950, the UN told MacArthur to cross the 38th parallel and reunite Korea.

The Chinese opposed UN forces moving into North Korea. China said it would not let the Americans near its border. The UN ignored the threat and advanced. Then Chinese troops entered North Korea. They drove UN forces back. In January 1951, the Communists recaptured Seoul.

For two years, fighting continued. But neither side advanced. MacArthur wanted to extend the war into China. He even suggested dropping atomic bombs on China. Truman was against this strategy. The Soviets were allies of the Chinese. Truman felt bombing China would start World War III.

MacArthur continued to argue for his plan. He spoke to the press and to Republican leaders. Truman felt that he could no longer allow MacArthur's *insubordination.* He fired MacArthur as commander. At first, the American public sided with MacArthur. Later, they came to agree with Truman's idea of a *limited war.*

Meanwhile, a cease-fire went into effect in June 1951. Both sides agreed on a *demilitarized zone* at the 38th parallel. An *armistice* was signed in July 1953. The agreement was a *stalemate.* Korea was still divided between Communist North Korea and non-Communist South Korea.

Many people felt that American lives had been lost for little gain. As a result, the American people rejected the party in power, the Democrats, in the 1952 election. Republican Dwight D. Eisenhower was elected president. Americans also became even more worried about Communist expansion abroad and Communist spies at home.

2. What was gained by the Korean War?

_____

_____

Skillbuilder

Use this picture to answer these questions.

1. What kind of leader do you think MacArthur was from looking at this photo?

_____

2. What does the quote from President Truman tell you about his feelings for MacArthur?

_____

"Mr. Prima Donna, Brass Hat, Five Star MacArthur" *Harry S. Truman*

Photo Credit: Carl Mydans, *Life* Magazine. Copyright © Time, Inc.

CHAPTER 18   Section 3 (pages 619–624)

The Cold War at Home

TERMS AND NAMES

HUAC House Committee on Un-American Activities

Hollywood Ten People called before HUAC who did not cooperate

blacklist List of people in the Hollywood film industry who were refused jobs because they did not cooperate with HUAC

Alger Hiss Former State Department official

Ethel and Julius Rosenberg Activists in the American Communist Party who were executed as spies

Senator Joseph McCarthy Republican Senator who claimed Communists were taking over the federal government

McCarthyism Term used to refer to tactic of accusing people of disloyalty without producing evidence

BEFORE YOU READ

In the last section, you read about the Cold War abroad.

In this section, you will read about the effects of the Cold War at home.

AS YOU READ

Fill in the diagram below with the causes of the Fear of Communism in the boxes to the left and the effects in the boxes to the right.

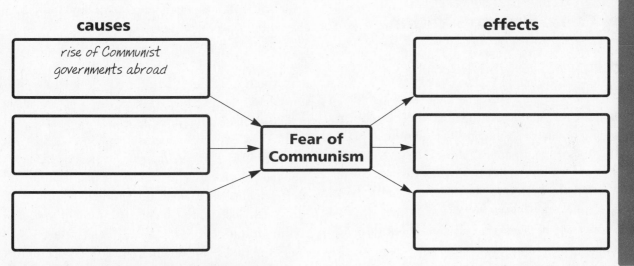

causes

rise of Communist governments abroad

Fear of Communism

effects

Fear of Communist Influence
(pages 619–621)

How did Americans react to the threat of Communist influence?

Many Americans felt threatened by the rise of Communist governments in Europe and Asia. Some even felt that Communists could threaten the U.S. government from within. These fears increased when people found out about some spies selling U.S. government secrets to the Soviets.

Republicans accused the Truman administra-

tion of being "soft on communism." In response to this pressure, Truman set up a Loyalty Review Board. The Board investigated over 3 million people. About 200 were fired. Many people felt that these investigations were unconstitutional. The accused were not allowed to see the evidence against them or to face their accusers.

In 1947, Congress set up the House Committee on Un-American Activities (HUAC). Its purpose was to look for Communists both inside and outside government. **HUAC** concentrated on the movie industry because of suspected Communist influences in Hollywood. Many people were brought before HUAC. Some agreed that there had been Communist *infiltration* of the movie industry. They *informed on* others to save themselves.

Ten people called before HUAC refused to testify. They said the hearings were unconstitutional. The **Hollywood Ten,** as they were called, were sent to prison for their refusal.

In response to the HUAC hearings, Hollywood executives created a list of some 500 people they thought were Communist-influenced. They refused to hire the people on this **blacklist.** Many people's careers were ruined.

In 1950, Congress passed the McCarren Act. It outlawed the planning of any action that might lead to a totalitarian dictatorship in the United States.

1. **What are three ways that the United States reacted to fear of communism at home?**

_____

_____

_____

Spy Cases Stun the Nation
(pages 621–623)

How did spies increase fear of communism?

Two spy cases added to the fear of communism sweeping the nation. One involved an official of the State Department named **Alger Hiss.** A former Soviet spy accused Hiss of spying for the Soviet Union. He had documents that *implicated* Hiss. Hiss claimed the documents were forgeries. Hiss was convicted of *perjury*—for lying about the documents—and went to jail.

In 1949, the Soviet Union tested an atomic bomb. Most people thought that it would take the Soviets much longer to develop their own atomic bomb. A British scientist admitted giving the Soviets secret information about the American bomb. He also implicated two Americans: **Ethel and Julius Rosenberg.**

The Rosenbergs were members of the American Communist Party. They denied the charges of spying. But they were convicted and sentenced to death. People from all over the world appealed for *clemency* for the Rosenbergs. They said the evidence against them was weak. The

Supreme Court refused to overturn the decision, and the Rosenbergs were executed in 1953.

2. **What two spy cases increased fear of communism in the United States?**

_____

_____

McCarthy Launches His "Witch Hunt" (pages 623–624)

Who was Senator McCarthy?

In the early 1950s, Republican Senator **Joseph McCarthy** made headlines. He claimed that Communists were taking over the government. He also said the Democrats were guilty of *treason* for allowing this Communist infiltration.

McCarthy never produced any evidence to support his charges. These unsupported attacks on suspected Communists became known as **McCarthyism.** Later, McCarthyism also came to mean the unfair tactic of accusing people of disloyalty without producing evidence.

Many Republicans encouraged McCarthy. They thought that a strong anti-Communist position would help them win the 1952 elections. But some complained that McCarthy was violating people's constitutional rights.

In 1954, McCarthy made accusations against the U.S. Army. The Senate *hearings* were broadcast on national television. The American people watched McCarthy bully witnesses but produce no evidence. McCarthy lost public favor. The Senate voted to condemn him.

There had been much support for Communist *witch hunts* in the early 1950s. Many people were forced to take *loyalty oaths* in order to get jobs. States passed laws making it a crime to speak of overthrowing the government. These laws violated the constitutional right of free speech. But people became afraid to speak their views. Fear of communism made many Americans willing to give up their constitutional rights.

3. What was McCarthyism?

_____

_____

CHAPTER 18 Section 4 (pages 625–629)

Two Nations Live on Edge

BEFORE YOU READ

In the last section, you saw how the fear of communism affected life in the United States.

In this section, you will see how Cold War tensions increased as both the United States and the Soviet Union tried to spread their influence around the world.

AS YOU READ

Fill in the time line below with events that show how the United States and the Soviet Union competed during the Cold War. Write Soviet actions above the line and U.S. actions below the line. Draw arrows to show how the two nations reacted to each other.

TERMS AND NAMES
H-bomb Hydrogen bomb
Dwight D. Eisenhower President of the United States
John Foster Dulles Secretary of state
brinkmanship Willingness to go to the edge, or brink, of war
CIA Intelligence-gathering, or spy, agency of the United States government
Warsaw Pact Military alliance of the Soviet Union and its satellite nations
Nikita Khruschev Soviet leader
Eisenhower Doctrine Policy of the United States that it would defend the Middle East against attack by any Communist country
Francis Gary Powers Pilot of an American U-2 spy plane
U-2 incident Downing of a U.S. spy plane and the capture of its pilot by the Soviet Union in 1960

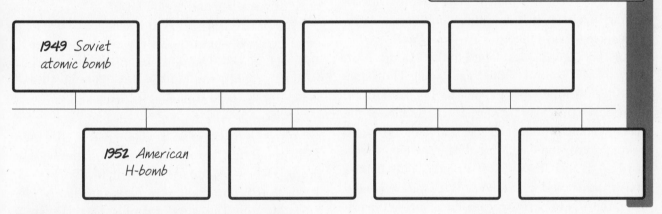

1949 Soviet atomic bomb

1952 American H-bomb

Brinkmanship Rules U.S. Policy

(pages 625–626)

What was the arms race?

The Soviet Union exploded its first atomic bomb in 1949. American leaders wanted to develop a more powerful weapon. In 1952, President Truman authorized work on the hydrogen bomb, or **H-bomb.** This bomb was much more powerful than the atomic bomb. It was ready in 1952.

But the Soviets tested their own H-bomb in 1953. **Dwight D. Eisenhower** was president. His Secretary of State, **John Foster Dulles,** was very anti-Communist. He said America must not com-

promise. The United States must be prepared to use all of its nuclear weapons against any aggressor. This willingness to go to the edge, or brink, of war was called **brinkmanship.**

The United States began making more nuclear weapons. So did the Soviet Union. This was called the arms race. Many Americans feared a nuclear attack at any time. They had *air-raid drills* and *fallout shelters* to prepare for these attacks.

1. Why did the arms race begin?

_____

_____

The Cold War Spreads Around the World (pages 626–628)

What events increased Cold War tensions?

The United States was in competition with the Soviet Union all over the world. President Eisenhower began to rely on the Central Intelligence Agency (CIA). The **CIA** used spies to get information abroad. It also carried out covert actions, or secret operations, to weaken or overthrow governments unfriendly to the United States.

One CIA action involved Iran. In 1951, the CIA convinced the Shah, or monarch, of Iran to get rid of a prime minister who was not friendly to the West. In 1954, the CIA took action in Guatemala. Eisenhower believed Guatemala was friendly to the Communists. The CIA trained an army that overthrew Guatemala's government.

Soviet dictator Josef Stalin died in 1953. At first, tensions eased between the superpowers. People called it a thaw in the Cold War. But when West Germany joined NATO, the Soviet Union formed a military alliance with its satellite nations in 1955. This alliance was called the **Warsaw Pact.**

In 1956, a crisis developed in the Middle East. Egypt seized control of the Suez Canal. The Canal was located in Egypt but owned by Britain and France, who had built it. Egypt was an ally of the Soviet Union. Britain, France, and Israel invaded Egypt to take the Canal back. The Soviets threatened to bomb Britain and France. The United States threatened to *retaliate*. War was prevented when the UN imposed a cease-fire. During the crisis, Eisenhower issued a warning, known as the **Eisenhower Doctrine.** It said the United States would defend the Middle East against Communist attack.

When the new Soviet leader, **Nikita Khrushchev,** criticized Stalin's *repressive* policies, many people thought the Soviet Union had changed. The satellite nation of Hungary demanded reforms. For a while, Khruschev seemed to agree. But when the Hungarians asked to leave the Warsaw pact in 1956, Soviet tanks rolled into Hungary. They crushed the reform movement. Many Hungarian reformers were killed, and others fled the country.

2. How did hostilities increase between the United States and the Soviet Union during the 1950s?

_____

_____

The Cold War Takes to the Skies
(pages 628–629)

What was the missile race?

The United States and the Soviet Union also competed in the skies. At first, the United States was sure it was ahead in military technology. But in 1957, the Soviets developed an ICBM, or intercontinental ballistic missile. This was a rocket that could travel much farther than American rockets and could carry nuclear weapons.

On October 4, 1957, the Soviets shocked the world by launching *Sputnik I*. It was the first artificial satellite to orbit the earth. Americans knew that it took a very powerful missile to launch this satellite—a missile that could reach the United States. This made Americans feel inferior to the Soviets in science and technology.

Americans responded by making changes in education. They improved the teaching of science and technology. American scientists also worked hard to catch up. On January 31, 1958, the United States successfully launched its first satellite.

Meanwhile, the United States had been flying spy missions over the Soviet Union. The CIA used U-2 aircraft that flew so high they could not be shot down. Or so the Americans thought. On May 1, 1960, a U-2 spy plane was shot down over the Soviet Union. The pilot, **Francis Gary Powers,** was captured and convicted of spying. However, he was soon released in exchange for a Soviet spy.

This **U-2 incident** happened right before a meeting between Eisenhower and Khrushchev. At the meeting, Khrushchev criticized the United States and walked out. The U-2 incident hurt Eisenhower's ability to deal with the Soviets.

3. In what two ways was the Cold War fought in the skies?

_____

_____

Glossary   CHAPTER 18 Cold War Conflicts

air-raid drills Practice of what to do during a bombing attack

armistice Temporary stop to fighting by agreement of both sides

clemency Mercy; reduction of a severe sentence given by a court

defensive Intended to withstand or protect against aggression or attack

demilitarized zone An area where military forces are not allowed

fallout shelters Underground living areas that give protection from the explosion and radiation of a nuclear attack

famine Drastic, wide-reaching food shortage, often resulting in the starvation of many people

hearing Session of an investigating committee at which testimony is taken from witnesses

hostage Person or persons held prisoner in order to get a ransom or agreement to certain demands

implicated Suggested the guilt of; incriminated

infiltration Process of entering gradually or secretly, in order to spy or gain control

informed on Implicated; gave incriminating information about others to the authorities

insubordination Act of disobeying authority

latitude Distance north or south of the earth's equator, measured in degrees

limited war War whose objective is less than the enemy's total defeat

loyalty oath Formal pledge of loyalty to the government, sometimes specifically denying membership in the Communist Party

offensive Attacking; starting a war

peasants Small farmers, tenant farmers, sharecroppers, and farm laborers

perjury False testimony under oath, as in a court of law or Congressional hearing; lying

repressive Stifling the free will and rights of a population

retaliate To strike back in kind; especially to return a military attack

reunification Recombining of the parts of a nation divided by force

Sputnik I First artificial satellite to orbit the Earth

stalemate Situation in which further action is blocked; a deadlock

superpowers Most powerful and influential nations, especially those that lead a power bloc

treason Betrayal of one's country, especially by aiding its enemies

the West Democracies of Western Europe and North America

witch hunt Investigation that says its purpose is to uncover illegal activities but is actually used to harm those whose views differ

AFTER YOU READ

Terms and Names

A. Write the name or term that best completes each sentence.

blacklist

containment

Mao Zedong

McCarthyism

NATO

satellite nations

Taiwan

Warsaw Pact

1. Stalin set up Communist governments in Soviet-dominated countries called _____. The United States tried to block Soviet influence in a policy called _____.

2. The United States, Canada, and ten European nations formed _____ to defend each other against Soviet aggression. Later, the Soviet Union and other Communist nations formed a military alliance called the _____.

3. Fear of Communist influence at home led to _____, a "witch hunt" in which many people were unfairly and unconstitutionally accused of being Communists. These people were sometimes put on a _____, which meant they could no longer find work.

4. _____ and his Communist forces won the civil war in China. They forced Chiang Kai-shek and his Nationalist forces to flee to the island of _____.

B. Write the letter of the name or term next to the description that explains it best.

a. Cold War

b. Korean War

c. John Foster Dulles

d. brinkmanship

e. CIA

f. Nikita Khrushchev

g. U-2 incident

_____ 1. The willingness to go to the edge of war in order to keep the peace

_____ 2. The period of competition and hostility between the United States and the Soviet Union

_____ 3. The shooting down of an American spy plane by the Soviets

_____ 4. The agency of the U.S. government that used spies to get information and to carry out secret actions abroad

_____ 5. The fighting between North Korean and Chinese Communist troops and UN forces for control of Korea

_____ 6. The leader of the Soviet Union who criticized Stalin but then crushed the reform movement in Hungary

_____ 7. President Eisenhower's secretary of state who developed the policy of brinkmanship

Main Ideas

1. What were the goals of U.S. foreign policy during the Cold War?

_____

2. What goals did the United States achieve by fighting in Korea? What goals did it fail to achieve?

_____

3. What actions of Senator Joseph McCarthy worsened the national hysteria about communism?

_____

4. By what means did the U.S. government, including the CIA, fight the Cold War around the world?

_____

Thinking Critically

Answer the following questions on a separate sheet of paper.

1. What was the Cold War? How did containment and the arms race contribute to the Cold War?

2. What were some effects of the fear of communism that swept the United States in the 1950s?

Postwar America

TERMS AND NAMES

GI Bill of Rights Law that provided financial and educational benefits for World War II veterans

suburb Residential town or community near a city

Harry S. Truman President after World War II

Dixiecrats Southern Democrats who left the party

Fair Deal President Truman's economic and social program

BEFORE YOU READ

In the last section, you read about the developments in the Cold War at home and abroad.

In this section, you will read about the economic boom in the United States after World War II.

AS YOU READ

Take notes on the chart below. List the postwar changes in various segments of American society.

SEGMENT OF AMERICAN SOCIETY	POSTWAR CHANGES
veterans	
economy	
labor	
civil rights	

Readjustment and Recovery
(pages 636–638)

How did the end of World War II affect America?

After World War II, millions of returning veterans used the **GI Bill of Rights** to get an education and to buy homes. At first, there was a terrible housing shortage. Then developers such as William Levitt built thousands of inexpensive homes in the **suburbs,** small residential communities near the cities.

Many veterans and their families moved in.

The United States changed from a wartime to a peacetime economy. After the war, many defense workers were laid off. Returning veterans added to unemployment. When wartime price controls ended, prices shot up. Congress eventually put back economic controls on wages, prices, and rents.

The economy began to improve on its own. There was a huge pent-up demand for consumer goods. People had been too poor to buy these goods during the Depression. Many items had not been available during the war. Now Americans bought cars and appliances and houses. The Cold War increased defense spending and employment.

1. What were three effects of the end of World War II on American society?

Economic Challenges; Social Unrest Persists (pages 638–641)

What were postwar problems?

President **Harry S. Truman** faced a number of problems immediately after the war. One was labor unrest. In 1946, a steel-workers' strike was followed by a coal miners' strike. In addition, the railroad unions threatened to stop all rail traffic in the nation.

Truman was pro-labor. But he would not let strikes cripple the nation. He threatened to draft striking workers into the army and then order them back to work. The unions gave in.

During this time, before the economy turned around, many Americans were disgusted with shortages, rising *inflation,* and strikes. Voters became more conservative. In the 1946 election, conservative Republicans gained control of Congress.

After the war, there was racial violence in the South. African-American veterans demanded their rights as citizens. Truman met with African-American leaders. They asked for a federal *anti-lynching law,* an end to the *poll tax,* and a commission to prevent discrimination in hiring.

Truman put his career on the line for civil rights. But Congress would not pass any of his civil rights measures. Finally, Truman acted on his own. In 1948, he issued an executive order to desegregate the armed forces. He also ordered an end to discrimination in hiring government employees.

Meanwhile, the Supreme Court said that African Americans could not be kept from living in certain neighborhoods. These acts marked the beginning of a federal commitment to deal with racial issues.

Truman was nominated for president in 1948. He insisted on a strong civil rights *plank* in the Democratic Party platform. This split the party. Many Southern Democrats left the Democratic Party. These **Dixiecrats** were against civil rights. They wanted to preserve the "Southern way of life." They formed the States' Rights Party. Some liberals left the Democratic party to form the Progressive Party.

It didn't look like Truman could win. But he took his ideas to the people. He criticized the "do-nothing Congress." Truman won a narrow victory. Democrats took control of Congress.

Truman tried to pass economic and social reforms. He called his program the **Fair Deal.** Health insurance and a *crop-subsidy program* for farmers were both defeated by Congress. But an increase in the minimum wage, extension of Social Security, and financial aid for cities passed.

2. What were some issues Truman fought for?

Republicans Take the Middle Road (pages 641–642)

Why did Eisenhower win?

Truman did not run for reelection in 1952. The big issues of that campaign were 1) the stalemate in the Korean War, 2) anti-Communist hysteria and McCarthyism, 3) the growing power of the federal government, 4) strikes, and 5) inflation. Voters wanted a change. The Republicans nominated war hero General Dwight Eisenhower. He easily beat Democrat Adlai Stevenson.

Eisenhower was a low-key president with middle-of-the-road policies. He did have to deal with one controversial issue—civil rights. In 1954, the Supreme Court ruled in *Brown* v. *Board of Education* that public schools could not be segregated. Eisenhower believed that the federal government should not be involved in desegregation. But he upheld the law. When the governor of Arkansas tried to keep African-American students out of a white high school, Eisenhower sent federal troops to integrate the school.

The America of the mid-1950s was a place of "peace, progress, and prosperity." Eisenhower won a landslide victory in 1956.

3. What two important civil rights actions occurred during Eisenhower's presidency?

CHAPTER 19 Section 2 (pages 643–649)

The American Dream in the Fifties

TERMS AND NAMES

conglomerate Major corporation that owns smaller companies in unrelated industries

franchise Company that offers similar products or services in many locations

baby boom Soaring birthrate from 1946 to 1964

Dr. Jonas Salk Developer of a vaccine to prevent polio

consumerism Excessively concerned with buying material goods

planned obsolescence Purposely making products to become outdated or wear out quickly

BEFORE YOU READ

In the last section, you read about the postwar boom in the United States.

In this section, you will read how many Americans achieved their dreams of material comfort and prosperity, but some found the cost of conformity too high.

AS YOU READ

Take notes on the chart below. Fill it in with examples of specific goals that characterized the American Dream for suburbanites of the 1950s.

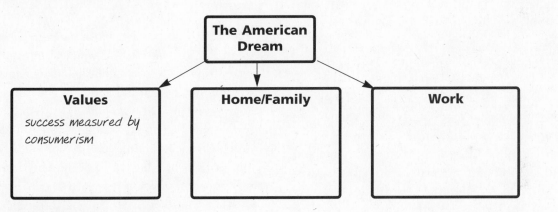

The American Dream

Values	Home/Family	Work
success measured by consumerism		

The Organization and the Organization Man (pages 643–644)

What changes took place in the American workplace in the 1950s?

The economy grew rapidly in the 1950s. By 1956, more Americans were *white-collar* workers in offices than were in *blue-collar* factory jobs. White-collar workers were paid better. They usually worked in service industries, such as sales and communications.

Businesses also expanded. They formed **conglomerates,** or major corporations that own smaller companies in unrelated industries. Other businesses expanded by franchising. A **franchise** is a company that offers similar products or services in

many locations, such as fast-food restaurants.

These large companies offered well-paying, secure jobs to certain kinds of workers. These workers were conformists, or team players. They were "company people" who would fit in and not rock the boat. Businesses rewarded loyalty rather than creativity. They promoted a sameness, or standardization, of people as well as products. Books such as *The Organization Man* and *The Man in the Gray Flannel Suit* criticized this conformity.

1. What changes occurred in the American work force and workplace in the 1950s?

_____

_____

_____

The Suburban Lifestyle (pages 644–647)

What was life like in the 1950s?

Many Americans enjoyed the benefits of the booming economy. Many worked in cities but lived in suburbs. They had the American dream of a single-family home, good schools, and a safe neighborhood with people just like themselves.

There was an increase in births called the **baby boom.** It was caused by the reuniting of families after the war and growing prosperity. Medical advances also wiped out childhood diseases. **Dr. Jonas Salk** developed a vaccine to prevent polio. Polio had killed or crippled 58,000 children a year.

The baby boom created a need for more schools and products for children. Suburban family life revolved around children. Many parents depended on advice from a popular baby-care book by Dr. Benjamin Spock. He said it was important that mothers stay at home with their children. The role of homemaker and mother was also glorified in the media. But many women felt alone and bored at home.

By 1960, 40 percent of mothers worked outside the home. But their career opportunities usually were limited to "women's fields." These included secretarial work, nursing, and teaching. Even if women did the same work as men, they were paid less.

Americans had more *leisure* time. They spent time and money on leisure activities, such as sports. They also watched sports on television and read books and magazines. Youth activities, such as Scouts and Little League, became popular too.

2. What was life like in the suburbs of 1950s?

The Automobile Culture
(pages 647–648)

Why were cars so important?

Easy credit for buying cars and cheap gasoline led to a boom in automobile ownership. In the 1950s, the number of American cars on the road grew from 40 to 60 million.

A car was a necessity in the suburbs. There was no public transportation. People needed to drive to their jobs in the cities. They also had to drive to shop and do errands. Therefore, more and better roads were also needed. In 1956, the United States began building a nationwide highway network. In turn, these roads allowed long-distance trucking. This led to a decline in the railroads.

Americans loved to drive. They went to drive-in restaurants and movies. They drove long distances on vacation. Motels and shopping malls were built to serve them. These new industries were good for the economy. But the increase in driving also caused problems. These included stressful traffic jams and air pollution. Many white people left the cities. Jobs and industries followed. This left mostly poor people in crowded inner cities.

3. How did cars change American life?

Consumerism Unbound (pages 648–649)

Why did Americans turn to consumerism in the 1950s?

By the mid-1950s, nearly 60 percent of Americans were in the *middle class*. They had the money to buy more and more products. They measured success by their **consumerism,** or the amount of material goods they bought.

American business flooded stores with new products. Some of them, such as polyester fabrics, teflon, and plastics, had been developed during the war. War-time developments in electronics also reached the marketplace. Among these electronic goods were household appliances, televisions, and hi-fi record players.

Manufacturers also tried a new marketing strategy called **planned obsolescence.** They purposely made products to become outdated or to wear out quickly. Americans began to throw away items in order to buy "new models." Easy credit, including the introduction of credit cards, encouraged people to buy. Private debt grew.

The 1950s were "the advertising age." Ads were everywhere—even on the new medium of television. They tried to persuade Americans to buy things they didn't need. They appealed to people's desire for status and for a sense of belonging.

4. How was consumerism encouraged in the 1950s?

CHAPTER 19   Section 3 (pages 652–657)

Popular Culture

BEFORE YOU READ

In the last section, you read about the American dream in the 1950s.

In this section, you will read that popular culture in the 1950s reflected white, middle-class America.

AS YOU READ

Fill in the chart with notes on what each group contributed to popular culture in the 1950s.

GROUP	CONTRIBUTION TO POPULAR CULTURE OF THE 1950s
Families shown on TV	
Beat generation	
Rock 'n' roll	
African Americans	

New Era of Mass Media
(pages 652–655)

What influence did TV have?

Mass media—the means of communication that reach large audiences—include radio, television, newspapers, and magazines. Television became the most important means of communication in the 1950s. It both showed and influenced popular culture of the time.

The number of homes with television jumped. It went from 9 percent of all homes in 1950 to 90 percent in 1960. At first, the number of television

stations was limited by the **Federal Communications Commission (FCC).** The FCC is the government agency that regulates the communications industry. Soon, however, TV stations spread across the country. Many shows became widely popular all over the nation.

The 1950s were the "golden age of television." Comedy shows starring Milton Berle and Lucille Ball were popular. Edward R. Murrow introduced on-the-scene reporting and interviews. There were also westerns, sports events, and original dramas. At first, all shows were broadcast live.

Advertisers took advantage of this new medium, especially of its children's shows. Young fans wanted to buy everything that was advertised on their favorite shows. TV magazines and TV dinners— frozen meals to heat and eat—became popular.

Television reflected the mainstream values of white suburban America. These values were secure jobs, material success, well-behaved children, and conformity. Critics objected to the *stereotypes* of women and minorities. Women were shown as happy, ideal mothers. African Americans and Latinos hardly appeared at all. In short, TV showed an idealized white America. It ignored poverty, diversity, and problems such as racism.

As dramas and comedies moved to TV, radio changed. It began to focus on news, weather, music, and local issues. The radio industry did well. Advertising increased and so did the number of stations.

The movie industry suffered from competition by television. The number of moviegoers dropped 50 percent. But Hollywood fought back. It responded by using color, stereophonic sound, and the wide screen to create spectacular movies.

1. Was the picture of America portrayed on television accurate?

_____

_____

A Subculture Emerges (pages 655-656)
What were the beat movement and rock 'n' roll?

Television showed the suburban way of life. But two *subcultures* presented other points of view. One was the **beat movement** in literature. These writers made fun of the conformity and materialism of *mainstream* American society.

Their followers were called **beatniks.** They rebelled against consumerism and the suburban lifestyle. They did not hold steady jobs and lived inexpensively. They read their poetry in coffee houses. Their art and poetry had a free, open form. Major works of the beat generation include Allen Ginsberg's long poem *Howl,* Jack Kerouac's novel *On the Road,* and Lawrence Ferlinghetti's *A Coney Island of the Mind.*

Some musicians also took a new direction. They added electronic instruments to the African-American music called rhythm and blues. The result was **rock 'n' roll.** The new music had a strong beat. Its lyrics focused on the interests of teenagers, including *alienation* and unhappiness in love. And teenagers responded. They bought millions of records. The biggest star of all—the King of Rock 'n' Roll—was Elvis Presley. He had 45 songs that sold more than one million copies.

Some adults criticized rock 'n' roll. They said it would lead to teenage crime and immorality. But television and radio helped bring rock 'n' roll into the mainstream.

2. In what ways did the beat movement and rock 'n' roll differ from mainstream America in the 1950s?

_____

_____

African Americans and Popular Culture (pages 656–657)
What role did African-American artists play in the 1950s?

Many of the great performers of the 1950s were African American. Nat "King" Cole, Lena Horne, Harry Belafonte, and Sidney Poitier were popular with white audiences. They led the way for later African-American stars. Jazz musicians like Miles Davis and Dizzy Gillespie also entertained audiences of both races. The most popular black performers were the early rock 'n' roll stars, like Little Richard and Chuck Berry.

Television was slow to integrate. One of the first programs to do so was Dick Clark's popular rock 'n' roll show *American Bandstand.* In 1957, *Bandstand* showed both black couples and white couples on the dance floor.

Before integration reached radio audiences, there were stations that aimed specifically at African-American listeners. They played the popular black artists of the day. They also served advertisers who wanted to reach black audiences.

3. How did African Americans fit into the entertainment industry of the 1950s?

_____

CHAPTER 19 Section 4 (pages 660–663)

The Other America

TERMS AND NAMES

urban renewal Plan to tear down decaying neighborhoods and build low-cost housing

bracero Farm workers entering the United States from Mexico

termination policy Federal government decision to end federal responsibility for Native American tribes

BEFORE YOU READ

In the last section, you read about mainstream American society in the 1950s.

In this section, you will read about Americans who were not part of the American mainstream.

AS YOU READ

Fill in the chart below with notes on the problems faced by each of the groups listed. Then circle the problems that all of the groups faced.

GROUP	PROBLEMS
Urban Poor	
Mexican Americans	
Native Americans	

The Urban Poor (pages 660–661)

What was the plight of the inner cities?

Prosperity reached many Americans in the 1950s. But it did not reach all Americans. In 1962, one out of every four Americans was poor. Many of these poor people were members of minority groups.

In the 1950s, millions of middle-class white people left the cities for the suburbs. This was called "white flight." Meanwhile, many poor African Americans moved from the rural South to Northern cities. Businesses—and jobs—followed whites out of the cities. Cities also lost the taxes these people and businesses had paid. City governments could no longer afford to keep up the quali-

ty of schools, public transportation, or other services. The urban poor suffered as their neighborhoods decayed.

Many suburban, middle-class Americans could not believe that a country as rich as the United States had such poverty in its cities. However, Michael Harrington's 1962 book *The Other America: Poverty in the United States* made many Americans aware of the problem.

One way the government tried to solve the problem of the *inner cities* was called urban renewal. Minorities could not afford the new homes that had been built in the suburbs during the 1950s. Also minorities were not welcome in the white suburbs. As a result, inner-city neighborhoods became very overcrowded.

Urban renewal was designed to tear down decaying neighborhoods and build low-cost housing. However, sometimes highways and shopping centers were built instead. The people who had lived in the old slums ended up moving to other *slums*—rather than into better housing.

1. What were some reasons for the decay of America's inner cities?

_____

_____

Mexican Americans and Native Americans (pages 661–663)

How were Mexican Americans and Native Americans treated?

During World War II, there was a shortage of laborers to harvest crops. The federal government allowed **braceros,** or hired hands, to enter the United States from Mexico. They were supposed to work on American farms during the war, and then go back to Mexico. However, when the war ended, many braceros stayed illegally. Many other Mexicans entered the United States illegally to find jobs. The government started a program to seize and return *illegal aliens* to Mexico.

Mexican Americans suffered prejudice and discrimination, too, even though they were citizens. When Mexican-American veterans came home from the war, they wanted to be treated fairly. They formed an organization to protest injustices. Other groups worked to help Mexican Americans register to vote. Pressure from these groups forced California to stop placing Mexican-American chil-

dren in segregated classes. Mexican Americans began to have a nationwide political voice.

Native Americans also struggled for equal rights. This struggle was complicated by federal involvement in Native American affairs. At first, the government had supported assimilation, or absorbing Native Americans into mainstream American culture. That forced Native Americans to give up their own culture. In 1934, the Indian Reorganization Act changed that policy. The government now wanted Native Americans to have more control over their own affairs.

In 1944, Native Americans formed an organization to work for their civil rights and for the right to keep their own customs. After World War II, Native Americans got less financial help from the government. Outsiders grabbed tribal lands for mining and development.

In 1953, the federal government decided to end its responsibility for Native American tribes. This **termination policy** stopped federal economic support. It also ended the reservation system and distributed tribal land among individual Native Americans. One result of this policy was that many acres of tribal lands were sold to developers.

As part of the termination policy, the Bureau of Indian Affairs also moved thousands of Native Americans to the cities. It helped them find jobs and housing. This program was a failure. Native Americans did not have the skills to succeed in the cities. They were cut off from medical care. And they suffered job discrimination. The termination policy was ended in 1963.

2. How did Mexican Americans and Native Americans work for equal rights after World War II?

_____

Poverty Thresholds for a Family of Four

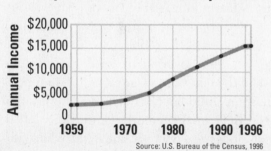

Source: U.S. Bureau of the Census, 1996

The poverty threshold, or poverty line, is the minimum amount of annual income that an individual or a family needs to survive in the United States.

Skillbuilder

Use the chart to answer the questions.

1. What was the poverty threshold in 1959?

_____

2. What was the poverty threshold in 1996?

_____

Glossary

alienation Feeling of being separate from or out of step with the majority or the mainstream

antilynching law Law to protect African Americans from being executed without due process of law, especially being hanged by a mob

blue collar Referring to workers who do manual labor and wear work clothes

crop-subsidy program Granted by the government to farmers to keep crop prices up

illegal alien Someone living in a foreign country without permission

inflation Continuing increase in consumer prices

inner cities Older, central parts of cities, with crowded neighborhoods of low-income, minority residents

leisure Freedom from time-consuming duties or activities

mainstream Most common attitudes and values of a society

middle class People whose economic situation places them between the working classes and the wealthy

plank One of the articles of a statement of the principles of a political party

poll tax Tax used to prevent African-Americans from voting

slums Poor, overcrowded urban areas with very bad living conditions

stereotype Oversimplified representation of what is typical of a person, group, or situation

subculture Group within a society that has its own set of customs, attitudes, and values

white collar Refers to workers who do not do manual labor and who wear "business dress"

AFTER YOU READ

Terms and Names

A. Write the letter of the phrase that best completes each sentence.

1. Followers of the beat movement were _____.

    a. nonconformist writers who criticized the American emphasis on material goods

    b. musicians who developed a rhythmic new style of popular music

    c. typical families shown on television

2. Manufacturers used the strategy of planned obsolescence to get people to _____.

    a. cater to teenagers

    b. plan carefully for their retirement

    c. throw away "out of date" products and buy new ones

3. The termination policy was _____.

    a. the canceling of credit for consumers

    b. a U.S. government plan to give up responsibility for Native American tribes

    c. the deporting of illegal aliens

4. The mass media include _____.

    a. radio, TV, and magazines

    b. business and labor

    c. sports, music, and fashion

5. Urban renewal was _____.

    a. migration of rural African Americans to the cities

    b. white flight to the suburbs

    c. a plan to rebuild the inner cities

B. Write the letter of the name or term next to the description that explains it best.

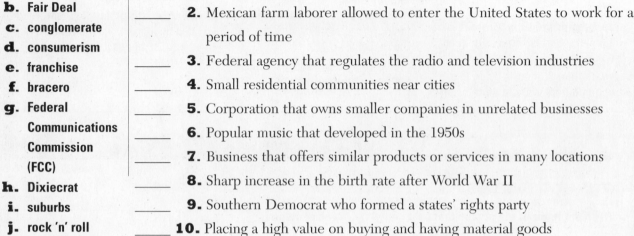

a. baby boom	_____ **1.** Truman's plan for economic and social reforms
b. Fair Deal	_____ **2.** Mexican farm laborer allowed to enter the United States to work for a
c. conglomerate	period of time
d. consumerism	
e. franchise	_____ **3.** Federal agency that regulates the radio and television industries
f. bracero	_____ **4.** Small residential communities near cities
g. Federal	_____ **5.** Corporation that owns smaller companies in unrelated businesses
Communications	_____ **6.** Popular music that developed in the 1950s
Commission	_____ **7.** Business that offers similar products or services in many locations
(FCC)	
h. Dixiecrat	_____ **8.** Sharp increase in the birth rate after World War II
i. suburbs	_____ **9.** Southern Democrat who formed a states' rights party
j. rock 'n' roll	_____ **10.** Placing a high value on buying and having material goods

Main Ideas

1. What domestic and foreign issues concerned voters during the 1952 presidential election?

_____

_____

2. What was portrayed as the American Dream in the 1950s.

_____

_____

3. How did the values of the beatniks differ from those of mainstream America?

_____

_____

4. How did many major cities change in the 1950s?

_____

_____

Thinking Critically

Answer the following questions on a separate sheet of paper.

1. What was the American Dream of the 1950s? How did television affect it?

2. How did the postwar boom of the 1950s affect most white Americans? What groups got left out, and why?

CHAPTER 20 **Section 1** (pages 670–676)

Kennedy and the Cold War

TERMS AND NAMES

John F. Kennedy 35th president of the United States

flexible response Policy of using nonnuclear weapons to fight a war

Fidel Castro Ruler of Cuba

Berlin Wall Barrier built to keep East Germans from fleeing to West Berlin

hot line Direct phone line between the White House and the Kremlin

Limited Test Ban Treaty Treaty that barred nuclear testing in the atmosphere

BEFORE YOU READ

In the last section, you read about the poverty that existed in the United States in the 1950s.

In this section, you will read how John F. Kennedy became president and how he handled a period of intense foreign affairs.

AS YOU READ

Use this diagram to take notes on the major foreign crises that the Kennedy administration faced.

CRISIS	KENNEDY'S HANDLING	OUTCOME
Bay of Pigs	*okays invasion, promises air support*	*invaders are captured; Kennedy is embarrassed*
Cuban Missile Crisis		
Berlin Crisis		

The Election of 1960 (pages 670–672)

How did Kennedy win the election?

In 1960, President Eisenhower's term came to a close. By then, many Americans were worried about the future. The economy was in a *recession*. In addition, the Soviet Union was gaining strength. As a result, some wondered whether the United States was losing the Cold War.

John F. Kennedy and Richard M. Nixon faced off in the 1960 presidential election. Kennedy was a Democratic senator from Massachusetts. Nixon was Eisenhower's vice-president. Kennedy won the election by a slim margin. Two main factors led him to victory.

The first factor was television. During the campaign, the two candidates held a televised debate. It was the first televised presidential election debate in the nation's history. During the debate, Kennedy appeared strong and forceful. Nixon appeared nervous and ill at ease. Kennedy's performance increased his popularity.

The second factor was Kennedy's response to the arrest of Dr. Martin Luther King Jr. in October 1960. King was emerging as a leader in the country's civil rights movement. An Atlanta judge sentenced King to four months in jail for demonstrating. Kennedy called King's wife to express his sympathy. The Kennedy campaign persuaded the judge to release King while he waited to appeal his sentence. Kennedy's actions won him widespread support from African Americans.

Upon entering the White House, Kennedy focused on foreign affairs. He urged a tough stand against the Soviet Union. He also supported a policy called **flexible response.** This policy called for the use of conventional weapons rather than nuclear weapons in the event of a war. Conventional weapons included jets, tanks, missiles, and guns. In order to build more conventional weapons, Kennedy increased defense spending.

1. What two factors helped Kennedy win the 1960 presidential election?

_____

_____

Crises Over Cuba (pages 672–675)

What two crises involving Cuba did Kennedy face?

Kennedy's first foreign policy test came from Cuba. Cuba's leader was **Fidel Castro.** Castro had seized power in 1959. Soon after that, he declared himself a Communist. He then formed ties with the Soviet Union.

Kennedy approved a plan to remove Castro from power. The plan called for Cuban exiles to invade Cuba and overthrow Castro. The U.S. government would supply air support for the exiles.

The attack failed. Many exiles were captured. The failed invasion became known as the Bay of Pigs. It left the Kennedy administration greatly embarrassed.

A year later, the United States and Cuba clashed again. Pictures from U.S. spy planes revealed that the Soviets were building nuclear missile bases in Cuba. Some bases already contained missiles ready to launch. These weapons could be aimed at the United States.

President Kennedy demanded that the Soviets remove the missiles. In October, 1962, he surrounded Cuba with U.S. Navy ships. These ships forced Soviet vessels trying to reach Cuba to turn around. A tense standoff followed. It appeared that war might break out. However, Soviet leader Nikita Khrushchev finally agreed to remove the missiles.

The crisis damaged Khrushchev's prestige in the Soviet Union and the world. Kennedy also endured criticism. Some Americans thought Kennedy had acted too boldly and nearly started a nuclear war. Others claimed he had acted too softly. These critics believed that Kennedy should have invaded Cuba and ousted Castro.

2. Name the two Cuban crises that the Kennedy administration faced.

_____

_____

The Continuing Cold War
(pages 675–676)

How did the U.S. and Soviets try to ease tensions?

Cuba was not Kennedy's only foreign policy problem. In 1961, the president faced a growing problem in Berlin. The city was still divided. East Berlin was under Communist control. West Berlin was under the control of Great Britain, France, and the United States. By 1961, almost 3 million East Germans had fled into West Berlin.

Khrushchev threatened to block all air and land routes into West Berlin. Kennedy warned the Soviet leader against such action. As a result, Khrushchev changed his plan. He built a large concrete barrier along the border between East and West Berlin. It was known as the **Berlin Wall.** It prevented any more East Germans from fleeing to West Berlin.

Despite their battles, Kennedy and Khrushchev did attempt to reach agreements. They established a **hot line** between their two nations. This telephone hookup connected Kennedy and Khruschchev. It allowed them to talk directly when a crisis arose. The two leaders also agreed to a **Limited Test Ban Treaty.** This treaty barred nuclear testing in the atmosphere.

3. Name two ways the U.S. and Soviet Union worked to ease tensions between them.

_____

_____

CHAPTER 20 Section 2 (pages 677–682)

The New Frontier

TERMS AND NAMES

New Frontier The name given to Kennedy's domestic program

mandate An overwhelming show of support by voters

Peace Corps A program that enlisted volunteers to help in poor countries

Alliance for Progress A program that supplied aid to Latin America

Warren Commission Body that investigated the assassination of President Kennedy

BEFORE YOU READ

In the last section you read about how President Kennedy dealt with explosive foreign matters.

In this section you will read about Kennedy's domestic agenda and how his presidency—and life—was cut short.

AS YOU READ

Use this diagram to take notes about Kennedy's New Frontier programs.

PROGRAM	DESCRIPTION
deficit spending	government spends more than it has in order to boost economy

The Camelot Years (pages 677–678)

How did the country react to the Kennedy family?

President Kennedy and his wife, Jacqueline, were a *glamorous* couple. They charmed many Americans with their elegance and grace. The Kennedys gave special recognition to arts and culture. They invited many artists, musicians, and celebrities to perform at the White House.

President Kennedy frequently appeared on television. His charm and wit made him popular with the American people. Much of the White House press corps also admired him. Their reports helped to boost Kennedy's public image.

The new first family fascinated the American public. Jacqueline Kennedy influenced fashion and culture. The nation's newspapers and magazines ran many pictures and stories about the Kennedy children. However, the Kennedy administration had its critics. They argued that his presidency was all style and no substance.

Kennedy surrounded himself with many intellectuals and businesspeople. He named his brother, Robert, as attorney general. Robert also served as the president's chief adviser.

1. Cite two examples of the country's fascination with the Kennedys.

_____

_____

_____

The Promise of Progress
(pages 678–681)

What were Kennedy's domestic plans?

President Kennedy called his domestic program the **New Frontier.** However, Kennedy had a difficult time getting Congress to support his program. Conservative Republicans and southern Democrats blocked many of his bills. These included bills to provide medical care for the aged, rebuild cities, and aid education.

One reason for Kennedy's difficulties was that he was elected by a small margin. As a result, he lacked a popular **mandate.** This was a clear indication that the voters approved of his plans. Because he lacked overwhelming support, Kennedy rarely pushed hard for his bills.

Kennedy did succeed with some proposals. To help the economy grow, the Kennedy administration used deficit spending. This occurred when the government spent more money than it received in taxes. Kennedy hoped that increased spending on defense would help boost the economy.

Kennedy also introduced the **Peace Corps.** This was a program of volunteers working in poor nations around the world. The purpose of this program was to decrease poverty *abroad*. It was also meant to increase goodwill toward the United States. The Peace Corps was a huge success. People of all ages and backgrounds signed up to work for the organization. By 1968, more than 35,000 volunteers had served in 60 nations around the world.

Another program was the **Alliance for Progress.** This program gave aid to Latin American countries. One reason for this program was to keep Communism from spreading to these countries.

In 1961 the Soviets launched a person into orbit around the earth. The news stunned America. A space race quickly began between the United States and Soviet Union. President Kennedy pledged that the nation would put a man on the moon by the end of the decade. That goal was reached on July 20, 1969, when Neil Armstrong stepped onto the moon.

The space race affected American society in many ways. Schools taught more science. Researchers developed many new technologies. The space race also contributed to economic growth.

The Kennedy Administration also tried to solve the problems of poverty and racism. In 1963, Kennedy called for a national effort to fight American poverty. He also ordered the Justice Department to investigate racial injustices in the South.

2. Name two successful programs of the Kennedy Administration.

_____

_____

Tragedy in Dallas (pages 681–682)

Who killed President Kennedy?

On November 22, 1963, President and Mrs. Kennedy arrived in Dallas, Texas. Kennedy had come there to improve relations with the state's Democratic Party. Large crowds greeted the Kennedys as they rode along the streets of downtown Dallas. Then, rifle shots rang out. Kennedy had been shot. The president died about an hour later at a nearby hospital.

The tragic news spread across the nation and then around the world. Millions of Americans sat glued to their televisions over the next few days. They watched on live television as a gunman shot and killed the president's accused killer, Lee Harvey Oswald.

The events seemed too strange to believe. Many people wondered if Oswald had acted alone or with others. Chief Justice Earl Warren headed a commission to investigate the assassination. The **Warren Commission** determined that Oswald acted alone. However, many people continue to believe that Oswald was part of a *conspiracy*.

3. What did the Warren Commission determine?

_____

_____

CHAPTER 20   Section 3 (pages 683–691)

The Great Society

BEFORE YOU READ

In the last section, you read about President Kennedy's domestic programs.

In this section, you will read about Lyndon Johnson's bold plan to reshape America.

AS YOU READ

Use this diagram to take notes about President Lyndon Johnson's Great Society programs.

PROGRAM	DESCRIPTION
Economic Opportunity Act	Created antipoverty programs

LBJ's Path to Power; Johnson's Domestic Agenda (pages 683–686)

How did Johnson wage "war" on poverty?

Lyndon B. Johnson, a Texan, was Senate majority leader in 1960. Johnson was a skilled lawmaker. He demonstrated a great ability to negotiate and reach agreements. During the 1960 presidential campaign, Kennedy's advisers thought that Johnson would make the perfect running mate. They believed that Johnson's connections in Congress and his Southern background would help

Kennedy's presidential chances. Kennedy asked Johnson to be his vice-presidential candidate. Johnson agreed. He helped Kennedy win important states in the South.

Upon Kennedy's death, Johnson became president. Under President Johnson's leadership, Congress passed two bills that President Kennedy had proposed. One was a tax cut to help stimulate the economy. The other was the Civil Rights Act of 1964.

Johnson then launched his own program—a "war on poverty." He worked with Congress to pass the **Economic Opportunity Act.** This law created youth programs, antipoverty measures, small business loans, and job training. The law also created the Job Corps youth training program and the VISTA (Volunteers in Service to America) program.

Johnson ran for president in 1964. He easily defeated his Republican opponent, Barry Goldwater.

1. **Name two programs created by the Economic Opportunity Act.**

Building the Great Society; Reforms of the Warren Court
(pages 686–690)

How did the Great Society and Warren Court change America?

President Johnson had a grand vision for America. He called it the **Great Society.** Throughout his term, Johnson introduced legislation to help him create his Great Society. Among other things, these laws:

- created **Medicare and Medicaid** to ensure health care for the aged and poor;
- funded the building of public housing units;
- lifted restrictions on immigration through the **Immigration Act of 1965**—which opened the door for many non-European immigrants to settle in the United States;
- required efforts to ensure clean water, through the Water Quality Act of 1965;
- offered increased protection to consumers, through the Wholesome Meat Act of 1967;
- established safety standards for automobiles and tires.

The wave of liberal reform that characterized the Great Society also affected the Supreme Court. Chief Justice Earl Warren took an active role in *promoting* more liberal policies. The **Warren Court** ruled school *segregation* unconstitutional. The court also banned prayer in public schools and strengthened the right of free speech.

The Warren Court also changed the area of congressional **reapportionment.** This is the way in which states redraw their election districts. The Court ruled that election districts in each state had to have roughly the same number of people in them. Because so many people lived in the cities, the court's ruling led to the creation of many new urban districts. As a result, political power shifted from the countryside to the cities.

The Warren Court also strengthened the rights of people accused of crimes. The Court ruled police had to read suspects their rights before questioning them. These rights are known as **Miranda rights.**

2. **Name one result of the Great Society and Warren Court.**

Impact of the Great Society
(pages 690–691)

How successful was the Great Society?

The Great Society and the Warren Court changed America. People disagree on whether these changes left the nation better or worse off than before. On one hand, Johnson's antipoverty measures helped reduce the suffering of many people. However, many of Johnson's proposals did not achieve their stated goals. Most people agree on one point: No president since World War II increased the power and reach of federal government more than Lyndon Johnson.

Eventually, some Americans began to question the increased size of the federal government. They also wondered about the effectiveness of Johnson's programs. Across the country, people became *disillusioned* with the Great Society. This led to the rise of a new group of Republican leaders.

3. **How did the Great Society affect the size of the federal government?**

Glossary — *CHAPTER 20* The New Frontier and the Great Society

abroad Outside of one's own country

conspiracy An agreement between two or more people to perform an illegal or evil act

disillusioned Let down or disappointed

glamorous Charming and romantic, exciting

promote To contribute to the progress or growth of

recession A temporary decline in economic activity

segregation Separation, including by race

AFTER YOU READ

Terms and Names

A. Choose the letter of the term or name that correctly fits the description or definition.

_____ **1.** The direct communication link between the president and the Soviet leader set up in the 1960s was
   a. the flexible response. **c.** massive retaliation.
   b. the hot line. **d.** reapportionment.

_____ **2.** The New Frontier program created to offer economic and technical assistance to help Latin American countries was
   a. the Peace Corps. **c.** Economic Opportunity Act.
   b. the Great Society. **d.** the Alliance for Progress.

_____ **3.** The way in which states redraw election districts based on the changing number of people in them is called
   a. reapportionment. **c.** the hot line.
   b. flexible response. **d.** the Miranda rights.

_____ **4.** The Chief Justice of the Supreme Court who oversaw liberal Court rulings was
   a. Richard Nixon. **c.** Earl Warren.
   b. Barry Goldwater. **d.** Robert Kennedy.

_____ **5.** This measure was not part of the Great Society.
   a. Medicare and Medicaid **c.** flexible response
   b. Immigrations Act of 1965 **d.** Wholesome Meat Act of 1967

B. Write the letter of the name or term that matches the description.

a. Nikita Khrushchev

b. Peace Corps

c. New Frontier

d. flexible response

e. Medicare and Medicaid

f. Great Society

_____ **1.** The Soviet leader who squared off against President Kennedy during the Cuban crisis

_____ **2.** The strategy intended to broaden America's range of options during international crises

_____ **3.** The name for Kennedy's domestic and legislative programs

_____ **4.** The program in which U.S. volunteers provided assistance to developing nations of the world

_____ **5.** Programs that provided low-cost health insurance to the aged and poor.

AFTER YOU READ (continued) *CHAPTER 20* The New Frontier and the Great Society

Main Ideas

1. Why did Kennedy have trouble getting much of his New Frontier legislation through Congress?

_____

_____

2. Describe the two international aid programs launched during the Kennedy administration.

_____

_____

3. How did The Great Society address the problem of poverty?

_____

_____

4. How did the Supreme Court strengthen the rights of people accused of a crime.

_____

_____

5. Why is the Great Society's legacy considered to be mixed?

_____

_____

Thinking Critically

Answer the following questions on a separate sheet of paper.

1. How important is a president's personality in his ability to lead? Consider how Kennedy's charm and mystique and Johnson's persuasive skills affected their success as presidents.

2. What do you see as the advantages and disadvantages of increasing the size and reach of the federal government?

Taking on Segregation

TERMS AND NAMES

Thurgood Marshall African American lawyer who led the legal challenge against segregation

Brown v. Board of Education Case in which court ruled segregated schools were unconstitutional

Rosa Parks Woman who helped start Montgomery bus boycott

Dr. Martin Luther King, Jr. Leader of the civil rights movement

Southern Christian Leadership Conference Civil rights organization

Student Nonviolent Coordinating Committee Civil rights organization formed by students

sit-in Protest tactic in which blacks occupied whites-only seats at lunch counters

BEFORE YOU READ

In the last section, you read about President Johnson's Great Society.

In this section you will read how African Americans challenged the nation's policies of segregation and racial inequality.

AS YOU READ

Use this diagram to take notes on the early civil rights battles.

INCIDENT	RESULT
Little Rock School Crisis	National Guard forces school to let in blacks
Montgomery Bus Boycott	
Lunch counter sit-ins	

The Segregation System
(pages 696–698)

How did World War II help start the civil rights movement?

By 1950, most African Americans were still considered second-class citizens. Throughout the South, Jim Crow laws remained in place. These were laws aimed at keeping blacks separate from whites.

During the 1950s, however, a civil rights movement began. This was a movement by blacks to gain greater equality in American society.

In several ways, World War II helped set the stage for this movement. First, the demand for soldiers during the war had created a shortage of white male workers. This opened up many new jobs for African Americans.

Second, about 700,000 African Americans had served in the armed forces. These soldiers helped free Europe. Many returned from the war ready to fight for their own freedom.

Third, during the war, President Franklin Roosevelt outlawed racial *discrimination* in all federal agencies and war-related companies.

World War II had given blacks a taste of equality and respectability. When the war ended, many blacks were more determined than ever to improve their *status*.

1. Name two ways in which World War II helped set the stage for the civil rights movement.

_____

_____

_____

Challenging Segregation in Court (page 698)

What did the Court rule in Brown v. Board of Education?

Even before the civil rights movement began, African-American lawyers had been challenging racial discrimination in court. Beginning in 1938, a team of lawyers led by **Thurgood Marshall** began arguing several cases before the Supreme Court.

Their biggest victory came in the 1954 case known as ***Brown v. Board of Education*** of Topeka, Kansas. In this case, the Supreme Court ruled that separate schools for whites and blacks were unequal—and thus unconstitutional.

2. What did the Supreme Court rule about separate schools for whites and blacks?

_____

_____

Reaction to the *Brown* Decision; the Montgomery Bus Boycott (pages 699–701)

Where did African Americans fight racial segregation?

Some Southern communities refused to accept the *Brown* decision. In 1955, the Supreme Court handed down a second *Brown* ruling. It ordered schools to desegregate more quickly.

The school desegregation issue reached a crisis in 1957 in Little Rock, Arkansas. The state's governor, Orval Faubus, refused to let nine African-American students attend Little Rock's Central High School. President Eisenhower sent in federal troops to allow the students to enter the school.

School was just one place where African Americans challenged segregation. They also battled discrimination on city buses. In Montgomery, Alabama, a local law required that blacks give up their bus seats to whites. In December 1955, Montgomery resident **Rosa Parks** refused to give her seat to a white man. Parks was arrested.

After her arrest, African Americans in Montgomery organized a yearlong *boycott* of the city's bus system. The protesters looked for a per-son to lead the bus boycott. They chose **Dr. Martin Luther King, Jr.,** the pastor of a Baptist Church.

The boycott lasted 381 days. Finally, in late 1956, the Supreme Court ruled that segregated buses were illegal.

3. Name two places that African Americans targeted for racial discrimination.

_____

_____

Dr. King and the SCLC; The Movement Spreads (pages 701–703)

Where did King get his ideas?

Martin Luther King, Jr. preached nonviolent resistance. He termed it "soul force." He based his ideas on the teachings of several people. From Jesus, he learned to love one's enemies. From the writer Henry David Thoreau, King took the idea of civil disobedience. This was the refusal to obey an unjust law. From labor organizer A. Philip Randolph, he learned how to organize huge demonstrations. From Mohandas Gandhi, King learned that a person could resist *oppression* without using violence.

King joined with other ministers and civil rights leaders in 1957. They formed the **Southern Christian Leadership Conference** (SCLC). By 1960, another influential civil rights group emerged. The **Student Nonviolent Coordinating Committee** (SNCC) was formed mostly by college students. Members of this group felt that change for African Americans was occurring too slowly.

One protest strategy that SNCC used was the **sit-in.** During a sit-in, African Americans sat at whites-only lunch counters. They refused to leave until they were served. In February 1960, African-American students staged a sit-in at a lunch counter at a Woolworth's store in Greensboro, North Carolina. The students sat there as whites hit them and poured food over their heads. By late 1960, students had desegregated lunch counters in 48 cities in 11 states.

4. Name two people from whom Martin Luther King, Jr. drew his ideas.

_____

_____

The Triumphs of a Crusade

BEFORE YOU READ

In the last section, you read how African Americans began challenging the nation's racist systems.

In this section, you will read how civil rights activists broke down many racial barriers and prompted landmark legislation.

AS YOU READ

Use this diagram to take notes on the achievements of the civil rights movement.

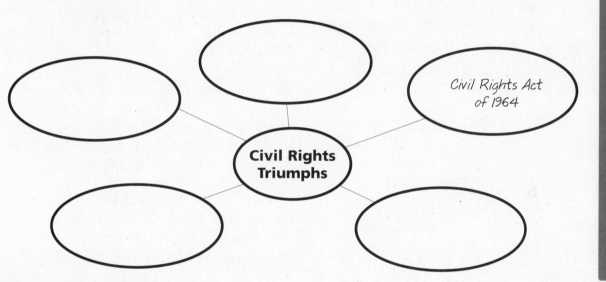

Civil Rights Triumphs

Civil Rights Act of 1964

Riding for Freedom (pages 704–705)

Who were the freedom riders?

The Congress of Racial Equality (CORE) was one of the nation's older civil rights groups. It was formed in 1942. As the civil rights movement of the 1950s and 1960s grew, CORE became more active.

In the 1960s, CORE decided to test the Supreme Court ruling that banned segregation on buses traveling national routes. White and black activists rode together on the buses into the South. These activists were known as **freedom riders.** Many riders were met by angry mobs that attacked and beat them.

As more attacks occurred, the Kennedy administration stepped in. It sent U.S. marshals to protect the freedom riders. The Interstate Commerce Commission, which regulated bus companies, also helped out. The Commission outlawed segregation in all interstate travel facilities. These included waiting rooms, restrooms, and lunch counters.

1. Name two ways the government helped the freedom riders.

_____

_____

Standing Firm (pages 705–707)

What happened in Birmingham?

Civil rights workers soon turned their attention to *integrating* Southern schools. In September 1962, a federal court allowed **James Meredith** to attend the all-white University of Mississippi. However, Mississippi's governor refused to admit him. The Kennedy administration sent in U.S. marshals. They forced the governor to let in Meredith.

Another *confrontation* occurred in 1963 in Birmingham, Alabama. There, King and other civil rights leaders tried to desegregate the city. Police attacked activists with dogs and water hoses.

Many Americans witnessed the attacks on television They were outraged by what they saw. Eventually, Birmingham officials gave in. They agreed to end segregation in the city.

The growing civil rights movement impressed President Kennedy. He became convinced that the nation needed a new civil rights law. Kennedy called on Congress to pass a sweeping civil rights bill.

2. What was the outcome of the demonstrations in Birmingham?

_____

_____

Marching to Washington
(pages 707–708)

What did the Civil Rights Act of 1964 do?

President Kennedy's civil rights bill outlawed discrimination based on race, religion, national origin, and gender. It also gave the government more power to push for school desegregation. Civil rights leaders wanted Congress to pass the bill. So they staged a massive march on Washington, D.C.

On August 28, 1963, more than 250,000 blacks and whites marched into the nation's capital. There, they demanded the immediate passage of the bill.

Dr. Martin Luther King, Jr., spoke to the crowd. He called for peace and racial harmony in his now-famous "I Have a Dream" speech.

Several months later, President Kennedy was assassinated. Lyndon Johnson became president. He won passage in Congress of Kennedy's **Civil Rights Act of 1964.**

3. Name two things the Civil Rights Act of 1964 did.

_____

_____

Fighting for Voting Rights
(pages 708–710)

Where did workers try to register African Americans to vote?

Civil rights activists next worked to gain voting rights for African Americans in the South. The voting project became known as **Freedom Summer.** The workers focused their efforts on Mississippi. They hoped to influence Congress to pass a voting rights act.

Robert Moses was a former New York City schoolteacher. He led the voter project in Mississippi. The project met with much opposition and violence.

Meanwhile, civil rights activists challenged Mississippi's political structure. At the 1964 Democratic National Convention, SNCC organized the Mississippi Freedom Democratic Party (MFDP). The new party hoped to unseat Mississippi's regular party delegates at the convention.

Civil rights activist **Fannie Lou Hamer** spoke for the MFDP at the convention. She gave an emotional speech. As a result, many Americans supported the seating of the MFDP delegates. However, the Democratic Party offered only 2 of Mississippi's 68 seats to MFDP members.

In 1965, civil rights workers attempted a voting project in Selma, Alabama. They met with violent resistance. As a result, Martin Luther King, Jr. led a massive march through Alabama. President Johnson responded by asking Congress to pass a new voting rights act. Congress passed the **Voting Rights Act of 1965.** The law *eliminated* state laws that had prevented African Americans from voting.

4. Name two states where civil rights workers tried to register blacks to vote.

_____

_____

Challenges and Changes in the Movement

BEFORE YOU READ

In the last section, you read about the triumphs of the civil rights movement.

In this section, you will read about challenges and changes to the movement and how it ultimately left a mixed legacy.

AS YOU READ

Use this diagram to take notes of the mixed legacy of the civil rights movement.

TERMS AND NAMES

de jure segregation Segregation by law

de facto segregation Segregation by custom or practice

Malcolm X African-American leader

Nation of Islam Group headed by Elijah Muhammad

Stokely Carmichael Leader of Black Power movement

Black Power Movement that stressed black pride

Black Panthers African-American group founded to combat police brutality

Kerner Commission Commission that reported on the state of race relations in America.

Civil Rights Act of 1968 Act that banned discrimination in housing

affirmative action Program aimed at hiring or including minorities

ACHIEVEMENTS	REMAINING PROBLEMS
full voting rights	high unemployment

African Americans Seek Greater Equality (pages 711–712)

What problems did African Americans in the North face?

By 1965, the civil rights movement had turned its attention to the North. In the South the problem had been **de jure segregation.** This was segregation by law. The problem in the North was **de facto segregation.** This was segregation that exists by practice or custom. This type of segregation was more difficult to overcome. It was easier to change laws than it was to change people's attitudes.

De facto segregation increased as African Americans moved to Northern cities after World War II. Many white people left the cities. They moved to suburbs. By the mid-1960s, many African Americans in the North lived in decaying urban slums. There, they dealt with poor schools and high unemployment.

The terrible conditions in Northern cities angered many African Americans. This anger led to many episodes of violence.

1. Name two problems African Americans in the North faced.

_____

_____

_____

New Leaders Voice Discontent
(pages 713–715)

Who were the new leaders?

During the 1960s, new African-American leaders emerged. They called for more *aggressive* tactics in fighting racism.

One such leader was **Malcolm X.** Malcolm preached the views of Elijah Muhammad. Muhammad was the head of the **Nation of Islam,** or the Black Muslims. Malcolm declared that whites were responsible for blacks' misery. He also urged African Americans to fight back when attacked.

Eventually, Malcolm changed his policy regarding violence. He urged African Americans to use peaceful means—especially voting—to win equality. In February 1965, he was assassinated.

Another new black leader was **Stokely Carmichael.** He introduced the notion of **Black Power.** This movement encouraged African-American pride and leadership.

In 1966, some African Americans formed a political party called the **Black Panthers.** The party was created to fight police brutality. They urged violent resistance against whites. Many whites and *moderate* African Americans feared the group.

2. Name two new civil rights leaders.

_____

_____

1968—A Turning Point in Civil Rights (pages 715–716)

Who was killed in 1968?

In April 1968, a gunman shot and killed Martin Luther King, Jr., in Memphis, Tennessee. Many leaders called for peace. But anger over King's death led many African Americans to riot. Cities across the nation erupted in violence.

A bullet claimed the life of yet another leader in 1968. In June, a man shot and killed Senator Robert Kennedy. Kennedy was a strong supporter of civil rights. The assassin was a Jordanian immigrant. He allegedly was angry about Kennedy's support of Israel. Kennedy had been seeking the Democratic nomination for president when he was killed.

3. Name two of the nation's leaders killed in 1968.

_____

_____

Legacy of the Civil Rights Movement (pages 716–717)

Why is the legacy of the civil rights movement considered mixed?

Shortly after taking office, President Johnson formed a group known as the **Kerner Commission.** The commission's job was to study the cause of urban violence. In March 1968, the commission issued its report. It named one main cause for violence in the cities: white racism.

What, then, did the civil rights movement achieve? The movement claimed many triumphs. It led to the passage of important civil rights acts. This included the **Civil Rights Act of 1968.** This law banned discrimination in housing.

The movement also led to the banning of segregation in education, transportation, and employment. It also helped African Americans gain their full voting rights.

Yet many problems remain. Whites continue to flee the cities. Throughout the years, much of the progress in school integration has been reversed. African Americans continue to face high unemployment.

The government has taken steps to help African Americans—and other disadvantaged groups. During the 1960s federal officials began to promote **affirmative action.** Affirmative-action programs involve making special efforts to hire or enroll minorities.

4. Name one goal the civil rights movement achieved and one that remains.

_____

_____

Glossary

aggressive Inclined to move in a hostile or angry manner

boycott To protest against something by refusing to buy or use it

confrontation To face with hostility and anger

discrimination The act of regarding someone as different due to various features, including race

eliminate To get rid of, remove

integrate To unify, to open to all races

moderate Mild, calm, reasonable

oppression The state of being kept down, or treated poorly

status The legal condition of a person

AFTER YOU READ

Terms and Names

A. Write the letter of the term that best answers the question.

a. Fannie Lou Hamer

b. *Plessy* v. *Ferguson*

c. Stokely Carmichael

d. Robert Moses

e. Civil Rights Act of 1968

f. *Brown* v. *Board of Education*

_____ **1.** What Supreme Court case declared segregation in schools unconstitutional?

_____ **2.** Who led the Freedom Summer project in Mississippi in 1964?

_____ **3.** Who spoke for the Mississippi Freedom Democratic Party in the 1964 Democratic convention?

_____ **4.** Who introduced the idea of Black Power?

_____ **5.** What was the legislation that banned discrimination in housing?

B. If the statement is true, write "true" on the line. If it is false, change the underlined word or words to make it true.

_____ **1.** The NAACP lawyer who argued the Brown v. Board of Education case in front of the Supreme Court was <u>Robert Moses</u>.

_____ **2.** In 1957, Dr. Martin Luther King, Jr., was one of the founders of the <u>Student Nonviolent Coordinating Committee</u>.

_____ **3.** In September 1962, <u>James Meredith</u> was the first African American to attend the University of Mississippi.

_____ **4.** Segregation that exists by practice and custom, not by law, is <u>de jure segregation</u>.

_____ **5.** The <u>Black Panthers</u> was a political party formed to fight against police brutality in the ghetto.

Main Ideas

1. How did the Montgomery Bus Boycott begin?

_____

_____

2. Describe Martin Luther King Jr.'s "soul force."

_____

_____

3. What was the objective of the freedom rides? of Freedom Summer?

_____

_____

4. What did Malcolm X preach?

_____

_____

5. What challenges still face the nation in the area of civil rights?

_____

_____

Thinking Critically

Answer the following questions on a separate sheet of paper.

1 A civil rights activist once said, "You can kill a man, but you can't kill an idea." How did the civil rights movement prove this?

2 What civil rights achievement do you consider most important? Explain your answer.

CHAPTER 22 Section 1 (pages 724–728)

Moving Toward Conflict

TERMS AND NAMES

Ho Chi Minh Leader of North Vietnam

Vietminh Communist group led by Ho Chi Minh

domino theory Eisenhower's explanation for stopping communism

Dien Bien Phu Major French outpost captured by the Vietminh

Geneva Accords Peace agreement that split Vietnam in two

Ngo Dinh Diem Leader of South Vietnam

Vietcong Communist rebel group in South Vietnam

Ho Chi Minh Trail Network of paths running between North and South Vietnam

Tonkin Gulf Resolution Resolution that allowed President Johnson to fight in Vietnam

BEFORE YOU READ

In the last section, you read about the legacy of the civil rights movement.

In this section, you will read how the United States became involved in Vietnam.

AS YOU READ

Use the diagram below to take notes on the important Vietnam-related events during the following years.

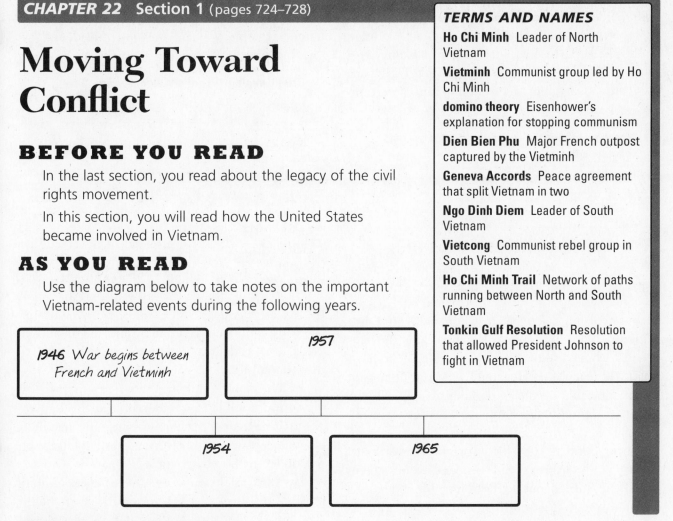

1946 War begins between French and Vietminh

1957

1954

1965

The Roots of American Involvement (pages 724–726)

Why did the U.S. get involved?

Vietnam is a long, thin country on a *peninsula* in southeast Asia. From the late 1800s until World War II, France ruled Vietnam. The French treated the Vietnamese badly. As result, the Vietnamese often rebelled. The Communist Party in Vietnam organized many of the rebellions. The group's leader was **Ho Chi Minh.**

In 1941, Japan conquered Vietnam. That year, the Vietnamese Communists combined with other groups to form an organization called the **Vietminh.** The Vietminh's goal was to achieve independence for Vietnam. In 1945, Japan was defeated in World War II. As a result, the Japanese left Vietnam. The Vietminh claimed independence for Vietnam.

However, France wanted to retake control of Vietnam. French troops moved back into the country in 1946. They conquered the southern half of Vietnam. The Vietminh took control of the North. For the next eight years, the two sides fought for control of the entire country.

The United States supported France during the war. America considered the Vietminh to be Communists. The United States, like other western nations, was determined to stop the spread of communism. President Eisenhower explained his country's policy with what became known as the **domino theory.** Eisenhower compared many of the world's smaller nations to dominoes. If one nation fell to communism, the rest also would fall.

The Vietminh defeated the French. The final blow came in 1954. That year, the Vietminh conquered the large French outpost at **Dien Bien Phu.**

Several countries met with the French and the Vietminh to negotiate a peace agreement. The agreement was known as the **Geneva Accords.** It temporarily split Vietnam in half. The Vietminh controlled North Vietnam. The anti-Communist nationalists controlled South Vietnam. The peace agreement called for an election to unify the country in 1956.

1. For what reason did the United States support France in the war?

The United States Steps In
(pages 726–727)

Who were the Vietcong?

Ho Chi Minh ruled North Vietnam. **Ngo Dinh Diem** led South Vietnam. When it came time for the all-country elections, Diem refused to take part. He feared that Ho would win. And then all of Vietnam would become Communist.

The United States supported Diem's decision. The U.S. government provided aid to Diem. America hoped that Diem could turn South Vietnam into a strong, independent nation. Diem, however, turned out to be a terrible ruler. His administration was corrupt. He also refused to allow opposing views.

By 1957, a rebel group had formed in the South. The group was known as the **Vietcong.** It fought against Diem's rule. Ho Chi Minh supported the Vietcong from the North. He supplied arms to the group along a network of paths that ran between North and South Vietnam. Together, these paths became known as the **Ho Chi Minh Trail.**

John Kennedy became president after Eisenhower. Kennedy continued America's policy of supporting South Vietnam. He, like Eisenhower, did not want to see the Communists take over Vietnam.

Meanwhile, Diem's government grew more *unstable.* The Vietcong rebels were gaining greater support among the peasants. The Kennedy administration decided that Diem had to step down. In 1963, military leaders overthrew Diem. Against Kennedy's wishes, they executed him.

Two months later, Kennedy himself was assassinated. Lyndon Johnson became president. The growing crisis in Vietnam was now his.

2. Briefly explain who the Vietcong were.

President Johnson Expands the Conflict (pages 727–728)

What was the Tonkin Gulf Resolution?

South Vietnam did not improve after Diem's death. A string of military leaders tried to rule the country. Each one failed to bring stability. Johnson, however, continued to support South Vietnam. The president was determined to not "lose" Vietnam to the Communists.

In August 1964, Johnson received reports of an incident in the Gulf of Tonkin off North Vietnam. A North Vietnamese patrol boat allegedly had fired torpedoes at a U.S. destroyer. President Johnson responded by bombing North Vietnam.

He also asked Congress for special military powers to stop any future North Vietnamese attacks on U.S. forces. As a result, Congress passed the **Tonkin Gulf Resolution.** The resolution granted Johnson broad military powers in Vietnam. In February 1965, President Johnson used his new power. He launched a major bombing attack on North Vietnam's cities.

3. What did the Tonkin Gulf Resolution grant President Johnson?

CHAPTER 22 Section 2 (pages 729–734)

U.S. Involvement and Escalation

BEFORE YOU READ

In the last section, you read how the United States became involved in Vietnam.

In this section, you will read about the war America fought in Vietnam.

AS YOU READ

Use this diagram to take notes on why the United States had trouble fighting the Vietcong.

TERMS AND NAMES

Robert McNamara Secretary of Defense under Johnson

Dean Rusk Secretary of State under Johnson

William Westmoreland Commander of U.S. troops in Vietnam

napalm Gasoline-based explosive

Agent Orange Chemical that destroyed jungle land

search-and-destroy mission Tactic in which U.S. troops destroyed Vietnamese villages

credibility gap Situation in which the U.S. public no longer believed the Johnson administration

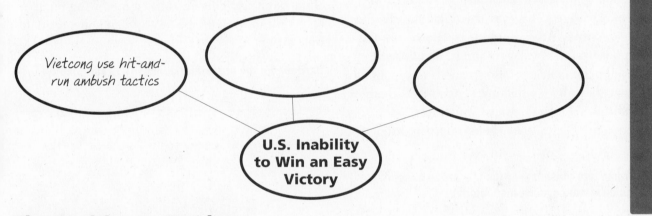

Vietcong use hit-and-run ambush tactics

U.S. Inability to Win an Easy Victory

The Decision to Escalate
(pages 729–730)

Who supported Johnson's decision to send U.S. troops to Vietnam?

In 1965, Johnson began sending U.S. troops to Vietnam to fight the Vietcong. Some of Johnson's advisers had opposed this move. They argued it was too dangerous.

But most of the president's advisers supported sending in troops. They included Secretary of Defense **Robert McNamara** and Secretary of State **Dean Rusk.** These men believed that America had to help defeat communism in Vietnam. Otherwise, the Communists might try to take over other countries.

Much of the public also agreed with Johnson's decision. Many Americans believed in stopping the spread of communism.

By the end of 1965, the United States had sent more than 180,000 troops to Vietnam. The American commander in South Vietnam was General **William Westmoreland.** He asked for even more troops. By 1967, almost 500,000 American soldiers were fighting in Vietnam.

1. Name two groups that supported Johnson's decision to use troops in Vietnam.

_____

_____

A War in the Jungle (pages 730–733)

Why did the war drag on?

The United States believed that its superior weaponry would lead to a quick victory over the Vietcong. However, several factors turned the war into a bloody *stalemate.*

The first factor was the Vietcong's fighting style. The Vietcong did not have advanced weapons. As a result, they used hit-and-run *ambush* tactics. The Vietcong struck quickly in small groups. They then disappeared into the jungle or an elaborate system of tunnels. These tactics frustrated the American troops.

The second factor was the Vietcong's refusal to surrender. Throughout the war, the Vietcong suffered many battlefield deaths. However, they continued to fight on.

The third factor was the American troops' inability to win the support of the Vietnamese peasants. In fighting the Vietcong, U.S. troops ended up hurting the peasants as well. For example, U.S. planes dropped **napalm,** a gasoline-based bomb that set fire to the jungle. They did this to expose Vietcong tunnels and hideouts. They also sprayed **Agent Orange.** This was a leaf-killing chemical that destroyed the landscape. Both of these weapons wounded villagers and ruined villages.

American soldiers also turned the peasants against them by conducting **search-and-destroy missions.** During these missions, soldiers destroyed villages they believed supported the Vietcong.

2. **Name two reasons why the U.S. failed to score a quick victory against the Vietcong.**

_____

_____

_____

The Early War at Home
(pages 733–734)

How did the war affect Johnson's domestic programs?

The number of U.S. troops in Vietnam continued to increase. So did the cost of the war. As a result, the nation's economy began to suffer. In order to pay for the war, President Johnson had to cut spending for his Great Society programs.

By 1967, many Americans still supported the war. However, the images of the war on television began to change that. The Johnson administration told the American people that the war was going well. But television told the opposite story. Each night, Americans watched the brutal scenes of the war on their television screens.

This led to a **credibility gap** in the Johnson administration. This meant that a growing number of people no longer believed what the president was saying.

3. **How did the war affect Johnson's Great Society?**

_____

_____

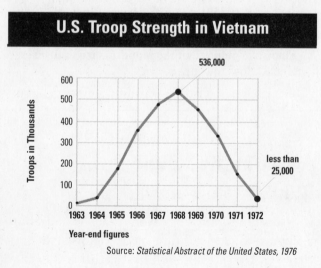

U.S. Troop Strength in Vietnam

536,000

less than 25,000

Troops in Thousands

600
500
400
300
200
100
0

1963 1964 1965 1966 1967 1968 1969 1970 1971 1972

Year-end figures

Source: *Statistical Abstract of the United States, 1976*

Skillbuilder

Use the graph to answer the questions.

1. **What year saw the largest number of U.S. forces in Vietnam?**

_____

2. **By the beginning of what year had the number of U.S. troops in Vietnam dropped below 200,000?**

_____

_____

CHAPTER 22 Section 3 (pages 735–740)

A Nation Divided

BEFORE YOU READ

In the last section, you read about America's war effort in Vietnam.

In this section, you will read about how the nation became divided over the war in Vietnam.

AS YOU READ

Use this diagram to take notes on the beliefs and actions of the New Left organizations.

Free Speech Movement

Students For a Democratic Society

New Left

A Working-Class War
(pages 735–737)

Who fought the war?

Most soldiers who fought in Vietnam were *drafted*. Because the war was growing unpopular, thousands of men tried to avoid the draft.

One of the most common ways to avoid the draft was to attend college. Most men enrolled in a university could put off their military service.

Many university students during the 1960s were white and wealthy. As a result, many who fought in Vietnam were lower-class whites or minorities. Nearly 80 percent of American soldiers came from lower economic levels. Thus, Vietnam was known as a working-class war.

Early on, a high number of African Americans served and died in Vietnam. During the first several years of the war, 20 percent of American soldiers killed were black. Blacks, however, made up only

about 10 percent of the U.S. population. This situation prompted protests from many civil rights leaders, including Martin Luther King, Jr. Many African-American soldiers also endured racism within their units.

The U.S. military in the 1960s did not allow women to serve in combat. However, nearly 7,500 women served in Vietnam as army and navy nurses. Thousands more volunteered in the American Red Cross and the United Services Organization (USO). This organization provided entertainment to the troops.

1. Name two groups of Americans who did most of the fighting in Vietnam.

_____

_____

The Roots of Opposition

(pages 737–738)

What were the New Left groups?

By the 1960s, American college students had become politically active. The growing youth movement of the 1960s was known as the **New Left.** The group took its name from the "old" left of the 1930s. That organization had tried to push the nation toward socialism. The New Left did not call for socialism. However, it did demand sweeping changes in American society.

One of the better known New Left organizations was **Students for a Democratic Society** (SDS). This organization called for greater individual freedom in America.

Another New Left group was the **Free Speech Movement** (FSM). This group was formed at the University of California at Berkeley. It grew out of a fight between students and administrators over free speech on campus. FSM criticized business and government institutions.

The strategies of the SDS and FSM eventually spread to colleges throughout the country. There, students protested mostly campus issues. Soon, however, students around the nation found one issue they could protest together: the Vietnam War.

2. Name two New Left groups.

_____

_____

The Protest Movement Emerges

(pages 738–740)

How did the hawks and doves differ?

Across America, college students rose up in protest against the war. They did so for various reasons. The most common reason was that the conflict in Vietnam was a civil war between the North and South. Thus, the United States had no business being there. Others believed that the war kept America from focusing on other parts of the world. Still others saw the war as morally unjust.

In April 1965, SDS helped organize a march on Washington, D.C. About 20,000 protesters participated. In November 1965, a protest rally in Washington drew about 30,000 protesters. Eventually, the antiwar movement reached beyond college campuses. Small numbers of returning veterans protested. Musicians took up the antiwar cause. Many protest songs became popular.

By 1967 Americans were divided into two main groups. Those who supported the war were called **hawks.** Those who wanted the United States to withdraw from the war were called **doves.** Other Americans took no stand on the war. However, they criticized doves for protesting a war in which U.S. troops were fighting and dying.

3. Briefly explain the position of the hawks and doves.

_____

_____

Skillbuilder

Use this cartoon to answer the questions.

1. Who is the person pictured on the poster?

_____

_____

2. Which group do you think designed it, the hawks or doves?

_____

_____

A parody of a U.S. World War I poster.
Credit: Peter Newark's American Pictures

1968:
A Tumultuous Year

TERMS AND NAMES

Tet offensive Series of Vietcong attacks during 1968 Tet holiday

Clark Clifford Lyndon Johnson adviser who became his secretary of defense

Robert Kennedy Democratic candidate for president in 1968

Eugene McCarthy Democratic presidential candidate who ran on antiwar platform

Hubert Humphrey 1968 Democratic nominee for president

George Wallace Third party candidate in 1968 presidential election

BEFORE YOU READ

In the last section, you read how the Vietnam War divided America.

In this section, you will read about the shocking events that made 1968 one of the most explosive years of the decade.

AS YOU READ

Use this diagram to take notes on the shocking events of 1968.

```
  ( Tet Offensive )                    (          )
                \                     /
                 \                   /
                  ( 1968 )
                 /    |    \
                /     |     \
    (        )  (        )  (        )
```

The Tet Offensive Turns the War

(pages 741–743)

How did the Tet offensive affect America?

January 30 was the Vietnamese equivalent of New Year's Eve. It was the beginning of festivities known as Tet. During the Tet holiday in 1968, a week-long war *truce* was called. Many peasants crowded into South Vietnam's cities to celebrate the holiday.

However, many of the peasants turned out to be Vietcong rebels. The rebels launched a massive attack on nearly 100 towns and cities in South

Vietnam. They also attacked 12 U.S. air bases. The attacks were known as the **Tet offensive.** The offensive lasted for about a month. Finally, U.S. and South Vietnamese forces regained control of the cities.

General Westmoreland declared that the Tet offensive was a major defeat for the Vietcong. From a military standpoint, he was right. The Vietcong lost about 32,000 soldiers during the attacks. The United States and South Vietnam lost only 3,000 soldiers.

However, the Tet offensive shattered America's confidence in the war. The enemy now seemed everywhere. Many Americans began to think that the war was unwinnable. The Tet offensive also shocked many in the White House. **Clark Clifford** was the president's new secretary of defense. After Tet, Clifford decided that America could not win the war.

The Tet offensive also hurt President Johnson popularity. By the end of February 1968, nearly 60 percent of the public disapproved of Johnson's handling of the war. In addition, nearly half the country said it had been a mistake to send troops to Vietnam.

1. How did the Tet offensive affect Johnson's popularity?

Days of Loss and Rage (pages 743–744)

Which events shocked the nation?

Even before the Tet offensive, an antiwar group in the Democratic Party had taken steps to *unseat* Johnson. The group looked for someone to challenge Johnson in the 1968 primary election. They asked **Robert Kennedy,** a senator from New York. Kennedy declined. However, Minnesota senator **Eugene McCarthy** agreed. He would run against Johnson on a *platform* to end the Vietnam War.

McCarthy surprised many people by nearly beating Johnson in the New Hampshire Democratic primary. Suddenly, Johnson appeared politically weak. As a result, Robert Kennedy declared himself a candidate for President. The Democratic Party was now badly divided.

President Johnson decided to address the nation on television. He announced that he would seek peace in Vietnam. Then he declared that he would not seek reelection as president. The country was shocked.

In the days and months ahead, several more incidents stunned the nation. On April 4, a gunman killed civil rights leader Martin Luther King, Jr. Two months later an assassin gunned down killed Robert Kennedy.

Meanwhile, antiwar protests continued to rock college campuses. During the first six months of 1968, almost 40,000 students on more than 100 campuses held demonstrations.

2. Name two events that shocked Americans in 1968.

A Turbulent Race for President
(pages 744–746)

What happened in Chicago?

In August 1968, the Democrats met in Chicago for their presidential convention. There, they would choose a presidential candidate. In reality, Democratic leaders had already decided on the candidate: Vice-President **Hubert Humphrey.** This angered many antiwar activists. They favored McCarthy.

About 10,000 antiwar protesters came to Chicago. Some protesters wanted to pressure the Democrats to create an antiwar platform. Others wanted to voice their opposition to Humphrey. Still others wanted to create violence to discredit the Democratic Party.

Violence eventually erupted at a downtown park away from the convention hall. There, police moved in on thousands of demonstrators. They sprayed the protesters with Mace. They also beat them with nightsticks. Many protesters fled. Others fought back.

The violence in Chicago highlighted the Democrats' division. The Republicans were more unified. They nominated former Vice-President Richard Nixon for president.

Nixon campaigned on a platform of law and order. He also assured the American people that he would end the Vietnam War. Nixon's campaign was helped by the entry of a third-party candidate, **George Wallace.** Wallace was a former governor of Alabama. He took many democratic votes away from Humphrey. In November, Nixon won the election. It was now up to him to resolve the Vietnam crisis.

3. Name two reasons that protesters came to Chicago for the Democratic convention.

CHAPTER 22 Section 5 (pages 747–753)

The End of the War and Its Legacy

BEFORE YOU READ

In the last section, you read about the explosive events of the year 1968.

In this section, you will read how the Vietnam War ended and what effect the war had on America.

AS YOU READ

Use this diagram to take notes on the important dates and events relating to the end of the Vietnam War.

TERMS AND NAMES

Vietnamization President Nixon's plan for ending America's involvement in the war

silent majority Those mainstream Americans who supported Nixon's policies

Pentagon Papers Government documents that showed the government had no real plan for leaving Vietnam

Henry Kissinger Nixon adviser who helped negotiate an end to the war

Khmer Rouge Communist group that took control of Cambodia

War Powers Act Act that forbids the president from mobilizing troops without Congressional approval

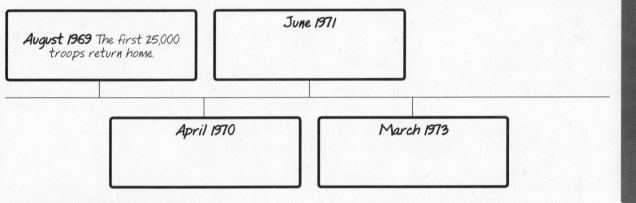

August 1969 The first 25,000 troops return home.

June 1971

April 1970

March 1973

President Nixon and Vietnamization (pages 747–748)

How did Vietnamization work?

Nixon's plan to end America's involvement in Vietnam was known as **Vietnamization.** The plan called for the gradual withdrawal of U.S. troops. It also called for the South Vietnamese to do more of the fighting. By August of 1969, the first 25,000 U.S. troops had returned home. Over the next three years, the number of American troops in Vietnam dropped from more than 500,000 to less than 25,000.

Nixon, however, did not want to lose the war. So as he pulled American troops out, he ordered a massive bombing attack against North Vietnam. Nixon also ordered that bombs be dropped on the neighboring countries of Laos and Cambodia. These countries held a number of Vietcong bases.

1. Name both aspects of the Vietnamization plan.

_____

_____

Trouble Continues on the Home Front (pages 748–750)

Which events weakened support for the war?

To win support for his war policies, Nixon appealed to what he called the **silent majority.** These were mainstream Americans who quietly supported the president's strategy. Many Americans did support the president. However, the war continued to divide the country.

In November of 1969, Americans learned of a shocking event. U.S. troops had massacred more than 100 unarmed Vietnamese in the village of My Lai. In April 1970, the country heard more upsetting news. President Nixon announced that U.S. troops had invaded Cambodia. They had tried to destroy Vietcong supply lines there. Upon hearing of the invasion, colleges exploded in protest.

A protest at Kent State University in Ohio turned tragic. To restore order on the campus, the local mayor called in the National Guard. Some students began throwing rocks at the guards. The guards fired into a crowd of protesters. Four students were killed.

Nixon's invasion of Cambodia cost him public support. It also cost him political support. Members of Congress were angry that he had invaded Cambodia without telling them. As a result, Congress repealed the Tonkin Gulf Resolution. This had given the president the freedom to conduct war policy in Vietnam on his own.

Support for the war declined even further in June of 1971. That month, a former Defense Department worker *leaked* what became known as the **Pentagon Papers.** These documents showed that the past U.S. presidents had never drawn up any plans to withdraw from Vietnam.

2. Name two incidents that weakened support for the war.

_____

_____

_____

America's Longest War Ends
(pages 750–751)

Who won the war?

1972 was a presidential election year. To win reelection, Nixon believed he had to end the Vietnam War. Nixon called on **Henry Kissinger,** his adviser for national security affairs. Kissinger negotiated a peace settlement with the North Vietnamese. In October 1972, Kissinger announced that peace was close at hand. A month later, Nixon was reelected president.

However, the promised peace in Vietnam did not come. South Vietnam objected to the proposed peace settlement. As a result, the peace talks broke down. Nixon responded by ordering more bombings against North Vietnam.

Eventually, the peace talks resumed. In January 1973, the warring parties signed a peace agreement. By the end of March, the last U.S. combat troops had left. For America, the Vietnam War was over.

Shortly after America left, the peace agreement collapsed. North and South Vietnam resumed fighting. In April 1975, North Vietnamese troops captured the South's capital, Saigon. Soon after, South Vietnam surrendered to North Vietnam.

3. What happened to South Vietnam after America left?

_____

_____

_____

The War's Painful Legacy
(pages 751–753)

How did the war affect America?

The Vietnam War cost both sides many lives. In all, about 58,000 Americans died in Vietnam. Another 365,000 were wounded. Vietnamese deaths topped 1.5 million.

After the war, Southeast Asia continued to experience violence and unrest. The Communists imprisoned hundreds of thousands of South Vietnamese. In Cambodia, a Communist group known as the **Khmer Rouge** took power in 1975. They attempted to transform the country into a peasant society. In doing so, they killed many government officials and intellectuals. The group is believed to have killed as many as 2 million Cambodians.

In the United States, the war resulted in several policy changes. In November 1973, Congress passed the **War Powers Act.** This law prevented the president from committing troops in a foreign conflict without approval from Congress. In a larger sense, the war made Americans less willing to become involved in foreign wars. The war also left many Americans with a feeling of mistrust toward their government.

4. Name two ways in which the war affected Americans.

_____

_____

_____

Glossary		**CHAPTER 22** The Vietnam War Years
ambush A surprise attack	**platform** A declaration of one's beliefs or principles	**unstable** Unsteady, weak
draft The selection of people for a duty, including war	**stalemate** A situation in which both sides are stuck; a deadlock	**unseat** To remove from office
leak To reveal secret information		
peninsula A land area surrounded on three sides by water	**truce** A temporary halt of fighting	

AFTER YOU READ

Terms and Names

A. Write the letter of the best answer.

_____ **1.** Which of the following gave the U.S. president broad military powers in Vietnam?

    a. Vietnamization

    b. Pentagon Papers

    c. domino theory

    d. Tonkin Gulf Resolution

_____ **2.** Which group is believed to have killed nearly 2 million Cambodians in the years following the Vietnam War?

    a. Vietminh

    b. Khmer Rouge

    c. Vietcong

    d. hawks

_____ **3.** What organization called for greater individual freedom in America?

    a. Free Speech Movement

    b. Students for a Democratic Society

    c. hawks

    d. doves

_____ **4.** Who ran as a third-party candidate in the 1968 election?

    a. George Wallace

    b. Eugene McCarthy

    c. Hubert Humphrey

    d. Robert McNamara

_____ **5.** What law prevented the president from committing troops in a foreign conflict without the approval of Congress?

    a. Tonkin Gulf Resolution

    b. Pentagon Papers

    c. War Powers Act

    d. Geneva Accords

B. Write the name or term that best completes each sentence.

Robert McNamara

New Left

silent majority

domino theory

Robert Kennedy

Eugene McCarthy

1. The idea that countries on the brink of communism were waiting to fall one after the other was called the _____.

2. An adviser to President Johnson who supported the sending of troops to Vietnam was _____.

3. The _____ was the term given to the growing youth movement of the 1960s.

4. _____ decided to join the 1968 Democratic race for president after seeing the surprising results in the New Hampshire primary.

5. President Nixon made a special appeal to the _____ to win support for his war policies.

Main Ideas

1. How did the Tonkin Gulf Resolution lead to greater U.S. involvement in Vietnam?

_____

2. Name three reasons why U.S. troops had difficulty fighting the Vietcong.

_____

3. Why were many African-American leaders opposed to the Vietnam War?

_____

4. Why was the Tet offensive considered the turning point of the war?

_____

5. What was an immediate and more lasting impact of the Vietnam War on America?

_____

Thinking Critically

Answer the following questions on a separate sheet of paper.

1. How did the division at home over the war demonstrate America's long-held belief in freedom of expression?

2. Do you agree or disagree with the War Powers Act? Explain your answer.

Name _____ Date _____

Latinos and Native Americans Seek Equality

TERMS AND NAMES

Cesar Chavez Leader of the farm worker movement

United Farm Workers Organizing Committee Union that fought for farm workers' rights

La Raza Unida Latino political party

American Indian Movement Group that fought for greater reform for Native Americans

BEFORE YOU READ

In the last section you read about the end of the Vietnam War.

In this section, you will read about how Latinos and Native Americans fought for greater equality.

AS YOU READ

Use the following diagram to take notes on the goals and tactics of the Latino and Native American movements.

GROUPS	GOALS	TACTICS
Latinos	better working conditions	formed workers union
Native Americans		

The Latino Presence Grows

(pages 760–761)

Who are Latinos?

Latinos are Spanish-speaking Americans. During the 1960s, the Latino population in the United States tripled—from 3 million to more than 9 million.

During this time, the nation's Mexican American population grew. Many were *descendants* of Mexicans who stayed on the land that Mexico surrendered to the United States in 1848. Others were the children and grandchildren of the Mexicans who arrived after Mexico's 1910 revolution. Still others came as temporary laborers during the 1940s and 1950s. Mexican Americans always have made up the largest group of Latinos.

About a million Puerto Ricans have lived in the United States since the 1960s. Most Puerto Ricans have settled in the Northeast, especially in New York City.

Many Cubans also settled in the United States during the 1960s. They had fled Cuba after the Cuban Revolution in 1959. Most Cubans settled in or near Miami.

Thousands of Salvadorans, Guatemalans, Nicaraguans, and Colombians immigrated to the United States after the 1960s. They came to escape political *persecution* and poverty at home. Wherever they settled, many Latinos experienced poor living conditions and discrimination.

1. Name two groups that make up the Latino community.

_____

_____

Latinos Fight for Change
(pages 761–763)

Which groups fought for change?

In the 1960s Latinos began to demand equal rights and respect. One such group was Mexican American farm workers. These men and women worked on California's fruit and vegetable farms. They often worked long hours for little pay.

Cesar Chavez was the group's leader. Chavez believed that the farm workers should organize into a union. In 1962, he helped establish the National Farm Workers Association. In 1966, Chavez merged this group with a Filipino agricultural union. Together, they formed the **United Farm Workers Organizing Committee** (UFWOC).

California's grape growers refused to recognize the farm workers union. As a result, Chavez called for a nationwide boycott of grapes. His plan worked. In 1970, the grape growers finally signed contracts with the UFWOC. The new contracts guaranteed union workers higher pay and other benefits.

Latinos also wanted greater recognition of their culture. Puerto Ricans demanded that schools offer classes taught in their native language. In 1968, Congress passed the Bilingual Education Act. This law funded *bilingual* and cultural programs for students who did not speak English.

Latinos also began organizing politically during the 1960s. Some worked within the two-party system. Others created an independent Latino political movement. José Angel Gutiérrez, for example, started **La Raza Unida** (the United People Party). The party ran Latino candidates and won positions in city government offices.

2. Name two organizations that fought to promote the cause of Latinos.

_____

_____

Native Americans Struggle for Equality
(pages 763–765)

What problems did Native Americans face?

Native Americans, like Latinos, are a diverse group. However, most Native Americans have faced similar problems. These problems include high unemployment rates, poor health care, and high death rates.

During the 1950s, the Eisenhower administration tried to solve some of these problems. The government thought that introducing Native Americans to more aspects of mainstream culture would help them. As a result, the government moved Native Americans from their reservations to the cities.

The plan failed. Most Native Americans who moved to the cities remained very poor. In addition, many Native Americans refused to mix with mainstream American society.

Native Americans wanted greater opportunity to control their own lives. In 1961, representatives from more than 60 Native American met to discuss their concerns. They demanded the right to choose their own way of life.

In 1965, President Johnson responded to their demands. He created the National Council on Indian Opportunity. The council's goal was to make sure that government programs reflected the needs and desires of Native Americans.

Many young Native Americans were not satisfied with the government's new policies. They wanted greater reform. They also wanted it more quickly. As a result, some young Native Americans formed the **American Indian Movement** (AIM). This organization demanded greater rights for Native Americans. Sometimes, the group used violence to make its point.

Meanwhile, Native Americans won greater rights through the court system. Throughout the 1960s and 1970s, they won legal battles that gave them greater education and land rights.

3. Name two problems that Native Americans faced.

_____

_____

CHAPTER 23 Section 2 (pages 768–772)

Women Fight for Equality

BEFORE YOU READ

In the last section, you read how Latinos and Native Americans fought for greater rights.

In this section, you will read how the nation's women also attempted to improve their status in society.

AS YOU READ

Use this diagram to take notes on the successes and failures of the women's movement.

TERMS AND NAMES

feminism The belief that women should be equal to men in all areas

Betty Friedan Author of *The Feminine Mystique*

National Organization for Women Organization that pushed for women's rights

Gloria Steinem Journalist who tried to help women gain political power

Equal Rights Amendment Amendment to U.S. Constitution that would prohibit discrimination against women

Phyllis Schlafly Equal Rights Amendment opponent

New Right A coalition of social conservatives

SUCCESSES	FAILURES
Government declares all-male job ads illegal	ERA is defeated

A New Women's Movement Arises (pages 768–770)

How did the women's movement emerge?

The theory behind the women's movement of the 1960s was **feminism.** This was the belief that women should have economic, political, and social equality with men.

The women's movement arose during the 1960s for several reasons. First, a growing number of women entered the work force. In the workplace, many women received less pay than men—even for the same job. Many women saw this as unfair.

Second, women had become actively involved in both the civil rights and antiwar movements. These movements led women to take action on behalf of their own beliefs. In addition, many men in these groups refused to give women leadership roles. As a result, many women became more aware of their *inferior* status.

In 1963, **Betty Friedan** published *The Feminine Mystique.* This book expressed the discontent that many women were feeling. Friedan's book helped to unite a number of women throughout the nation.

1. Name two factors that helped launch the women's movement.

_____

_____

The Movement Experiences Gains and Losses (pages 770–772)

What were the movement's successes and failures?

In 1966, several women formed the **National Organization for Women** (NOW). The group's goal was to more actively pursue women's goals. NOW pushed for more child-care facilities. It also called for more educational opportunities.

The organization also pressured the federal government to enforce a ban on *gender* discrimination in hiring. The government responded by declaring that male-only job ads were illegal.

In 1972, Congress passed a ban on gender discrimination in higher education. As a result, several all-male colleges opened their doors to women. In 1973, the Supreme Court's decision in the case *Roe* v. *Wade* granted women the right to choose an abortion.

Women also attempted to gain political strength. In 1971, Journalist **Gloria Steinem** helped found the National Women's Political Caucus. This group encouraged women to run for political office.

The women's movement also met with some failure. It failed to win passage of the **Equal Rights Amendment** (ERA). The ERA was a proposed *amendment* to the U.S. Constitution. It would have outlawed government discrimination on the basis of sex. One prominent ERA opponent was **Phyllis Schlafly.** Schlafly called the ERA the work of *radical* feminists.

In addition, the women's movement angered many of the nation's *conservatives*. In response, these conservatives joined together to form a movement known as the **New Right.** This movement emphasized traditional social, cultural, and moral values. Throughout the 1970s, the New Right gained support for its social conservatism.

2. Name one success and one failure of the women's movement.

_____

_____

The Movement's Legacy (page 772)

What was the movement's legacy?

Despite the ERA's failure, the women's movement achieved many of its goals. In 1970, for example, only about 8 percent of medical school graduates were women. Only 5 percent of law school graduates were female. By 1992, about 36 percent of medical school graduates were women. By 1992, 43 percent of law school graduates were female.

The movement also changed the way women looked at work and careers. In the 1950s, most women who took jobs had done so to help out with family finances. By the 1970s, many women were preparing themselves for lifetime careers.

The women's movement also led to an increase in the number of women holding elected office. Finally, the women's movement helped many women open their lives to countless possibilities.

3. Cite two examples of how the women's movement helped women improve their standing in society.

_____

_____

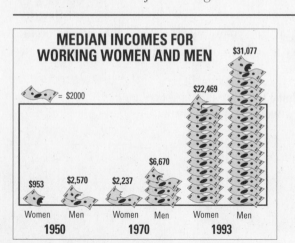

MEDIAN INCOMES FOR WORKING WOMEN AND MEN

= $2000

$953	$2,570	$2,237	$6,670	$22,469	$31,077
Women	Men	Women	Men	Women	Men
1950		**1970**		**1993**	

Skillbuilder

Use the graph to answer the questions.

1. How much more did the average woman make in 1993 than she did in 1970?

_____

2. How much less did the average woman make than the average man in 1993?

_____

CHAPTER 23 Section 3 (pages 773–777)

Culture and Counterculture

BEFORE YOU READ

In the last section, you read about the women's movement that emerged in the United States in the 1960s.

In this section, you will read about the emergence of the counterculture movement—and how the nation reacted to it.

AS YOU READ

Use this diagram to take notes on how the counterculture affected America

IMMEDIATE EFFECT	LONG-TERM EFFECT
Mainstream America blamed it for decline of traditional values.	Rock 'n' roll became a part of mainstream culture.

The Counterculture (pages 773–775)

What characterized the counterculture?

During the 1960s, many young people adopted values that differed from those of mainstream society. These Americans were part of a movement known as the **counterculture.**

The movement was made up mostly of white middle-class youths. Members of the counterculture were known as "hippies." Many hippies shared some of the beliefs of the New Left. They took part in demonstrations against the Vietnam War. However, a majority of hippies chose to turn their backs on America. They wanted to establish a new society based on peace and love.

The main characteristics of the hippie culture were rock 'n' roll, colorful clothes, and the use of drugs. Many also chose to live in large groups called communes. Many hippies moved to San Francisco's **Haight-Ashbury** district. This community was popular mainly because of the availability of drugs.

After a few years, the counterculture movement began to decline. Some aspects of the movement became violent. Many urban communes grew dangerous. The widespread use of drugs also led to the decline of the movement.

More than anything else, hippies eventually found that they could not survive outside mainstream America. They needed money to live. For

many, this meant returning to mainstream society—
and getting a job.

1. Name two characteristics of the counterculture.

_____

_____

A Changing Culture (pages 775–776)

How did the counterculture affect America?

The counterculture movement collapsed after only a few years. However, some aspects of it had a lasting effect on mainstream culture.

The movement affected the worlds of art and fashion. The 1960s saw the rise of popular, or pop, art. The counterculture also lived on in the way Americans dressed and groomed themselves. Many Americans wore longer hair and more colorful clothing. They also began wearing blue jeans. Today, jeans are a basic part of American wardrobes.

The most lasting legacy of the counterculture movement was its music. Rock 'n' roll continues to be a popular form of entertainment. Perhaps the most influential band was **The Beatles.** The British group helped rock music became part of mainstream America.

A dramatic example of rock 'n' roll's popularity was an event known as **Woodstock.** This was a massive outdoor rock concert in upstate New York. It occurred during the summer of 1969. More than 400,000 people attended—far more than expected.

The counterculture movement affected Americans' social attitudes as well. The American media began to address the subjects of sex and violence. Before this time, few Americans discussed these topics.

2. Name two areas of society affected by the counterculture.

_____

_____

The Conservative Response
(page 776–777)

Why did mainstream America attack the counterculture?

In the late 1960s, many mainstream Americans criticized the counterculture. They blamed the movement for the decline of traditional American values.

Some conservative groups called the movement a threat to law and order. They also accused members of the counterculture of being *immoral.*

Mainstream America's anger toward the counterculture affected the country's political scene. In 1968, the Republicans nominated Richard Nixon as their presidential candidate. Nixon ran on a platform of law and order, and conservative values. His ideas appealed to many voters. As a result, Nixon won the election. He then set the nation on a more conservative course.

3. Cite two reasons why Americans criticized the counterculture.

_____

_____

Glossary

amendment A revision or change

bilingual Able to speak two languages

conservative Moderate, cautious, traditional

descendant An offspring, someone derived from an ancestor

gender Relating to male or female

immoral Evil, characterized by bad behavior

inferior Lower, lesser rank

persecution The act of oppressing or treating badly

radical Extreme, carried to the furthest limit

AFTER YOU READ

Terms and Names

A. If the statement is true, write "true" on the line. If it is false, change the underlined word or words to make it true.

1. _____ In the 1970s, <u>La Raza Unida</u> fielded Latino candidates and won positions in several city governments.

2. _____ A major opponent of the Equal Rights Amendment was <u>Betty Friedan</u>.

3. _____ <u>Phyllis Schlafly</u> helped found the National Women's Political Caucus.

4. _____ A popular British band, <u>The Beatles</u>, helped propel rock 'n' roll into mainstream America.

5. _____ Young Native Americans formed a group known as <u>the New Right</u>, which helped fight for Indian rights.

B. Write the letter of the name or term that matches the description.

a. counterculture

b. Woodstock

c. Cesar Chavez

d. National Organization for Women

e. American Indian Movement

f. New Right

_____ **1.** The person who organized Mexican-American farm workers

_____ **2.** A sometimes violent Native-American rights organization

_____ **3.** An organization created to pursue the goals of the women's movement

_____ **4.** Movement made up of white middle-class youths, who were fed up with mainstream America

_____ **5.** A massive outdoor concert in 1969 that highlighted rock's popularity

AFTER YOU READ (continued) **CHAPTER 23** An Era of Social Change

Main Ideas

1. Name the different ways in which Latinos fought for greater equality.

_____

_____

2. Why did President Eisenhower's Native American plan fail?

_____

_____

3. What achievements did the women's movement make?

_____

_____

4. Why did the counterculture decline?

_____

_____

5. How did many Americans view the counterculture? How did this view affect the nation's political scene?

_____

_____

Thinking Critically

Answer the following questions on a separate sheet of paper.

1. How were the Latino and Native American movements similar? How were they different?

2. A stereotype is a generalization made about a group. What stereotypes do you think hippies and mainstream Americans made about each other? Why?

CHAPTER 24 Section 1 (pages 786–792)

The Nixon Administration

BEFORE YOU READ

In the last section, you read about the counterculture.

In this section, you will learn about President Nixon and his attempts to move the country in a more conservative direction.

AS YOU READ

Use the web below to take notes about the major policies of Richard Nixon as president.

TERMS AND NAMES

Richard M. Nixon 37th president

New Federalism Plan to give federal power back to the states

revenue sharing Plan for the federal government to share money with state and local governments

Family Assistance Plan Nixon welfare reform proposal to give direct relief to poor families

Southern strategy Nixon's effort to attract Southern votes by opposing desegregation

stagflation Occurs when unemployment and inflation rise at the same time

OPEC Organization of nations that export oil

realpolitik Realistic politics

détente Policy aimed at easing Cold War tensions

SALT I Treaty Treaty to limit nuclear weapons

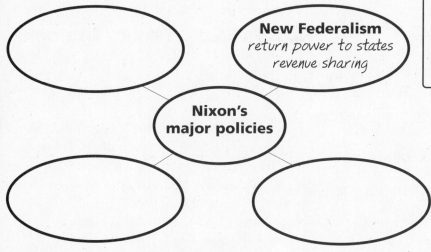

Nixon's New Conservatism
(pages 786–788)

How did Nixon pursue conservative policies?

President **Richard M. Nixon** wanted to turn the United States in a more conservative direction. He tried to decrease the power of the federal government. Nixon's plan was called **New Federalism.** Its goal was to give federal power to the states.

Nixon introduced **revenue sharing.** The federal government usually told state and local governments how to spend their federal money. Under revenue sharing, state and local officials could spend their federal dollars however they saw fit with few limits.

Nixon also wanted to reform welfare. He supported the **Family Assistance Plan** (FAP). Under this plan, every family of four with no income would receive a payment of $1,600 a year, and could earn up to $4,000 more a year. But this plan failed to pass Congress.

When Nixon first took office he cooperated with Congress. But he soon refused to spend money that Congress wanted to spend on programs that he did not like. Federal courts ruled that Nixon's action was unconstitutional. They ordered that Nixon spend the money on the programs.

Nixon also followed "law and order" policies to stop riots and antiwar protests. He used the Central Intelligence Agency (CIA) and the

Internal Revenue Service (IRS) to harass people. He created an "enemies list." And he had the CIA and IRS target people on this list. The list included liberals and other opponents of his policies.

1. What conservative programs did Nixon support?

_____

_____

Nixon's Southern Strategy
(pages 788–790)

What was the Southern strategy?

Nixon wanted to make sure he would get reelected in 1972. He used what he called a **Southern strategy** to win the support of Southerners.

To attract white voters, Nixon tried to slow school desegregation. But the Supreme Court ordered the administration to move more quickly. Nixon also opposed the extension of the Voting Rights Act of 1965. But Congress extended the act.

Nixon believed that the Supreme Court under Chief Justice Earl Warren was too liberal. During his presidency, four justices, including Warren, left the Court. This gave Nixon an opportunity to appoint more conservative justices.

2. How did Nixon hope to win Southern support?

_____

_____

Nixon Confronts a Stagnant Economy (page 790)

What is stagflation?

One of the biggest problems facing Nixon was a weak economy. Between 1967 and 1973, *inflation* and unemployment increased. This situation is known as **stagflation.**

Stagflation had several causes. Unemployment increased because *trade competition* increased. This made it harder for Americans to sell their goods overseas. The nation also had trouble finding jobs for millions of baby boomers who reached working age.

Inflation increased for two main reasons. First, more government spending on social programs and

the war in Vietnam raised prices. The second cause was the nation's need for foreign oil. The United States received much of its oil from the Middle East. Many of these countries belonged to a *cartel* called **OPEC.** During the 1960s OPEC gradually raised oil prices. Then in 1973 a war broke out, with Israel against Egypt and Syria. The United States sent military aid to Israel.

The OPEC nations sided with Egypt and Syria. They stopped selling oil to the United States. This led to problems in the United States. Between the fall of 1973 and March 1974, motorists faced long lines at the gas stations. Some factories and schools closed. When OPEC started selling oil to the United States again, the price had *quadrupled*.

3. How did OPEC affect the U.S. economy?

_____

_____

Nixon's Foreign Policy Triumphs
(pages 791–792)

What is realpolitik?

Nixon's main foreign policy advisor was Henry Kissinger. Kissinger based his foreign policy views on a philosophy known as **realpolitik.** This meant that Kissinger dealt with other nations in a practical and flexible manner. Kissinger believed it was practical to ignore a country that was weak. But it was important to deal with strong nations.

Realpolitik was a change from the policy of containment. Nixon and Kissinger changed U.S. relations with Communist countries. They called their policy **détente.** This policy was aimed at easing Cold War tensions.

In 1972, Nixon visited Communist China. Before this, the United States had refused to recognize the Communist government. Three months later, Nixon went to the Soviet Union. Nixon and the Soviet leader signed the **SALT I Treaty.** This five-year agreement limited nuclear weapons. Nixon's successes in foreign affairs helped him win reelection.

4. How did Nixon try to ease Cold War tensions?

_____

_____

CHAPTER 24 Section 2 (pages 793–797)

Watergate: Nixon's Downfall

TERMS AND NAMES

Watergate Scandal that forced Nixon to resign

H. R. Haldeman Advisor to Nixon

John Ehrlichman Advisor to Nixon

John Mitchell Attorney general and director of Nixon's campaign committee

Committee to Reelect the President Nixon's campaign committee

Judge John Sirica Judge in the trial of the Watergate burglars

Saturday Night Massacre Nixon's firing of Justice Department officials, including the special prosecutor investigating Watergate

BEFORE YOU READ

In the last section, you read about President Nixon's approach to politics and the Cold War.

In this section, you will learn about the Watergate scandal.

AS YOU READ

Use the diagram below to take notes about the causes and effects of the Watergate scandal.

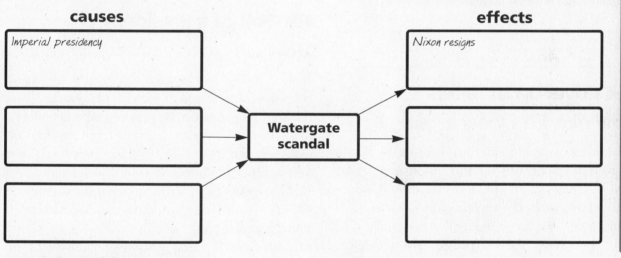

causes

Imperial presidency

Watergate scandal

effects

Nixon resigns

President Nixon and His White House (pages 793–794)

What was Watergate?

The **Watergate** scandal was the attempt to *cover up* a burglary of the Democratic National Committee (DNC) headquarters.

By the time Richard Nixon became president, the executive branch had become powerful. Nixon expanded the power of the presidency. He confided in a small group of very loyal advisers. These advisers included **H. R. Haldeman,** chief of staff; **John Ehrlichman,** chief domestic adviser; and **John Mitchell,** the attorney general. These men helped Nixon get reelected. They also shared Nixon's desire for power. This would lead Nixon

and his advisers to cover up their role in the Watergate burglary.

1. Define Watergate scandal.

_____

_____

The Drive Toward Reelection
(pages 794–795)

What was the CRP?

Nixon campaign aides were determined to win the 1972 election. They hired five men to raid Democratic party offices in the Watergate complex in Washington, D.C. The men were caught photographing files and placing wiretaps on phones.

The press soon discovered that the group's leader, James McCord, was a former CIA agent. He was also an official of a group known as the **Committee to Reelect the President** (CRP). John Mitchell, who had been attorney general, was the CRP's director.

Nixon and his staff tried to hide the link to the White House. Workers shredded evidence. Nixon and his staff asked the CIA to urge the FBI to stop its investigations into the burglary.

The Watergate burglary was not a big issue in the 1972 election. Only two reporters kept on the story. In a series of articles, the reporters found information that linked members of the administration to the burglary. The White House denied any connections.

2. Why did the CRP order the burglary of the Democratic National Committee headquarters?

_____

_____

The Cover-Up Unravels (pages 795–796)

How did Nixon get caught?

After Nixon's reelection, the cover-up began to unravel. In January of 1973, the Watergate burglars went to trial. All of the burglars except James McCord changed their pleas from innocent to guilty. McCord was found guilty by a jury. The trial's presiding judge, **Judge John Sirica,** believed that the burglars did not act alone. Then in March 1973, McCord sent a letter to Sirica, stating that he had lied under oath. He also stated that the White House was involved in the cover-up.

Soon the public interest in the Watergate burglary increased. In April 1973, three top Nixon aides resigned. The President then went on television and denied any cover-up. He also announced that he was appointing Elliot Richardson as the new attorney general. And he was authorizing Richardson to appoint a *special prosecutor* to investigate Watergate.

In May 1973, the Senate began its own investigation of Watergate. The Senate hearings were televised live. In the hearings, one of Nixon's aides said that Nixon knew about the cover-up. Then it was revealed that White House meetings had been tape-recorded. The Senate committee demanded the tapes. Nixon refused to release them.

Court battles over the tapes lasted a year. Archibald Cox, the special prosecutor, took the president to court in October 1973 to get the tapes. Nixon refused and ordered Richardson to fire Cox. In what became known as the **Saturday Night Massacre,** Richardson refused the order and resigned. The deputy attorney general also refused and resigned. Solicitor General Robert Bork finally fired Cox. But his replacement, Leon Jaworski, was also determined to get the tapes.

3. What did Nixon do during the investigation?

_____

_____

The Fall of a President (pages 796–797)

How did Nixon's presidency end?

In March 1974, a grand jury charged seven Nixon aides with *obstruction of justice* and *perjury.* Nixon released more than 1,250 pages of taped conversations. But he did not release the conversations on some key dates. In July 1974 the Supreme Court ordered the White House to release the tapes.

Three days later a House committee voted to impeach President Nixon. If the full House of Representatives approved, Nixon would go to trial in the Senate. If Nixon was judged guilty there, he would be removed from office. When the tapes were finally released, they proved that Nixon had known of the cover-up. On August 8, 1974, he resigned.

Watergate produced distrust about the presidency. A poll taken in 1974 showed that 43 percent of Americans had lost faith in the presidency. In the years after Vietnam and Watergate, Americans developed a deep distrust of government officials.

4. Why did President Nixon resign from office?

_____

_____

The Ford and Carter Years

BEFORE YOU READ

In the last section, you learned about Watergate.

In this section, you will read about the presidencies of Gerald Ford and Jimmy Carter.

AS YOU READ

Use the time line below to take notes about the major events of the Ford and Carter administrations.

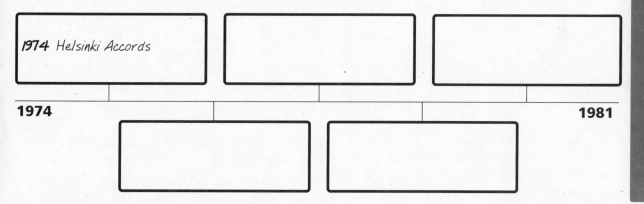

1974 Helsinki Accords

1974

1981

Ford Travels a Rough Road
(pages 800–801)

What did Ford as president?

Gerald R. Ford replaced Richard Nixon as president. Ford was likable and honest. But he lost public support when he *pardoned* Nixon.

The economy had gotten worse by the time Ford took office. Ford invited the nation's top economic leaders to the White House to discuss what to do. Ford promoted a program to slow inflation by encouraging energy conservation. This program failed. Ford then pushed for higher interest rates. This triggered the worst recession in 40 years.

In foreign affairs, Ford relied on Henry Kissinger, the secretary of state. Ford continued talks with China and the Soviet Union. In 1974 he participated in a meeting in Helsinki, Finland. There, 35 countries, including the Soviet Union,

signed the Helsinki Accords. These were agreements that promised greater cooperation between the nations of Europe.

1. What did Ford do about the economy?

_____

_____

Jimmy Carter Enters the White House (pages 801–802)

Why did Carter get elected?

Ford ran for election in 1976 against Democrat **Jimmy Carter.** Carter ran as an outsider, or someone apart from Washington politics. Carter promised he would never lie to Americans. Carter won a close election with this message.

Carter stayed in touch with the people by holding "fireside chats" on radio and television. But Carter did not try to reach out to Congress. He refused to take part in deal-making. As a result he angered both Republicans and Democrats in Congress.

2. Why did Carter win the 1976 presidential election?

_____

_____

Carter's Domestic Agenda
(pages 802–804)

How did Carter try to fix the economy?

Carter believed that energy policy should be his top priority. He signed the **National Energy Act.** It placed a tax on gas-guzzling cars. It removed price controls on oil and natural gas. It also funded research for new sources of energy.

But in 1979, violence in the Middle East caused another shutdown of oil imports. High prices made inflation worse. Carter tried voluntary price freezes and spending cuts, but these measures did not stop inflation.

Other changes in the economy caused problems in the 1970s. Greater *automation* meant fewer manufacturing jobs. Competition from other countries cost American jobs, too. Many companies moved their factories from the Northeast to the South and West. They were looking for lower energy costs and cheaper labor.

3. How did Carter try to solve the nation's economic problems?

_____

_____

A Human Rights Foreign Policy
(pages 804–806)

How did human rights affect Carter's foreign policy?

Carter tried to follow moral principles in his foreign policy. He believed the United States should promote **human rights.** Human rights are freedoms and liberties like those listed in the Declaration of Independence and the Bill of Rights.

Carter cut aid to countries that violated the rights of their people. He supported a treaty with Panama to give control of the Panama Canal to that country. Carter signed a nuclear arms treaty—called SALT II—with the Soviets. The treaty was opposed by the Senate. But when the Soviets invaded Afghanistan, Carter refused to fight for the treaty. It was never ratified.

4. What was Carter's foreign policy based on?

_____

_____

Triumph and Crisis in the Middle East (pages 806–807)

What did Carter do about the Middle East?

In 1978, Carter arranged a meeting between the leaders of Egypt and Israel. The two nations had been enemies for years. After several days of talks, Carter and the two leaders reached agreements known as the **Camp David Accords.**

In 1979, Muslim fundamentalists and their leader **Ayatollah Ruhollah Khomeini** overthrew the *shah* of Iran. In October of 1979, Carter allowed the shah to enter the United States for cancer treatment. This angered the revolutionaries. On November 4, 1979, they took control of the American embassy in Tehran, Iran's capital, and took 52 Americans **hostage.** They demanded that the United States send the shah back to Iran in return for the hostages.

Carter refused. A long standoff followed. Carter could not get the hostages released. They were held for 444 days. The hostages were freed just minutes after Ronald Reagan was inaugurated president on January 20, 1981.

5. Name one success and one defeat in the Middle East for Carter?

_____

_____

CHAPTER 24 Section 4 (pages 808–813)

Environmental Activism

BEFORE YOU READ

In the last section, you learned about Presidents Ford and Carter.

In this section, you will see how Americans addressed their environmental concerns.

AS YOU READ

Use the web below to take notes about important events for the environmental movement in the United States.

TERMS AND NAMES

Rachel Carson Environmentalist leader in the U.S.

Earth Day Annual day to celebrate the environment

environmentalist Person who actively tries to protect the environment

Environmental Protection Agency Federal agency formed to decrease pollution

Three Mile Island Site of a nuclear plant that released radiation into the air

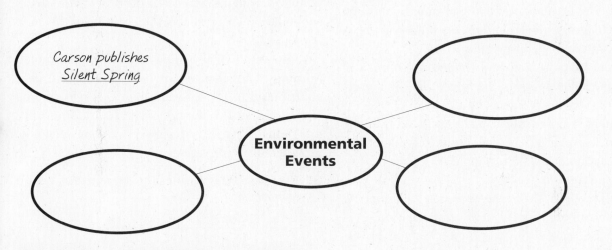

The Roots of Environmentalism
(pages 808–809)

What is environmentalism?

Concern for the environment was increased by the 1962 book *Silent Spring*, written by **Rachel Carson.** That book argued that *pesticides* were poisoning food and killing birds and fish. *Silent Spring* sold nearly half a million copies within months.

Carson's book was an awakening to many Americans. President Kennedy set up a committee to investigate the situation shortly after the book's publication. In 1963, Congress passed the Clean Air Act. This law regulated *emissions* from cars and factories. Carson's work helped to outlaw the use of DDT, a harmful pesticide, in 1972.

1. How did *Silent Spring* encourage environmentalism?

_____

_____

Environmental Concerns in the 1970s (pages 809–812)

What were the key environmental issues of the 1970s?

On April 22, 1970, Americans celebrated **Earth Day** for the first time. Earth Day became a yearly event to highlight environmental issues.

Richard Nixon was not an **environmentalist**—someone who takes an active role in protecting the environment. But he did recognize the nation's concern over the environment. In 1970, he created the **Environmental Protection Agency.** This agency had the power to regulate *pollution* standards and to conduct research.

Nixon also signed the 1970 Clean Air Act. This law required industry to reduce pollution from factories and automobiles. Other new laws to protect the environment also passed.

In 1968 oil was found in Alaska. In 1974, oil companies began building a pipeline to carry the oil 800 miles across the state. The discovery of oil and the construction of the pipeline created many new jobs and increased state revenues.

But the pipeline raised concerns about Alaska's environment and the rights of Alaska's native peoples. In 1971, Nixon signed the Alaska Native Claims Settlement Act. This law gave millions of acres of land to the state's native tribes.

In 1978, President Carter set aside 56 million more acres in Alaska as national monuments. In 1980, Congress added another 104 million acres to Alaska's protected conservation areas.

In the 1970s, some people believed that nuclear energy was the energy of the future. They believed that it was cheap, plentiful, and safe.

Others opposed nuclear energy. They warned that nuclear plants were dangerous to humans and the environment. These people also feared accidents and nuclear waste.

On March 28, 1979, the concerns of opponents of nuclear energy appeared to come true. An accident caused one of the nuclear reactors on **Three Mile Island,** in Pennsylvania, to release *radiation* into the air. An investigation showed that workers at the plant had not been properly trained. It also showed that some safety measures were not taken. Afterwards, the government strengthened nuclear safety regulations.

2. What did the government do after the accident at a nuclear reactor on Three Mile Island?

_____

_____

A Continuing Movement (page 813)

Have the goals of the environmental movement changed?

The debate over the environment continues today. In the 1990s, Americans began addressing new environmental problems. Scientists warned that pollution from industries was destroying the earth's ozone layer. This protects the earth from the sun's most dangerous rays.

Some studies also showed that the continued burning of fossil fuels (such as oil and coal) was contributing to global warming. This is a general rise in the earth's temperature. Today Americans are trying to strike a balance between economic growth and conservation.

3. What issue faces Americans today regarding the environment?

_____

_____

Environmental Progress in Los Angeles Region

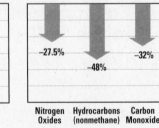

Ozone-Alert Episodes

Number of Days

- 1977: 121
- 1986: 80
- 1996: 7

Air Pollution Reduction, 1976–1990

- Nitrogen Oxides: −27.5%
- Hydrocarbons (nonmethane): −48%
- Carbon Monoxide: −32%

Source: California Air Resources Board

Skillbuilder

Use the charts to answer these questions.

1. How many days in 1996 did people in Los Angeles face ozone-alert episodes?

_____

_____

2. How much did carbon monoxide pollution decrease in Los Angeles between 1976 and 1990?

_____

_____

Glossary

automation Making things with machines rather than people

cartel An organization that controls enough of the production of an item to set the price

cover-up To hide or conceal

emissions Something that is given off or sent out

hostage A person held against his or her wishes

inflation Increase in prices

obstruction of justice Preventing legal work from proceeding

ozone One layer of the atmosphere

pardoned Excused or forgave

perjury Lying under oath

pesticides Chemicals used to kill insects and rodents

pollution Waste or harmful material

quadrupled Made four times greater

radiation Possibly dangerous energy that is sent out

shah Ruler of Iran before the 1979 revolution

special prosecutor Lawyer appointed to investigate public officials

trade competition Competition from other nations to sell goods

AFTER YOU READ

Terms and Names

A. Write the letter of the term that best answers the question.

a. John Sirica
b. environmentalist
c. realpolitik
d. Jimmy Carter
e. stagflation
f. Gerald Ford

_____ **1.** What is the foreign policy in which nations deal with each other in a practical and flexible manner?

_____ **2.** What is the economic term that refers to the double problems of rising inflation and unemployment?

_____ **3.** Who was the judge in the trial of the Watergate burglars?

_____ **4.** Who was the president who based much of his foreign policy on human rights?

_____ **5.** Who is a person who takes an active role in advocating measures to protect the environment?

B. Write on the blank the name or term that best completes each sentence.

Earth Day
Saturday Night Massacre
Rachel Carson
revenue sharing
Camp David Accords

1. Through Richard Nixon's plan of _____, state and local governments were allowed to spend their federal dollars however they saw fit within certain limitations.

2. When Archibald Cox sued to obtain Nixon's tapes, Nixon set off the _____, by ordering the attorney general to fire Cox.

3. President Jimmy Carter negotiated the _____ between Israel and Egypt.

4. The book *Silent Spring*, written by _____, prompted Americans to address environmental issues.

5. On April 22, 1970, thousands of communities celebrated the first _____ by having some type of environmental awareness activity.

AFTER YOU READ (continued)   CHAPTER 24   An Age of Limits

Main Ideas

1. How did Nixon try to help the economy?

_____

_____

2. What were the effects of the Watergate scandal?

_____

_____

3. How did Ford handle the economy?

_____

_____

4. Describe one success and one failure of Carter's foreign policy?

_____

_____

5. What happened at Three Mile Island?

_____

_____

Thinking Critically

Answer the following questions on a separate sheet of paper.

1. What do you think were President Nixon's successes? What were his failures?

2. How did Rachel Carson's book *Silent Spring* contribute to the environmental movement?

An Age of Limits

CHAPTER 25 Section 1 (pages 818–821)

A Conservative Movement Emerges

BEFORE YOU READ

In the last section, you read about the environmental movement.

In this section, you will learn about the growth of the conservative movement in the 1960s and 1970s.

AS YOU READ

Use the web below to take notes about conservatives and their political beliefs.

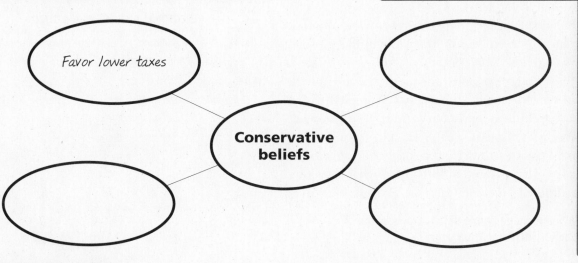

The Conservative Movement Builds (pages 818–820)

Why did conservatism grow?

American history has been marked by swings between liberal and conservative policies. During times when liberals held power, the federal government took strong action to reform society. During more conservative times, Americans tried to have less government activity. From the late 1960s onward, conservatives steadily gained power. In 1980, conservatives won a great victory: **Ronald Reagan** was elected president.

Many Americans resented the cost of **entitlement programs.** These are programs that

guaranteed benefits to particular groups. By 1980, one out of every three households was receiving benefits from government programs. Americans were unhappy paying taxes to support these benefits. They were also upset about high inflation.

Some people also became frustrated with the government's civil rights policies. The Civil Rights Act of 1964 was meant to end racial discrimination. But over the years some court decisions extended the act. Some opposed laws that increased minority opportunities in employment or education. They called this **reverse discrimination,** discrimination against white people and specifically white men.

During the 1970s, several conservative groups

formed across the country that opposed liberal programs. They thought these programs hurt the economy and other aspects of life. Together these groups were known as the **New Right.** Some members of the New Right fought any government action at all.

Members of the New Right often promoted one issue that had to do with their own interests. Many members opposed legal abortion and the proposed Equal Rights Amendment (ERA). Some called for prayer in public schools.

Right-wing groups tended to vote for the same candidates. These voters formed the **conservative coalition.** This was an alliance of some intellectuals, business interests, and unhappy middle-class voters.

Members of the conservative coalition shared some basic positions. They opposed big government, entitlement programs, and many civil rights programs. They also believed in a return to traditional moral standards.

Religious groups, especially Christian fundamentalists, played an important role in the conservative coalition. Some of these groups were guided by television preachers. Some of them banded together and formed the **Moral Majority.** They interpreted the Bible *literally.* They also believed in absolute standards of right and wrong. The Moral Majority criticized a decline in national morality. They wanted to bring back what they saw as traditional American values.

1. What basic positions did members of the conservative coalition share?

_____

_____

Conservatives Win Political Power (pages 820–821)

Why was Reagan popular?

The conservatives found a strong presidential candidate in Ronald Reagan. He won the 1980 nomination and chose **George Bush** as his running mate.

Reagan had been a movie actor and a spokesman for General Motors. He won political fame with a speech for Barry Goldwater during the 1964 presidential campaign. In 1966, Reagan was elected governor of California. He was reelected in 1970.

In the 1980 election, Reagan ran on a number of issues. Supreme Court decisions on abortion, the teaching of evolution, and prayer in public schools all upset conservative voters. Reagan also had a strong anticommunist policy.

Reagan was an extremely effective candidate. High inflation and the Iranian hostage crisis also helped Reagan. Reagan easily won the election. The election also gave Republicans control of the Senate.

2. What factors helped Reagan win the presidential election in 1980?

_____

_____

_____

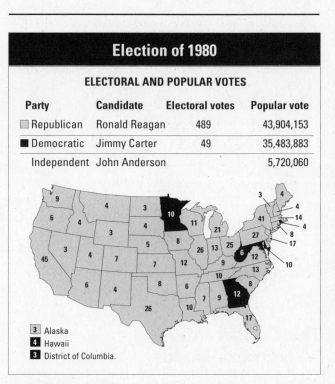

Election of 1980

ELECTORAL AND POPULAR VOTES

Party	Candidate	Electoral votes	Popular vote
Republican	Ronald Reagan	489	43,904,153
Democratic	Jimmy Carter	49	35,483,883
Independent	John Anderson		5,720,060

3 Alaska
4 Hawaii
3 District of Columbia.

Skillbuilder

Use the map to answer the questions

1. Did Ronald Reagan win more than 50% of the popular vote?

_____

2. Name three states that Jimmy Carter won.

_____

Name _____   Date _____

Conservative Policies Under Reagan and Bush

BEFORE YOU READ

In the last section, you saw how conservative power grew before the presidential election of 1980.

In this section, you will read how President Reagan put in place conservative policies.

AS YOU READ

Use the chart below to take notes on the effects of Reaganomics.

TERMS AND NAMES

Reaganomics Reagan's economic policies

supply-side economics Economic theory that tax cuts will increase jobs and government revenues

Strategic Defense Initiative Proposed system to defend the United States against missile attacks

trade imbalance When a nation imports more than it exports

Sandra Day O'Connor First woman Supreme Court justice

William Rehnquist Chief Justice of the Supreme Court

Geraldine Ferraro Democratic vice-presidential candidate in 1984

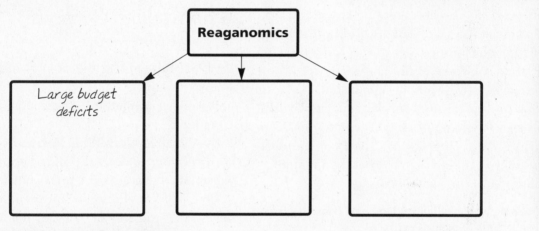

Reaganomics

Large budget deficits

"Reaganomics" Takes Over
(pages 822–824)

What was Reaganomics?

Reagan tried to reduce the size and power of the federal government. He wanted to make deep cuts in government spending on social programs. He convinced Congress to lower taxes. This approach was called **Reaganomics.**

Reaganomics depended on **supply-side economics.** This theory said that cutting taxes would motivate people to work, save, and invest. More investment would create more jobs. More workers would mean more taxpayers, which would cause government **revenues** to increase.

Reagan also increased military spending. Between 1981 and 1984, the Defense Department

budget almost doubled. In 1983, Reagan asked the country's scientists to develop a defense system that would keep Americans safe from enemy missiles. The system became known as the **Strategic Defense Initiative,** or SDI.

The economy grew. Interest rates and inflation rates dropped. Government revenues, however, did not increase as much as Reagan hoped. So the federal government ran up huge budget deficits.

During the Reagan and Bush years, the size of the government debt more than doubled. This meant that the United States had a larger national debt than any other nation in the world.

Interest payments on this debt accounted for about 21 percent of the national budget. This limited the amount of money available for investment in many projects, including houses, roads, businesses, and schools.

The United States also faced a large **trade imbalance.** This meant that the nation was importing more goods than it was exporting.

1. What was the main idea of Reaganomics?

_____

_____

Judicial Power Shifts to the Right (page 824)

What kind of judges did Reagan and Bush nominate?

Reagan made conservative appointments to the Supreme Court. He nominated **Sandra Day O'Connor,** Antonin Scalia, and Anthony M. Kennedy to fill the seats of retiring justices. Reagan also nominated Justice **William Rehnquist** to the position of chief justice.

President George Bush later made the Court more conservative when he nominated David H. Souter to replace the retiring justice William Brennan. He also nominated Clarence Thomas to take the place of Thurgood Marshall. In many decisions, the Court moved away from the more liberal rulings of the previous 40 years.

2. What was the result of Reagan's and Bush's appointments to the Supreme Court?

_____

_____

Deregulating the Economy
(page 825)

What was deregulation?

Reagan tried to reduce the power of the federal government through **deregulation.** Reagan removed price controls on oil and gas. He deregulated the airline industry.

Reagan ended government regulation of the savings and loan industry. Savings and loan associations (S & Ls) were allowed to invest in *commercial* real estate. This included shopping malls and office buildings. Some S & Ls made risky loans. Even if

they made risky investments, the government insured investors for up to $100,000.

When the economy slowed down, many of these risky investments went bad. This forced many S & Ls into bankruptcy. The government paid the cost of insuring the losses.

Reagan also reduced environmental regulation. He cut the budget of the Environmental Protection Agency (EPA). He ignored requests from Canada to reduce acid rain.

3. What was the result of the deregulation of the savings and loan industry?

_____

_____

Conservative Victories in 1984 and 1988 (page 826)

Who won the elections of 1984 and 1988?

By 1984, Reagan had the support of conservative voters who approved of his policies. These voters helped Reagan win the 1984 election. He defeated Democrat Walter Mondale. Mondale chose Representative **Geraldine Ferraro** of New York as his running mate. Ferraro became the first woman on a major party's presidential ticket.

In 1988, Vice-President Bush ran for the presidency. He won the Republican nomination. The Democrats nominated Massachusetts governor Michael Dukakis.

During the campaign, Bush built on Reagan's legacy of low taxes by saying, "Read my lips: no new taxes." Most Americans saw little reason for change. George Bush won the election with 53 percent of the popular vote and 426 electoral votes.

4. What did the presidential elections of 1984 and 1988 show about the mood of the country?

_____

_____

American Society in a Conservative Age

BEFORE YOU READ

In the last section, you read about the conservative policies of Reagan and Bush.

In this section, you will learn about the social problems that existed in the 1980s.

AS YOU READ

Use the chart below to take notes about social issues during the 1980s and how Americans responded to them.

TERMS AND NAMES

AIDS (acquired immune deficiency syndrome) Disease without a cure whose victims were mostly homosexual men and drug abusers

pay equity Plan to ensure women receive equal pay for equal work

L. Douglas Wilder Nation's first African-American governor

Jesse Jackson Civil rights leader and presidential candidate

affirmative action Efforts to overcome discrimination

Selena Quintanilla-Perez Singer

SOCIAL ISSUES	AMERICANS' RESPONSES
Drugs	• Prosecute users and dealers • Antidrug education

Health, Education, and Cities in Crisis (pages 827–830)

What problems did Americans face in the 1980s?

A scary health issue that arose in the 1980s was **AIDS (acquired immune deficiency syndrome).** The disease is caused by a virus that destroys the *immune system* that protects people from illness. Most of the victims of AIDS were either homosexual men or *intravenous* drug users who shared needles.

Another issue that concerned Americans was abortion. In the 1973 *Roe* v. *Wade* decision, the Supreme Court said women had the right to have an abortion. Opponents of legalized abortion described themselves as "pro-life." Supporters of legalized abortion called themselves "pro-choice."

Reagan and Bush declared a war on drugs. Reagan supported laws to catch drug users and drug dealers. In 1988, Congress passed a law cutting off some benefits for marijuana users. Congress also funded antidrug education in the schools.

Bush's program stressed stopping drugs at the nation's borders. It also called for jailing drug users and giving the death penalty to drug dealers.

Education remained an important issue. In

1983, a report entitled *A Nation at Risk* criticized the nation's schools. The report showed that American students' test scores lagged behind those of students in other nations. Many people agreed that the nation's schools were not doing a good job. But they did not agree on solutions.

The nation's cities were also in crisis. Many poor and homeless people lived in cities. Budget cuts had eliminated earlier federal programs to aid the cities. Welfare payments to the poor had not kept up with rising prices.

1. How did Americans respond to the problems of the 1980s?

_____

_____

The Equal Rights Struggle
(pages 830–831)

Did women's lives improve in the 1980s?

Women continued to try to improve their lives. Women's groups were unable to get the Equal Rights Amendment ratified. But more women were elected to Congress.

By 1992 nearly 58 percent of all women had entered the work force. But women still earned only 76 cents for every dollar a man earned. New divorce laws and social conditions increased the number of single women heading a household. Many of these women lived in poverty.

Women's organizations and unions called for **pay equity.** This was an idea to make sure that women would earn the same pay as men doing the same work.

Under the pay equity system, jobs would be rated according to the skills and responsibilities they required. Employers would set pay rates to reflect each job's requirements. Women also called for benefits to help working mothers.

2. What political losses and gains did women have in the 1980s?

_____

_____

The Fight for Rights Continues
(pages 831–833)

How did minority groups fight for their rights?

Members of many minority groups achieved greater political power during the 1980s. Hundreds of communities had elected African Americans to serve in public offices. In 1990, **L. Douglas Wilder** of Virginia became the first African-American governor in the United States. The Reverend **Jesse Jackson** ran for the Democratic presidential nomination in 1984 and in 1988.

But the income gap between white Americans and African Americans was larger in 1988 than it was in 1968. In addition, Supreme Court rulings further limited **affirmative action.**

Latinos became the fastest growing minority group during the 1980s. Like African Americans, Latinos gained political power during the 1980s.

Latino culture also influenced mainstream culture. Salsa dancing and music became popular in the 1980s. So did Tejano music. The murder of the Tejano singer **Selena Quintanilla-Perez** in 1995 was even the subject of a special issue of *People* magazine.

Native Americans faced cuts in federal aid. Some opened casinos on their reservations to earn money. Asian Americans made economic advances but did not gain much political power.

During the 1970s and 1980s, homosexual men and women worked for laws to protect their rights. By 1993, seven states and 110 communities had outlawed discrimination against homosexuals.

3. What were some political and social gains made by Latinos during the 1980s?

_____

_____

Name ______________________ Date ______________

CHAPTER 25 Section 4 (pages 836–841)

Changes in America's Foreign Policy

TERMS AND NAMES

Mikhail Gorbachev Last leader of the Soviet Union

INF Treaty Treaty to reduce nuclear weapons

glasnost Gorbachev's policy of openness in discussing problems in the Soviet Union

perestroika Gorbachev's policy of reforming the economy in the Soviet Union

Commonwealth of Independent States Federation of new nations that formed after the collapse of the Soviet Union

Tiananmen Square Place in Beijing where Chinese protesters demonstrated against the Communist government

Sandinista Communist rebel group that took power in Nicaragua

Contras Rebel forces supported by Ronald Reagan to overthrow the Sandinistas

Operation Desert Storm The 1991 U.S. attack on Iraq to force the Iraqis out of Kuwait

BEFORE YOU READ

In the last section, you learned about some of the social problems Americans faced in the 1980s.

In this section, you will see how American foreign policy changed after the Cold War.

AS YOU READ

Use the chart below to take notes about U.S. foreign policy in different regions of the world.

MIDDLE EAST	LATIN AMERICA	EUROPE
Refuse to sell arms to Iran		

The Cold War Ends (pages 836–838)

What ended the Cold War?

In March 1985, **Mikhail Gorbachev** became the leader of the Soviet Union. He started talks with the United States to lessen Cold War tensions. Gorbachev thought this would allow the Soviets to cut their military spending. It would also let them reform their economy.

Talks led to the **INF Treaty** (Intermediate-Range Nuclear Forces Treaty). Reagan and Gorbachev signed the treaty in December 1987. The Senate ratified it in May 1988.

Gorbachev supported ***glasnost*** (openness in discussing social problems) and ***perestroika*** (economic *restructuring*) in the Soviet Union. He let private citizens own land. He also allowed more free speech and held free elections.

The weakness of the economy and Gorbachev's reforms led to the collapse of the Soviet Union. All the republics that were in the Soviet Union became independent nations. Then they formed a loose confederation called the **Commonwealth of Independent States.**

The collapse of the Soviet Union ended the Cold War. In January 1993, Russia and the United States signed the START II treaty. This treaty cut both nations' nuclear weapons by 75 percent.

Communists were knocked from power throughout Eastern Europe. Germany reunited. Other Eastern European nations enacted democratic reforms.

Students in China demanded freedom of speech. In April 1989, protesters held marches to voice their demands. The marches grew into large demonstrations in Beijing's **Tiananmen Square.** The Chinese military crushed the protesters. Soldiers killed hundreds of them and arrested others. People all over the world watched these actions. They were upset by what they saw.

1. What events in the Soviet Union led to the end of the Cold War?

_____

_____

Central American and Caribbean Policy (pages 838–839)

How did the United States act toward its neighbors?

In 1979, **Sandinista** rebels overthrew the Nicaraguan government. President Carter sent aid. So did the Soviet Union and Cuba. In 1981, President Reagan charged that the Sandinista government was Communist. He supported the **Contras,** a group trying to defeat the Sandinistas. After years of conflict, a peace agreement was signed and free elections were held in 1990.

Reagan sent U.S. troops to Grenada in 1983. He feared its government had ties with Cuba. The U.S. troops overthrew the pro-Cuban government. They set up a pro-American government in its place.

In 1989, President Bush sent more than 20,000 U.S. troops to Panama. He wanted to overthrow Panamanian dictator Manuel Noriega. He also

wanted to arrest him for *drug trafficking.* Noriega was taken by the American military. They took him to Miami. He was tried, convicted, and sentenced to 40 years in prison.

2. How did the United States influence affairs in Grenada?

_____

_____

Middle East Trouble Spots
(pages 839–841)

How did the United States act toward the Middle East?

In 1983, terrorists linked to Iran took some Americans hostage in Lebanon. Reagan condemned Iran. He called on U.S. allies not to sell Iran weapons for its war against Iraq.

Three years later, the American people found out that Reagan was breaking his own policy. Some of his staff had sold missiles to Iran. They were trying to free the hostages in Lebanon. Also, some of the profits from the sale were sent to the Contras in Nicaragua. These illegal activities were called the Iran-Contra affair.

In the summer of 1987, Congress investigated Iran-Contra. Some of Reagan's staff were convicted of crimes in the scandal. In 1992, President Bush pardoned some of these people.

In 1990, Iraq invaded Kuwait. On January 16, 1991, with the support of Congress and the United Nations, President Bush launched **Operation Desert Storm** to fight Iraq and to free Kuwait.

The United States and its allies staged air strikes against Iraq. On February 23, they also launched a ground attack. On February 28, President Bush announced a cease-fire. The Persian Gulf War was over. Kuwait was freed.

3. What was the purpose of Operation Desert Storm?

_____

_____

Name _____ Date _____

commercial Related to trade or business

deregulation Cutting back on federal regulation

drug trafficking Delivering illegal drugs

immune system Part of the body that fights off illness

intravenous Through the veins

literally Exactly, precisely

restructuring Reform or reorganization

revenues Incomes

AFTER YOU READ

Terms and Names

A. If the statement is true, write "true" on the line. If it is false, change the underlined word or words to make it true.

_____ **1.** An <u>entitlement program</u> is one that guarantees benefits to particular people.

_____ **2.** <u>Reaganomics</u> led to an increase in the national debt.

_____ **3.** President Reagan nominated <u>Sandra Day O'Connor</u> to the position of Chief Justice of the Supreme Court.

_____ **4.** The <u>pay equity</u> system was proposed by unions and women's rights organizations to close the income gap that left so many women poor.

_____ **5.** The actions of Iraq against Kuwait led the United States and its allies to start the <u>INF Treaty</u>.

B. Write the letter of the best answer on the line.

_____ **1.** Which of the following was an alliance of conservative groups that opposed liberal programs?
   a. the New Left
   b. the New Right
   c. affirmative action
   d. Silent Majority

_____ **2.** The theory that tax cuts would increase government revenues was called
   a. affirmative action.
   b. entitlement programs.
   c. supply-side economics.
   d. reverse discrimination.

_____ **3.** The first woman to run on a major party's presidential ticket was
   a. Sandra Day O'Connor.
   b. Anita Hill.
   c. Peggy Noonan.
   d. Geraldine Ferraro.

_____ **4.** What was the policy that was intended to correct the effects of discrimination in the employment and education of minority groups and women?
   a. affirmative action
   b. pay equity
   c. entitlement program
   d. deregulation

_____ **5.** What was the policy set up by Mikhail Gorbachev that called for openness in discussing social problems in the Soviet Union?
   a. perestroika
   b. affirmative action
   c. glasnost
   d. reverse discrimination

Main Ideas

1. Why did Reagan win the election of 1980?

_____

_____

2. Name two key policies of Reaganomics.

_____

_____

3. Define deregulation.

_____

_____

4. Name two gains made by women in the 1980s.

_____

_____

5. What caused the collapse of the Soviet Union?

_____

_____

Thinking Critically

Answer the following questions on a separate sheet of paper.

1. What were two goals of the conservative movement in the late 1970s?

2. How did the conservative policies of the Reagan and Bush administrations affect women and
minority groups in the 1980s?

Name _____ Date _____

The Clinton Presidency

TERMS AND NAMES

Bill Clinton 42nd president

Twenty-seventh Amendment
Prevents Congress from getting a pay raise until after an election has occurred

Hillary Rodham Clinton Wife of Bill Clinton

NAFTA Trade agreement between Canada, Mexico, and the United States

Newt Gingrich Speaker of the House of Representatives

Contract with America Republican plan for political reform

BEFORE YOU READ

In the last section, you learned about American foreign policy at the end of the Cold War.

In this section, you will read about Bill Clinton's presidency.

AS YOU READ

Use the time line below to take notes about the major events of Clinton's first term.

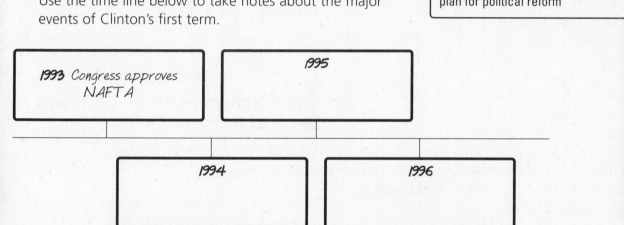

1993 Congress approves NAFTA

1995

1994

1996

Clinton Wins the Presidency
(pages 846–847)

Why did Clinton win the 1992 election?

President George Bush was very popular after the Persian Gulf War. But his support dropped when the economy weakened. The Democrats nominated Arkansas governor **Bill Clinton** to face Bush in the 1992 presidential election.

There was great concern over the economy. This created an opening for a third-party candidate— Texas billionaire H. Ross Perot. He won support from voters who were unhappy with politicians.

In fact, people's distrust of government led to the passage of the **Twenty-seventh Amendment.** This amendment prevented Congress from getting a pay raise until after an election occurred.

Clinton faced *ethical* problems during the race.

Some people criticized his efforts to avoid military service in Vietnam. They also questioned his actions in a real-estate deal called Whitewater.

Clinton won the election anyway. He took 43 percent of the popular vote and won easily in the electoral college.

1. What was the major issue in the 1992 presidential election?

_____

_____

The Clinton Record (pages 847–849)

What issues did Clinton face?

Clinton took steps to simplify the federal *bureaucracy.* He also appointed many women and minorities to his cabinet.

But Clinton's most important goal was to strengthen the economy. This included changing the *health-care system.* The system needed change because nearly 40 million Americans did not have health insurance.

Clinton named his wife, **Hillary Rodham Clinton,** to lead a task force on health care. It developed a plan to offer health insurance for all Americans. Conservatives criticized the plan, and it never got a vote in Congress.

The economy grew during Clinton's presidency. Low interest rates, low inflation, low unemployment, and small budget deficits contributed to the growth. Clinton raised taxes on wealthy Americans. He also slowed growth in federal spending. The Clinton plan cut the federal budget deficit in half between 1992 and 1996.

In 1993, Congress approved **NAFTA** (North American Free Trade Agreement). This treaty with Canada and Mexico made trade easier between the three countries. Some people said the treaty would cost American workers their jobs.

Clinton tried to shape a new foreign policy after the Cold War. Warfare broke out in many regions, including the former Yugoslavia. The United States, NATO, and the United Nations tried to bring peace to these regions. Many Americans did not want to send troops to dangerous places.

2. What were four reasons why the economy improved during the Clinton administration?

_____

_____

The Republican Congress
(pages 849–851)

What did the Republicans in Congress want to do?

In 1994, Clinton faced several problems. He still faced questions about Whitewater. He was also hurt by the failure of his health plan.

Newt Gingrich, a Republican congressman from Georgia, took advantage of Clinton's troubles. Behind Gingrich's leadership, the Republicans won control of both Houses of Congress in the 1994 elections.

Gingrich was elected Speaker of the House. He

and the Republicans tried to pass the **Contract with America.** The contract promised to reform Congress, reform welfare, and pass tougher crime laws.

Some of these bills did not pass the House or the Senate. Clinton vetoed others. Clinton and the Republicans disagreed on many issues. When Clinton refused to accept a Republican budget, the federal government shut down three times.

During 1996, Clinton and Congress worked together better. Congress passed and Clinton signed a bill that changed the nation's welfare system. A modest health-insurance reform bill also became law.

3. What issues were addressed in Gingrich's Contract with America?

_____

The Election of 1996; Clinton's Second Term (pages 851–852)

What issues did Clinton face in his second term?

In the 1996 presidential campaign, Clinton held a large lead in public opinion polls. Clinton won reelection against Republican Bob Dole and Ross Perot. Clinton won 49 percent of the popular vote. But Republicans kept control of Congress.

During Clinton's second term, Democrats and Republicans continued to attack each other. Congress investigated the fundraising activities of both political parties. Some representatives and senators came up with plans to reform campaign *financing.*

Clinton and Congress continued to try to balance the budget. In August 1997, they agreed on a bill that achieved a balanced budget. It also included tax cuts.

4. Describe two issues Clinton faced in his second term.

_____

_____

Name _____ Date _____

The New Global Economy

BEFORE YOU READ

In the last section, you learned about the presidency of Bill Clinton.

In this section, you will read about the economic issues that Americans faced in the 1990s.

AS YOU READ

Use the web below to take notes about the major changes that occurred in the U.S. economy during the 1990s.

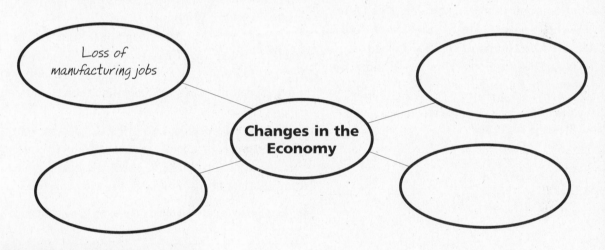

Loss of manufacturing jobs

Changes in the Economy

The New Service and High-Tech Economy (pages 853–856)

What changed for American workers?

Americans heard a great deal of good news about the economy in the 1990s. But many American workers still struggled. Ten million new jobs had been created. But many families now needed two incomes to make ends meet. And the average family income decreased.

Some economists blamed the problems of workers on companies that made their goods in countries with lower labor costs. Other economists blamed people's problems on high taxes. They said these taxes kept companies from growing faster and creating jobs.

Places of work changed in the 1990s. One change was the loss of jobs in *manufacturing*. This is the part of the economy that makes goods such as automobiles.

There was an increase of jobs in the service sector. The **service sector** is the part of the economy that provides services to people. By 1996, more than 60 percent of American workers held jobs in the service sector. The largest growth in the service sector came in jobs that pay low wages. These include jobs such as sales clerks and janitors.

Many companies **downsized**—reduced staff in order to cut costs. They hired temporary workers to replace full-time staff. This had serious *consequences* for the workers. Most temporary workers had lower wages, little job security, and few benefits. This led many workers to feel insecure about their jobs.

Starting in the 1970s, jobs in the manufacturing sector began to disappear. In the 1990s, machines did many jobs that people used to do. The loss in jobs in manufacturing led to a drop in union membership. Workers with high-paying jobs saw no need to join unions. Workers with low-paying jobs were too worried about losing their jobs to join unions.

Workers in high-tech fields such as computers, made up about 20 percent of the work force. These new high-tech jobs demanded that workers have special skills. Most workers who had high-tech jobs earned high salaries.

By the 1990s, some people who had creative ideas about computers made fortunes. **Bill Gates** was one of these people. He founded Microsoft, a computer *software* company. By 1997 he had assets of more than $39 billion. This made him the wealthiest man in the world.

1. What were three changes in the workplace in the United States in the 1990s?

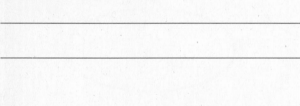

Change and the Global Economy (pages 856–857)

What is the global economy?

Improvements in transportation and communication allowed people, goods, and information to move around the world faster than ever. One of President Clinton's major foreign policy goals was to expand trade.

In 1994, the United States joined other nations in signing a world trade agreement called **GATT** (General Agreement on Tariffs and Trade). GATT lowered tariffs. It also set up the World Trade Organization (WTO). This organization was created to settle trade disputes.

Many people believed that GATT would be good for the U.S. economy. But many American workers feared they would lose their jobs. They thought it would help companies make products in countries where wages are low.

Many low-wage American jobs were lost as a result of NAFTA. But exports to Canada and Mexico increased. By 1997 there were 300,000 more jobs in the United States than there had been in 1993.

Developing nations also offered some businesses the chance to avoid laws on the environment. For example, in Mexico, many assembly plants dumped dangerous chemicals on Mexican soil.

2. In what way did President Clinton try to expand trade?

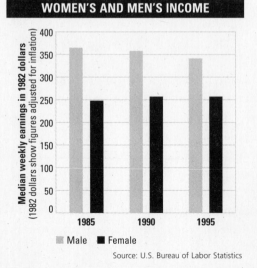

WOMEN'S AND MEN'S INCOME

Median weekly earnings in 1982 dollars (1982 dollars show figures adjusted for inflation)

■ Male ■ Female

Source: U.S. Bureau of Labor Statistics

Skillbuilder

Use the graph to answer the questions.

1. How much money did the average woman earn each week in 1985?

2. Were women's wages closer to men's wages in 1985 or 1995?

CHAPTER 26 Section 3 (pages 860–865)

Technology and Modern Life

TERMS AND NAMES

information superhighway Popular name for a proposed computer network

Internet Worldwide computer network

e-mail Electronic notes and messages

Telecommunications Act Controversial law to reform the communications industry

magnetic resonance imaging New method of seeing inside the human body

genetic engineering Method of changing the genes of living cells

BEFORE YOU READ

In the last section, you saw how the American economy changed in the 1990s.

In this section, you will learn how technology has changed Americans' lives.

AS YOU READ

Use the chart below to take notes on the technological changes described in this section and how these changes have affected your life.

CHANGES	EFFECTS
Information superhighway	• Internet • e-mail

Technology and Communications (pages 860–862)

How have new technologies affected communications?

President Clinton wanted to create an **information superhighway.** This was a computer *network* that linked people from around the world. The network would link cable, phone, and computer systems to provide entertainment and information.

Clinton appointed Vice-President Gore to over-see the government's role in creating the information superhighway. They wanted private *entrepreneurs* to build the network. But they believed the government should protect people's rights to use it.

Most people took part in the information superhighway through the **Internet,** a worldwide computer network. By 1996, experts expected that 24 million Americans regularly used the Internet to send **e-mail**—electronic notes and messages.

New technologies let many Americans work in their homes instead of going to an office every day.

They also gave Americans many entertainment options. Cable television gave people more television channels. The Internet has provided people with new video games.

The changes in communications caused the growth of many communications companies. Congress passed the **Telecommunications Act** in 1996 to make sure people get good service. The law allowed telephone and cable companies to enter each others' industries. One of the results of the law was an increase in *mergers*. This cut the number of competing companies.

Congress passed the Communications Decency Act as part of the Telecommunications Act. Congress called for a *"V-chip"* to be placed in television sets. This computer chip would allow parents to block TV programs that they do not want their children to see.

The communications industry liked the Telecommunications Act. But some people believed that the law allowed a small number of people to control the media. Civil rights activists thought the Communications Decency Act limited free speech.

1. How did the Internet and cable television affect Americans?

_____

_____

Technology Enriches Lives
(pages 862–864)

How does technology affect daily life?

Technology changed many other areas of life, too. New treatments and new ways of diagnosing—discovering—illnesses were developed in the 1990s.

Doctors found better ways of tracking the spread of HIV, the virus that causes AIDS, in the body. **Magnetic resonance imaging** (MRI) helped doctors get a better view of the inside of the body.

Some advances caused controversy. One of these advances was **genetic engineering**—the artificial changing of the cells of a living thing. This procedure was used to *alter* some foods. Many people feared the changes in these foods. They also feared that these foods would create *allergic* reactions in people who ate them.

New technologies offered people new types of entertainment. CD-ROM (Compact Disk Read-Only Memory) technology improved communication and research.

A single CD-ROM had enough memory to hold all the information in two encyclopedias. CD-ROMs also gave people a great way to play video games on their computers.

Technology affected other areas of life, too. Computers were placed in more classrooms across the country. Improved air bags made cars safer.

The space program also made progress. In 1993, American astronauts repaired the Hubble Space Telescope. This telescope provided scientists with great views of the universe.

2. What were some important technological advances in the United States?

_____

_____

Progress on the Environment
(pages 864–865)

How can technology protect the environment?

Some new technologies helped the environment. The most popular way of protecting the environment was through recycling. This helped to reduce waste in the country.

Automakers developed an electric car to reduce air pollution. Also, researchers looked for cleaner sources of energy. They tried to find energy sources— such as nuclear, wind, and solar power— to take the place of coal, gas, and oil.

3. What was the most widespread way in which Americans protected the environment?

_____

_____

Name _____ Date _____

CHAPTER 26 Section 4 (pages 866–871)

The Changing Face of America

> **TERMS AND NAMES**
> **urban flight** Movement of people away from cities
> **telecommute** To work at home

BEFORE YOU READ

In the last section, you learned about the ways technology affects modern life.

In this section, you will read about the changes facing Americans at the start of the 21st century.

AS YOU READ

Use the web below to take notes about the changes occurring in the United States.

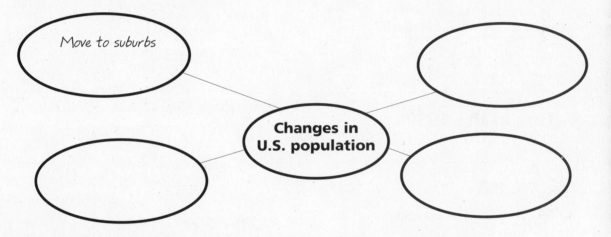

The Suburban Nation (pages 866–868)

Why did people move to suburbs?

Between 1950 and 1970, Americans experienced **urban flight,** where Americans left the cities and moved to the suburbs. By 1990 more than half of all Americans lived in the suburbs. Many people left the cities because they were crowded. Some people moved to the suburbs so that their children could attend newer schools.

One result of this growth was *suburban sprawl.* Over time, the number of people from minority groups living in the suburbs increased.

As more people moved to the suburbs, some high-tech industries moved their factories there. This removed many jobs from the cities. But

people in cities often did not have any way to get to jobs in the suburbs.

Suburbs competed with each other to attract companies that would provide jobs for their workers. The cities grew poorer as the suburbs grew wealthier. Also, many cities' downtown areas were falling apart.

During the 1990s, many workers began to **telecommute.** They used new communications technology to work from their homes.

1. How did urban flight change the nation's cities?

_____

_____

The Graying of America (page 868)

How will aging affect America?

As the baby boomers—people born between 1946 and 1961—got older, Americans were living longer. The increase in the number of older Americans caused problems for American leaders.

They needed to find ways to fund programs like Social Security and Medicare for the future. The cost of these programs in 1995 was more than $150 billion.

In 1996, three workers made Social Security contributions to support every retired person. But experts expect that by 2030, there will be only two workers to support each retired person. Social Security will begin to pay out more than it takes in. As a result, some people want to reform the Social Security system.

2. How does the increase in the number of elderly people affect Social Security and Medicare?

_____

_____

Immigration in the 1990s
(pages 869–870)

How has immigration affected America?

Between 1970 and 1995, the population of the United States increased from 204 million to more than 260 million. Much of this increase was because of immigration. Most of these immigrants came from Latin America and Asia.

Experts believed that immigration will change the ethnic and racial makeup of the United States. They predicted that by 2050, *non-Latino whites* will make up 53 percent of the population, down from 74 percent in 1996. They expect the Latino population to increase from 10 percent of the population in 1996 to 25 percent in 2050. The Asian population is expected to increase from 3 percent to 8 percent. The African-American population is expected to increase from 12 percent to 14 percent.

In 1994, almost two-thirds of Americans wanted to cut back immigration. Some people feared that immigrants took jobs away from Americans born in the United States.

Another problem was illegal immigration. By the early 1990s, about 3.2 million illegal immigrants came to the United States.

3. How is immigration changing the United States?

_____

_____

America and the New Millennium (pages 870–871)

What challenges do Americans face in the 21st century?

At the end of the 20th century, Americans faced many challenges. One problem was *terrorism*. Bombings in Oklahoma City, New York City, and Atlanta have made Americans feel threatened at home and abroad.

Americans were also concerned about environmental issues. Scientists warned about the dangers of global warming, acid rain, and the loss of the ozone layer.

Americans were also concerned about poverty. This remains a problem as some jobs in the country are cut and government antipoverty programs are cut.

But Americans also saw many new opportunities for the 21st century. They hoped that the economy would continue to grow. They also hoped this growth would help reduce the problems of poverty.

Americans also looked with hope to better education and new technologies to help them meet the challenges of the new *millennium*.

4. What challenges faced Americans at the end of the 20th century?

_____

_____

Glossary   CHAPTER 26   The United States in Today's World

allergic Related to allergies

alter To change

bureaucracy An agency or department to deal with an issue

consequences Effects, results

developing nations Countries that are building industries

entrepreneurs People who use their own money to create a new business

ethical Relating to good or bad behavior

financing The way something is paid for

health-care system Hospitals, doctors, insurance companies, and government programs that provide health care

manufacturing Making goods such as automobiles

merger Joining together

millennium A period of 1,000 years

network Group of connections

non-Latino whites White people who are not Latinos

software Programs that make computers work

suburban sprawl The expansion of suburbs away from a city

terrorism Use of violence to create political change through fear

V-chip Computer chip to allow parents to prevent children from watching some shows

AFTER YOU READ

Terms and Names

A. Write the letter of the name or term that matches the description.

a. urban flight

b. GATT

c. telecommute

d. NAFTA

e. Internet

_____ **1.** Agreement that ended trade barriers between the United States, Canada, and Mexico

_____ **2.** Treaty that lowered tarrifs and set up the World Trade Organization (WTO)

_____ **3.** A worldwide computer network

_____ **4.** When Americans left the cities and moved to the suburbs

_____ **5.** To use new communications technology to work from home

B. Write the name or term that best completes each sentence.

genetic engineering

downsize

Hillary Rodham Clinton

magnetic resonance imaging

service sector

1. President Clinton appointed _____ to head the task force on health care.

2. The 1990s saw a decrease of jobs in manufacturing and an increase in jobs in the _____.

3. In the 1990s, doctors used _____ to see the inside of the body better.

4. The use of _____ to alter food caused concern in the 1990s.

5. Companies that tried to cut costs would often _____ their staffs.

AFTER YOU READ   *CHAPTER 26*   The United States in Today's World

Main Ideas

1. What did the Twenty-seventh Amendment do?

_____

_____

2. Why did some American companies downsize?

_____

_____

3. Describe two ways that technology changed people's lives in the 1990s.

_____

_____

4. How did urban flight affect cities?

_____

_____

5. What percentage of Americans do experts think will be Latinos in 2050?

_____

_____

Thinking Critically

Answer the following questions on a separate sheet of paper.

1. Describe three ways that the U.S. economy changed by the 1990s.

2. What are some possible effects of the graying of America?

Name ______________________________ Date ______________

Foreign Policy After the Cold War

TERMS AND NAMES

democracy Government elected by the people

human rights Basic freedoms to which all people are entitled

double standard Set of principles granting greater opportunity or liberty to one than to another

Most Favored Nation (MFN) Privileged trading status

BEFORE YOU READ

In the last section, you read how Americans were looking for new ways to deal with the nation's problems.

In this section, you will read about the changing role of the United States in world affairs.

AS YOU READ

Fill in the chart below with the three goals of American foreign policy after the Cold War. Take notes on the different points of view about each issue.

FOREIGN POLICY GOAL	ARGUMENT FOR	ARGUMENT AGAINST
promoting democracy	*democracies make world safe*	*democracy not "good fit" for all nations*

Historical Perspective (page 878)

How did the United States contain Communism?

The United States came out of World War II ready to play an active role in world affairs. The next 45 years were marked by the Cold War. That was a time of competition—and sometimes confrontation—between the United States and the Soviet Union. During that time, U.S. foreign policy concentrated on stopping the spread of Communism around the world.

These key foreign policy actions were based on that goal:

- Marshall Plan and NATO (1949) to protect against the Communist threat in Europe
- Korean War (1950s) and Vietnam War (1960s) to contain Communism in Asia
- Forcing Soviets to remove missiles from Cuba (1962) and support of Contra rebels in Nicaragua (1980s) to remove Communist threat in Western Hemisphere
- Improving relations with China and the Arab nations (1970s) to weaken Soviet influence
- Nuclear arms reduction (1970s and 1980s) to limit Communist military threat

By 1992, the Soviet Union had broken up. The Cold War was over. The United States no longer had to concentrate on the Communist threat. U.S. foreign policy needed new goals.

1. What were three American foreign policy actions designed to prevent the spread of Communism?

_____

_____

Foreign Policy Goals (pages 878–879)

What are the goals of U.S. foreign policy?

There have been three major goals of American foreign policy since the end of the Cold War. They are 1) promoting democracy around the world, 2) protecting human rights, and 3) opening world markets to American goods. Americans have sometimes disagreed on how to deal with these issues.

Many American leaders have felt that the United States should be active in promoting **democracy,** or governments elected by the people. They believe that the more democratic nations there are the safer the world will be. That is because democratic governments are more likely to keep their international agreements. They are also less likely to engage in war and terrorism.

The opposing view does not think that the American style of democracy is a "good fit" for all nations. They do not believe it is reasonable to expect democratic governments everywhere. Those who want to spread democracy respond by pointing to the rise of new democratic governments in places as different as Taiwan and Argentina. According to them, people naturally want to govern themselves.

The United States has tried to make sure that people worldwide enjoy basic **human rights.** These are the freedoms to which all people are entitled. Such freedoms are found in the Declaration of Independence and the Bill of Rights. Most people agree about this goal. But there is disagreement about the way the United States has acted in support of this goal.

Some argue that the United States has a **double standard** on the issue of human rights. Certain acts are considered bad when they are done by one nation but not when they are done by another. For example, the United States puts pressure on small nations to correct human rights problems. But American policy often ignores the same human rights abuses by larger nations that are economically or politically important to it. Critics argue that the United States should not trade with nations that abuse human rights.

Other people argue that trade improves the lives of people in both nations. They feel that American companies help raise the standard of living in such countries.

Trade—including opening world markets to American goods—is sometimes tied to the issue of human rights. For example, the United States wants to get its share of new markets in China. That country has a very poor record on human rights. Even so, China continues to receive **Most Favored Nation** (MFN) status, a privileged trading status. That means that China enjoys low tariffs, or import taxes, on goods it sells in the United States.

Some people want to take away China's MFN status because of its human rights abuses. Others believe that would just make China angry. They feel that nations that trade with China should put pressure on the Chinese to correct human rights problems. They feel that the United States can be a leader in this effort.

2. What are the three major goals of U.S. foreign policy?

_____

_____

EPILOGUE Section 2 (pages 880–883)

The Debate Over Immigration

TERMS AND NAMES

bloc Group

ethnic Relating to people sharing racial, national, religious, or cultural heritage

asylum Safe place for people fleeing an oppressive foreign government

BEFORE YOU READ

In the last section, you read about the foreign policy goals of the United States.

In this section, you will read about the debate over immigration.

AS YOU READ

Use the chart below to take notes on the arguments for and against limiting immigration.

ARGUMENTS	FOR LIMITING IMMIGRATION	AGAINST LIMITING ARGUMENTS
Economic	immigrants take jobs from American workers	low-paying jobs that Americans don't want
Political/ Cultural		
Moral		

Historical Perspective and Recent Trends (page 880)

How have native-born Americans reacted to immigrants?

It is often said that the United States is a nation of immigrants. All groups helped build the nation and create its culture. And Americans have always felt pride in immigrants. Yet, limiting immigration has often been popular. Americans have worried about the numbers of people entering the nation since the time of Benjamin Franklin in the 1700s. Later, there was the anti-immigrant *nativist* movement in 1840s. Then there were the immigration quotas of the 1920s. More recently, economic troubles and

rapidly growing population in Asia and Latin America have led people from those areas to come to the United States. In 1965, restrictions on immigration were loosened. Since then, 20 million immigrants have entered the country.

During much of that time, the American economy was growing slowly. Unemployment was up. Wages were falling. Some Americans blamed the large numbers of immigrants for these problems. The debate over immigration limits began again.

1. How have Americans traditionally felt about immigrants?

_____

_____

Illegal and Legal Immigration
(page 881)

What has been the reaction to illegal immigrants?

By the 1990s, several million immigrants had entered the country illegally. They posed an economic burden. Many had low-paying jobs, seasonal work, or no jobs at all. Yet, states provided them with health care, education, welfare, and other services. Californians voted to limit services to illegal immigrants in 1994. In 1996, Congress voted similar limits.

Most Americans want to stop illegal immigration. But they disagree on whether to limit legal immigration. The debate focuses on economic, political, cultural, and moral issues.

2. How did California react to illegal immigrants?

Economic Arguments (page 882)

What are the economic arguments over immigration?

People who want to limit immigration say that immigrants take jobs from American workers. Others argue that those are low-paying jobs that Americans don't want. They say that unemployment went down when immigration was high.

Immigrants have always worked for low wages. Some say that drives down wages for everyone. Economists think other factors are more important in lowering wages. They also point out that low wages result in lower prices for consumers.

Government support for immigration is hotly debated. Some people say that many immigrants are poor. They take more in welfare, Social Security, Medicare, and other services than they pay in taxes. Others say that immigrants are an economic gain, not a drain. They pay more in federal taxes than they get in services. But supporters of immigration limits point out that immigrants use more state and local resources than federal services. And they pay little in state and local taxes.

3. How might immigrants be an economic drain?

Political and Cultural Arguments (page 883)

What are the political and cultural arguments over immigration?

Those who favor limits on immigration complain that many immigrants do not become citizens. They feel it is unfair for immigrants to enjoy the privileges of living in the United States without the responsibilities of voting, serving on juries, and so on. However, since 1996, immigrants have been becoming citizens at a more rapid rate.

When they become citizens, some people argue, immigrants tend to vote in blocs, or groups. Earlier immigrants had done the same thing at first. Later, their voting became more independent.

Some people feel that Americans will lose their common culture because of the mix of peoples entering the country. Or they complain that immigrants do not mix but stay in *ethnic* neighborhoods. They stay with people who share their racial, national, religious, or cultural heritage. Others feel the ethnic mix makes American culture richer.

4. What are the political and cultural arguments for and against limiting immigration?

Moral Arguments (page 883)

What are the moral arguments over immigration?

Some people feel that there are moral reasons for allowing immigration. One is offering **asylum,** a safe place for people fleeing an oppressive foreign government. But those fleeing economic hardship are often turned away. Many people feel that is unfair.

People also disagree over allowing relatives of immigrants into the country. Many complain that they are often very young or old or have no skills. They become an economic burden on the nation.

Finally, some people simply feel there are too many immigrants. Others say that the United States is a nation of immigrants. It should allow others to follow the same path.

5. What are the moral arguments over immigration?

Crime and Public Safety

BEFORE YOU READ

In the last section, you read the debate over immigration.

In this section, you will read about the problem of crime and concerns about public safety.

AS YOU READ

Use the chart below to organize your notes on the ideas and facts you learn about crime in this section.

HEADING	MAIN IDEAS	SUPPORTING FACTS
A New Crime Wave?		
Gun Control		
Getting Tough on Crime	locking up offenders prevents crime	lenient prison sentences in Britain led to more crime
Terrorism		

Historical Perspective and Recent Success Against Crime
(pages 884–885)

What factors cause crime rates to rise and fall?

Americans consider crime one of the nation's worst problems. Crime rates were going up during the 1970s. Then, in the 1980s, an increase in drug abuse—particularly of crack cocaine—drove up the crime rate even more. This increase continued into the mid 1990s.

Then crime began to drop. Experts see four reasons for this. First, there are fewer people in the group most likely to commit crime—males 18 to 29. Second, the use of crack cocaine dropped.

Third, unemployment went down. But the most important factor in the drop in crime is new policing methods.

These policing methods include putting officers back on the street, walking a beat. Officers take a more active role in the neighborhood. Also the police work to prevent crime. Counseling programs try to find and help young people who are likely to turn to crime before any crimes occur.

1. What factors drove the crime rate up in the 1980s and down in the 1990s?

_____

_____

Public Alarm Remains (page 885)

Why is the public still concerned about crime?

In spite of dropping crime rates, people still worry about it. One reason is that rates are still high. Second, the prison population is soaring. Also, according to many critics, the media overemphasize crime. For example, TV news shows run many more stories on crime today than they did when the crime rate was higher. This promotes a widespread fear of crime.

2. What are three reasons for the public fear of crime?

_____

_____

Continuing Efforts Against Crime (pages 885–887)

What are the main ideas about preventing crime?

Some experts believe that a new crime wave is coming. Violent crime is up among young teenagers. There is a large population of children under ten who will be teenagers soon. Also, drug abuse among young teenagers is going up.

Other experts disagree. They think the share of teenagers in the population in the near future will be about the same as it was 1994. Some of these experts feel that it is not the number of kids that is the problem. They think keeping guns out of their hands is more important.

Gun control, limiting people's ability to own handguns legally, is a controversial issue. In 1993, the **Brady Act** became federal law. It called for a waiting period for the sale of handguns. During that time, police check to see if the buyer has a criminal record. If so, he or she cannot buy the gun. Many people credit this and similar state laws for the drop in the crime rate.

Others disagree. The **National Rifle Association (NRA)** is against gun control. They claim the Brady Act has had little effect. It does not apply to places with their own gun laws. Those are the places that have the highest crime rates. The Supreme Court also ruled that the federal govern-

ment could not force local officials to do the background checks required by the Brady Act.

Gun control raises a constitutional question. The Second Amendment protects the rights of the people to "bear arms." The NRA argues that gun-control laws violate this right. Others say that the purpose of the Amendment was not to protect personal weapons. Its purpose was to allow states to have their own military units.

Some people support another way to cut crime. They want criminals caught and locked up for a long time. This is the "get tough on crime" theory. Another approach is the "broken window" theory. People who believe this theory think minor crimes lead to major ones. They feel that crime will be discouraged if police crack down on *vandalism* and *graffiti*.

Another "get tough" measure is the "three strikes and you're out" laws. Persons who have been convicted of two previous crimes get a stiff sentence if they are convicted of a third crime. Some people oppose these laws. They say criminals who are afraid of getting caught a third time are more likely to shoot police officers. And they claim that these laws are used against blacks more than against whites. They point to the high percentage of African Americans in prison even though they are a small percentage of the population.

Finally, a new kind of violent crime is beginning to affect Americans. It is **terrorism,** or the use of violence against people or property for *ideological* or political reasons. The 1990s saw terrorist bombings at the World Trade Center in New York, in Oklahoma City, and at the Atlanta Olympics. As a result, President Clinton signed a bill giving the FBI more power to fight terrorism. Both civil liberties groups and Republicans protested parts of this bill. They do not like the idea of giving the federal government too much power.

3. What are the pros and cons of some current ways of fighting crime?

_____

_____

Exploring Education Today

BEFORE YOU READ

In the last section, you read about the continuing concerns about crime.

In this section, you will see how Americans feel about education and schools.

AS YOU READ

Take notes on the formal outline below. List the three most important education issues and the different opinions about how to deal with those issues.

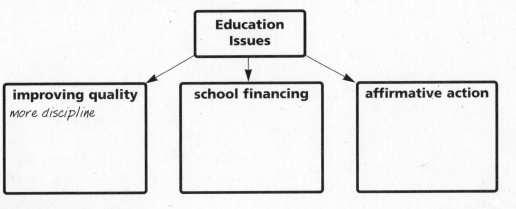

Historical Perspective and Key Issues (page 888)

What problems are American public schools facing?

America's leaders have always thought that education is important. It is a necessity for a free and democratic society. A system of government-supported public schools was set up in the 19th century. By the 1960s, there were severe problems. Achievement levels had begun to drop. Inner city schools did not have the resources of richer suburban schools. Violence and drugs threatened safety. And integration of white and minority students did not always go smoothly. In 1983, a government report declared American schools in crisis.

The debate over public education has focused on three issues: improving quality, school financing, and **affirmative action,** or programs intended to remedy past discrimination.

1. What problems did public schools begin to face in the 1960s?

_____

_____

Improving Quality (pages 888–890)

What do people think are the major problems with schools?

Many people say that lack of discipline in the schools is a major problem. One proposed solution is school uniforms, to prevent fights caused by students wearing gang colors. Other people focus on access to information. They say schools should be hooked up to the internet.

Two different ways to change the educational system have also been suggested. One is **charter schools.** These are schools that get permission, or a charter, from the state to try new ways to teach. One advantage of a charter school is the commitment of parents, teachers, and students to the philosophy of their school. But some of these schools are also businesses. And poor management can be a problem. Also, the schools are small with few facilities and extracurricular activities.

Another approach is the **voucher system.** States give parents a certificate worth a certain amount of money. The parents give the voucher to the public or private school of their choice. The state then pays the school. This makes schools compete to attract students. Many people feel that this competition will improve the overall quality of all schools. Some are not sure what impact vouchers would have. Also there is disagreement over whether vouchers should be available only to the poor or to everyone.

Other reform ideas focus on what students should be learning. In 1989, government leaders set educational goals for the year 2000. This **Goals 2000** plan said that schools must have higher standards that demand more from their students.

2. What are three suggestions for improving the quality of the nation's schools?

Financing Education (page 890)

How are public schools financed?

Some education reformers are concerned that schools do not receive equal resources. Schools in poorer towns and cities get less money than those in wealthy areas. That is because most schools are supported by local property taxes. Real estate has higher value in wealthy areas. Also, these town are often willing and able to pay a higher tax rate to support their local schools.

Reformers feel that all students are entitled to the same educational resources, no matter where they live. Court cases have challenged unequal school funding in more than 20 states.

In 1993, Michigan voters approved a new plan. They now support their schools out of state funds. That helps to even out inequities, or unfair differences. However, many people still want local school systems to decide how the money is spent.

3. How does the way schools are financed affect their quality?

Affirmative Action (page 891)

What is the purpose of affirmative action?

Unlike public schools, students compete to enter private schools and colleges. There, it has been difficult to solve the problem of discrimination against women and minorities. One approach has been affirmative action. It is a policy that is supposed to correct the effects of past discrimination. It does this by favoring the groups who were previously disadvantaged. Most Americans support giving these groups new opportunities. However, many Americans disapprove of what they consider to be a quota system. Quotas set aside a certain number of college admissions for minority students.

In 1978, the Supreme Court ruled race could be one factor among others considered in college admissions. Recently, a federal court ruled against separate admission tracks, or requirements, for white and minority students. The court said this discriminates against whites. In 1996, California passed an *initiative* that banned race or gender preferences in college admissions.

Opponents of affirmative action argue that it is unfair to use gender or race for decisions about jobs or college admissions. They say a "race-blind" society is fairer. Others disagree. They say that there is still too much discrimination against African Americans and other minorities. And affirmative action is necessary to correct the balance.

4. What are the main arguments for and against affirmative action?

Name _____ Date _____

Curing the Health Care System

TERMS AND NAMES

universal health insurance
Guaranteed health insurance for everyone

Medicare Federal program paying for health care for the elderly

Medicaid Federal program paying for health care for the poor

BEFORE YOU READ

In the last section, you read about America's concerns for its schools and education.

In this section, you will read about the problems in the American health care system.

AS YOU READ

Use the chart below to take notes on how the federal government is involved in health care for its citizens.

MEDICAL PROGRAM	FEDERAL INVOLVEMENT
Universal Health Insurance	• Trumam proposed/Congress, defeated, 1945 •
Medical Care for the Poor	
Medical Care for Elderly	

Historical Perspective and Health Reform Today (page 892)

What is univeral health insurance?

In 1945, President Harry Truman proposed **universal health insurance,** or guaranteed *health insurance* for everyone. Congress did not pass it. In 1965, Medicare and Medicaid were established to help pay for medical care for the elderly and for the poor.

In the early 1990s, health care costs were rising. But the economy was not doing well. President Clinton was concerned about the large numbers of Americans not covered by health insurance. Many of them did not get medical care because they could not afford it. Clinton proposed a complex plan of universal health insurance. Congress defeated the plan in 1994. The defeat of this plan was due to *lobbying* by private insurance companies and to the public not wanting another big government program.

Only a few years later, the situation had changed. The American economy was doing better. Health costs were not rising as fast. Fewer people were losing their jobs and, therefore, losing their health insurance. In 1996, a new federal law was passed. It required employers' health insurance plans to cover new employees who had had health insurance before they changed jobs. That meant people could not be denied insurance because of *preexisting conditions*—medical problems they had before applying for this new insurance.

1. **What were two reasons for the defeat of universal health insurance?**

_____

_____

Medicare and Medicaid (page 892–893)

Why are Medicare and Medicaid in crisis?

By the 1990s, the federal programs of **Medicare** (which pays for health care for the elderly) and **Medicaid** (which pays for health care for the poor) were taking a large share of federal spending. Medicare is actually running out of money. The reasons are rising costs and population changes.

Americans are living longer. Seniors form a larger percentage of the population. There are proportionally fewer young people working and paying the taxes that support Medicare. Therefore, the Medicare program is in financial crisis.

Several solutions have been proposed. One is to raise the tax rate. Another suggestion is to increase the share that the elderly pay for their Medicare insurance. But some argue that increased payments will push many elderly people into poverty. Others suggest raising the age at which people can get Medicare from 65 to 70.

Medicaid faces a similar financial problem.

Much of its spending goes to the elderly poor. As the population ages, Medicaid's costs go up too. Also recent changes in welfare laws may increase the number of poor people who will need Medicaid.

2. **What are two reasons why Medicare and Medicaid are facing financial crisis?**

_____

_____

The Uninsured Millions (page 893)

Why are millions of Americans uninsured?

The number of Americans without health insurance is rising. Many political leaders feel that the government does not have the resources to cover everyone. But they are willing to cover children.

About 10 million children have no health insurance. The result is that they get poor medical care. Government leaders agree that money spent on these "gap kids" is a good investment. Every dollar spent on preventive care saves $10 in later costs to treat an illness that could have been prevented.

3. **Why are government leaders willing to support health insurance for children?**

_____

_____

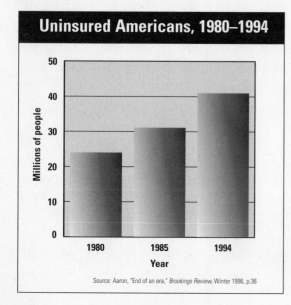

Uninsured Americans, 1980–1994

Millions of people / Year

Source: Aaron, "End of an era," *Brookings Review,* Winter 1996, p.36

Skillbuilder

Use the graph to answer the questions.

1. **Is the number of uninsured Americans going up or going down?**

_____

2. **How many Americans were uninsured in 1980? In 1985? In 1994?**

_____

Name _____ Date _____

Women and the Glass Ceiling

> **TERMS AND NAMES**
> **glass ceiling** Limit that prevents women from advancing to the upper levels of their chosen careers
> **upward mobility** Ability to move to top-level jobs

BEFORE YOU READ

In the last section, you read about the crisis in the health care system.

In this section, you will read how working women still meet obstacles to equal pay and promotion up the corporate ladder.

AS YOU READ

Use the chart below to take notes on the progress—or lack of progress— women have made in equal pay, promotion, and entering "men's fields." Give reasons if possible.

	PROGRESS/LACK OF PROGRESS	REASONS
equal pay for equal work		
promotion to top management	*limited advancement: only 10% of senior jobs*	
entering "men's fields"		

Historical Perspective (page 894)

How have women's work and pay compared to men's?

A 1961 commission reported that women were paid less than men for equal work. It also said that women were not usually promoted to top positions. Over 30 years later, another commission found little improvement in pay. And women held only 10 percent of the most senior jobs in the nation's largest companies. Even so, the percentage of women working outside the home continued to grow.

Women have often found it difficult to advance in their chosen fields. They describe a **glass ceiling** that limits their progress. It is glass because

they can see through to the upper levels. But it is still a ceiling, preventing them from rising higher.

1. Traditionally, how have women's pay and job opportunities compared to men's?

_____

_____

Positive Trends (page 894)

Has the employment picture for women improved?

Women have seen some improvement in their employment picture in recent decades, They are entering new fields. Some of these areas, such as construction, used to be almost totally male. Women are also better represented on college and university faculties. And they are going into the sciences. This will give them opportunities in the high-tech industries of the future.

Another trend is the increase of women "knowledge workers." These are managers, professionals, and those who use technology. Today, women hold almost half of these jobs. These kinds of jobs will be important in the future. Some people feel that women will achieve powerful positions in these fields.

2. How have women's opportunities changed in recent decades?

Money and Upward Mobility
(page 895)

What are the areas of inequality for working women?

There are two important issues in women's employment today. One is unequal pay. The other is the lack of **upward mobility**—the ability to advance to top-level jobs.

The gap in earnings between men and women remains. In 1970, men earned about three times, or 300 percent, what women did. Today, men still earn about 50 percent more. And women's earnings are lower than men's in a wide variety of careers. Some people say that women are paid less because they are more likely to be part-time work-

ers. In addition, women often take time out of the labor force to care for young children.

Women are also still not rising to the top jobs in America. They hold only 10 percent of senior jobs in the *Fortune 500 companies*. And only 2.4 percent of the *chief executive officers* of those companies are women.

Men and women explain this situation differently. Men feel that women don't advance because they lack management experience. They also say that women have not been in the work force long enough. Women blame the situation on male stereotypes of women.

Women also blame the so-called *old-boys' network*. This is a loose association of friendships formed in men's schools, men's sports activities, men's clubs, and in mostly male corporate offices. Because managers tend to hire and promote people they know—or people recommended by people they know—this network is a business asset. And women are not part of it.

Women have made more progress in being appointed to *corporate boards of directors*. The reason is *demographics*, or the characteristics of different segments of the population. Companies want to understand the needs of their customers. Many of their customers are women. Companies are slowly realizing that they benefit if their managers reflect the population they are targeting.

3. What are some reasons for the lack of equality for women in the work place?

Women's and Men's Average Earnings in Selected Careers

Career	Women	Men	Career	Women	Men
Accountant	$28,496	$38,844	Magazine art director	$40,546	$40,625
Advertising copywriter	53,000	58,000	Pediatrician	119,660	137,065
Computer operator	20,384	27,404	Personnel specialist	30,212	35,932
Cook	12,376	13,988	Pharmacist	53,650	52,200
Engineer	49,100	50,000	Real estate salesperson	26,832	33,800
Financial manager	33,020	48,984	Registered nurse	36,036	37,180
High school teacher	33,124	37,596	Retail sales worker	13,156	18,980
Insurance salesperson	23,556	40,404	Travel agent	23,600	28,200
Lawyer	49,816	60,892	University professor	57,790	65,080

Source: "1997 salary report," Working Woman, January 1997, pp. 31–33, 69, 71, 73–76.

Skillbuilder
Use the chart to answer the questions

1. What pattern in earnings do you see?

2. In what five careers is pay almost equal?

Breaking the Cycle of Poverty

TERMS AND NAMES

working poor People with low-paying jobs that provide few benefits and no health insurance.

enterprise zones Targeted areas in poor neighborhoods where the government gives tax breaks to companies that locate there

BEFORE YOU READ

In the last section, you read that women still face problems of equality in the workplace.

In this section, you will read about poverty and the attempts of governments to reform the welfare system.

AFTER YOU READ

Use the chart below to take notes on who is poor in America and the causes of poverty.

WHO IS POOR IN AMERICA	CAUSES OF POVERTY
Working Poor	low pay, no benefits

Historical Perspective and Americans in Poverty (pages 896–897)

How has the federal government tried to help the poor?

Many Americans were poor during the Great Depression of the 1930s. So Congress created the Social Security system to help. This was the first time the federal government offered to give aid to the poor. But poverty did not go away. In the 1960s, President Lyndon Johnson's War on Poverty created more programs to help the poor. Nevertheless, by the 1970s, the poverty rate was going up again. Also, prices were rising at the same time that many Americans feared losing their jobs. These workers

did not want their tax money going to poor people who did not work. They demanded *welfare* reform.

However, many poor Americans do work. About 30 million are the **working poor**—people with low-paying jobs that provide few *benefits* and no health insurance. Children make up a large share of the poor. The homeless and the unemployed also account for a large number of those in poverty.

1. Who are the poor in America?

_____

_____

Some Causes of Poverty (page 897–898)

What are the leading causes of poverty?

Many poor people do not have *marketable skills*. That fact keeps them from finding and keeping jobs. They need training in the skills that are in demand in the work place. Many of the poor also need training in good work habits, such as getting to work on time and following instructions.

Some experts feel that the poverty level drops during times of economic growth. More jobs are available. Others argue that high welfare payments discourage people from working at low-paying jobs.

Some people who do want to work and can find a job still face problems. Mothers often cannot afford to pay someone to care for their children while they are at work. They do better financially when they stay home and live on welfare than when they go to work for a low salary and pay for child care. The 1996 welfare law included funding for day care to help solve this problem.

Another factor that limits the ability of poor people to find jobs is their lack of a good education. Three-fourths of people on welfare have very poor *literacy*. They can hardly read. That makes it almost impossible for them to perform most jobs in today's economy. Some experts feel that improved education is the key to breaking the *cycle of poverty*.

Racial discrimination has kept many members of minority groups in poverty. Even when minority workers got hired, they seldom got promoted above the lowest-paying jobs. The Civil Rights Act of 1964 banned the most obvious forms of discrimination. But subtle discrimination still exists.

2. **What are the major causes of poverty in the United States?**

_____

_____

Welfare Reform by the States and Federal Welfare Reform

(page 898–899)

How are governments getting people off welfare?

The states took the lead in welfare reform.

Wisconsin began welfare reform in 1987. Its welfare rolls went down by half. One reason is that Wisconsin's economy was growing at the time. But a more important reason was that the state helped former welfare recipients find jobs. Wisconsin and many other states encourage businesses to hire former welfare recipients. These states give tax credits to employers and help pay workers' wages.

In 1996, President Clinton and Congress agreed on a federal welfare reform bill. This law did three things. 1) It cut more than $55 million in welfare spending. 2) It put a five-year limit on how long people could get welfare payments. 3) It cut benefits to people who did not find a job within two years.

The federal government also did three things to encourage businesses to hire people who had been on welfare. 1) It gave tax credits to employers. 2) It also helped pay the wages of these new workers. 3) It set up **enterprise zones.** These zones are targeted areas in poor neighborhoods. The government gives tax breaks to companies that locate there.

Many critics felt that the old system encouraged people to become dependent on welfare payments. These efforts at welfare reform are designed to encourage people's self-reliance.

3. **What are the main points of welfare reform?**

_____

_____

Effects of Welfare Reform (page 899)

What are the effects of welfare reform?

There are critics of the new welfare reforms. Some liberals fear that the cuts in welfare will hurt children. Conservatives argue that the benefits of the new reforms are worth any costs. Still others think the new welfare law will cause increased homelessness. Most observers are watching carefully to see the long-term results of welfare reform.

4. **What are two criticisms of the new welfare law?**

_____

_____

Tough Choices About Entitlements

BEFORE YOU READ

In the last section, you read about state and federal efforts to reform welfare.

In this section, you will read about problems with government entitlement programs.

AS YOU READ

Use the diagram below to fill in the problems of Social Security and some proposed solutions.

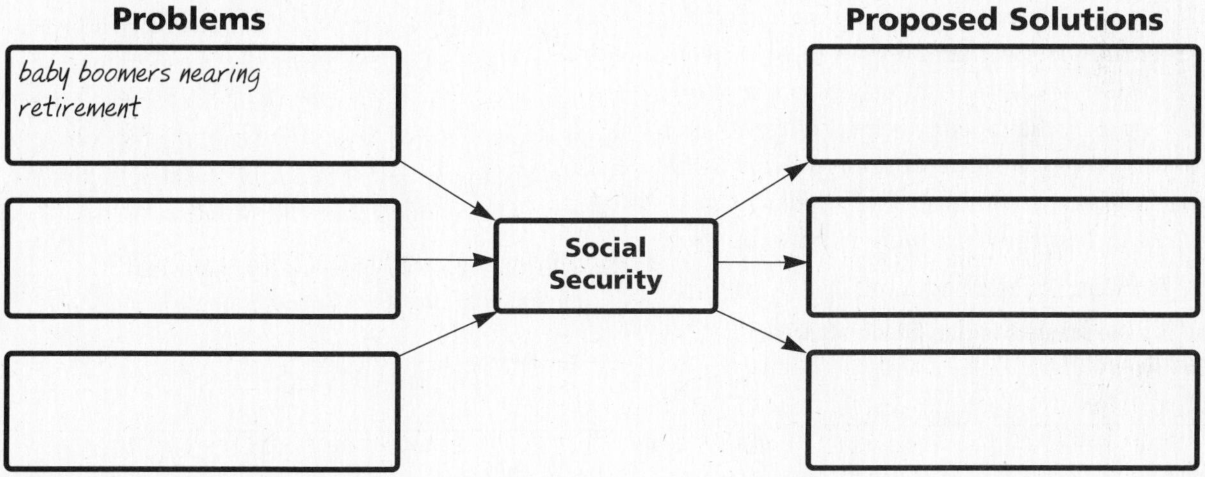

Problems

baby boomers nearing retirement

Social Security

Proposed Solutions

Historical Perspective (page 900)

What are entitlements?

In the 1935 Social Security Act, the federal government promised to pay a *pension* to retired Americans. The money would come from taxes these workers and their employers paid into the Social Security system. In 1965, the government added health care payments. Medicare would pay health care costs for the elderly. Medicaid would pay for health care for the poor.

These programs are called **entitlements.** In entitlement programs, benefits are guaranteed by law. Congress does not have to approve them each year as *appropriations.* Many people feel that enti-

tlement programs like Social Security, Medicare, and Medicaid are in financial trouble. That is because the U.S. population is aging. One way to understand why this increase in the number of older persons threatens entitlement programs is to use Social Security as a case study.

1. What seems to be threatening the financial health of entitlement programs?

_____

_____

Social Security: A Case Study
(pages 900–901)

Why is Social Security in trouble?

The threat to Social Security comes mainly from three factors. First, baby boomers (the large number of Americans born between 1946 and 1964) will reach retirement age soon. This large number of people retiring at once will be a big drain on the money in the Social Security system.

Second, Americans now live longer than ever before. That adds to the number of people entitled to Social Security payments. It also means that the share of benefits a person will receive over a lifetime is greater than in the past.

Third, there is slow growth in the rate of employment. That means that less tax money is coming into the Social Security system.

Some experts predict a disaster. They say that by 2020 there will be more money going out of the Social Security system than coming in to it. That means the system will have to use its **trust fund.** That is the money that Social Security currently has left over after it pays out pensions. Trust fund money is invested for future Social Security payments. Critics fear the trust fund will also be used up early in the 21st century.

2. What are the reasons for the financial threat to Social Security?

_____

_____

_____

Options for Change (page 901)

What are suggestions for "saving" Social Security?

Other experts don't see disaster on the horizon. They think that a small increase in payroll taxes will provide enough money to keep Social Security *funded* for a while. They suggest several other ways to help Social Security in the long run. These include increasing taxes, cutting benefits, and raising the retirement age. They also include investing some of the Social Security trust fund in stocks. Another suggestion requires workers to invest in an extra retirement program. Some suggestions involve letting workers control and invest part of their Social Security taxes themselves.

Many of these proposals involve **privatization.** Privatization is putting some income from payroll taxes into investments in the *private sector,* such as the stock market. Those who support privatization say that the Social Security fund could earn far more in the stock market than it currently does. Others point out that stocks don't always go up. If stocks go down, Social Security could actually lose money. This would make the situation worse.

3. What are three suggestions for improving the financial health of Social Security?

_____

_____

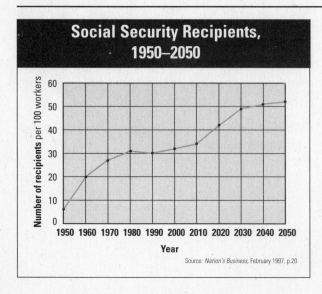

Social Security Recipients, 1950–2050

Number of recipients per 100 workers

Year

Source: *Nation's Business,* February 1997, p.20

Skillbuilder
Use graph to answer questions

1. How many people were receiving Social Security benefits in 1950?

_____

_____

2. What is the trend for receiving Social Security benefits?

_____

Glossary   *EPILOGUE* Issues for the 21st Century

appropriations Legislative acts authorizing payment of a certain amount of public funds for a specific purpose

benefits Retirement and health insurance programs provided by an employer to employees

case study Detailed study of a sample person, group, or unit that can be used as a model of a larger group or similar units

cycle of poverty Condition of poverty repeated generation after generation

day care Daytime supervision, recreation, and education for children of preschool age

funded Setting aside sufficient money

graffiti Drawing or writing on a wall or other surface, usually so as to be seen by the public

health insurance Agreement by which an insurance company pays some or all doctor's or hospital costs in exchange for monthly premiums, or fees, paid in advance by the insured

homeless, the People who live on the street, in parks, or in shelters because they do not have permanent homes

initiative Law proposed by a petition of citizens and then submitted to the voters

literacy Ability to read and write

lobbying Efforts to influence legislators or other public officials in favor of a particular cause or industry

marketable skills Skills that employers are willing to pay for; skills used on the job

nativist Favoring the interests of native, or indigenous, inhabitants over those of immigrants

pension Sum of money paid regularly as a retirement benefit

preexisting conditions Medical problems that a person has before he or she applies for health insurance

preventive care Medical care that can prevent or slow the course of disease, such as vaccinations, early treatment of infections, and nutritional supplements.

private sector Part of the economy controlled by individuals and businesses, not by the government

tax credit Reduction in taxes for a specific reason, such as an action the government wants to encourage

welfare Financial aid given by the government to people considered unable to support themselves

vandalism Destruction of public or private property in order to harm others or out of spite

AFTER YOU READ

Terms and Names

A. Fill in the blanks with the term or name that best completes the sentence.

affirmative action

glass ceiling

gun control

human rights

quotas

upward mobility

Most Favored Nation (MFN)

National Rifle Association (NRA)

1. The _____ opposes the Brady Act and other forms of _____, which they say violate the right of American citizens to bear arms.

2. Many Americans have supported _____ to make up for past discrimination, but they are against _____, or setting aside certain college admissions "slots" for minorities.

3. Some people feel that nations that do not respect the _____ of their own citizens should not be given special trading status, or _____ by the United States.

4. Many women claim that a _____ prevents their _____, so they cannot rise to top management positions in many U.S. companies.

Name _____ Date _____

B. Write the letter of the term or name next to the description that explains it best.

a. voucher system

b. working poor

c. entitlements

d. terrorism

e. universal health insurance

f. enterprise zones

g. privatization

_____ **1.** People who hold low-paying jobs that do not have benefits such as health insurance

_____ **2.** The use of violence for ideological or political reasons

_____ **3.** Guaranteed health insurance for everyone

_____ **4.** Government programs that guarantee and provide benefits for certain groups

_____ **5.** Changing from government control to private enterprise

_____ **6.** Areas in poor neighborhoods that receive government help in attracting development

_____ **7.** A government program that gives parents certificates to be used in paying for the schools of their choice

Main Ideas

1. What have been the purposes of most foreign policy actions of the United States since the end of the Cold War?

_____

2 What are the major problems facing education?

_____

3. What factors are threatening Medicare and Medicaid programs?

_____

4. What is the main concern about the future of entitlements?

_____

Thinking Critically

Answer the following questions on a separate sheet of paper.

1. Which one of the eight issues covered in this Epilogue do you think is the most important problem for the United States in the 21st century? Why?

2. Explain how one of the following groups of issues are related:

   (a) foreign policy after the Cold War, immigration, and the crime of terrorism

   (b) problems in the health care system, poverty, and entitlements

   (c) equality of opportunity in education, for women, and in breaking the cycle of poverty